BLACK POWER AT WORK

BLACK POWER AT WORK

Community Control,
Affirmative Action, and
the Construction Industry

**Edited by David Goldberg
and Trevor Griffey**

ILR PRESS
AN IMPRINT OF
CORNELL UNIVERSITY PRESS   ITHACA AND LONDON

First published 2010 by Cornell University Press
First printing, Cornell Paperbacks, 2010

Printed in the United States of America

Library of Congress Cataloging-in-Publication Data

Black power at work : community control, affirmative action, and the construction industry / edited by David Goldberg and Trevor Griffey.
    p. cm.
  Includes bibliographical references and index.
  ISBN 978-0-8014-4658-0 (alk. paper) — ISBN 978-0-8014-7431-6
(pbk. : alk. paper)
  1. African American construction workers.   2. African American labor union
members.   3. Construction workers—Labor unions—United States.
4. Affirmative action programs—United States.   5. Labor movement—United
States.   6. Black power—United States.   7. Civil rights movements—United
States.   I. Goldberg, David A., 1972–   II. Griffey, Trevor, 1975–   III. Title.
  HD9715.U52B53   2010
  331.6'396073—dc22   2010011806

Cornell University Press strives to use environmentally responsible suppliers and materials to the fullest extent possible in the publishing of its books. Such materials include vegetable-based, low-VOC inks and acid-free papers that are recycled, totally chlorine-free, or partly composed of nonwood fibers. For further information, visit our website at www.cornellpress.cornell.edu.

Cloth printing   10 9 8 7 6 5 4 3 2 1
Paperback printing   10 9 8 7 6 5 4 3 2 1

For Leo Fletcher, Herbert Hill, and Tyree Scott

Contents

Acknowledgments

We are grateful to the anonymous reviewers who read our book proposal and the manuscript, and provided thoughtful comments and guidance that helped strengthen the volume. In particular, we thank the contributors to this volume for their patience and understanding, and Fran Benson, our editor at Cornell University Press, for supporting our project and remaining a joy to work with throughout the process.

Trevor Griffey

I especially thank David Goldberg for being the driving force behind this volume and for challenging me to grow as a colleague and a scholar. And I thank my family for their faith and support.

I also thank James N. Gregory, Nikhil Singh, Moon-Ho Jung, Michael Mc-Cann, John Findlay, Quintard Taylor, and Susan Glenn at the University of Washington (UW) for their academic guidance, feedback, and inspiration. In addition, I thank Jessie Kindig for being an outstanding colleague.

Critical support for my research came from various UW institutions: the Simpson Center for the Humanities; the Harry Bridges Center for Labor Studies; the Graduate School Alvord Fellowship; the Center for the Study of the Pacific Northwest; and the History Department Burg Scholarship, Rondeau-Evans Fellowship, and Travel Awards.

I am indebted to innumerable archivists, but my research would have been impossible without the following individuals: Don Davis of the American Friends Service Committee, Kathleen Crosman at National Archives Regional Archives (NARA) in Seattle, Gregory Cumming at the Richard Nixon Presidential Library and Museum, and Karyl Winn at the Special Collections of the UW Library.

Most of all, I am indebted to the activists themselves, who trusted me to share their stories and whose guidance has transformed not only my scholarship but also my life: Todd Hawkins, Michael Woo, Bev Sims, Harold Wright, Michael Fox, and Dillard Craven in Seattle; Michael Simmons in Philadelphia; James Pannell in Shreveport; and Michael Conley, Walter Block, Ruford Henderson, and LaRue Thompson in Tulsa.

David Goldberg

This book began as an idea in my thick skull, but germinated into a viable project once I pulled Trevor Griffey away from his dissertation. As the table of contents shows, Trevor went above and beyond the call of duty. I thank him for his hard work, for making the volume immeasurably better, and for being a wonderful scholar and friend.

I also thank Shawn Alexander, Ernest Allen, Aaron Anderson, Shannon Anderson, Ian Anderson, Jay Anderson, General Baker, Jackson Bartlett, Beth Bates, Melba Joyce Boyd, John H. Bracey, Dana Brenner-Kelly, Raydin Brenner-Kelley, Eric Kelley, Sundiata Cha Jua, Liz Faue, Edward Finman, Willie Green, Jennifer Hamer, Zhandarka Kurti, Clarence Lang, Tricia Loveland, Daniel McClure, Kelli Morgan, Timothy O'Neil, Leah Raab, James Smethurst, Manisha Sinha, Thomas Sugrue, Monica White, and Rhonda Y. Williams for their feedback, friendship, support, and guidance during the creation of this book.

This project could not have been completed without generous financial support provided by Central Michigan University; the Department of African American Studies at the University of Illinois, Champaign-Urbana; and the College of Liberal Arts and Sciences and the Department of Africana Studies at Wayne State University.

Finally, I want to thank and honor my beloved late grandmother, Helen Brenner, and my mother, Elaine Rosenblat, for their unfailing love and support. I am forever indebted to my mother, who is currently battling terminal cancer, for always being there and for serving as both my mother and my father. While she may never see this book, she will always be with me. I thank you and love you dearly, Mom.

BLACK POWER AT WORK

CONSTRUCTING BLACK POWER

David Goldberg and Trevor Griffey

The construction industry has provided extraordinary opportunities for class mobility in the United States, but those benefits have been largely restricted to white men and their families. After World War II, home ownership became, along with Social Security, one of the few entitlements that the political culture of the Cold War allowed to be considered "American." From the 1940s through the 1960s, generous federal government home-loan programs, highway construction, and tax incentives heavily underwrote residential construction in the United States (particularly in its suburbs). As numerous studies have shown, the racial exclusivity of the post–World War II federal subsidies for home ownership, combined with the lack of fair housing laws, ensured that the unprecedented class mobility afforded to Americans in the postwar era disproportionately benefited white families. The resulting disparate levels of wealth accumulation from the 1940s to the 1960s ensured that, as the middle class expanded, it remained predominantly white and suburban.[1]

But the question of who owned homes or benefited from real estate speculation does not fully explain the role that the construction industry has had in shaping U.S. society. The growth of U.S. homeownership after World War II provided jobs that allowed millions of blue-collar workers and their families to participate in a new consumer society. Building trades unions facilitated this transition while restricting access to it. Construction industry unionization was at its apex in 1940–1960, when half of all construction jobs were union and unions controlled the industry in many cities outside the South. The fact that this was also a time when federal government construction spending was at its apex is hardly a coincidence. Federal law, and many similar state laws, required that government contractors pay the "prevailing wage," which in turn provided unions extraordinary leverage to organize the construction industry. These organizing campaigns did more than ensure that construction workers received a fair portion of the profits from the construction industry boom. They also wrested away employer prerogatives to train, hire, fire, and discipline workers from contractors. As a result, building trades unions exerted extraordinary power to control wages and worker access to an industry that during the post-war boom provided close to 10 percent of male employment.[2]

Thus, although the construction industry literally paved the way for the emergence of a postwar service-based economy, black workers remained largely trapped in industrial jobs that provided lower wages and few, if any, opportunities to ascend the ranks into management. The "racial welfare state" of the New Deal—which subsidized racially segregated homeownership and discriminatory employers and granted labor rights to racially exclusive unions—deepened racial segregation by limiting economic and social mobility to white men, thus producing "a mostly white and propertied proletariat in the suburbs, and a poor, inner city working class of people of color."[3] Black unemployment increased rather than decreased, even during the heyday of the postwar boom, because of the segregation of blacks into low and semiskilled jobs and inner-city neighborhoods made vulnerable to layoffs produced by automation, the relocation of factories to the suburbs, and deindustrialization.[4]

It was in this context that black activists in Philadelphia, frustrated with the glacial pace of post–World War II racial liberalism and the gradualist politics of the established civil rights leaders, built a largely working-class, grassroots movement incorporating the politics of disruption and direct action to confront institutionalized racism in the construction industry. Incorporating ideological and tactical approaches as well and constituents from nationalist and community-based activism and boycotts of the 1950s, "Philadelphia's branches of CORE and the NAACP" in April 1963 began a two-month series of protests and construction shutdowns to demand "the inclusion of black workers in city-sponsored construction projects." These protests brought mass direct-action tactics to large-scale, publicly funded construction projects in the North. In the process, they "attacked the very core of postwar Keynesian economics: business and unions reliant on government spending" and fundamentally transformed the northern freedom movement.[5]

The 1963 Philadelphia protests helped launch a six-year, nationwide movement for "affirmative action from below" that became rooted in Black Power and community control politics. Construction protests spread to other job sites in the northeast during the summer, including the Downstate Medical Center in

Brooklyn and the Barringer School in Newark, campaigns chronicled in this volume. Throughout the summer, activists, many of them associated with the Congress of Racial Equality (CORE), became "impatient with the pace of change" and experimented "with new, more militant forms of protest."[6] According to Elliot Rudwick and August Meier, the 1963 protests precipitated a series of "changes that involved not only a stress on the grievances of the black poor, but also an escalation of tactics, the beginning of an erosion in the commitment to nonviolence, and a tendency towards black separatism." What emerged in their wake was a movement of local movements that frequently blurred the lines between civil rights and black power while also placing the two in increasing tension with one another.[7]

Although they are connected with much longer struggles for jobs and justice and community-centered labor organizing, the 1963 protests and those that followed do not fit neatly within a history of the "long civil rights movement." The expulsion of black radical labor organizations and leaders from the labor movement during the Red Scare created a generational vacuum between the 1940s- and 1950s-era black radicals and 1960s activists. Cold War unionism, dominated by the building trades unions, further limited the options available to the civil rights leaders and unionists who remained. Internal efforts to reform the building trades unions through voluntarism, liberal-labor coalitions, or remaining race-based caucuses such as the Negro American Labor Council proved futile, and racially progressive allies within the labor movement were scarce and enfeebled.

The 1963 building trades protests were central to the "Negro Revolt of 1963" and represented the limits of civil rights unionism and fair employment politics. Activists organized outside the formal labor movement to demand "that racial equality in construction" and local jobs for local people "be measured by results" rather than procedure.[8] When these demands were not met and federally funded urban renewal projects continued, activists, including mainline civil rights organizations, increasingly turned to Black Power labor politics and community control organizing to gain access to jobs as well as control of the economic and physical development of inner cities.[9]

As the contributors to this book show, confrontations with the building trades unions became a critical axis for the rise of Black Power and community control politics, and provide a means for us to rethink the history of Black Power through the fusion by the movement of community control and labor organizing. By tracing the evolution of these activists' organizing methods and analysis, we show that African American grassroots struggles to desegregate the construction industry provided a major, and in some cities *the,* means through which Black Power movements became ascendant in African American urban politics.

Only through close attention to local politics are these profound cultural and political shifts visible. Because of their decentralized quality, the movements for community control of the construction industry varied by city, based on the idiosyncratic nature of the specific African American communities and political networks from which they emerged. These differences were accentuated by weak federal enforcement of affirmative action plans, which relied on a strategy of localism that placed the origin, evolution, and fate of construction industry affirmative action plans primarily in the hands of local actors and courts.[10]

The chapters in this book thus provide case studies whose sum is greater than their parts. Their focus on local politics contribute to a growing body of literature focusing on expanding our understanding of civil rights histories beyond charismatic leaders to understand how local people's participation in the black freedom movement drove much of its intellectual and political evolution. Our regional focus on the urban North stems from the fact that campaigns to desegregate the construction industry did not enter the South until the early 1970s, and emerged largely in response to federal government intervention.[11] Inspired by the southern civil rights activism, the campaigns to desegregate the building trades galvanized local movements in the North in ways that voting registration and direct action campaigns against public segregation politicized local people in the South.[12]

The ascension of community control and Black Power perspectives within local movements to desegregate the building trades during the early and mid-1960s are chronicled at length in the first three chapters of this book, which present case studies of Brooklyn, Newark, and the San Francisco Bay Area. Chapters 4 and 5, studies of Detroit and Chicago, continue this approach, but chronicle the development and activities of the Black Power construction coalitions formed in wake of spreading urban uprisings, whose campaigns facilitated the implementation of affirmative action in the building trades beginning in 1969. These chapters, along with chapter 6, on the hard hat movement, the Nixon administration, and affirmative action policy, contextualize how and why affirmative action was so quickly compromised. Activists, however, responded to this turn of events by using direct action and construction shutdowns in an attempt to revive and gain control of the implementation of affirmative action programs during the 1970s, as detailed in chapter 7, a study of Seattle's movement.

Black Power at Work chronicles the profound impact that these grassroots movements had on national political culture and the social-movement origins of affirmative action politics. At their peak in the 1960s and early 1970s, these movements were diverse and diffuse, spread by activists in loose communication with one another rather than being directed by a single organization, coalition, or government actor from the top down.[13] At the local level, militant tactics that halted work on billions of dollars of federal construction created a crisis for civil rights moderates and liberal-labor political coalitions. Deeming the gradualism of the liberal establishment to be ineffective and racist, black militants' calls for power and not promises created fissures in Democratic Party coalition that helped set in motion new forms of urban politics. "The protesters," Thomas Sugrue argues, "were not, in a strict sense, the architects of affirmative action. They did not draft executive orders and federal regulations. But, by taking their grievances to the streets and construction sites," they made affirmative action politically possible.[14]

Yet these grassroots campaigns not only drove the creation of affirmative action but also sought to connect the desegregation of the building trades with the broader Black Power movement goals of black community control and economic and political self-determination. The case studies in *Black Power at Work* locate the development of the Black Power construction struggles as a process beginning in 1963 and extending into the early 1970s, but they strongly refute the notion that Black Power contributed to the declension of the movement. Rather, the studies show that the community-based labor politics and grassroots organizing of these local Black Power movements served as the catalyst that pushed building trades struggles and civil rights litigation beyond their prior limitations.[15]

Taken together, the chapters in *Black Power at Work* unsettle a number of assumptions that have informed the history of civil rights, Black Power, affirmative action, the labor movement, and 1960s social movements. First, they remove affirmative action history from the world of public policy by placing its origins within the context of black radical and nationalist community organizing during the 1960s and 1970s. Second, by highlighting the community organizing strategies of Black Power activists in the 1960s and early 1970s, specifically around the politics of employment and unionization, the studies in this book show the centrality of the labor question to the evolution of Black Power. The question of building black independent and political power, for example, was often directly connected to debates about how to best organize black workers to fight against economic marginalization and discrimination, both within and outside the "house of labor." Third, by treating affirmative action law as *both* labor law and civil rights law, the case studies provide a means for us to see Black Power labor activism not as antiunion—as some labor historians have derided it—but as an important form of labor radicalism.

From Inclusion to Community Control

What we now think of as affirmative action was first implemented on Public Works Administration (PWA) and U.S. Housing Authority (USHA) projects in the 1930s and early 1940s, but it was supplanted as a remedy for employment discrimination when liberal activists focused on securing fair employment legislation during and after World War II.[16] The 1963 job-site protests, however, resurrected quotas or goals as a remedy for employment discrimination by using direct action and construction shutdowns to demand specific percentages of jobs in inner-city construction. These often protracted and large-scale protests drew violent responses from white tradesmen and police, as well as the attention of the federal government. Yet, although they raised awareness of discrimination in the building trades, these initial protests produced little in terms of tangible results. When confronted with discrimination charges, unions denied having bias or responsibility but pledged to police themselves, and local authorities deferred to the unions. Similarly, President John Kennedy's Executive Order 11114, a direct response to the Philadelphia protests, called for affirmative action against discrimination on publicly funded projects but failed to define what this entailed or to provide an enforcement mechanism.[17]

The liberal political machines and the federal government proved themselves either unwilling or unable to effectively respond to the challenge to union racism posed by African American communities. From late 1963 forward, activists in cities across the country incorporated "militant strategies and rhetoric" from the emerging Black Power and community control movements. Increased funding for inner-city construction, in the form of Lyndon Johnson's Great Society programs—first the Office of Economic Opportunity and later also Model Cities—contained provisions requiring the "maximum feasible participation" of community residents, which local activists organized to test and expand.

The Newark Coordinating Committee (NCC), a coalition group formed in 1963 by Newark members of CORE that had led the Barringer protests, moved "beyond merely exposing discrimination and demanding redress" by fighting to gain oversight of apprenticeship training and placement as well as community control of local health services and urban renewal programs. The failure of the initial direct action campaigns and protests had a similar impact on activists elsewhere. At the national level, the unwillingness of the federal government to "take affirmative action" against racial discrimination in the building trades unions led James Farmer, CORE director, to consider sponsoring independent unions in 1964 to "put pressure on established unions that discriminate in admitting new members."[18] CORE never established independent construction unions for fear of drawing the ire of the American Federation of Labor–Congress of Industrial Organizations (AFL-CIO) and losing important financial support, but it did embark on a "pilot project" in Boston that created "a voluntary organization cutting across racial lines…to obtain more construction contracts for Negro contractors, more construction jobs for the skilled Negro worker, and more apprenticeship opportunities for the unskilled Negro worker."[19] In addition, in 1966 in the San Francisco Bay Area, Justice on Bay Area Rapid Transit (JOBART) activists staged protests to demand access to jobs on the construction of the regional rail system (Bay Area Rapid Transit, BART), part of a larger effort to "rebuild the black community in place by using development money attached to major projects like BART."[20]

A specific trajectory within the long civil rights movement historiography refutes the dominant narrative that depicted Black Power and black nationalism as reactionary post-1965 phenomena that caused the declension of the "the good" civil rights movement. This scholarship rightfully revives the long ignored pre-1960s black radical tradition, and depicts a long Black Power movement by linking the Garvey movement; the Brotherhood of Sleeping Car Porters; Don't Buy Where You Can't Work campaigns; National Negro Congress; National Negro Labor Council; black internationalism; Nation of Islam; and local black nationalist, radical, and self-defense organizations and activists to the development of Black Power in the 1960s.[21]

The contributors to *Black Power at Work,* however, make a conscious distinction between prior instances of black nationalist, community-centered, and black radical politics and the Black Power movement. We recognize that 1960s-era black nationalism, as John Bracey argued nearly forty years ago, resulted "from a long historical development and" was "not merely a specific response to immediate conditions."[22] Yet linking earlier movements to the Black Power movement often obscures the "strategic vision, goals, objectives, leaders and followers, practices, symbols and discourses" of each movement while failing to adequately address the specific historical contexts in which they were operative.[23] The movements that developed around the building trades in the 1960s shifted tactically and ideologically as activists experimented with and responded to local and national social, political, and cultural currents that were very different than those encountered by prior activists.[24] For example, although black labor organizations such as the Brotherhood of Sleeping Car Porters may (or may not) have represented workplace-based Black Power in decades prior, during the 1960s they sought to work within the existing labor movement and its institutions and discouraged black independent labor organizing.

This insider approach to racism within organized labor failed to change discriminatory practices within the AFL-CIO, particularly the craft unions, thus providing the inspiration for calls for self-determination and independent unionism by the Black Power movement. In fact, the challenge posed by Black Power unionism was so great that civil rights unionists (including Bayard Rustin, the A. Philip Randolph Institute, and the Workers Defense League) actively sought to *shorten* the Black Power movement by working in conjunction with building trades unions to usurp grassroots leaders during "hometown plan" affirmative action negotiations.[25]

Black Power and Black Mondays

The successes and limitations of the civil rights movement and the complicity of liberalism in the expansion of institutionalized racism at home and abroad during the 1960s bolstered the growth of a Black Power movement that "thought globally and acted locally."[26] Black workers, activists, institutions, and businessmen, frustrated with the deleterious effects of continued white economic and political control of urban areas—particularly in cities with rapidly expanding black populations—were attracted to the goals and rhetoric of community control rather than integration. But they lacked the vast resources needed to establish black economic and political self-determination in inner-city neighborhoods struggling with the crippling effects of deindustrialization and second ghettoization. By seeking control over urban renewal projects, contracts, and the jobs they created, local Black Power activists fought to ensure that federally construction projects of the mid-1960s would be as politically and economically beneficial to inner cities and their residents as the urban renewal programs of the 1950s had been for white suburbanites. This approach gained increased currency as urban unrest and state repression escalated.

Civil unrest and "long hot summers" had dominated U.S. urban politics from 1963 to 1968. Inner-city "riots," most often triggered by incidents of police brutality, began in Birmingham, Alabama, in 1963 and spread a year later to Harlem and Rochester, New York, and then to Philadelphia. Following the Watts (Los Angeles) uprising of 1965, hundreds of similar rebellions took place during the next three years in cities throughout the country. White Americans, however, including political leaders, proved ambivalent at best about substantively addressing the rampant racial discrimination in housing, employment, and education, along with widespread police brutality, that had enraged urban black communities. The mass upheavals in Detroit and Newark in 1967 were the largest, and they were followed by unrest around the country after the assassination of Martin Luther King Jr. in April 1968. By mid-1968, these rebellions showed few signs of abating, and many if not most observers at the time assumed that they would persist for years to come.[27]

Instead, a change took place in African American urban politics between 1968 and 1969 that has yet to be adequately explained. Rather than persisting, the rebellions largely came to a halt and were replaced by well-organized grassroots political campaigns. The possibility for violence, which gave the militant demands made by Black Power activists attention that they otherwise would have lacked, have also caused contemporaries and historians to overlook the significance of the local organizing traditions that Black Power advocates solidified in the wake of the rebellions. Instead of looting, everyday people rose up to demand jobs. Instead of setting fires, the poor residents of racially segregated African American cities across the country demanded control of the rebuilding of their communities. Instead of promoting uprisings that expressed black frustration and powerlessness, local Black Power activists, in concert with activists across the nation, organized campaigns that mobilized hundreds, and sometimes thousands, of people to demand control over the policies and institutions that impacted their lives and communities. Across the country, Black Power, already operative in several local construction struggles, went to work.

These processes gained a wider expression and a more specific formulation when, on August 29, 1968, over 3,000 black activists met in Philadelphia to attend the Third National Conference on Black Power, whose theme was "Black Self-Determination and Black Unity through Direct Action." An observer from the press described the four-day event, with its roughly fifty different plenary and workshop sessions, as being different in tone from the "loud rhetoric" and bluster that defined the Black Power conference held in Newark the previous year. With the meanings of Black Power already theorized and the need for implementation and organization clear, conference attendees in Philadelphia participated in "intense and serious discussion...[about] programs of action in which blacks at all levels—both moderates and militants—can become involved." Seizing control of the political, economic, and social institutions whose everyday operation allowed white people to exercise control over black urban communities, activists believed, would harness the rise in black militancy that followed the outbreak of the urban rebellions in a common struggle to end "internal colonization" and establish black self-determination and "community control."[28]

Formulating an economic program for Black Power played a significant role in shaping how conference attendees framed what Black Power and community control entailed. Conference attendees linked the call for jobs with the call for political power and the development of black businesses and job opportunities with larger demands for power beginning at the local neighborhood level. Federal government funding of urban renewal projects and the reconstruction of postrebellion inner cities through the Model Cities Program deeply implicated the U.S. government in the razing of African American communities in the name of social progress. Conference attendees attacked existing "federally funded institutional expansions, highway development and urban renewal" as coordinated attempts to fragment and weaken black communities, institutions, and voting power as the concentration of black citizens in urban areas expanded.[29] Activists rejected these federal projects as a form of "colonization," a "neo-plantationism" created by "the systematic effort of racist planners and politicians to isolate, confuse and destroy Black people socially, economically, mentally and spiritually."[30]

But Black Power activists also saw organizing potential in federal redevelopment projects. Community control groups, if effectively organized at the grassroots level, could demand that every aspect of such projects—from policy making to labor—be placed under black control. To work toward this objective, activists dedicated themselves to taking control of or blocking Model Cities programs at the local level while also developing "trade training institutions, programs and unions" on a nationwide basis to create a material foundation for community economic development and self-determination.[31] This call for action, and the subsequent movement building that took place across the country, set the stage for a looming confrontation among Black Power activists, racially exclusive skilled trades unions, and the U.S. government.

From July to September 1969, Black Power activists around the country organized a wave of direct action protests against employment discrimination in the U.S. construction industry. Demanding the immediate implementation of affirmative action programs to fund black contractors and hire and train black (and sometimes also Puerto Rican) workers on federally funded construction projects in inner-city neighborhoods, protesters shut down billions of dollars of government projects in many of the largest U.S. cities. Beginning in Chicago and Pittsburgh in July, spreading to Philadelphia in August, and inspiring similar actions throughout the urban North from Seattle to New York City in September to coincide with Black Monday protests called by activists in Pittsburgh, this wave of direct action campaigns was directly responsible for the breakthrough of affirmative action at the federal level.[32]

What little has been written about the wave of construction-site closures in 1969 tends to describe them as *both* riots and protests, as an extension of the "long hot summers" and a transformation of them, even though actual violence was rare and burning and looting were nonexistent.[33] Black Power activists intentionally mobilized protests to capitalize on white people's fears of racial violence in the wake of urban rebellions. In cities such as Detroit and Washington, D.C., the scale of the previous rebellions and fear of continued racial unrest were so great that the mere threat of protest was sufficient to provide activists with leverage to demand community control of, and federal intervention in, pending inner-city redevelopment projects.

Black Power at Work

Histories of affirmative action written since the early 1990s have documented how the political crisis that protesters created made the Philadelphia Plan—the first affirmative action plan ever imposed by the federal government—politically possible. The imposition by the U.S. Labor Department of the Philadelphia Plan, which imposed goals and timetables for the hiring of black construction workers on federal contractors in Philadelphia, opened the door for similar affirmative action plans in other cities as both riot prevention and a civil rights policy alternative to the War on Poverty.[34] At the same time, officials in the Richard Nixon White House hoped to flood the construction industry with low-wage nonunion labor as a means of controlling the contribution of high construction industry wages to inflation.[35] But regardless of Nixon's goals, the tactic he introduced proved uncontrollable. In conjunction with the increasingly expansive interpretation of Title VII of the Civil Rights Act by the federal courts, the Philadelphia Plan moved the metric for discrimination from individual acts of discrimination to workplace diversity statistics and shifted the object of reform in fair employment law from individual actions to institutionalized patterns and practices of racial discrimination.

Yet, despite the significance of the 1969 protests to this change in federal policy, most histories have taken these movements out of affirmative action history. Intellectual and policy studies of affirmative action invoke civil rights campaigns (if at all) mainly to describe them as a pretext for action by the Nixon White House. They largely omit what preceded or followed the Black Monday protests as if the movements had no role in the subsequent development or enforcement of affirmative action.[36] Similarly, the voluminous histories of civil rights, Black Power, and 1960s social movements of the last forty years have almost totally ignored the Black Monday protests.

Perhaps one reason why these protests have been overlooked by historians is that telling their history requires rethinking the declension narratives of the civil rights movement and African American urban politics that have structured so many histories of the late 1960s and 1970s. By demanding jobs and not welfare, power and not proclamations of equal opportunity, Black Monday protest leaders cut against the stereotypes of hopelessness, passivity, criminality, and a "culture of poverty" that have dominated popular discussions of African American ghettos and the development of the so-called underclass during the post–civil rights era.[37] Instead of being the passive victims of capital flight (urban deindustrialization) and white flight (urban depopulation), the participants in these campaigns imagined a new direction and purpose for both inner cities and the black freedom movement. The Black Monday protest leaders were local activists, not national media icons. Their organizations were so new that they seemed almost ad hoc, and they blended community and labor politics in a way that often blurred the boundaries among civil rights organizations, black nationalist organizations, independent labor unions, and social service agencies. They were led by a combination of black youth (often involved in War on Poverty job training programs), community activists, and black construction workers and contractors who do not fit neatly into the standard organizational genealogies of the civil rights, Black Power, and the labor movement. Their mobilizations gave everyday people the means to put forward their own vision to confront institutionalized racism and the so-called urban crisis. Affirmative action in the construction industry had been a goal of the black freedom struggle since 1963, but the Black Monday protests produced what six years of prior protests and shutdowns had paved the way for but failed to secure.

By linking the development of alternatives to the urban crisis to the engagement by the Black Power movement with labor movement politics, the case studies in *Black Power at Work* contribute to the emerging field of Black Power studies. Recent works in this field have highlighted the relationship of the Black Power movement to prior struggles and its varied meanings and manifestations among community organizers and theorists, black feminists, cultural nationalists, student organizers, and clergy, as well as its influence on the development of "rainbow radicalism."[38] These works have begun shifting attention away from a prior focus on familiar national figures, singular activists and organizations, and titillating tales of violence and declension. Yet more still needs to be done to describe Black Power's labor politics and the impact that the campaigns for jobs had on the history and development of the movement locally and nationally. With the exception of school decentralization campaigns, the movements for community control of the construction industry secured more mass support than most of the better-known and more iconic campaigns of the Black Power movement. The chapters in this book provide a starting point for documenting this history as part of the broader project of connecting it to the robust and complicated Black Power community-organizing tradition.[39]

Peter Levy locates the origins of Black Power labor politics in deindustrialization and the limits of liberalism, arguing that industrial "social activist unions, which had stood at the front of the fight for civil rights and economic reform, bore the brunt of the Black Power critique because they were the unions that were most susceptible to the structural changes taking place." The construction unions, which "had the worst records on civil rights," were in Levy's estimation "less affected by structural changes and thus escaped part of Black Power's wrath."[40] But the Black Monday protesters' use of direct action at the point of production and their focus on community control of inner-city construction directly challenge such narrowly focused definitions of Black Power and Black Power unionism. And, although Black Power unionism did not replace civil rights unionism or end the long civil rights movement, even these movements and the shifting historical contexts in which they operated cannot be understood without first acknowledging the ways in which Black Power rhetoric and organizational activities influenced black workers both within and outside the "house of labor."[41]

The Chapters

Black struggles for inclusion in the northern building trades unions and the construction industry began long before the rise of direct action protests during the 1960s. During the first half of twentieth century, black tradesmen in the North and West were restricted from working in all but the low-skill "trowel trades" and were forced into segregated locals that lacked power on the job and lacked influence within their respective unions. When individual attempts to join unions proved fruitless, as Erik S. Gellman (chap. 5 in this volume) discusses, some black tradesmen formed independent worker associations that served as parallel labor organizations, not unlike those found among black craftsmen in other segregated industries in the early twentieth century. Or, as John J. Rosen (chap. 3) and David Goldberg (chap. 4) document, black tradesmen sought greater control over their work through state or local licensing to become independent construction contractors.[42]

White contractors and the unions, through labor and contractor federations, generally colluded at the local level to refuse to admit black workers to skilled trades and to marginalize their voluntary worker and contractor organizations. At the national level, in 1935 the AFL, in which the building trades unions had long played an essential part, threatened to withdraw its support for the Wagner Act (which legalized union organizing for the first time) if an amendment that made racial discrimination an unfair labor practice was not removed from the bill. With no explicit prohibition of union racism, and with the exclusion of domestic and farm laborers (nearly two-thirds of all black workers at the time) from union rights, the Wagner Act became "the Magna Carta for white labor."[43]

Practices of racial discrimination in the building trades thus remained firmly intact despite the establishment of racial quotas on PWA and federally funded public housing projects. Subsequent fair employment campaigns led by local chapters of the National Negro Congress, National Association for the Advancement of Colored People (NAACP), and Urban League during the 1930s and 1940 had little impact.[44] As a result, black tradesmen largely remained restricted to working with small black contractors on piecemeal, short-term jobs in black communities. Well into the post–World War II era, the racial exclusivity of the building trades unions, much like the skilled trades in the railroad and printing industries, remained stark. An Urban League survey of plumbers unions, for example, found *no* black journeymen in twenty of the twenty-three cities it surveyed. Bricklayers, although mildly better outside the South, had twenty-five formally segregated southern locals in 1962. In New York City, a number of trades had "for white only" and "father-son only" apprenticeship clauses, and many others followed this practice in deed rather than words.[45]

In 1956, following the merger of the AFL and CIO, NAACP Labor Secretary Herbert Hill found little support for the proposals he frequently offered to eliminate racial discrimination in the building trades unions.[46] Hill's appeals to the international building trades unions were continually rebuked, and George Meany, AFL-CIO president, regularly "defended the practices of the building trades councils." This included the defense by Meany and the AFL-CIO Civil Rights Committee of Milwaukee Bricklayers Local 8 even after local courts ruled that the union was in violation state antidiscrimination laws. The AFL-CIO also refused to intervene when presented with evidence that East St. Louis Plumbers Union Local 630 had completely barred blacks from membership. Meany did help three black youths in Cleveland gain entrance to an apprenticeship program for the electricians union in 1957 by threatening to decertify the union, but this was a rare exception that proved the rule. Ten years later, for example, the 1,200-member local still had only two black journeymen and two black apprentices.[47] Even Walter Reuther, the president of the United Auto Workers (UAW) and prominent supporter of the southern civil rights movement, "failed to lift a finger during AFL-CIO council meetings" on building trades union discrimination.[48]

"By the end of 1959," Gilbert Jonas explains, "the NAACP and Labor Secretary Hill had abandoned hope that racial justice in the workplace could be accomplished under the leadership of white labor leaders."[49] During the early 1960s, Hill stepped up his efforts to expose the racism of the building trades unions in speeches and widely publicized studies. But, rather than appealing to the conscience of the AFL-CIO, Hill began promoting aggressive litigation and grassroots organizing in local NAACP branches.[50]

In 1963, CORE, the most militant of the civil rights organizations in the North in the early 1960s, accelerated the work of Hill and the NAACP. CORE chapters were important pioneers in using direct action to challenge racism in the construction industry, sparking the initial protests in Philadelphia and participating in the movements that followed.[51] Inspired by CORE and NAACP protests in Philadelphia and New York City, Brooklyn CORE, with the help of a local black ministerial alliance, halted construction on the Downstate Medical Center in summer 1963. This campaign, as Brian Purnell (chap. 1 in this volume) argues, represented an unstable fusion of civil rights and Black Power perspectives and tactics. The Downstate Medical Center protests, although failing to secure jobs for local residents, pushed CORE and other movement participants in a variety of different directions in the years that followed. Brooklyn CORE, for example, went from being half white in summer 1963 to being predominantly black, working class, and more radical and community-centered as a result of the Downstate campaign. At the individual level, Sonny Carson, Brooklyn CORE member and Downstate activist, went on to become a major force in the community control and Black Power movements, later serving as the chairman of the economics workshop at the Third National Conference on Black Power in Philadelphia in 1968.[52]

The history of CORE and the Newark Coordinating Committee (NCC) similarly helps us see the gradual development of Black Power and its intersections with the civil rights movement prior to the late 1960s.[53] CORE members' involvement in building trades protests in New Jersey moved younger militant activists from the margins to the center of the Newark freedom movement. As Julia Rabig (chap. 2 in this volume) shows, the formation of the NCC challenged the gradualist, integrationist approach to civil rights taken previously by the Newark democratic machine, established civil rights leaders, and the business elite. What is more, their protests at the construction of Barringer High School in 1963 set off a series of changes within the Newark freedom movement so that calls for affirmative action became connected to calls for community control. These demands were advanced by the development of autonomous and parallel institutions, ideological and tactical approaches that expanded following the 1967 Newark rebellion.

The increasing significance of community control and Black Power politics in construction struggles resulted largely from the failure of previous efforts of blacks to gain inclusion in the trades. Government officials generally approached the topic of discrimination in the building trades unions by deferring to union supporters. Although the Department of Labor authorized the Bureau of Apprenticeship Training (BAT) to decertify discriminatory programs in 1963, BAT, headed by a former official of the New York Bricklayers' Union, refused to do so. This approach produced token results while maintaining union control of access, training, placement, and jobs.[54]

Between 1963 and 1968, "protests and policy innovations reinforced each other in a feedback loop"[55] that eventually took the enforcement of civil rights law to uncharted territory. Herbert Hill, of the NAACP, provided the public face for the diffuse movements in the urban North, leading protests that called for strengthened federal policy while also fighting for the rigorous enforcement of existing mandates. Hill pushed for litigation against building trades unions, crafting some of the very first lawsuits seeking to enforce Title VII of the 1964 Civil Rights Act.[56] He also helped organize and publicize a wave of 1965 protests.[57] And while continuing to provide information, organizational support, and resources to civil rights activists around the country, by the late 1960s, Hill had helped foster the development of independent black worker unions and black contractor associations in an attempt to bypass the building trades unions and to make workers' calls for community control of construction a reality.[58]

Efforts to desegregate the building trades generally attracted the guarded attention of policymakers—but only after construction protests were joined by large-scale civil disorders and rising black militancy. Job site and union hall shutdowns occurred in St. Louis, Cincinnati, Cleveland, Newark, and the Bronx in 1964 and summer 1965, but the federal government did not intercede.[59] But on August 11, 1965, when rebellion broke out in the Watts neighborhood of Los Angeles, national political discourse finally began to debate the consequences (and, less often, the causes) of African Americans being forced to live in highly segregated and impoverished neighborhoods located in the center of the wealthiest U.S. metropolitan regions. Roughly six weeks later, President Johnson intervened by issuing Executive Order 11246, which reaffirmed Kennedy's prior order and created the Office of Federal Contract Compliance (OFCC) to enforce it.

The OFCC, located within the U.S. Department of Labor, had substantially more power than the free-floating and underfunded agency created to enforce Title VII, the Equal Employment Opportunity Commission (EEOC). It was granted the power to cancel contracts with contractors who had failed to take affirmative action against discrimination when subcontracting labor, but it refused to enforce this provision. Instead, it began crafting plans "to enforce compliance on construction contracts" for St. Louis and San Francisco in 1966 and for Cleveland and Philadelphia in 1967.[60]

By targeting cities that were already hotbeds for construction protests and Black Power organizing, the OFCC programs ended up contributing further to Black Power organizing. These plans expanded the ineffectual model created by BAT, giving credence to radicals' demands for community control. OFCC programs were funded by the Labor Department's Manpower Administration and were overseen in collaboration with the building trades unions and moderate black organizations such the Urban League, Workers Defense League, Trade Union Leadership Council, and Opportunities Industrialization Centers. They focused on increasing the pool of minority applicants to apprenticeship programs, but had little effect on the placement of minority workers in jobs or their admission into unions.

Federally imposed remedies were slow in developing and strongly resisted by both the building trades unions and segments of the government.[61] The building trades unions responded to the implementation of the St. Louis Plan by walking off the Gateway Arch construction site, provoking a protracted legal dispute. The Cleveland and Philadelphia plans crafted a year later—the former was later "recommended to the Kerner Commission"[62] as a means of combating unemployment and rioting and served as a model for the latter—were stronger. Both required contractors to present affirmative action plans based on preaward manning tables, but the Philadelphia Plan included a provision that authorized federal officials to "visit job sites and conduct head counts"[63] to ensure compliance. Comptroller General Elmer Staats, however, declared both illegal in 1968.

The proliferation of independent worker and contractor organizations in the mid- to late 1960s was indicative of the growing influence of community control and Black Power politics as well as the attempt to link them to the implementation of affirmative action plans. In the San Francisco Bay Area, for instance, where Black Power is often associated with the founding of the Black Panther Party for Self-Defense in 1966 and the Black Student Union–led strike at San Francisco State in 1968, the construction industry desegregation battles played an important but overlooked part in the local shift in African American political culture in the late 1960s. As a community organization founded in 1966 to demand jobs for San Francisco and West Oakland residents on the construction of BART, "JOBART spoke the language of community power," historian Robert Self argues, and it initiated, prior to the Black Panthers, "a discursive and tactical turn that replaced liberal individualist legal remedies with place-based political organizing and action."[64]

Although the OFCC response to JOBART demands was largely ineffectual, its call to "encourage minority subcontractors" to work in tandem with the development of War on Poverty redevelopment programs, as John J. Rosen (chap. 3 in this volume) shows, facilitated the rise of black contractor activism. In the Bay Area, black contractors responded to OFCC efforts by organizing across craft lines in 1966 to form the General and Specialty Contractors Association to assist one another in securing bonding and bidding on federally sponsored construction projects. They joined with JOBART activists and situated themselves as the primary vehicle for training and placing inner-city residents on construction jobs. They then used this experience to found one of the first national minority contractors' associations. Although their organizations emerged from a dialog between local community control politics and affirmative action politics, Nixon administration policies soon separated worker and contractor affirmative action plans, influencing the development of Black Power and community control politics in the 1970s in complex ways.

The rise of black-run independent institutions around the country in the late 1960s also dovetailed with Black Power activists' attempts to take control of urban renewal and Model Cities programs in the wake of the Newark and Detroit uprisings in 1967. As David Goldberg (chap. 4 in this volume) demonstrates, these programs overlapped in important but heretofore overlooked ways in Detroit, with black autoworkers in the League of Revolutionary Black Workers allying with black construction workers and contractors to demand community control of the postrebellion rebuilding process. Invoking a black nationalist, anticolonial analysis of inner-city segregation, the Detroit movement sought independent black control of every aspect of the post-1967 construction, including building, planning, and the training and placement of labor.[65] The radicalism of the Detroit movement sparked direct confrontation with the building trades unions, unsettling the labor-liberal politics of the city and inspiring the intense repression of the movement. Black construction worker radicalism in the wake of the urban rebellions proved similarly unsettling in other cities—especially Washington, D.C., where black anticolonial critiques of urban segregation overlapped with a statehood movement and targeted the construction of federal government buildings rather than just federally funded urban renewal.[66]

By the late 1960s, War on Poverty programs to train and occupy the time of the "hardcore unemployed"—young black men whose unemployment, according to liberal planners, made them susceptible to Black Power politics and likely to participate in violent rebellions—proliferated. These jobs programs, rather than creating a liberal alternative to the Black Power movement, unintentionally transformed and linked the desegregation of the building trades with Black Power struggles. Jill Quadagno, political sociologist, has called people who participated in job programs or filed suit against racist employers and unions "agents of equal opportunity."[67] William Gould has called them "private attorney generals."[68] But whatever the term used, the effect was that the limitations of federal agencies to substantively rectify employment discrimination had, at the same time, challenged and partly empowered African Americans to enforce the law themselves. In Seattle, black contractors in the Central Contractors Association were organized by Model Cities administrators to bid for Model Cities construction projects, but turned to direct action when they realized that they were still powerless to overcome the regional labor agreements that made it impossible for them to hire black workers. In Pittsburgh, the Black Construction Coalition, which issued the call for the nationwide spread of the Black Monday movement, grew out of Operation Dig, a federal jobs training program.[69] And in Chicago, as Erik S. Gellman (chap. 5 in this volume) argues, neighborhood gang members exposed to the skilled trades when they participated in a million-dollar War on Poverty job training program in 1967 later played a pivotal role in the Coalition for Community Action (CUCA) massive direct action campaigns in 1969.[70]

The construction coalitions that emerged around the country following the 1969 direct action protests in Chicago, Pittsburgh, Philadelphia, and Seattle contributed to a national debate regarding the role that labor unions played in contributing to the racially fractured nature of the working class in the United States. Yet it was the rapid development of construction coalitions in Detroit,

San Francisco, New York, Boston, Newark, Cleveland, Milwaukee, and Buffalo following the Black Monday protests that made it politically possible for Arthur Fletcher, the Philadelphia Plan's lead advocate in the Department of Labor, to expand it to the rest of the country.[71] And it was their continued participation in attempts to enforce the Department of Labor affirmative action plans that helped make the Philadelphia Plan so contentious among elected officials.

Although still in alliance with established civil rights organizations or radical Black Power organizations, self-organized black workers and contractors challenged the legitimacy of the traditional unions as spokesmen for the working class. When accused by building trades union leaders of representing "dual unionism" or of being used by antiunion contractors (who also, not coincidentally, happened to be black), black construction coalitions frequently responded by framing their advocacy of affirmative action as an antiracist remedy for the historic exclusivity of the AFL craft unionism. Don Newsom, a contract-compliance officer for the Seattle Model Cities Program, expressed a view common to construction coalition supporters around the country when he told a reporter, "the black workers' struggle for construction jobs is simply an extension of the labor movement....The building trades unions have lost sight of their real role in this system: to champion the cause of *all* workers."[72] To them, the expansion and enforcement of the Philadelphia Plan grew out of debates not just over formal versus substantive justice and also over the conservative and exclusive legacy of craft unionism and of the labor movement in general.

This distinction was often lost on building trades union leaders, who saw the Philadelphia Plan as a violation of their collective bargaining rights and who saw no problem with their completely controlling the desegregation of their own unions. It was also lost on leaders in the AFL-CIO, whose president, George Meany, had himself come from an all-white plumbers union in New York City. The effectiveness of grassroots movements against the Philadelphia Plan by building trades union members and their ability to mobilize political alliances in self-defense stifled attempts to use affirmative action to reform the labor movement from the outside. In the process, their success helped stigmatize affirmative action by eliding its supporters claims to be pro-union.

In Chicago, as Erik S. Gellman (chap. 5) shows, construction-site closures led by militant political gangs forced a debate over craft union racism that had long been suppressed by the powerful political allies of the building trades. But Mayor Richard Daley, with assistance from the Chicago Police Department antigang unit, coopted that debate and compelled local activists to sign off on a weak Chicago Plan, which served as a model for how building trades union leaders around the country could undermine the expansion of the Philadelphia Plan from within.

As Trevor Griffey (chap. 6 in this volume) shows, when Arthur Fletcher sought to overcome the failed hometown plan process shaped by the Chicago Plan, building trades union leaders in New York City made their political alliance with Richard Nixon in support for the Vietnam War contingent on having Fletcher removed from the Department of Labor. Nixon capitulated to their demand, noting privately to his adviser that "The Philadelphia Plan is right, but it hurts us."[73] Building trades union resistance to affirmative action, Griffey concludes, played a significant role in Nixon's decision to pursue a "post-southern strategy" to mobilize racial antagonism among members of the white working class in the North to his advantage in his 1972 reelection campaign.

So, although African American movements to desegregate the construction industry made affirmative action politically possible, that moment of possibility was exceptionally brief. In most instances, the creation of affirmative action policy in the construction industry provided cover for repressing Black Power activists rather than empowering them. Violent repression of the African American activists who led the 1969 construction-site closures—by the police in Chicago and by union thugs, especially in cities where the building trades were controlled by organized crime—accompanied the hollowing out of the implementation of affirmative action, making it much more difficult and dangerous to sustain a campaign against the ongoing racism in the building trades. And in some cities, including Chicago and Pittsburgh, African Americans serving on the staff of weak hometown plans tended to focus their efforts more on personally benefiting from illegal kickbacks than on fighting for meaningful compliance.

Black men's movements to desegregate the construction industry in the 1960s opened the door for women to enter the trades, but only slightly. Although the male-centered grassroots movements of the 1960s and 1970s provided women with inspiration as well as legal leverage, the debate over hiring in the construction industry remained largely about competing claims of manhood. Women thus had to fight their own struggles against workplace sexism and harassment, sexism within existing minority coalitions, and the low priority that federal bureaucrats gave to enforcing nondiscrimination laws for women seeking employment in the construction industry.

But the legacy of the Philadelphia Plan is not just its having helped provide grist for the white working-class backlash against the black freedom movement and the women's movement. In Seattle, where activists relied less on the Department of Labor and more on Title VII litigation, the United Construction Workers Association (UCWA) created an innovative community-organizing model that sought to combat union resistance to affirmative action. As Trevor Griffey (chap. 7 in this volume) shows, that model of fusing class-action lawsuits with community organizing and giving the objects of affirmative action plans (the minority workers) a substantial role in the implementation of affirmative action, had a significant influence on the development of the left in Seattle in the 1970s. As we argue in the conclusion to this volume, this example, as well as those previously chronicled, have much to teach those seeking to build power at work and a labor movement rooted in inclusion and social justice today.

The interventions in the histories of the civil rights and Black Power movements in this book build on as well as depart from previous scholarship on grassroots mobilizations of affirmative action law, especially as it relates to the complicated mobilization of black workers to desegregate white workers' unions. As Nancy MacLean has shown, affirmative action emerged from the black freedom movement, and its enforcement inspired a movement of everyday people whose assertion of their new rights on the job weakened the "culture of exclusion" from high-skilled and high-paying work that for centuries had relegated women and nonwhite men to second-class citizenship.[74]

A number of other studies have documented the significance of individual struggles for racial and gender desegregation in the workplace in the 1960s and 1970s—especially through the use of Title VII law.[75] Yet the struggles against the culture of exclusion are not so easily grouped together as movements for inclusion, especially when the objects of such struggles are labor unions that have their own histories of invoking class differences to challenge liberal universalism. As numerous chapters in this book document, those community activists who organized direct action protests to desegregate the construction industry in the 1960s saw affirmative action plans that granted them inclusion without power as doomed to failure because such plans continued to put racists in charge of desegregating their own unions. We need to take activists' radical and, in some ways, utopian visions seriously, lest we conflate the goals of these social movements with the liberal political and legal compromises—which sometimes provided cover for union-busting—that employers and politicians used to manage and coopt them.

Even though the Black Power campaigns to desegregate the construction industry were largely unsuccessful, they nonetheless helped lay a legal, organizational, tactical, and philosophical foundation for other aggrieved and underrepresented groups of workers. By separating ideas of race and class, and too often suggesting that affirmative action undermined class consciousness by promoting identity politics, historians critical of affirmative action have failed to take seriously the ways in which a new kind of labor radicalism emerged through community control, Black Power, and affirmative action politics.[76]

The campaigns of the Black Power movement against the nepotistic, racist, and politically conservative building trades unions, although largely thwarted by machinations at both the local and national levels, played a significant role in the larger development of an identity-based working-class politics that linked the politics of work with the politics of community. These campaigns attempted to confront white identity politics and, in the process, democratize the labor movement.

This is perhaps the least appreciated legacy of the Black Power movement—its contribution to a new working-class radicalism through which leftists of different stripes came to see the desegregation of work and organized labor as key to the revitalization of labor in the 1970s. Rather than dividing the labor movement, the "movement of movements" that Black Power was a part of and helped inspire actively challenged racism and sexism in the labor movement and in society as a whole. These movements represented, and continue to represent, the best hope we have for a more just labor politics and society. The lesson is as relevant today as it was then: "racism, not racially defined activism, is the real threat to workers and the labor movement."[77]

"REVOLUTION HAS COME TO BROOKLYN"

Construction Trades Protests and the Negro Revolt of 1963

Brian Purnell

In 1963, the national civil rights movement experienced several key turning points. That spring, the violent suppression of peaceful demonstrators in Birmingham, Alabama, was televised across the nation as citizens watched firefighters blasting black people with high-pressure water hoses and police dogs mauling nonviolent protesters. This dramatic campaign, and Martin Luther King's stirring "Letter from a Birmingham Jail," in which he reminded moderates that "freedom is never voluntarily given by the oppressor; it must be demanded by the oppressed," sent a heroic message to citizens around the country regarding the moral righteousness of nonviolence. In August, ten weeks after Byron De La Beckwith assassinated Mississippi civil rights leader Medgar Evers, the nonviolent movement reached its apotheosis when more than 200,000 people participated in the triumphant March on Washington. But a little over two weeks later, again in Birmingham, the nation witnessed the horrific murder of four young girls in the dynamite attack on the Sixteenth Street Baptist Church. That shocking event became a rhetorical symbol in public denunciations of the nonviolent approach of the civil rights movement. More violence followed in November when President John F. Kennedy was assassinated, but that catastrophe made Lyndon Johnson president. In less than two years, Johnson pushed through and signed into law the monumental legislation of the movement. In retrospect, the key events and images—the heroism, the speeches, the setbacks

I thank Clarence Taylor, Jeanne Theoharis, David Goldberg, Trevor Griffey, and the anonymous reviewers for commenting on earlier drafts of this chapter.

turned into successes—of 1963 are among the most iconic symbols of the legacy of the movement.[1]

But triumph from tragedy and progress toward legal victories are only part of the story that watershed year tells. If we include northern protests in the historical narrative of the civil rights movement, 1963 is also the year in which we witness increased militancy within protest organizations and more attention given to issues of economic justice. Northern activists, frustrated over the slow pace with which elected officials and labor leaders addressed widespread employment discrimination, demanded that black workers have immediate access to jobs historically closed to African Americans. This was especially true in the construction trades. In spring and summer 1963, northern activists organized picketers at major construction sites and implemented aggressive, antagonistic tactics to demand the entrance of minority workers into all-white unions and immediate employment for unemployed black laborers. In the goals and tactics of these demonstrations, we see how, several years before Black Power became a rally cry for the departure from interracial organizations and nonviolent protest, activists in the urban North initiated increasingly antagonistic and militant campaigns for economic justice. With northern protests for jobs part of the post–World War II U.S. historical narrative, we can see that demands for economic justice, compensatory hiring practices, and affirmative action were present in both the civil rights *and* Black Power movements. Rather than the Black Power movement's supplanting the civil rights movement, which is often how this part of history is rendered, the inclusion of the northern protests for economic justice reveals how civil rights and Black Power coexisted and were in conversation with one another throughout the Revolt of 1963.

The spring and summer months of 1963 offer an ideal window through which to view the blurred lines between the civil rights and Black Power movements. While Martin Luther King Jr. was leading desegregation demonstrations in Birmingham, local activists in the National Association for the Advancement of Colored People (NAACP) and the Congress of Racial Equality (CORE) were launching large demonstrations against racial discrimination in the building trades unions in New York, Philadelphia, Newark, Trenton, and Cleveland. For these northern urban activists, this was the most important civil rights issue.[2] Most black construction workers—the few who were able to attain steady employment or even union membership—were segregated into menial, low-skilled jobs. Rarely could black workers gain access to the skilled professions in the construction industry or to union protections and benefits, all of which provided salaries that facilitated many white construction workers' entrance into the U.S. middle class as homeowners.[3]

Thus, the attack by the black freedom movement against employment discrimination in the building trades industry marked a significant moment when activists applied pressure tactics for blacks' immediate entrance into one of the most racially segregated and well-paying sectors of the U.S. workforce. In the short run, these protests achieved little in terms of breaking down the racial barriers in construction unions. But over the long term, they transformed many first-time demonstrators into lifelong activists, some of whom became significant radical leaders in the modern black freedom movement. These campaigns also helped created new, more militant organizations, such as Harlem Fight Back, which spent decades struggling to secure jobs for black workers in the building trades. And last, these campaigns against discrimination in the construction trades focused the attention of the black freedom movement on employment discrimination, job-creation initiatives, and calls for economic justice through affirmative action. Economic justice did *not* first emerge as a national civil rights issue in the mid-1960s after the movement had secured voting rights and cities exploded in violence. Breaking down racial barriers in employment had always been an important goal of the black freedom movement. And in the early 1960s, this long-term goal gained much needed energy, direction, and attention through northern efforts to desegregate the construction trades unions.

"A New Push"

In 1963, national leaders from NAACP and CORE expressed their displeasure with politicians' and labor leaders' consistent foot-dragging and back-peddling when faced with demands that they desegregate the construction trades. In early June 1963, NAACP Labor Secretary Herbert Hill upbraided specific unions in New York City, such as Local 28 of the Sheet Metal Workers, which had close to 3,300 members, none of whom was an African American, and the Kennedy administration, which failed to use its power and prestige to address national patterns of segregation and discrimination. "For years," Hill declared, "we have attempted through conferences, memoranda, and interminable negotiations to make progress for Negro workers in the building trades' craft unions. This has been an exercise in futility."[4] James Farmer, the CORE national chairman, appeared on a televised news program called *The Open Mind*, hosted by Richard Heffner, and argued that "it is necessary for there to be a new push" in the national movement, one that forced employers and government leaders to begin "compensatory, preferential hiring" in industries that for years had excluded African American laborers. Farmer argued that employers and trade unionists had a responsibility "to seek qualified Negroes, and if they are not qualified for the specific job to help train them, and to admit them to apprenticeship training classes." When Heffner stated that Farmer's arguments sounded like demands for something "more than equality," the CORE spokesman's baritone shot back

that black people in the United States had received "special treatment of a negative nature for 300 to 400 years," and that "now we're asking for the kind of special treatment that is positive and affirmative."[5]

For northern urban civil rights activists, the building trades industries and
construction unions were perfect targets against which to mount aggressive campaigns for jobs. Historically, African Americans had worked in the "trowel trades"
of the construction industries as low-skilled, menial laborers. Although black
workers earned good wages hauling materials, excavating rock, or performing
other low-end construction work, jobs in the "trowel trades," and even construction jobs that required specialized skills, were rarely permanent and always physically taxing and dangerous. When day laborers were no longer needed at a work
site they were cut loose. With no union protection or job placement assistance,
they wandered from site to site, or even city to city, in search of work. African
American construction workers in the postwar era found it almost impossible
to advance to positions that required more skills and paid higher wages. Unlike
many whites, they could not use construction work to climb the economic and
social ladder into the U.S. middle class.

In New York state during the early 1960s, this discrimination made a record
$345 million in construction work practically unavailable to African Ameri-
cans and Puerto Ricans. Whites dominated the industry; in 1960, they made up
92 percent of the 189,122 workers enrolled in the 121 New York City building
trades unions. As African Americans and Latinos grew to almost one-quarter
of the city population, they still held only just under 8 percent of city construction jobs, mostly in the lowest, meanest positions available. Some unions
had no black members, or only a token number: Local 1 Plumbers had 3,000
members total and only 9 blacks; Local 2 Plumbers and Steamfitters had
4,100 members total and only 16 blacks; Local 28 Sheet Metal Workers had
no blacks among its 3,300 members. Only the forty-two Carpenters and Joiners locals had a sizable number of black members; out of 34,000 members,
5,000 were African American. At a time when the construction industry was
booming thanks to government-funded building projects, unions excluded
African Americans from lucrative jobs, denied them access to apprenticeship
programs, and barred them from advancement in one of the most promising
labor markets for unskilled men with little or no specialized education.[6]

Throughout the construction industry, from the union locals that ran apprenticeship programs and trained new workers to the small contracting firms or
large companies that employed them, networks built through friendship, famil-
ial ties, organized crime, and political cronyism determined who received jobs,
and the type of work they performed. The highly skilled, best-paying jobs such
as electricians, steamfitters, and sheet metal workers were passed down from

fathers to sons, uncles to nephews, and among cousins and neighborhood buddies as ethnic groups created specified niches within the construction industry and its unions. Over time, Italian, Irish, and Polish Americans amassed political power and became economically mobile, in part through their monopolization of construction jobs.[7]

In New York City, the industry was almost entirely white. Black workers had made some gains during World War I and World War II, but those advances receded quickly during the Great Depression and the postwar periods. Some union locals made no attempt to cover up their exclusion of blacks. Local 3 of the electrical workers outright refused to admit African Americans. Plumbers Local 2 enforced racial exclusiveness by not issuing licenses to black workers who had gained experience or completed apprentice programs in other states. Sheet Metal Workers Local 28 was strictly a father-son local with no black members at all. Carpenters were a less-skilled group and had more black workers, but their unions also segregated members. After World War I, black carpenters were assigned to Local 1888, a mixed local based in Harlem. As whites transferred out, the local became exclusively black, and union councils relegated black workers to jobs in Harlem, limiting the number of work sites available to them. As a result, black membership in the Carpenters' local fell from 440 members in 1926 to an abysmal 65 members in 1935.[8]

For Gilbert Banks, a man who became a significant leader in the efforts to crack the New York City construction industry color line, the subtle informal methods of racial discrimination that denied construction jobs and advanced training to African Americans became all too clear when he left the army in 1953. An expert diesel mechanic during World War II, Banks could not find work in his field after his nine years of service and becoming a high-ranking noncommissioned officer. He searched for any type of work on construction sites, but foremen usually hired blacks only when they were behind schedule. Men such as Banks got sporadic work in the worst jobs that provided the least pay. Sometimes, he found temporary jobs as a "chipper." Chippers operated a pneumatic hammer that broke concrete, which was one of the most basic, dangerous, and unhealthy jobs at a building site. Banks noticed that men who had been chippers for years did not live long. Many developed silicosis from breathing in dust from the machines and spending hours in deep holes with little or no ventilation. Whenever Banks asked for work that was permanent or more related to his expertise, foremen and unions gave him the same run-around: "They'd say, 'Have you got a (Union membership) book?' I'd say, 'No.' 'Well,' they said, 'Go get a book and we'll give you a job.' And I'd go to the Union and ask them for a book. They'd say, 'Listen if you get the job, we'll give you a book.' There was no way of fighting it."[9]

Banks's memory of black workers being systemically barred from work in the construction trades seemed true for New York City at the start of summer 1963. After multiple reports and statements from the Urban League, NAACP, and Negro American Labor Council criticizing the inaction and apathy of elected officials and labor leaders, New York politicians and union power brokers responded with tough talk about equal opportunity but empty promises regarding enforcement. "Whatever we have been doing in the field of human rights until today is still not enough for tomorrow," Mayor Robert F. Wagner declared in a statement to aides charged with monitoring racial discrimination in private organizations that had contracts with the city. "By law and by mayoral direction," he proclaimed, "every agency and department is under mandate to advance the cause of equal rights and equal opportunity." James J. McFadden, the New York labor commissioner, echoed the mayor's sentiments. "Statistic after statistic," he wrote to twenty-four construction union leaders, "clearly indicate that right here in New York City many of our Negro and Puerto Rican workers are making little true progress in the vital fields of wages and employment." Blacks and Puerto Ricans were under-represented in construction unions, McFadden argued, because of the "histori-cal hiring patterns that have been allowed to develop." "The time to correct this inheritance is now," he declared. "Change is long over due." And in a separate meeting with two of the most powerful city labor leaders, Peter J. Brennan, presi-dent of the Building and Construction Trades Council, and Harry Van Arsdale, president of the Central Labor Council, Mayor Wagner demanded "more jobs and more job opportunities for members of the minorities who have a much greater unemployment ration the rest of the city's population." "The goal," Wag-ner exclaimed, "is not headlines." Nonetheless, no jobs or investigations into pat-terns of bias came out of these meetings, and their statements did not inspire any tangible changes.[10]

The failure of more mainstream civil rights groups to negotiate a workable plan for desegregating the construction industry inspired more militant activists to increase pressure on the mayor and leaders of the building trades unions. New York City CORE chapters led the way, taking to the streets in Harlem to demand that contractors immediately hire qualified African American and Puerto Ricans as construction workers. In early June, 150 demonstrators shut down work at the Harlem Hospital annex. Protestors blocked entrances to the work site and forced police to carry them from the scene. Minor scuffles broke out, and fears of a riot brought three hundred police officers to the scene. The head contractor suspended work for the day. The following day brought even more protestors and police officers to the construction site. While tensions mounted in Harlem, Mayor Wagner attended a conference in Hawaii. In his absence, Paul Screvane, the acting mayor, officially shut down the Harlem Hospital project. Concern for "public safety," he said, was the reason for his decision. Screvane suspended work on the annex until the mayor could confer with labor leaders and investigate the demonstrators' charges. Protestors in Harlem cheered when they heard Screvane's decision.[11]

Brooklyn CORE activists wanted to build on the momentum generated by the Harlem Hospital demonstration. Their target was the Downstate Medical Center construction project slated by the state to upgrade the sprawling Kings County Hospital complex with a new 350-bed teaching hospital and renovations to the State University of New York (SUNY) medical school campus housed in the Kings County facilities. These construction projects were part of the $353 million earmarked by the state in 1960 to expand the entire SUNY system by 1965. Upgrading the two state medical schools was the main priority of this overhaul. Albany had allocated $20 million for the construction costs of new facilities at SUNY Downstate Medical Center in Brooklyn and $22 million for its counterpart, the SUNY Upstate Medical Center in Syracuse. With these improvements, SUNY Downstate would be able to increase its student capacity from 587 to 800 and SUNY Upstate would expand from 308 to 400.[12]

The massive, multimillion dollar, state-funded Downstate Medical Center project seemed to be a boon for almost everyone: the SUNY system administrators; the Kings County Hospital complex; city residents who wanted affordable medical school training; and the citizens of Brooklyn, who received a new state of the art medical facility. But one group that criticized the construction project was unemployed black laborers, especially those who lived in the black residential areas of north central Brooklyn—the neighborhoods of Bedford-Stuyvesant, Crown Heights, Brownsville, Fort Greene, and East New York—which bordered the Flatbush section of the borough where Downstate was located. Throughout most of the post–World War II period, Flatbush itself was a largely white residential neighborhood, but small numbers of African Americans from the surrounding black enclaves slowly found housing in the community. Nonetheless, Brooklyn CORE activists found that the workforce for the Downstate project was almost entirely white. Most of the workers came from white areas of Brooklyn and Queens, but some commuted to Downstate from as far away as Long Island, Connecticut, and New Jersey. Yet black workers such as Gilbert Banks could not attain jobs a quarter mile from their homes.

Staging a demonstration at Downstate would be difficult. The main work site was a seven-story medical school facility and teaching hospital annex embedded in a sprawling complex four city blocks wide and one large block long. To further complicate matters, the site had several entrances. Four leaders in Brooklyn CORE investigated the scene: Oliver Leeds, the chapter president; Gilbert Banks; Maurice Fredericks; and Vincent Young. Leeds saw hundreds of workers, large cement trucks, bulldozers, and cranes constantly entering and leaving the site. Except for a handful of carpenters' assistants, there were few black workers. They immediately realized that the site was too large for Brooklyn CORE to picket alone. At most, the chapter had thirty to forty members, only ten or twelve of whom could be counted on to attend every meeting and demonstration. If Brooklyn CORE wanted to stage an effective protest and disrupt construction at Downstate, it would need hundreds of participants. As a result, its leaders sought support from other local civil rights organizations and black churches.[13]

Leeds first contacted Warren Bunn, president of the Brooklyn chapter of the NAACP, and John Parham, leader of the local the Urban League chapter. In early July, the three went to the Downstate construction site to gather more data. After walking around the work area, they witnessed how the few black workers there did only menial labor. Bunn, Leeds, and Parham took their complaints to leaders of local construction unions and tried to convince them to recruit more black workers. The union leaders' responses were not pleasant. "They wouldn't even listen to us," Leeds recalled. "One of them almost threw us down the stairs."[14]

The three men went back to Downstate and planned their demonstration strategy. The main construction area had one large entrance on its far west side. A large picket line in front of that area could effectively slow down the work site, and if enough people sat down in front of trucks, they could repeat the success of the Harlem protest. But Leeds knew Bunn and Parham could not rally enough members to pull off that type of disruption. According to him, "Johnny Parham's Urban League had no troops" and "the NAACP had a big paper membership, but it undoubtedly couldn't get 10 people out there on a Monday morning at 7 o'clock." Brooklyn CORE could guarantee twenty people, but Leeds knew it would not be enough. Demonstrators would have to maintain the picket line from 7 a.m. to 4 p.m., five days a week. It would take hundreds, if not thousands, of people to make a protest at Downstate as successful as the protest at Harlem Hospital. Leeds had the foresight to reach out to the black churches in Brooklyn, several of which had over 1,000 members. With support from their ministers, Leeds felt confident they would have enough troops to lead an effective protest at Downstate.[15]

But getting the ministers to support a Brooklyn CORE project was its own struggle. For the most part, black church leaders in Brooklyn held conservative views about civil disobedience. With the exception of the Reverend Milton Galamison, black Brooklyn clergy rarely participated in Brooklyn CORE civil rights activities, which tended to be confrontational. More prominent ministers, moreover, did not want to risk their reputation by being associated with militants in Brooklyn CORE. The two ministers with the most political power in Brooklyn were Reverend Sandy F. Ray and Reverend Dr. Gardner Taylor. Ray, the sixty-five-year-old pastor of Cornerstone Baptist Church, was an avid supporter of Governor Nelson Rockefeller. The governor made annual visits to Cornerstone and had spoken there several times during the campaign season. Taylor, pastor of Concord Baptist Church, was a leading Democrat in Brooklyn and had a close relationship with Mayor Wagner. In 1958, the mayor had appointed Taylor to the Board of Education and in 1962 made him Democratic Party leader in Brooklyn. Like Ray and Taylor, most of black ministers in Brooklyn thought of themselves as moderate power brokers. They felt they could use their influence over thousands of black voters as leverage with elected officials. Brooklyn CORE had a reputation for rabble rousing and militancy. If the ministers participated in anything led by CORE, they risked losing their clout with their friends in City Hall and Albany.[16]

The Harlem Hospital demonstration, however, had made fighting against racial discrimination in the building trades the most important civil rights issue in the city. Other demonstrations sprang up all over Manhattan. East River CORE, a chapter in the Lower East Side of Manhattan, began a similar protest at the construction site of the Rutgers housing projects, and a coalition of activists from different organizations began a round-the-clock sit-in at the mayor's and governor's downtown offices. Calling themselves the Joint Committee for Equality, they demanded that New York elected officials enforce the state antidiscrimination laws, especially in the building trades. By early July, Leeds remembered, "you couldn't pick-up a newspaper anywhere in New York City without seeing demonstrations at construction sites all over the city, all over, except Brooklyn." Leeds intimated that if the ministers did not support the Brooklyn CORE demonstration at Downstate that they would be seen as meek during the high point of civil rights activism.[17]

Not wanting to lose face, fourteen of the Brooklyn African American ministers agreed to encourage their congregations to support the Downstate campaign. Most, like Gardner Taylor, hesitated when Leeds approached them with the idea for the CORE protest. "Well Ollie," Leeds remembered Taylor saying, "I think that's a good idea. I'll do the best I can. I got a busy schedule. I don't know if I can make it, but I'll give it a try."[18] Eventually, however, he and other ministers not only gave the campaign their full support but also became its most ardent spokesmen and leaders.

Many factors influenced their change of heart. According to Clarence Taylor, a historian, the ministers were inspired by the example of Martin Luther King, whose leadership in the South motivated clergymen around the country to see nonviolent direct action as a powerful weapon for social and political change. The Brooklyn ministers were also motivated by the opportunity to show the power of their local influence. They were confident that they could get hundreds, if not thousands, of their members to participate nonviolently in the demonstration and take the media spotlight off the contribution of Brooklyn CORE. They formed the Ministers' Committee for Job Opportunities and planned to make their first appearance on the picket lines on Monday, July 15, using the previous day's sermons to drum up support.[19]

The members of the Ministers' Committee positioned themselves to become the de facto leaders of the campaign. Not wanting to feel controlled by outsiders, Brooklyn CORE members organized their own picket line in front of Downstate on Wednesday, July 10. By 7 a.m. that morning, only thirty people had shown up. Some blocked the entrance to the work site, but they failed to disrupt the site for long. Police arrested Gilbert Banks for disorderly conduct when he sat down in front of an on-coming truck. Elaine and Jerome Bibuld, a married couple, both staunch members of Brooklyn CORE, were also present with their children. Both were arrested for allegedly assaulting police officers. The *New York Times* reported that "Mrs. Bibuld had kicked one policeman and her husband had punched two others when the policeman tried to move them out of the path of cement-mixing trucks." Elaine Bibuld's side of the story is that an officer pointed at her and her husband and said to his partner, "Get those two." When Jerome and their oldest son, Douglass, passed the police officer, Elaine saw him push at the boy. Jerome came to Douglass's defense and wrestled the cop to the ground. The officer rolled on top of Jerome Bibuld, pressed a knee into his groin, and used Jerome's jacket zipper to choke his neck. When Elaine saw this, she said, she sprang into action. "I personally had not, up until that point, been ready to attack anybody," she recalled, "but that was my husband and my child! I was going to kick this cop's testicles as far up through his head as I could get them. I meant to hurt him, but he was getting up just as my foot was connecting so my foot hit him in the middle of his back."[20] During Elaine Bibuld's arraignment, the judge lectured her on the impertinence of civil disobedience. "You know who you are?" Elaine screamed at the African American judge. "You're Uncle Tom with Jim Crow sitting on his shoulder!" The judge held her in contempt and sentenced her to ten days in the Women's House of Detention. Elaine was pregnant at the time, and the trauma of the fight and prison sentence proved too much; shortly after her release, she miscarried.[21]

Elaine Bibuld's actions on the picket line—and in court—illustrates how frustrated, impatient, and bold some Brooklyn CORE members had become and how this dynamic could have a powerful effect on the tenor of the Downstate demonstration. The ministers felt that their leadership could control the picket lines and keep the participants from becoming too brash. From July 15 on, they effectively took over as leaders of the Downstate campaign. Still, the Downstate protest attracted certain participants who were neither interested in following the ministers' direction nor willing to adhere to the CORE principles of nonviolence. This element, more than Brooklyn CORE tactics or the ministers' moral authority and political power, did a great deal to shape the outcome of the campaign.

Direct Action at Downstate

From the start, newspaper reporters and politicians treated the members of the Ministers' Committee as the titular leaders and practically ignored the role of Brooklyn CORE in organizing the protest. Most of the participants in the demonstration came from various congregations, and the churches themselves served as bases of operation. The ministers held rallies in their church halls, raised bail money from members for at Sunday services, and inspired congregants with weekly sermons on the righteousness and justness of their cause.[22]

Still, the Brooklyn CORE members were a significant force at the picket line. Their experiences during earlier campaigns made them much more experienced than the ministers in working with the press and devising tactics to disrupt the work site. On the picket lines, Brooklyn CORE members' tactics garnered three solid weeks of media attention. The ministers, on the other hand, were overly cautious when it came to disrupting work at the site. Protective of their reputations, they tried to choreograph their every move on the picket line, including the exact day they would get arrested. They even sought to control the demonstrators' behavior, a task that became more difficult as time went on.[23]

Monday, July 15 was the first day at Downstate for the Ministers' Committee and fourteen of the most prominent black clergymen in Brooklyn arrived at the site at 7 a.m., along with over seventy-five people from their churches. The ministers planned to make their presence known by giving interviews to reporters and posing for pictures, but they wanted to wait to get arrested until Wednesday, July 17. By that time, the ministers thought, they could generate sufficient buzz in the media and they would be perceived as leading the campaign to greater militancy.[24]

Media attention would be essential for the success of the campaign. The CORE leaders and the ministers wanted photographers and television cameras to capture images of demonstrators lying in front of trucks, blocking entrances, singing freedom songs, and being carried away by police officers. Images of the most prominent black ministers in Brooklyn engaged in civil disobedience would be one of the most important weapons of the campaign. The public had seen similar images from the South, and such pictures had swayed northerners' opinions to support the southern civil rights movement. Brooklyn CORE and the ministers hoped their demonstration at Downstate would rouse public support for increased employment opportunities for African American and Puerto Rican workers on publicly funded construction projects.[25]

On that first morning, the ministers and demonstrators formed a picket line and marched peacefully for an hour. Some newspaper reporters and one television crew arrived. Gardner Taylor and the other ministers approached Leeds and made plans to return on Wednesday and get arrested then. Years later, Leeds referred to this staged arrest as the "big show." Taylor blamed the low turnout by the press for their premature exit from the picket line. "We've got to stop this discrimination in these construction places, and I don't mind going to jail for it but if I go to jail I'd like to get my picture took [sic]," Leeds recalled him saying. The ministers were ready to leave the demonstration when Leeds saw a truck about to enter the site. "I'll go for the 'big show' Wednesday," he told the departing ministers, "but I'm taking this one *today*." Leeds went by himself, sat down, and blocked the large truck. All fourteen ministers followed him and sat down too.[26]

They blocked the truck for over an hour. During that time, more reporters and photographers arrived at the scene. The arrest of fourteen of the most prominent Brooklyn ministers on the first major day of picketing was a dramatic event. It inspired twenty-seven others to lie down and block trucks until police arrested them too. A story appeared on the front page of the *New York Times*, which lauded the Reverend Dr. Taylor as "one of the most prominent Negro religious leaders in the city" and highlighted the minister's leadership of the protest. The *Times* also featured a picture of ministers who went limp and forced police officers to carry them into the wagon, a tactic they probably copied from Brooklyn CORE members arrested earlier that day.[27]

Later in the day, over four hundred people attended the ministers' arraignment at the Brooklyn Criminal Court. The Reverend George Lawrence, who was absent from the day's action, arrived at the courthouse just in time to greet reporters as the demonstrators' spokesman. He mentioned that "the Bedford-Stuyvesant section is on the brink of a very violent outburst" but that he and the other ministers would do their best to maintain peace. "The reason why our clergymen took part [in the demonstration] is that we feel anything concerning our people is our concern since they look to us for leadership and guidance. The militant action was forced upon us by the inaction of the Governor and the Mayor." Reporters also interviewed Dr. Taylor, who emphasized the ministers' role in bringing about justice: "Most of the prophets spent time in jail. This is a long tradition. When a government is corrupt, as this one is about discrimination, it must be challenged, particularly by those who love it and certainly by religious people."[28]

That evening, a postdemonstration rally at Bethany Baptist Church attracted over 1,500 people, and the members of the Ministers' Committee became the public leaders of the campaign when they issued the following demand: Governor Rockefeller, Mayor Wagner, and Building Trades Council President Brennan had to make the workforce on all publicly funded construction jobs at least 25 percent African American and Puerto Rican. If the New York political and labor leaders refused, the ministers would continue the protest, which they promised would lead to a record number of arrests. "We need more jailbirds for freedom," George Lawrence told the crowd. He encouraged the twenty-six ministers in attendance to support this campaign by leading their congregations in sit-ins at Downstate. Other ministers hinted that uncontrollable violence might also result. Dr. Taylor exclaimed that "blood may flow in the streets of Brooklyn, and if it does the streets will be cleansed. If necessary we will die like heroes."[29] The ministers allowed Oliver Leeds to speak, and he recalled that he made one of the most memorable speeches of the evening, one that made construction industry racism the symbol of the failure of the United States to hold true to its democratic principles:

> I went in the Army and I tried to join the Tank Corps. When I got down to Louisiana I found I was in the Corps of Engineers. And you know what we do? We *worked* to win the war. We built anything that could be built: bridges, tunnels, houses, officers' quarters, mess quarter, roads, and airstrips. We loaded and unloaded ships. We did anything in the way that involved *work, construction work.* You know, when I got back to the United States, after the war, I couldn't get a job in construction, that there was no union that would let me in? And there was damn little that I couldn't do in the way of construction work. They'll take you and turn you into construction workers in the army, in a *segregated* army, and then when you get back into civilian life, you can't get a construction job.[30]

While he appealed to his audience's patriotism, Leeds remembered that the ministers had distanced themselves from him and Brooklyn CORE for being too radical. "They wanted to control it," he declared years later. They wanted to "be able to say that this was a civilized, well-organized demonstration, no radicals, nothing wild about it, even though it was wild. They were well intentioned but they wanted to control it, and within days they took it over."[31]

Brash Tactics Revive the Campaign and Attract New Participants

The ministers felt confident that the members of their churches would supply most of the troops for the protest and keep the numbers high at the demonstration.

The ministers also worked in their speeches and mass meetings to define the broader historical significance of the protest. A rally held on Sunday, July 21 in Bedford-Stuyvesant's Tompkins Park drew over 6,000 people. Reverend Sandy Ray declared that the Downstate campaign was a part of the national struggle for civil rights and human dignity. "We are here in response to the call of history," he exclaimed. "There will be no turning back until people in high places correct the wrongs of the nation." Dr. Taylor, a magnificent orator, also placed Downstate in the context of the national civil rights movement: "We're ready!" he shouted. "We're not going another step and America is not going anywhere without us!" "Revolution has come to Brooklyn!" he shouted. "Whatever the cost, we will set the nation straight....The protest will be peaceful, but if the ruling white power structure brings it about, our blood will fill the streets." The crowd responded with loud cries of "Yes sir!" and "Amen!" The ministers were also superb fundraisers. At the Tompkins Park rally, they announced that over $2,000 had been collected and another $3,140 was pledged to assist with legal fees. Those donations did not go to waste. Downstate made history for the high number of people arrested for disruptive acts of civil disobedience. On July 22, over 1,200 people attended the demonstration and over 200 were arrested. This was the largest mass arrest of African Americans in New York since 500 people were jailed during the Harlem riot on August 1, 1943.[32]

Still, as inspirational and powerful as the ministers were, they were less adept at sustaining a prolonged campaign. Participation waned over time. Days with hundreds of people on the picket line and many arrests—143 were arrested on July 23 and 84 on July 25—were followed by days with low turnouts and few arrests. By July 25, there were only 150 protestors on the picket line, and fewer than 50 people were arrested on July 30. For the protest to be effective, hundreds of demonstrators had to occupy the site all day. But, because most of their parishioners were working people who could not afford to lose more than a day's pay, drawing hundreds of participants to the site proved too difficult for the ministers to organize. On days when there were thin numbers on the picket lines, newspaper reporters ignored the demonstration. The campaign was in danger of fading from the headlines and politicians' attention. Protestors had to think of new ways to disrupt the worksite and maintain the momentum of the campaign.[33]

During these low points, Brooklyn CORE members revitalized the campaign. CORE members and other protestors who were not beholden to the ministers kept the media focused on the demonstration by using innovative tactics the ministers thought were too outrageous, inappropriate, or antagonistic. At a strategy meeting, some members of the Ministers' Committee suggested using children in the sit-downs, similar to the way children in Birmingham had filled the jails during desegregation protests that summer. Eventually, the committee rejected this idea because a majority felt it was too dangerous and that they might lose public support if people saw pictures of children sitting in front of steamrollers and bulldozers. But Brooklyn CORE did not go along with their decision. On a day when only sixty people attended the picket line and there were only twenty-seven arrests for blocking entrances to the site, two members of Brooklyn CORE organized seventeen children to block the main entrance and get arrested. Barbara Weeks, a member of Brooklyn CORE since the chapter was formed in 1960, and Isaiah Brunson, a twenty-one-year-old from Sumter, South Carolina, who had joined Brooklyn CORE during the Downstate campaign, orchestrated the children's demonstration. When patrolmen asked them to escort the kids away from the entry roadway, Weeks and Brunson refused. Police charged them with endangering the lives of minors. The tactic made the front page of the newspaper.[34]

On another day with a low turnout, fourteen picketers chained their wrists together and refused to move from the work-site main entrance. They chanted, "Jim Crow must go," and sang "The Battle Hymn of the Republic." Two women at the site also grasped one another's arms and locked their legs together as they sat in front of a truck. They struggled and kicked as police attempted to separate and arrest them. On another occasion, Arnold Goldwag, a young white college-age member of Brooklyn CORE who served as the chapter community relations director, along with six others, climbed to the top of a crane shovel, which prevented it from bringing bricks into the work area. Twenty police officers climbed up after them. After a long struggle, police arrested the seven demonstrators. All the major city newspapers featured a picture of the dramatic scene. Shelly Spector, a young white woman who had joined Brooklyn CORE during the Downstate campaign, climbed the crane with Goldwag that day. Spector felt excited and invigorated to participate in such a dramatic fashion. Climbing that crane, she remembered, made her feel "the exhilaration of doing something meaningful and being part of a dedicated community."[35]

Veteran members of CORE expressed a similar sense of pride in participating in Downstate. Maurice Fredericks worked as a postal carrier from 6 a.m. until 2 p.m. Every day after work, he went home, changed his clothes, and attended the picket line. Sometimes he had to use vacation days or sick time when his arrests prevented him from going to work. Many in Brooklyn CORE viewed being arrested at Downstate as an honorable, even heroic act. Some of the younger members, such as Goldwag and Brunson, were arrested multiple times. Oliver Leeds claimed that Brunson and Goldwag, "were arrested every day, literally every day, and sometimes twice a day at Downstate." Leeds's probably exaggerated their arrest records, but other CORE members also remembered that going to jail during Downstate became a source of pride and a way they built camaraderie.

"You'd be ashamed if you didn't get arrested," Rioghan Kirchner, another Brooklyn CORE member since the chapter began in 1960, remarked. She was arrested twice at Downstate, once after she had called in sick to the public library where she worked. She almost lost her job when her supervisor recognized Kirchner's picture in the next day's newspaper. "Everyone at work kept saying, 'Gee that looks like you,'" she recalled. "I said, 'No. No I was so sick.'"[36]

Losing their employment was one fear that many had, but getting killed was another. "They would rev the engines, make you think they were going to run over you," Kirchner recalled. Maurice Fredericks was confident no one would be killed. "Honestly, I didn't expect to get killed," he remembered, "because there were a lot of people there and a whole lot of cops. You just assumed that the man wasn't going to run you over." His confidence also stemmed from his belief that white people in the North, unlike whites in the South, would not kill demonstrators. "There was always a more humane white person in the North than in the South," he argued. "That was our feeling anyway." Cameras and reporters also protected the demonstrators. "Whatever we were doing, there was plenty of press there," Elaine Bibuld recalled. With so much public attention on Downstate, the police and union leaders were extra cautious to prevent any fatal accidents.[37]

Daily news coverage of dramatic, heroic acts of civil disobedience and record-number arrests made the atmosphere at Downstate a magnet for activists from all over the city. Malcolm X attended the protest daily, but never participated in the demonstration. Some Brooklyn CORE members approached him and invited him to join the picket line, but he declined because the lines were interracial. According to Maurice Fredericks, Malcolm X told him, "I'd be only too happy to walk with you just as soon as you get them devils off your line." Fredericks and other black members of Brooklyn CORE who were committed to interracial solidarity, assured him that was impossible. "We were fighting against discrimination," Fredericks explained, "and we couldn't possibly do that."[38]

But Malcolm X's presence helped shape the evolution of Brooklyn CORE, even though he remained on the sidelines at the protest and preached about the futility of integration and nonviolent demonstration. The militant nature of the Downstate campaign tactics did not cause most veteran participants to reject principles such as interracial organizing or nonviolence that had shaped years of their political life, but it did attract new activists who were less committed to those ideals. While at the demonstration, Malcolm X caught the eye of a young Sonny Carson, who was drawn to the Downstate protest because of the militancy and dramatic tactics of Brooklyn CORE. A former street hustler and member of a gang called the Bishops, Carson was fresh from prison (for robbing a UPS worker) when the Downstate protests began. Meeting Malcolm X that day turned him into a political activist. Malcolm X approached him, shook his hand, and, according to Carson, "looked at me and said, you look like you can get something done." That inspired the young man to direct his energies and leadership abilities towards black nationalist politics and militant activism. For Carson, even as an emerging nationalist, the only protest organization that was worth joining was Brooklyn CORE. "Brooklyn CORE was in the papers more so than anybody else," he recalled. Carson also appreciated the boldness of Brooklyn CORE and its willingness to be confrontational; these appealed to the young militant's personality.

> Their sit-ins weren't all together non-violent. Non-violence prevented me from joining many groups because I just didn't believe in the concept. And at some of the (Brooklyn) Congress of Racial Equality's sit-ins or programs that were challenged by the white folks, it became confrontational and some them fought back. That caused me to look longer at them, then to look at some of the others like the NAACP and all those organizations that were talking about—when he hits you, don't hit him back. I'm not one of those kinds of people because when he hits me I'm *going* to hit them back. So the only group that I'd seen that could stand the way I felt, more so than anybody else, was CORE. And I meant Brooklyn CORE, because there were some CORE chapters that I didn't want anything to do with because of their leadership. But I think Brooklyn CORE was more suitable and appropriate for me at that moment. As I began to get more involved, the more I got involved, the more I began to see that there was room for new thought.[39]

For Carson and others, the boldness of Brooklyn CORE at Downstate signaled the arrival of a newer, more confrontational approach to civil rights activism. The campaign attracted many young people and first-time activists, some with nationalistic tendencies, like Carson, and others who just wanted to get involved in something exciting and meaningful. For Yuri Kochiyama and Frances Crayton, who were also not members of the local churches, participation in the Downstate protest was a chance to do something they felt would make a contribution to the larger freedom struggle. Their motivation also stemmed from personal experiences with racial discrimination and the inspiring examples of others at Downstate.

In 1963, Yuri Kochiyama was a forty-two-year-old Japanese American living in Harlem with her husband and six children. She had been politically active since her internment in one of the prison camps established for Japanese American citizens during World War II. Her activism in the camp, however, was mostly as a journalist and social events coordinator. Afterward, she and her husband Bill organized letter-writing campaigns to free Japanese American political prisoners.

During the late 1950s and early 1960s, Kochiyama read a great deal about the southern civil rights movement, but it was not until she and her husband moved to an apartment in a Harlem housing project that she became involved in the black freedom movement. She attended local political meetings and met key people who were leaders in the national movement. The Kochiyamas hosted social gatherings on Saturday nights at their apartment, which attracted many prominent activists including Ossie Davis, Ruby Dee, Malcolm X, and Bayard Rustin. Arnold Goldwag of Brooklyn CORE was also a regular. He remembered that "anyone who was anyone in the movement knew Saturday night at the Kochiyamas' was the place to hang out. This was the place where you brought a bottle of wine, you sat there and you bullshitted." James Peck, the famed CORE leader who was hospitalized in Birmingham, Alabama, during the Freedom Rides, began visiting the Kochiyamas' Saturday night socials in 1961. They became good friends, and Yuri Kochiyama developed a deep respect for CORE and its action-oriented activities. When the Downstate campaign began she volunteered to stand on the picket line. Kochiyama was inspired by the charged atmosphere of the demonstration. She brought her children to the picket line every day. The nonviolent methods and interracial protestors of the demonstration motivated Yuri to get arrested for the first time; she and her oldest son Billy were carried off by police for blocking a truck. Kochiyama said she felt proud and excited to "be a part of the actions, to be doing something to fight discrimination."[40]

Another person who was introduced to protest politics and Brooklyn CORE at the Downstate campaign was Frances Crayton. Born in 1943 in Columbus, Georgia, Crayton moved to Bedford-Stuyvesant with her mother and sister in 1956. While living in the South, Crayton's family had shielded her and her sister from the nastiness of Jim Crow racism. She spent most of her childhood in environments that were all black. When she went shopping in the city, Crayton recognized the segregated busses and second-class treatment blacks received in stores, but she also remembered that her mother and grandmother "made sure that we were never in a position of being insulted or accosted in any way." The older women in her family had mastered southern mores well enough so that Frances never had serious trouble with whites, that is, until she moved to Brooklyn.[41]

Crayton attended George Wingate High School, a new school in the Crown Heights section of Brooklyn. To get there, she traveled by bus and walked through white residential areas. Crayton felt tortured as young whites yelled slurs at black Wingate students who walked in their neighborhoods. In the afternoons, Crayton recalled, some white teenagers would drive around and "throw rocks at us and say, get out of our neighborhood, niggers go home." The experience stuck with her: "It always bared heavy on my mind that we weren't wanted in the neighborhood, that we were treated differently, that we were told that we better not be there after sundown. And it reminded me of the kind of thing that I had been hearing about in the South." When the demonstrations began at Downstate, she empathized with the African Americans who could not get work, whom she assumed were also ostracized and terrorized as minorities in all-white environments. "I knew how those workmen must feel," she recalled. "I mean, the fact that we can't get jobs there and when we do get jobs we're chased and told that we shouldn't be there." She joined Brooklyn CORE during Downstate and over the next few years became one of its most militant young members.[42]

But Brooklyn CORE members' outlandish tactics, bold spirit, and strong camaraderie, which kept alive the Downstate campaign during its slowest points and inspired new members and demonstrators such as Carson, Kochiyama, and Crayton, also appealed to a rowdier element that neither CORE nor the ministers were prepared to deal with. After three weeks of demonstrating, some on the Ministers' Committee felt they might no longer be able to control people in the crowds, which increasingly comprised people who were not members of their churches. Many ministers also wanted to end the protest because they felt the demonstration was taking up too much of their time and causing them to neglect their parish duties. Others, such as Gardner Taylor, argued that the campaign lacked a proper exit strategy. They did not know what to do if Rockefeller, Wagner, and Brennan chose to ignore the demand that 25 percent of construction workers on publicly funded projects had to be African American and Puerto Rican. Taylor publicly remarked that some of the ministers were "not particularly wedded to the quota idea." He probably leaked this information because, after 691 arrests, politicians and labor leaders continued to ignore the ministers' demands. Rockefeller and Wagner repeated their commitment to enforcing the existing legislation and supporting investigative committees, but that was as far as they would go. Brennan denounced the 25 percent demand as blackmail. His only concession was to establish a six-man panel to screen job applicants, which replaced the old system in which newcomers needed two current members to sponsor them into the union. The Ministers' Committee wanted to negotiate while they still had at least a modicum of influence with elected officials. They were looking for a way out of the campaign that allowed them to save face with their political contacts and parishioners. An opportunity came at the end of July.[43]

During the last few days of July, as the campaigned threatened to fizzle without any gains, some activists wanted to employ more destructive and violent measures to gain politicians' and labor leaders' attention. On July 31, the picket lines at Downstate erupted into a "near riot." Most of the antagonists were young people who heckled and fought with police. Teenagers also started a new technique that day. Ten of them locked arms and blocked a truck until police asked them to disperse, which they did. Quickly, after they left, another ten appeared in their place. Officers became so frustrated that they formed a double column and used their batons to ram protestors away from the path of the trucks. The crowd of about one hundred demonstrators spilled into the streets, scuffled with police, and taunted them with repeated chants of "storm trooper!" One protestor kicked a cop in the groin, which sent the officer to the hospital. Reverend Jones tried to calm the crowd and halt the demonstration. He climbed on top a stack of lumber and proclaimed, "This proves there's no difference between New York and Alabama, no difference between the United States and South Africa. This nation is going straight to hell!" Gardner Taylor blamed the police for the disturbance. Later he sent a telegram to the governor and the mayor that said, "Violence has occurred at Downstate Medical Center. People can no longer be restrained. Police apparently cannot be controlled. Public safety is threatened."[44]

This incident was the breaking point for the ministers. Oliver Leeds attended the Ministers' Council meeting that night at Berean Baptist Church. "The tenor of the meeting was that everyone was looking for an excuse to get out," he remembered. Sandy Ray voiced concern over the ministers' loss of control and the potential for more violence. "Anything violent take[s] place, I am out," Leeds recalled him saying. Rumors flew around the room that unknown militants were threatening to destroy construction property at Downstate. After over twenty minutes of this type of talk, Milton Galamison got the ministers refocused on the next day's plans. Leeds recounted that he stood up and shouted, "As far as I'm concerned we are only responsible for our congregations. When I bring my people down there they do what I tell them. When you bring your congregation down they do what you tell them. We're not responsible for anything else. And he says if somebody wants to burn up some trucks or blow up Downstate, *LET 'EM!*" The Ministers' Committee stayed involved for the next few days, but took precautions to avoid more serious violence. Many members eagerly anticipated their meeting with Governor Rockefeller on August 6 and spent the rest of the meeting planning a solution to end the campaign.[45]

But before they officially withdrew from the demonstration, the ministers collaborated with the police to target demonstrators who did not meet their approval. On the morning of August 1, Reverend Jones informed Deputy Chief Inspector Wynn, the police officer in charge at the scene, that they expected troublemakers to attempt to disrupt the protest. He also promised the police that the ministers would help remove unwanted demonstrators. Four young men, not affiliated with the ministers, arrived at 10:15 a.m. They carried four or five dozen eggs in a paper bag. The ministers quickly notified the police of their presence. When a patrolman tried to question the four men, they pelted him with the eggs and tried to run away. All four were arrested.[46]

One young man, twenty-five-year-old Donald Washington, wanted to do more than just throw eggs at cops. On August 5, he went to the picket line and on five different occasions sat down in front of trucks, leaving each time officers threatened to arrest him. As he walked away, he taunted the cops. Once he asked a patrolman to "come around the corner for five minutes with me and I'll show you some black supremacy." Later that evening, Washington attended a Brooklyn CORE meeting where he proposed sabotaging equipment at the work site. According to Leeds, he wanted to "put some bombs underneath some trucks and put a match to it." CORE members refused to actively participate in his plan, but, as Oliver Leeds remembered the conversation, some had no moral objection to destroying equipment and even offered to help financially. "On the day you want to blow up a truck," Leeds said he told Washington, "stop by and pick up a dollar from me and let me know so I won't be there. You can blow the truck up. I have no problem with that, just don't do it in the name of CORE or the civil rights movement."[47]

Despite the explicit commitment of national CORE to nonviolence, Leeds and most other Brooklyn CORE members, like many civil rights activists, saw nonviolence as a useful tactic, not a way of life. Many in Brooklyn CORE were not opposed to using violence, especially in self-defense, but they understood that there was no way they could maintain public support and convince politicians to negotiate if the campaign became associated with the destruction of property. The Brooklyn CORE leaders felt these tactics were counterproductive to their cause, even though destroying construction equipment seemed like a logical thing to do to some of the more radical Brooklyn CORE members. Nonetheless, a majority of the members of the chapter valued their affiliation with the national organization and did not want to participate in something that would alienate the chapter from its allies in the movement or besmirch its reputation as an effective nonviolent protest group. The threat of intense violence, however, did give the ministers some leverage in their negotiation with the governor. They tried to use the potential for more violence to force the governor's hand, but their efforts were largely futile. Unwilling to push the demonstrations in the militant directions that Brooklyn CORE had initiated, the ministers largely hid behind the fear of violence and used it as an excuse to quickly end the protest.

"We Struggled in Vain"

Having distanced themselves from CORE and aided in the police crackdown on militant demonstrators, the Ministers' Committee met with Governor Rockefeller on August 6, dropped its demands for the quota, and after three hours worked out a compromise that ended the campaign. In exchange for an immediate end to the demonstration, the governor agreed to appoint a representative to monitor the construction industry and report cases of discrimination to the State Commission on Human Rights. Rockefeller also promised a special investigation into charges of racial discrimination in the Sheet Metal Workers Local 28, a union notorious for its discrimination against blacks. Last, a recruitment program would be created to place qualified African Americans and Puerto Ricans in unions and apprenticeship programs. Except for the promised recruitment program, nothing new had resulted from these talks. Moreover, there was no guarantee that the Building Trades Council or the unions, which retained their power to discriminate without penalty, would support the governor and the ministers' apprenticeship program.[48]

The ministers held a rally that evening and announced their victory. They invited Oliver Leeds to speak and publicly endorse the settlement, which he did. In a letter to Galamison, Leeds remarked that "the accord was less than satisfactory [but] it was nevertheless, a good beginning." Twenty-five years later, Leeds regretted his decision, calling it "the biggest mistake I've ever made in my life." Logistically, Leeds realized that the demonstration was over without the ministers. "Basically, I felt what the hell, I can't carry it by myself," he said. "CORE can't carry it. The NAACP isn't anywhere. Urban League's got no troops and the ministers are pulling out. What's left? There's nothing. So I agreed to go along." Members of Brooklyn CORE who were standing in the back of the church burst into a chorus of protest. Some believed that it was still possible to win hiring percentages or at least push for some immediate hires. They accused the ministers of selling out just when tangible signs of victory seemed possible.[49]

The outrage of the Brooklyn CORE members carried over to its next meeting, which attracted over one hundred people and helped transform the organization. People spilled out the door of the tiny storefront office. For many of the attendants, it was their first time at a CORE meeting. Because Brooklyn CORE did not follow strict rules on voting or decision making, the raucous assembly rejected a resolution to support the ministers' settlement. Everyone there wanted the demonstration to continue. Leeds put the question to a vote, and the decision was unanimous. Some of the older members of CORE were doubtful that the demonstration would have any meaningful effect without the ministers' involvement. "I just didn't believe that those hundred people would be out there the next morning," Leeds remarked.[50]

His prediction was correct. Only forty-four demonstrators arrived at the site on August 8, and by the end of the week the attempted resurgence was over. To be successful and effective, the Downstate campaign required a steady stream of hundreds of people able to demonstrate all day and go to jail for disrupting the site. Brooklyn CORE could not generate the necessary numbers after the ministers abandoned the campaign. And CORE members became pariahs in the eyes of many churchgoing African Americans after the ministers publicly denounced the call by the chapter for renewed demonstrations.[51]

In many ways, Downstate might seem like a failure. The promised apprenticeship programs failed to produce many jobs, at least initially. After the settlement, Gilbert Banks worked hard to get unemployed black construction workers into the union programs. He remembered that the unions and politicians "got a construction team to review the 2,000 people who applied for these jobs. There were 600 who could do anything they wanted: electrician, plumbers, carpenters, steamfitters; all that stuff. The deputy mayor got this committee together, and two years later, nobody was hired. So we had struggled in vain."[52]

But it would be incorrect to view the Downstate campaign as an insignificant struggle, even though it did not result in immediate construction jobs for black workers. One of the most important contributions of Downstate was that the demonstrations infused Brooklyn CORE, and the black freedom movement in general, with energized, excited activists, many of them young and willing to continue the antagonistic militant style of radical protest that they had experienced on the construction site picket lines. Yuri Kochiyama went on to become involved in Malcolm X's Organization of Afro-American Unity and was present when Malcolm X was assassinated in 1965. A photo of Kochiyama cradling the murdered militant leader's head in her arms became one of the most memorable symbols of that fateful day. Kochiyama and her husband spent decades involved with radical human rights organizations and international campaigns for social justice. Her lifelong involvement in radical movements for social change gained its foundation in militancy through her arrest at the Downstate protest.[53] Kochiyama remained friends with Brooklyn CORE activists such as Arnold Goldwag and Oliver Leeds for the rest of her life.

Frances Crayton also remained connected to the militant chapter and participated in many of the local actions of the group throughout the rest of the 1960s. In the mid-1960s, she accepted a paid position as a field organizer for national CORE and ventured south to Baltimore, Maryland, during the late 1960s, where she worked on the CORE campaign to desegregate housing, restaurants, bars, and hotels in Baltimore. Downstate had prepared her for that experience. "At least in Brooklyn," she recalled, "the only foes we had to deal with were the police, but once we got out of Brooklyn it became real serious and real dangerous." In Baltimore, Crayton remembered, she received threats from Ku Klux Klan members and witnessed police officers severely beating arrested CORE demonstrators. She remembered these experiences being "much more dangerous than I can ever think of anything in Brooklyn CORE being," but the solidarity she experienced going to jail at Downstate had readied her to go to jail with activists in Baltimore. After her time in CORE, Crayton became a leader in New York City early childhood education programs, and eventually she became an assistant commissioner in the Administration for Children's Services as well as the director of all Head Start programs. Had it not been for the strong camaraderie and daring nature of the protest at Downstate Medical Center, Frances Crayton would never have become involved in protest politics, which became the basis for her long career in social services and child advocacy.[54]

Last, Sonny Carson emerged as a dynamic black nationalist leader in both local and national Black Power movement organizations. In the late 1960s, Carson became the chairman of Brooklyn CORE and brought the chapter in line with the dominant trends of the Black Power movement when he repudiated interracial memberships and nonviolent tactics. When the city became embroiled in a prolonged teachers' strike over the continuance of an experimental community control district in a predominantly African American and Puerto Rican section of Brooklyn, Carson emerged as a public spokesperson for the black community. His comments to reporters and at rallies secured his position as one of the most trenchant critics of the teachers' union and of racially integrated schools, in general, in the community control movement. Those positions earned him a reputation as an anti-Semitic black supremacist, labels that stuck with him until he died in 2002. But in spite of his critics and his flamboyant personality (or perhaps because of it), for decades Carson remained a forceful, albeit highly controversial, figure in black radical politics. In the early 1990s, he organized boycotts against Korean grocery stores in Brooklyn that allegedly harassed and exploited black customers. During that time, he also organized a public community initiative to rid black communities in Brooklyn of the crack epidemic. On the national level, after leaving CORE in 1968 Carson became involved in the Revolutionary Action Movement (RAM), an underground revolutionary black nationalist organization. Like Kochiyama, Crayton, and hundreds of others who participated in the campaign, Carson's militant public activism began at the Downstate protests.[55]

But, aside from the people it drew into radical politics, the Downstate campaign was also an important catalyst in the long history of activism against employment discrimination in the building trades. The members of Brooklyn CORE who played leading roles in the Downstate campaign, especially Gilbert Banks, learned important lessons about the intransigence within the building trades industry and the uphill battle they needed to fight to gain entrance in the construction unions and to attain skilled jobs on worksites. Banks eventually became a founding member of Harlem Fight Back, a protest organization that zealously advocated for more black and minority workers in the building trades. For over forty years after the Downstate protest, Banks and other leaders in Fight

Back sat in, sat down, and shut down worksites throughout the city, and in the process slowly opened up the industry to more black workers.

Thus, even though Downstate and the other protests that occurred throughout the country during summer 1963 were not immediately successful, they marked an important starting point in what soon became a prolonged, aggressive, and militant struggle to win better-paying jobs for black workers in a historically racist industry. What may have seemed to Gilbert Banks like a "struggle in vain" in 1963 was really the beginning of a protracted fight, one that continues in the twenty-first century and deserves a pride of place in the history of the black freedom movement.

"THE LABORATORY OF DEMOCRACY"

Construction Industry Racism in Newark
and the Limits of Liberalism

Julia Rabig

Four summers before the 1967 Newark uprising left twenty-six people dead, before Newark became an emblem of the urban crisis, two hundred activists amassed at a construction site for the new Barringer High School. It was a small protest, but one at which activists planted seeds for what would become the Newark Black Power movement, influential nationwide. Nearly all the construction workers—also two hundred in number—were white. Arriving for their jobs on the morning of July 3, 1963, they encountered demonstrators organized by the Newark Coordinating Committee (NCC), a coalition of local civil rights groups, in picket lines at every entrance to the new $6.5 million-dollar school building. The workers charged toward the picketers, leading with their fists.[1]

The violence prompted democratic Mayor Hugh J. Addonizio and Harold Ashby, the first African American president of the Board of Education, to take the unprecedented step of suspending work on the school until the Newark Human Rights Commission could investigate the NCC claims of discrimination. Lest the protesters interpret his response as a victory, Addonizio insisted that the NCC "is not interested in resolving the problem but rather in prolonging and aggravating the differences that now exist."[2]

Addonizio's scolding tone contrasted with the optimism he had expressed in September 1962, when he had testified before U.S. Commission on Civil Rights hearings held in Newark.[3] Among the numerous manifestations of discrimination discussed by the forty-five participants at the hearing, the most striking was the near-total absence of African Americans in the city's construction trades. Union leaders denied responsibility, asserting that members of the largest

minority of the city, soon to become its majority, rarely applied for union apprenticeships.[4] Mayor Addonizio conceded that much remained to be done, but
pledged to uphold his record for supporting civil rights legislation, established
during his thirteen years as a congressman.[5] "Newark is the working laboratory
of democracy," he had told the commissioners. "What we learn and develop here
will be used in every major community throughout the world."[6]

Newark would become a laboratory, although not the type Addonizio had en-
visioned. The Barringer High School protest represented the opening salvo in a
prolonged struggle in which civil rights activists experimented with proto–Black
Power strategies. They launched three campaigns over the next seven years that
sought an immediate end to discrimination in the building trades and eventually
extended beyond the union hall and the construction site. The protest at Barringer High School ushered in widespread direct action by newly formed civil
rights groups. It effectively challenged—but did not completely displace—the
gradualism practiced by the established Newark civic organizations, corporations, and municipal officials. The second campaign, at the construction site for
the Rutgers Law School and the Newark College of Engineering, framed employment discrimination on publicly funded construction within the larger fight
against African Americans' exclusion from the use of public goods and services
for which they paid taxes. Finally, protests around the construction of the New
Jersey College of Medicine and Dentistry merged employment discrimination
into a broad-based criticism of the city's urban renewal program. Activists in
all three protests targeted construction projects identified with the decade-long
city urban renewal agenda not only because they promised to generate well-paying
jobs but because they highlighted African Americans' exclusion from the planning and construction of massive, publicly funded institutions. These three
protests show how activists honed strategies for building Black Power in civic
agencies, unionized trades, and neighborhood institutions long before it became
a familiar rallying cry.

Construction Activism in Context: 1950–1970

Democratic officials in Newark rallied around urban renewal in the 1950s and
1960s. Supplied with millions of federal dollars, they demolished old buildings,
erected high rises, and redirected traffic to speed travel to and from the suburbs.
They promised new university campuses, a research hospital, and other institutions that would make Newark into an intellectual hub and sustain downtown
commerce. But many African American residents came to perceive urban renewal as the work of machine thugs and arrogant technocrats who reshaped

downtown with little regard for the displaced. Construction trade protests in the 1960s increasingly underscored how the prevailing models of urban revitalization, coupled with a gradualist approach to civil rights reform, excluded African Americans from liberal visions for the future of the city at the very moment that Newark became a majority black city.[7]

The pursuit of unionized construction jobs on these projects therefore became a cornerstone of broader black demands for community control of urban redevelopment policies. For Newark activists, Black Power was a concept that gradually accumulated meaning and force; with each protest, they advanced an increasingly comprehensive analysis of where construction jobs fit into the rebuilding of a more equitable city, one in which new development responded to the needs of African American communities.

This arc of protests underscores the centrality of employment to black mobilization. African Americans involved in these protests demanded not only a fair share of public jobs but also a voice in the economic development policies of the city. All three protests revolved around the construction trades, but activists moved beyond merely exposing discrimination and demanding redress to taking on roles as enforcers and institutional builders. They developed multilayered critiques of the Newark economy, illuminating how political marginalization, top-down urban renewal, and employment discrimination acted as self-reinforcing processes. Through protesting specific instances of discrimination, activists came to conclude that such political marginalization was not a flaw in the urban renewal process but integral to it, a would-be whitening of the city to which Black Power seemed like the most reasonable response.

These campaigns altered the landscape of civil rights advocacy in the city, bringing more militant leaders and organizations into prominence and generating tension between moderates and militants, established leaders and younger upstarts. Yet a close reading of the period does not support a neat ideological differentiation between the civil rights and Black Power phases of the black freedom movement. Indeed, activists were already experimenting with many of the strategies that would make Newark a touchstone of the Black Power movement in the late 1960s and its movement an exemplar of Malcolm X's call for "operational unity."[8]

These three protests also prove that civil rights activists early on recognized that the liberal reforms generated by corporate and union voluntarism were insufficient for the kind of community-based leverage many Newark African Americans believed was necessary to change the course of public work and public works. The groundwork laid during these protests allowed activists to take advantage of the political currency that their demands gained after the 1967 uprising, when officials and corporate leaders scrambled for funds and programs to assuage discontent.[9] They also prepared residents to embrace the much more self-conscious, grassroots black nationalism embodied by poet and playwright Amiri Baraka, who became one of the most outspoken of Black Power activists on the national scene and a major force behind the election of African American officials, including Kenneth Gibson, the first black mayor of Newark, in 1970. Even beyond the election of local officials, activists advanced a version of Black Power that incorporated calls for community control and parallel African American institutions into local political struggles.

The Barringer High School Protest: Reconfiguring Newark Civil Rights Activism

In 1963, Newark had a population of about 382,000, a decline from its mid-century peak. The city economy had begun to waver even earlier, but it retained a strong sector of small manufacturers and large white-collar employers into the 1960s. The Prudential Insurance Company and Mutual Benefit Life Insurance Company anchored the bustling downtown, along with department stores such as Bamberger's, S. Klein, and Kresge's. The Newark unemployment rate was 7 percent, which exceeded the national rate of 5–6 percent in the early 1960s.[10] The unemployment rate among African Americans, who made up 34 percent of the city population by 1960, was around 13 percent. The construction industry employed only 4 percent of Newark workers in 1960, but stood at the center of the urban renewal building frenzy that many hoped would bring jobs for inner-city residents.[11] Compensation in the Newark construction industry had nearly doubled between 1949 and 1963, far outpacing the cost of living in the city or its suburbs.[12] Construction jobs were, therefore, of major economic and political importance to the Newark black citizenry.

The construction industry was also intimately connected to the physical creation of community: schools, hospitals, public housing, and other institutions that had so frequently denied African Americans their full rights. Barringer High School was especially significant in this respect. Black parents sought to enroll their children in Barringer, one of the best schools in Newark, despite threats from the predominantly white student body.[13] By asserting that African American workers were entitled to construction jobs at Barringer, the Congress of Racial Equality (CORE) implicitly challenged the idea that black students would be interlopers there or at any of the city schools. Black workers would help build the schools of the city, and their children would attend them.[14]

Newark leaders were well aware of the racial and ethnic barriers in their city in the years prior to the Barringer protest. Throughout the 1950s, they spoke of their own efforts—public tolerance programs and studies of prejudice—as part of the ongoing struggle for equal rights, one on which a U.S. victory in the Cold War depended. These programs sustained a small activist community and kept the issue of civil rights alive in a political culture that prized complacency. But the same anticommunist reasoning that made moderate progress on civil rights essential to protecting the national image in the Cold War inhibited radicalism and dampened a sense of urgency. The effectiveness of these activists was often inversely related to the loft of their rhetoric, in part because they lacked recourse to any meaningful enforcement mechanisms that would have allowed them to move beyond condemnations of personal prejudice to combat deep structural discrimination.

The experience of the Mayor's Commission on Human Relations captures their dilemma. In 1950, the Newark municipal government created the commission, in part to respond to the transformations wrought by black migration from the South. African Americans made up 11 percent (45,760) of the city population of 429,760 in 1940 and 17 percent (74,964) of the population of 438,776 in 1950. Whereas the overall Newark population began a long decline during the 1950s, the black population climbed steadily. In 1960, African Americans made up approximately 34 percent (138,035) of the city population of 405,220. By 1970, African Americans were the city majority, making up 54 percent (207,408) of the population, which had declined to 382,417.[15] The Mayor's Commission was the product of officials' concerns about the political consequences of this population shift and pressure from the National Association for the Advancement of Colored People (NAACP), Urban League, and other groups to fashion a more comprehensive response to problems that new residents faced.

Charged with implementing the city Fair Practice Ordinance, the commission insisted that the protection of civil rights was not only mandated by the constitution and the moral bonds of "brotherhood" but also constituted a bulwark for national security.[16] At a U.S. Senate subcommittee hearing in 1954, David M. Litwin, the commission chairman, compared prejudice to a "cancerous body" and warned "the invasion or violation of any one of our civil rights gives the communistic countries an advantage for propaganda purposes in their cold war of attrition." Yet, even though the commission asserted its responsibility to prevent discrimination, it had no significant enforcement powers and had to resort—with limited success—to private negotiations with resistant employers. Litwin and the commission walked a tightrope between emphasizing the need for stricter federal antidiscrimination laws and insisting that such mechanisms would rarely be fully used—that the mere existence of a federal law would pressure employers into preemptive voluntary compliance.[17] The Mayor's Commission denounced discrimination, but offered few details about its actual response.

The commission instead emphasized communication and compromise. The tone of the commission publications—earnest, measured, and optimistic—was intended to ease white residents' anxiety about their future in an increasingly black city while assuring black residents that they had the ear of the administration.

Some commission members publicly chafed against the constraints of their roles, but the organization ultimately conveyed an apolitical enthusiasm that served as a rhetorical panacea rather than a foundation for effective action.[18] Absent government power to enforce the nondiscrimination law, the Urban League emerged as the most effective, although still quite limited, organization in Newark assisting individual African American and Puerto Rican job seekers. Thousands of workers registered with the Urban League in the late 1950s and early 1960s, and the group annually placed approximately one hundred of them—mostly skilled and professional workers—in positions.[19]

By 1963, the Barringer controversy brought together Newark activists frustrated by the narrow scope of established organizations and the limits of liberal leadership. In response, they turned to the newly formed Essex County chapter of CORE. CORE attracted militant working-class activists and young college-educated men and women who began pursuing more direct tactics and immediate solutions.

Robert Curvin, one of the early founders of CORE and an organizer of the Barringer protest, had a history of challenging the northern New Jersey racial conventions. While in high school during the 1950s, Curvin and his circle of politically active friends, both black and white, joined the NAACP Youth Council and used its meetings to launch informal direct actions against segregated swimming pools and roller rinks.[20] Curvin served several years in the army and returned to Newark to attend Rutgers in 1957, gravitating to the "more activist" CORE rather than the NAACP. As in many other cities, Newark CORE boycotted businesses that refused to hire blacks or that relegated their black employees to the worst jobs.[21] CORE also publicized instances of police brutality, advocated for citizen review boards, and protested housing discrimination. Its members organized actions around all these problems in summer 1963.[22] Members also regularly protested hiring bias at a local White Castle hamburger stand, holding aloft signs that read "More jobs now" and "We want a Black and White Castle" and yelling at black customers who bypassed their pickets that they "weren't ready for freedom."[23] Propelled by a heady sense of spontaneity and formidable stamina, CORE staged protests across the city—often on short notice—at the suggestion of members who knew or had themselves been victims of employment discrimination.[24]

CORE moved from the margins to the center of the Newark civil rights movement during 1963. The Barringer protest spanned several months of intermittent picketing and caustic negotiations and marked, according to the *Newark Evening News*, the official arrival of the civil rights movement in Newark.[25] Although this designation obscured the civil rights advocacy that had persisted since the Second World War, it had some merit.[26] The protest publicized the inadequacy of voluntary programs to enforce antidiscrimination laws and exposed the shallow racial liberalism of Addonizio's administration. To younger activists, the Barringer protest confirmed that liberal reform efforts not only failed to address the needs of growing Newark black communities but actively reinforced their political and economic marginalization. NCC's tactics contrasted with the tepid emphasis on tolerance that characterized so much of the civil rights discourse and provided an alternative for activists dismayed by the essentially toothless options offered by the Mayor's Commission. The NCC leadership of the Barringer protest marked the increasing influence of civil rights leaders who gained a foothold in the local movement by introducing mass direct action. Established black leaders, who had supported Addonizio and hoped to secure concessions from his administration, viewed these upstart activists with suspicion.[27] Irvine Turner, the only African American on the Newark City Council, publicly opposed the pickets and criticized Curvin specifically. Most significantly, the Newark NAACP, averse to conflict, initially refused to join the NCC-led protest.[28] At one "very tense meeting," Curvin was ejected at the insistence of Larrie Stalks, a prominent NAACP member and Addonizio appointee, after Curvin asked to talk about the CORE plans to bring young activists into the city for a summer organizing project.[29]

Like the NAACP leadership, most of the Newark black clergy initially refused to support the NCC.[30] But there were exceptions, including Reverend Dr. Eustace L. Blake, who told his 2,000 congregants at St. James AME Church that "the price of freedom is not cheap" and urged them to join the NAACP, the Southern Christian Leadership Council (SCLC), or even CORE.[31] Reverend John Collier, a young AME minister and leader of Ministers' Alliance for Progress, went further, becoming a spokesman for NCC.[32]

Once the pickets were up and construction was stalled, negotiations with the mayor, unions, and contractors became increasingly likely. The politics of the Newark civil rights movement shifted—NCC gained more clout as the naysayers now supported the protest. The Urban League agreed to compile lists of skilled black tradesmen to apply for jobs at Barringer, and NAACP President Carlton Norris said that he approved a freeze on the Barringer project until additional black workers were added. And even as Irvine Turner continued to dismiss NCC activists as troublemakers, he announced plans for his own investigation of the Barringer matter.[33]

During the first weeks of July, school board members, city officials, and construction contractors met to discuss the NCC demands. The construction trades responded angrily. The Essex County Building and Construction Trades Council (EBTC) insisted that the Board of Education and the project contractors had excluded labor from the initial decision to stop construction. They argued that the work stoppage was illegal; some members threatened to boycott future school construction.[34] As the Mayor's Commission investigated the NCC claims, Addonizio sought to placate union officials by stacking the commission board with representatives of the local construction trades unions. Nonetheless, the commission announced on July 10 that its investigation had, in fact, revealed racial bias in the industry and urged the mayor to take action.[35]

The NCC had forced employment discrimination onto the municipal agenda and attracted support from other civil rights organizations, but it was still not universally recognized as legitimate. Although Norris of the NAACP, James Pawley of the Urban League, and Reverend Blake of St. James AME—all men Addonizio considered "responsible members of the Negro community"[36]—had by now expressed support for NCC, its members were still excluded from meetings with the mayor and slots on the Citizens Negotiating Committee (CNC), the team of civil rights leaders that was to negotiate with the trades unions.[37] But as the "responsible" black leadership of Newark increasingly criticized Addonizio, its purportedly "irresponsible" counterpart eventually gained representation. In mid-July, Addonizio invited Reverend Collier, a member of two NCC affiliates (the Ministers' Alliance for Progress and CORE) to join the CNC. A month later, the CNC was finally reshuffled and NCC gained substantial representation, replacing some of Addonizio's hand-picked appointments.[38]

In late July, the CNC proposed that African Americans and Puerto Ricans should make up half the workforce on municipal construction jobs to correct "an imbalance of decades." The EBTC called this proposal "arbitrary, unrealistic, and unreasonable."[39] The NCC vowed to picket Barringer until the unions agreed to eliminate discrimination, and Louis Vehling, president of EBTC, threatened to withdraw from negotiations unless the pickets stopped. Vehling also asserted that the unions would "not lower our standards...or grant any group super-seniority."[40] He told the press, "unless more jobs are created, the cost of eliminating discrimination will mean the loss of a job by someone else. We have no intention of permitting civil rights leaders...to play musical chairs with the job opportunities or employment status of the members of the union."[41]

Reverend Collier argued that Vehling had misconstrued the CNC proposal as an illegitimate seizure of jobs for unqualified black and Puerto Rican workers. In fact, Collier said, the CNC had only asked that the unions to consider skilled minority tradesmen or apprentices who had been vetted by the Urban League and met union requirements. Both Vehling and Collier often couched their positions in the language of liberal individualism—Collier spoke of the skilled African American tradesman unfairly denied a job, whereas Vehling spoke of the white union member possibly denied work because the union had been forced to take on too many apprentices. But both leaders actually understood that union membership did not merely protect individual workers but also advanced the communities that the unions represented.

Vehling often argued that civil rights activists wanted the unions to abandon their objective meritocratic hiring standards and give apprenticeships to less-qualified workers in the name of rectifying hiring bias. Collier questioned the objectivity of union membership criteria and pointed out that Vehling's defense of union meritocracy obscured the whole structure of interpersonal relationships that gave white workers an advantage. Many white workers, Collier noted, had successfully relied on relatives to inform them of job openings and sponsor their apprenticeships or "unofficial" training programs.[42] Although he disputed Collier on this point, Vehling and other union leaders had freely acknowledged as much during their testimony before the U.S. Commission on Civil Rights, admitting that the professed commitment of the unions to strict meritocracy did not prevent them from bending apprenticeship rules for the relatives of current union members.[43] Vehling used the language of liberal individualism to defend his unions even though the benefits of union membership accrued precisely because they had more expansive aims—union membership provided job security not just for individuals but for multiple generations. In this way, Collier and Vehling—although on different sides of the dispute—shared a conception of what union power could achieve.[44] For Collier and the NCC, the protest was not merely about the employment of a few tradesmen but a recognition that the trades unions could play a significant role in reducing economic inequality and defining what the freedom promised by the civil rights movement would entail.

For the black civic leaders drawn together by the negotiations, the Barringer protest opened up new possibilities for unity, but it also highlighted abiding schisms. Councilman Irvine Turner, for instance, acknowledged the persistence of discrimination, but consistently fell behind Addonizio in criticizing those who exposed it.[45] Meanwhile, some civil rights activists on the CNC supported the protest in general, but clashed with the NCC over strategy, warning that continued picketing would derail negotiations. Curvin rejected critics' claims that the forcefulness of the NCC jeopardized slow and steady reform on the part of white leaders or imperiled a heretofore unified black movement. Noting that the unions had yet to make any substantive concessions to the protesters, Curvin remarked, "the only thing we're wrecking is 100 years of misery."[46]

In addition to local leaders, officials from around the state weighed in on the Barringer protest. The New Jersey Civil Rights Division angered unions by insisting that they supply information on the race and ethnicity of their apprentices under threat of subpoena. Leaders of the New Jersey American Federation of Labor–Congress of Industrial Organizations (AFL-CIO) also alienated Essex County trades unions by siding with the NCC in the dispute.[47] The Barringer protest also drew federal officials to the city in August 1963. David S. North of the Labor Department met with Addonizio and urged him to start a referral system for minority apprentices similar to those instituted in New York, Cincinnati, Cleveland, and Pittsburgh. North reminded Addonizio that he could revoke the federal certification of union training programs throughout the city if the unions failed to comply with President John Kennedy's recently issued Executive Order 11114.[48]

A breakthrough finally occurred in mid-August when the building trades agreed to devise a response to the CNC proposal if NCC refrained from picketing.[49] Optimistic about this turn of events, civil rights groups began preparing young men to take advantage of the new opportunities they hoped would open up. Whereas "picket lines, sit-ins, and boycotts had taken center stage in the civil rights drama," the *Newark Evening News* reported, "a great deal of less spectacular action has been going on behind the scenes." The NAACP Youth Council descended upon the Reverend William P. Hayes Homes and encouraged residents to fill out applications for construction jobs, and the Negro American Labor Council (NALC) encouraged Essex County high schools to implement "on-the-job training programs" and collected information about openings from its trade union membership.[50]

Persistent agitation had also compelled the city private sector to respond to the local movement demands. NCC had threatened to picket downtown businesses and establish a boycott if Newark businessmen refused to use their own clout to encourage the construction trades to alter hiring practices. Although department store executives had refused to become publicly involved in the Barringer dispute, they privately consented to speak to union leaders and pressure Addonizio to stall construction until black workers were hired. In exchange for store protests' being called off, businessmen also agreed to participate alongside civil rights activists, such as Curvin, as well as leaders of the Urban League and other social service agencies, in the Business and Industrial Coordinating Council (BICC) to open up more jobs across the city.[51] By fall 1963, the BICC had placed a few dozen African Americans in jobs as department-store buyers, porters, clerks, kitchen workers, and bank tellers.[52]

The well-established white-collar Newark businesses had multiple incentives for joining BICC. First, the BICC conformed to the programmatic and ideological consensus that the federal government advanced to persuade the private sector that integration in the workplace could proceed peacefully and profitably.[53] In this respect, BICC resembled a more grassroots version of Plans for Progress. A corollary to the President's Committee on Fair Employment, Plans for Progress had commenced in 1962 with annual conferences at which corporations made voluntary pledges to hire minority workers.[54] Second, BICC also represented attempts by white-collar Newark businesses to influence the political incorporation of African Americans, a process that took on added urgency after the 1967 uprising as white executives recognized that an African American mayor was likely to lead future efforts to revitalize the city.[55]

Finally, some companies also found modest steps toward integration good for business. Curvin, who worked on over a dozen CORE-led efforts to persuade executives to hire more black workers, recalled that corporations proved more receptive than most unions to the CORE demands that they intensify recruiting in African American schools and communities. Unlike construction unions, which sought to control the labor supply, corporations such as Bell Telephone and General Electric benefited from relationships with civil rights organizations, which helped them to access large pools of entry-level workers and to recruit college-educated math and engineering majors from historically black colleges. Meanwhile, department stores conceded to some hiring demands to avoid embarrassing negative publicity that would turn away customers; nevertheless, entrenched racial barriers remained. CORE activists found that increasing the numbers of black workers in entry-level positions proved easier than securing promotions for those already employed.[56]

In early September 1963, a few days after the historic March on Washington For Jobs and Freedom drew 250,000 people, the NCC reached a tentative—but ultimately fleeting—pact with the EBTC: the unions agreed to consider apprentices screened and referred by the city Youth Career Development Center as well as skilled minority craftsmen vetted by the State Employment Service. Companies bidding on municipal contracts would be required to prove that all employees were hired through a nondiscriminatory process.[57] State officials promised to monitor the implementation of the plan.[58] Measured against the demands issued at the start of the Barringer protest, the agreement lacked immediacy and specificity, and it resulted in only a few hires.[59] Numerous contingencies remained to prevent applicants from proceeding from the referral and screening stage to acceptance as an apprentice or journeyman because unions in both cases refused to alter their hiring policies to immediately place African Americans and Puerto Ricans on jobs.[60] Buildings rose while agreements languished, the evolving Newark skyline serving as a symbol of minority workers' exclusion.

During the course of the Barringer protests, the NCC had reoriented the Newark civil rights leadership and prepared an African American constituency divided by class, status, and ideology to make sustained collective demands on municipal and state officials in the years ahead. Yet the prominence of the NCC does not bolster a straightforward narrative of increasing radicalization among civil rights leaders. The moderate membership of the NAACP continued to grow.[61] Rather than displacing established civil rights leaders, the Barringer protests unfolded in a way that seemed to codify the dynamic of the militant and the moderate. Groups such as NCC and CORE served as weapons—threatening pickets, boycotts, and, some municipal officials feared, violence—if the demands of their moderate colleagues went unheeded. Their efforts resulted in few jobs and more often demonstrated—especially in case of the construction trades unions—both the unwillingness and inability of local officials to enforce the New Jersey employment laws. But the protest did shift the tenor of the local freedom movement in the years that followed. It clarified the limitations of the civic infrastructure of the city in a way that helped reorient its activists toward Black Power strategies. The Barringer protest, then, represents both the fruit of an existing movement and the emergence of something new—a campaign that soon expanded beyond integration of the unions to include calls for community control over health services and urban renewal.

The Rutgers Law School and Newark College of Engineering Protests: Taking It to the Governor, Forging Broader Alliances

In 1964, Edward Andrade and Rebecca Doggett, a young couple from neighboring Orange, New Jersey, who were active in civil rights and electoral politics, complained to Ernest "Big Train" Thompson about the limits of Barringer agreement. A former organizer with the United Electrical Workers (UE) and National Negro Labor Council (NNLC) leader, Thompson had survived the McCarthy era to become a mentor to young African American activists, bridging the Old Left and Black Power in the making. Thompson urged younger activists to analyze the problem structurally, identifying what he called a "three-party conspiracy" among the contractors, their employers, and the unions that maintained status quo hiring policies.[62] NCC could not win solely by confronting union leaders or the mayor, Thompson warned; rather, it had to also target the contractors, those that hired them, and the authorities at the state and local level that funded and regulated construction. Most important, Thompson urged, activists needed to lay the foundations for such confrontations by forging alliances with public officials before taking to the streets.[63]

Between 1964 and 1966, NCC entered a new phase in its struggle against discrimination as the activists' reach extended to state officials and their tactics grew more sophisticated. Under Thompson's guidance, NCC attempted to recast the discrimination on the construction sites at Rutgers Law School and Newark

College of Engineering as a problem that not only concerned minority job seekers but also the broader taxpaying public. Edward Andrade wrote in 1964 that the
construction projects at Rutgers Law School and Newark College of Engineering
"hold out for us the prospect of adding a new dimension to our arsenal[,]...the
use of Negro and allied political power to smash job Jim Crow where the taxpayers'
money is involved." NCC, Andrade wrote, would pressure the government agencies and university authorities to aggressively enforce antidiscrimination stipulations in their own contracts "instead of initially attacking the unions and thus
pitting white workers against Negro workers."[64] NCC pointed beyond workers'
competition for union slots, targeting the role of the state in permitting or prohib-
iting discriminatory practices. NCC also began recruiting and preparing African
American and Puerto Rican workers for the apprenticeship tests, a role in which
state agencies and existing organizations had only dabbled.

Over the next two years, NCC pressured Louis Danzig, the director of the
Newark Housing Authority (NHA) and domineering urban renewal strategist,
to insist that contractors abide by antidiscrimination laws. NCC also sought support for the hiring of minority workers from both the Newark College of Engineering and Rutgers Law School. College of Engineering officials agreed only
after NCC picketed, but C. Willard Heckel, the dean of Rutgers Law, was enthusiastic.[65] Heckel called for contractors and unions to submit lists of minority
workers before construction on the school began, and when they stalled, Heckel
threatened to halt construction. The list they finally submitted to Heckel revealed
that the only minority workers were unskilled laborers.[66] The unions and the
contractors were attempting to use the mere presence of African Americans on
the site to mask the reality of a two-tiered labor system.

Under pressure from Heckel and NCC, several unions agreed to reexamine
their apprenticeship criteria and to bring Puerto Rican and African American
apprentices into the trades. Others, especially the iron workers and plumbers,
resisted. NCC demanded that Heckel file a discrimination complaint with the
State Division of Civil Rights, and they won an important symbolic victory when
they persuaded prominent local black Democrats, including Councilman Turner
and Larrie Stalks of the NAACP, to join picketers at the construction sites on a
brutally cold day in January 1965.[67] The presence of Turner, who less than two
years earlier had condemned the Barringer demonstrations, illustrates that the
protests had begun to reorder the civil rights leadership of the city, bringing into
the streets some of the very leaders who had previously denounced NCC.[68]

By winter 1965, Governor Richard Hughes, in the midst of a reelection campaign, had grown eager to resolve the construction crisis. Hughes had previously
proposed that all involved simply air their complaints at a public hearing, but he
now reluctantly agreed with NCC and Heckel that the Rutgers State University

system should file discrimination charges with the state Division of Civil Rights. NCC deemed Hughes's support a "worthwhile step" and called off the protests.[69] The group also attempted to exploit the subtle give and take with state officials in the service of more dramatic reform: the immediate hiring of black apprentices, new contract stipulations (enforceable by executive order) to permit parties to halt construction if hiring goals were not met, and a promise by the federal President's Committee on Equal Opportunity to ensure the enforcement of antidiscrimination measures.[70]

But even with the threat of a lawsuit and pressure from Governor Hughes, the plumbers' and iron workers' unions refused to budge. No African Americans passed their summer apprenticeship tests.[71] The activists responded with demands for standardized tests administrated by third parties, but they also recognized that many minority applicants lacked the educational advantages of white applicants.[72] Unions committed to diversifying their memberships, NCC argued, would have to revise the admissions criteria. At the same time, NCC recognized an immediate need for "training, preparation, and counseling" for minority applicants. Without this kind of support, NCC activists wrote, "even where we win we lose."[73] NCC thus began advocating for state-funded training centers in the New Jersey inner cities and providing remedial math courses, a significant departure from the prior strategy of the group, which had revolved almost exclusively around direct-action protest that called attention to discrimination.[74]

But by fall 1965, the NCC campaign to increase minority employment at the construction sites at Rutgers Law and the Newark College of Engineering began to unravel. State officials reneged on their promise to file formal complaints against segregated apprenticeship programs, and Charles Danzig, special counsel for the state, announced he would no longer resort to an injunction to compel contractors to hire workers from nonunion sources. Instead, he would merely seek a public hearing on the matter.[75] To justify this retreat, Danzig offered evidence of exceedingly modest success—Plumbers Local 24 had at last hired a single African American apprentice, and the sheet metal workers planned to "screen" nonwhite applicants.[76]

NCC acknowledged that the Rutgers Law and the College of Engineering campaigns had produced procedural improvements and small numerical increases at the bottom tiers of the workforce. "Some of the lily-white unions have yielded to placing non-whites on the job and have adopted a fairer standard of test." But, overall, NCC activists were dismayed. The retreat by the state, NCC argued, permitted the completion of the buildings while unemployed black and Puerto Rican workers waited for yet another airing of well-established facts.[77]

The Rutgers Law School campaign illustrates how union leaders' and contractors' resistance to antidiscrimination policies and commitment to local control over apprenticeship programs combined with tepid—or aggressive and poorly executed—stabs at enforcement on the part of federal and state officials to ensure that change would come slowly, if at all. It would also require direct and persistent intervention by local activists and officials. The activists' understanding of what was at stake in publicly funded construction and their tactics in subsequent protests were shaped by three developments that unfolded in the years before the 1967 Newark uprising: the infusion of War on Poverty funding, which briefly encouraged a black-led opposition to the established Newark Democratic Party leadership; the translation of this opposition into third-party tickets and new coalitions; and growing resistance to the Newark urban renewal regime. By the time of the uprising, these three sources of opposition had merged into an increasingly coherent vision of Black Power in which the construction industry played a significant role.

When the War on Poverty took off in 1964, its community action programs represented both a boon and a threat to established Democratic Party politics in Newark, as in other cities. Mayor Addonizio and city councilmen at first welcomed the millions in federal funding. But they also clashed with local activists over how much control they would wield over the United Community Corporation, the official War on Poverty agency of the city, and who would serve on neighborhood area boards created to enable maximum feasible participation of the poor as mandated by the legislation. (Antipoverty initiatives employed veterans of NCC, such as Rebecca Doggett; C. Willard Heckel of Rutgers Law served as the first chairman of the United Community Corporation.[78]) Federal, state, and municipal leaders eventually reasserted their authority over the War on Poverty by holding up funding, launching investigations, and amending legislation. Still, the Newark War on Poverty had cultivated new community leaders and strengthened opposition to Democratic Party regulars, some of whom sought to rein in community action as their strategy for weakening the emerging Newark black majority.[79]

The growing political strength of Newark's black voters was evident in the challenges to Democratic Party regulars mounted by African American candidates in the mid-1960s. In 1964, Donald Payne, who later served multiple terms as a U.S. representative from New Jersey's tenth district, won a county committee seat running as a "New Breed Democrat."[80] The next year, a coalition of "dissident blacks, Puerto Ricans, and 'civil rights-oriented whites'"—many of whom had developed their vision of liberalism in the more controversial city community action programs—launched the United Freedom Ticket and drafted George Richardson, the former state assemblyman and NCC activist, and several other black candidates to run for city and county offices.[81] Richardson had broken with the Democratic Party establishment several years earlier over Addonizio's failure to address discrimination and police abuse.[82] In 1966, a civil engineer named

Kenneth Gibson ran for mayor. Although the United Freedom Ticket and Gibson were both soundly defeated, the campaigns expressed at the polls residents' long-standing frustration with the inadequate response of the city to slum housing, policing, and poor city services.[83] In the wake of Gibson's failed campaign, black leaders formed the United Brothers, a nearly all-male, semisecret organization that met regularly to devise ways to mobilize discontent and elect a black mayor and city council in 1970. Their membership drew from a diverse range of black leaders. It included Amiri Baraka, the poet and emerging cultural nationalist who had recently returned to his hometown after directing the Black Arts Repertory Theater (BARTS) in Harlem; Robert Curvin of CORE; Eulis "Honey" Ward and other prominent Democratic ward leaders; Junius Williams, a graduate of Yale Law School who had originally come to the city to work with the Students for a Democratic Society (SDS), and other young radicals; Harold Wilson, a Central Ward storeowner; and David Barrett, a Newark-born computer programmer who had left a promising job at General Electric to return to Newark and re-build his hometown.[84] The United Brothers prompted a new phase of coalition-building among black and a few Puerto Rican organizations, which bridged, but did not displace, the militant and moderate dynamic of early 1960s.

New Jersey College of Medicine and Dentistry: Urban Renewal Protests, the 1967 Uprising, and the "Magna Charta" of Newark

Disputes over the War on Poverty, fresh (although unsuccessful) electoral challenges, and an emerging Black Power movement offered fertile ground for the third protest—the campaign against the New Jersey College of Medicine and Dentistry (hereafter referred to as the Medical School). An enormous project slated for the Newark Central Ward, the Medical School threatened to displace upward of 20,000 residents.[85] At the same time, it held out the promise of jobs building and operating a major new institution. The struggle over the Medical School drew men and women from a range of community organizations into a historic fight that put construction jobs and community control over urban renewal projects at the center of an emerging Black Power politics.

In 1966, Mayor Addonizio offered the state of New Jersey 150 acres of municipal land for the construction of the Medical School. Addonizio perceived the Medical School as his crowning achievement to the city's urban renewal: a first-rate medical training facility in the Central Ward that would deliver huge federal and state grants as well as jobs and prestige to his faltering, cash-strapped city. It would also provide low-cost medical care for the Newark poor, who were primarily served by the City Hospital, which was known in the black community as the "Butcherhouse" or the "Slaughterhouse" because of its overcrowded facilities and low standards.[86] But Central Ward residents—many of whom had been carelessly relocated to the area in preparation for earlier urban renewal projects— were not so enthusiastic. The Medical School would require the displacement of thousands of residents, the majority of whom were African American, and threatened to compound crowding in a city that already had a deficit of livable low-income housing. Given their prior experience with urban renewal, few residents believed they would actually benefit from the medical services provided by the Medical School or ever work building or operating the facility.[87]

The mayor responded to these concerns with boilerplate boosterism and, not surprisingly, the Medical School came to represent to many Central Ward residents the arrogant and even punitive nature of the municipal leadership.[88] They formed yet another coalition of organizations, broader still than the previous attempts at unity and including the Committee Against Negro and Puerto Rican Removal, CORE, the Student Nonviolent Coordinating Committee (SNCC), the Newark Area Planning Association, and the New Jersey NAACP, to oppose the Medical School proposal—but to little effect.

On July 12, 1967, as the fight over the Medical School escalated, two white policemen arrested John Smith, a black cab driver, for driving around their double-parked car. When Smith protested the charge, the policemen shoved him into their car, beat him into semi-consciousness with their fists and nightsticks, broke his ribs, and bruised and cut his face before driving him to the fourth precinct in the Central Ward.[89] Angry residents gathered around the precinct house in response to accounts of passersby, who had seen a bloodied and unconscious Smith dragged from the car and believed he was dead. They ignored civil rights leaders, who attempted to calm them, and began throwing bottles and bricks at the precinct house. Police surged forward, chasing the crowd into the streets. Looting and arson followed over the next two days, and the riot accelerated on July 14 when Governor Richard J. Hughes activated the New Jersey National Guard. Ill-prepared young guardsmen rolled into the city over the opposition of civil rights activists, who feared their presence would only result in more violence. When the National Guard left on July 17, 1,500 people had been arrested and nearly 1,000 had been injured. Springfield Avenue, a major commercial corridor, had been laid to waste by fires, looting, and police-led assaults. Twenty-six people died in the uprising and all but two of the dead, a police detective and a fire chief, were African Americans.[90]

The proximate and underlying causes of the Newark uprising are numerous, but nearly all accounts assign significant blame to local, state, and federal officials, who dismissed residents' opposition to the Medical School and helped create the conditions and frustrations that boiled over in July 1967.[91] In the wake of the Newark uprising, however, officials who previously depicted the development of the Medical School as a foregone conclusion began taking residents' opposition more seriously.[92] With an estimated cost of around $60 million, the Medical School depended on a complicated process of financial leveraging coordinated by multiple agencies; Newark would dedicate part of the funding it had procured from the Department of Housing and Urban Development (HUD) under the Model Cities program to clear the land for the Medical School, and the state of New Jersey would supply some of the funding, supplemented by grants set aside for medical education by the Department of Health, Education, and Welfare (HEW) and the Public Health Service.[93]

The extraordinary act of bureaucratic choreography required to build the Medical School provided community activists with many points of leverage to influence or subvert the project. Federal and state officials also brought their influence to bear on the residents' behalf. Paul Ylvisaker, the director of the New Jersey Department of Community Affairs mediated among Newark residents, Governor Hughes, and municipal officials. In a subsequent letter to the governor, Robert C. Wood, undersecretary of HUD, and William J. Cohen, undersecretary of HEW, under the authority of the Model Cities Act, threatened to withhold federal funds until college officials and municipal leaders could prove the project would alleviate, not compound, the problems that the Central Ward residents faced. The Wood-Cohen letter set the conditions for the Medical School to proceed.[94]

The coalition won many of its demands and negotiated every one of the points that had been laid out in the Wood-Cohen letter. The provision of jobs for the many unemployed and underemployed residents of the Central Ward figured prominently in residents' vision of community control over the Medical School. Gustav Heningburg, an executive of the NAACP Legal Fund who had been drawn into the Medical School dispute, worked alongside the coalition to persuade municipal authorities and college officials to stipulate that minority Newark residents occupy one-half of apprenticeships and one-third of the journeymen positions on the construction crews, and to provide training for Central Ward residents in a range of occupations in the new hospital.[95]

The agreement they reached represented the first victorious challenge to the Newark urban renewal regime, which had been the target of largely unsuccessful protests and lawsuits by neighborhood groups since the late 1950s.[96] Part of the reason that the coalition won was that it drew what appeared to be separate grievances together into a systemic critique. Activists involved in the Medical School dispute made few distinctions between community efforts to expose the negative consequences of urban renewal and efforts to end employment discrimination and increase substantive political representation. One community negotiator deemed the Medical School agreement the "Magna Charta of Newark.... For the first time the people had a voice in making policy that affected them....it gave the black community a feeling of being somebody."[97] According to one commentator, the black community and its negotiators had "displayed considerable unity."[98] In the course of the Medical School dispute, activists advanced a campaign against employment discrimination in federally funded construction projects that had been ongoing since the early 1960s and linked equal employment opportunities to the physical construction of cities.[99] But success was not just the product of sophisticated coalition politics and a project that offered multiple points of leverage. The riot had increased the stakes involved in community disputes that officials had previously ignored. Reflecting back a year later, Junius Williams of the United Brothers and Newark Area Planning Association perceptively argued, "None of this would have happened without last summer's rebellion, when black people tried to burn the town down."[100]

At first glance, the Medical School agreement represented the pinnacle of the organizing project begun during the 1963 Barringer High School demonstration—residents' protest yielded significant influence in the scope of the project and an assurance that the Medical School would be obligated to serve and employ residents in the surrounding community. But the actual enforcement of the agreement still required the kind of parallel structures that Black Power theorists were now advocating.[101]

Even as the Medical School agreement was praised by its adherents, contractors and unions undercut it by failing or refusing to employ minority workers.[102] Following "two years of fruitless efforts," Heningburg joined with George Fontaine, a fellow activist, to create the Black and Puerto Rican Construction Coalition (BPRCC) to pursue the enforcement of the Medical School agreement.[103] The BPRCC called on the Labor Department to directly intervene and on other federal agencies to freeze federal funding for the project until contractors were in compliance with existing antidiscrimination laws and requirements. BPRCC also demanded that Governor Hughes halt construction on the project with an executive order, but Hughes refused. The Medical School was crucial to the recovery of Newark, he argued, and must proceed. Instead, Hughes chose a less immediately disruptive strategy, pursuing a gradual legal solution beginning in January 1969.[104]

For Heningburg and other advocates of affirmative action, Hughes's stance amounted to a capitulation to the status quo that they had fought so hard to change. Irreplaceable opportunities were lost each day that construction continued without minority workers. The losses represented not just a few days' wages but the chances for hundreds of workers to become apprentices, to learn trades that would provide stable incomes, and possibly to become members of the union. In a city with an unemployment rate of 13 percent, these were immediate benefits that no drawn-out lawsuit, no matter how favorable the settlement, could replace.[105] Hughes's justification also betrayed a curious blindness. The Medical School negotiations had shown that it was not the building alone that that was crucial to the recovery of Newark but the formation of a coalition capable of delivering real benefits to the Central Ward that stood as the distinctive accomplishment of the city.

Over the next few years, the implementation of the employment plan at the heart of the Medical School settlement was interrupted by work stoppages, accusations of bad faith, and several protracted lawsuits. Union leaders did not budge, refusing to accept referrals for African American and Puerto Rican workers who had not received training from union tradesmen. Heningburg and George Fontaine created a parallel training structure for African American and Puerto Rican workers. With approval from the Department of Labor, they established the Newark Construction Trades Training Corporation in a former Bell Telephone building on the site of the Medical School. By hiring semiretired union members to prepare young blacks and Puerto Ricans for entry into a formal union apprenticeship program, this "pretraining" system undermined claims made by union apprenticeship sponsors that black and Puerto Rican applicants were unacceptable because they had no familiarity with union standards. It increased the number of minority tradesmen working on the Medical School, but union apprenticeship sponsors found other criteria—mainly age—for rejecting applicants.[106] Then, in December 1970—not long after the election of Kenneth Gibson, the first black mayor of Newark—a district court decision upheld the legality of the affirmative action plan meted out during the course of the Medical School dispute three years earlier and asserted the prerogative of the court to enforce integration, requiring unions to accept minority journeymen as members.[107] This decision fortified the Medical School model for minority hiring throughout the city, which later became known as the Newark Plan, but its implementation in subsequent construction projects still necessitated grassroots vigilance.

Construction trades activism had focused on breaking barriers in a small cluster of occupations, but it simultaneously contributed to the ambitious vision of community control of urban renewal codified in the Medical School agreement. In the wake of the 1967 uprising, the development of comparatively autonomous coalitions and parallel institutions rooted in earlier protests enabled residents to seize a brief moment when government officials were especially alarmed by residents' anger and receptive to community-based solutions. In this moment, residents pushed through the vacuum of fictive meritocracy to increase the numbers of unionized African American and Puerto Rican tradesmen—first by tens, then hundreds.

"WORK FOR ME ALSO MEANS WORK FOR THE COMMUNITY I COME FROM"

Black Contractors, Black Capitalism, and Affirmative Action in the Bay Area

John J. Rosen

In summer 1995, residents of Oakland, California, received news that their city would once again house a professional football team. Having lost the Raiders to Los Angeles thirteen years earlier, local football fans were thrilled at the prospect of the team's return. "Fans roared, grown people cried and a stereo system blared The Boys Are Back In Town, as members of the Raiders' faithful got the good news Friday: The Silver and Black is back in Oakland," the *St. Petersburg Times* reported.[1] Yet not everyone welcomed the team with open arms. "If they put taxpayer money at risk, the benefit to our community, and the black community, has to be substantial, and I don't see that," Joseph Debro warned. An African American construction contractor, Debro was upset because the Oakland Alameda County Coliseum Commission had awarded an $80 million contract for renovating the Raiders' home field to a personal friend of Al Davis, the Raiders' managing general partner, without requiring a competitive bid. "This is an affirmative action program that Al Davis has," Debro protested. "It's incredible that he'd be allowed to select the contractor and spend our money on his contractor."[2] City and county officials saw things differently. In their view, Debro was merely a disgruntled contractor who was jockeying for his own piece of the action on the stadium renovation project. "It's a shakedown," Oakland City Councilman Ignacio De La Fuente said of Debro's attempt to put the Raiders deal to a countywide vote. "This guy is damaged goods," added Don Perata,

I thank Eric Arnesen, John Flores, Sam Mitrani, Joseph Lipari, Trevor Griffey, and Joseph Debro for their comments on earlier drafts of this chapter.

former Alameda County supervisor. "He's got an ax to grind with the city of Oakland, he's in bankruptcy and he needs to get healthy."[3] But for Debro *ad hominem* attacks such as these only obscured the larger issue at stake. "I'm selfish and am looking for work," he countered, "but work for me also means work for the community I come from."[4]

It was fitting that Debro was at the center of such a controversy in the 1990s. During the three previous decades, he had been active in local and national campaigns to help African American contractors obtain a larger share of U.S. construction work. When he began this crusade in the mid-1960s, the construction industry seemed to present an ideal opportunity for government officials to combine inchoate affirmative action policies in employment with policies aimed at assisting the development of minority-owned businesses. After all, the specter of white contractors using white work crews on inner-city urban redevelopment projects while unemployed blacks stood by and watched ranked among the most potent symbols of racial inequality in the urban United States at the time. The use of black and other minority contractors on such projects, Debro and his peers asserted, would naturally result in more jobs and money for inner-city communities. Moreover, unlike other industries, construction was not confined to a single locale. Thus, black contractors reasoned, as they expanded their operations and achieved parity with white contractors they would be able to provide good jobs for African Americans outside the ghettos. Whereas E. Franklin Frazier, the African American sociologist, had famously classified the potential of black-owned businesses to create jobs and money for African American communities as a "social myth," black contractors felt that they could turn that myth into a reality.[5]

In this chapter, I examine the actions of black contractors in the 1960s to better understand why contractors such as Debro were still struggling to make this point three decades later. The activism of African American construction contractors is an important—if often overlooked—piece of the broader history of racial exclusion in the national construction industry.[6] In most accounts, black contractors do not enter the picture until the advent of—and controversy surrounding—minority set-aside programs in the 1970s and 1980s.[7] Yet, even in this context, they seldom receive consideration as agents of historical change. By focusing on black builders in the San Francisco Bay Area, I highlight here the role of African American construction contractors in the local and national campaigns for fair employment, minority business enterprise, and Black Power and community control in the 1960s and 1970s. More generally, this study of African American contractors provides a distinct grassroots perspective from which to view the relationship between black business and black labor.

The African American contractors whose stories fill the following pages advanced a theory of black capitalism that diverged in important respects from those of the policymakers in Washington, D.C. African American contractors offered a model of affirmative action for the construction industry that accorded black and other minority contractors a central role in racially integrating the skilled building trades and rebuilding America's inner cities. Only in the 1970s did the minority contractor and minority worker struggles for affirmative action diverge. Explaining this divergence, and the fate of minority contractors' campaign to combat racial discrimination in the construction industry, highlights a path not taken for the black freedom movement. It also explains the limited scope that modern affirmative action policy took during its formative stage.

African American contractors' historic link to black workers was a central component of their activism in the late 1960s and early 1970s. By the time that civil rights activists launched mass protests that shut down construction sites in the 1960s, black workers and interracial civil rights organizations in the San Francisco Bay Area had spent roughly two decades trying to compel the lily-white building trades unions to open their doors to nonwhite workers. Although the history of racial exclusion in organized labor dated back to the nineteenth century, in places such as the Bay Area the issue became particularly acute beginning in the 1940s with the massive wartime migration of African Americans from the South and Midwest. As James Gregory has recently stressed, many of the southern black migrants who transformed the racial composition of the urban North and West in the decades surrounding the two world wars were skilled workers.[8] The tens of thousands of black Americans who migrated to the Bay Area in the decades surrounding World War II were no exception, and their ranks included experienced and skilled plumbers and pipe fitters, electricians, painters, and plasterers who sought work in the booming shipyards and expanding commercial and residential construction markets. But, like their counterparts who arrived in other union strongholds such as New York, Chicago, Pittsburgh, and Seattle during the First and Second World Wars, these migrants found the opportunities to ply their trades severely curtailed by racially restrictive labor unions that proved obstinate when faced with external pressure to reform.

When confronted with union discrimination, black craftsmen responded in a variety of ways: some looked for work in another industry or trade or accepted lower-paying and less-skilled construction work as hod-carriers or common laborers; others sought assistance from civil rights organizations such as the Urban League or the National Association for the Advancement of Colored People (NAACP); and still others filed complaints with government agencies such as the Fair Employment Practices Committee (FEPC). But aside from a successful campaign against the San Francisco hod-carriers' union, the mid-century actions of the FEPC and civil rights groups in the Bay Area did not result in substantial and permanent gains for African Americans in skilled craft unions.[9] Moreover, when black craftsmen did gain admittance to unions, they usually found themselves passed over for jobs unless the client was also an African American.[10] Most scholarship has focused on these forms of activism when discussing black activism against racially biased skilled craft unions, but skilled black construction workers could also exercise another option—contracting.

The decision to become contractors grew out of the reinforcing pillars of racial discrimination and economic necessity. By setting up shop for themselves, African Americans who took the state contractors' licensing exam improved their chances of avoiding union discrimination and gaining a greater degree of autonomy and control over their work lives.[11] As a black master plumber who tried to join Local 445 in Oakland in 1945 recounted, "I was told that the union could not put me to work because most of the people (white) requesting plumbing work done in their home definitely did not want a Negro plumber. At this time there were no Negroes in the union. Rather than join the union and face the possibility of not getting any calls I decided to take the state examination for a license to contract." Another contractor who joined the Pile Drivers Union in 1934 left the local eight years later "after being told that the contractors did not want to work Negroes." A black plasterer who fought his way into Oakland Local 112 and worked on government contracts during the war "decided to take the state board and contract on my own" when "the government jobs were over" and "chances of working with white painting contractors would be very poor." Added a black carpenter who "experienced many forms of discrimination" as a member of Local 33 in Oakland, "Because of the discriminatory practices, I decided to take the state board and begin contracting on my own. I still retain my union card but do not depend upon the union for men to any great extent."[12]

As African American contractors bettered their chances to earn a living in the construction industry, they also created important roles for themselves as employers and mentors for black workers who found their opportunities to work and training curtailed by unions. Because of their own experiences with union discrimination and their general preference—and economic need—for using nonunion labor, many black contractors felt responsible for hiring and training other black workers. "After passing the state board I made it a point to train as many Negroes as possible for the trade and was determined to use them on jobs," a black plumbing contractor explained. "Finally two of these trainees were allowed to join the union as a result of working exclusively with me." Black contractors, who typically ran modest operations, also tried to "give each other a day or two when work is slack." As one general contractor explained, "Whenever one of us is in a little bad luck we try to help each other in every way we can.... That is one reason why most of the Negro contractors retain their union card after becoming a contractor."[13] Through their close relationships with black workers,

African American contractors established an important link to the growing Bay Area black communities—a connection that they looked to draw on as they sought larger government projects in the 1960s and 1970s.

The black contractors who emerged in the postwar decades illustrate historian Judith Walker's point that the "history of black business in America is primarily one of small enterprise."[14] Indeed, there was little difference between a black contractor and a craftsman. "The Negro firm is for the most part a single proprietorship, the owner being his own best worker," a 1954 study concluded. "He operates with virtually no administrative staff and with a minimum amount of capital and equipment." The majority of black contractors in this period built one or two homes a year and spent most their time performing repairs and "patch work."[15] During the 1960s, another observer noted, a typical black contractor was "still working out of his car trunk, off his truck bed and has offices in a room of his home or garage. Because of insufficient capital his home phone may serve a dual purpose. He can't afford a secretary, so his wife pitches in, and he has no accountant, bookkeeper, or lawyer."[16] According to a 1968 estimate of the Small Business Administration (SBA), only 8,000 of the nation's approximately 870,000 construction firms were minority-owned.[17] Of these, few were general building contractors. Rather, most worked as subcontractors specializing in electrical, carpentry, plumbing, painting, masonry, and other specific trades.[18]

The disparity between black and white contractors widened throughout the 1960s as, in the Bay Area and across the country, single-family residential construction stagnated while large-scale—and especially government-financed—construction expanded.[19] Beginning in 1956, Congress appropriated $2.2 billion per year for construction of the Interstate Highway System. The federal government spent even more money on housing and redevelopment. The 1959 Housing Act appropriated $650 million for urban renewal projects. When the Act was renewed in 1961, that amount increased to $2 billion while an additional $500 million was added for the construction of community facilities. Additionally, the Area Redevelopment Act provided $394 million for the improvement of impoverished cities and rural areas.[20] By 1968, according to *Fortune* magazine, construction was an $80-billion dollar industry that produced one-tenth of the nation's GNP.[21] Moreover, it showed no sign of slowing, leading a 1969 presidential Cabinet on Construction to predict that the "United States will put in place in the next thirty years as much construction as there has been from the founding of the Republic to now."[22] Yet black contractors stood to gain little from this construction boom. According to a 1967 report, for instance, minority contractors accounted for less than $500 million of the $80 billion U.S. construction industry.[23] This disparity was evident in the Bay Area, where by 1968 not one of the approximately 125 black contractors in the region was working on a large publicly financed job.[24]

In cities across the country, a small number of black contractors and business leaders sought to bridge this gap. Chief among them was Joseph Debro. Born in Jackson, Mississippi, Debro migrated to the Bay Area with his parents and thousands of other African Americans during World War II. In contrast to most of the African Americans who became contractors in the 1940s and 1950s, Debro entered the field with advanced university training and without a background in a particular trade. After obtaining an undergraduate degree in engineering and a master's degree in biochemistry from the University of California, he became interested in large-scale building contracting while working as an engineer on the construction of Interstate 580 in the East Bay during the 1950s. In the years that followed, he developed a keen interest in the problems confronting black building contractors and emerged as one of the leading advocates for black and other minority contractors.[25]

Beginning in the mid 1960s, Debro focused his work on overcoming the four major obstacles that prevented black contractors from expanding their operations and obtaining lucrative government contracts: lack of skilled labor, lack of technical management skills, lack of capital, and bonding requirements. The lack of skilled workers was a direct result of the building trades unions, which controlled the primary avenue to apprenticeship training. Most skilled construction workers were unionized, and small-scale black contractors could find it difficult to meet their wage scales. Yet, even if they could, they would have hesitated to use white workers on the job because they felt "that they cannot use union labor until their brothers and neighbors are admitted to union training programs and regular union membership," Debro stated in 1970.[26] As small-scale contractors, African Americans also needed technical assistance to meet the technical and managerial skills that large contracts required. "A large job requires full-time attention to the books, to the arranging of financing, bonding, and the on-site work," Debro explained. "Technical assistance is needed by the minority contractors if they are to develop their full potential." Similarly, if black contractors were going to take on larger jobs, they needed "seed money" to meet the insurance, material, and payroll requirements of a large contract. "Working capital is crucial," Debro and his colleagues maintained, "for it limits the size of the job a contractor can do."[27]

The fourth obstacle—bonding requirements—proved the most troublesome for black contractors and their supporters to overcome. Large construction contracts open to bidding (and following passage of the Miller Act in 1935 all federal contracts valued at least $2,000) required contractors to obtain surety bonds to insure the completion of the project, payment for their workforce, payment for their material suppliers, and in some cases for the bid itself. The surety companies that issued these bonds viewed them as a line of credit awarded to the contractor to protect the investment of the client. Typically, a construction company needed to demonstrate that it had liquid cash in the amount of 10 percent of the total cost of the project. Because of their historical lack of capital and technical training, black contractors claimed that the bonding requirements created a vicious circle in which most black contractors lacked the experience, capital, and managerial capability required to obtain the bonds they needed to qualify for the very types of projects that would give them that experience. Bonding companies justified their policies on the grounds that sound business practices necessitated that they minimize risks as much as possible when issuing bonds. They claimed to evaluate a contractor based on the "three C's": character, capital, and capacity.[28] However, surety firms also considered other factors. For instance, in a candid 1968 unpublished memorandum, the American Insurance Association stated that it believed "that it will serve no useful purpose, economic or sociological, for surety companies to issue contract bonds indiscriminately to all applicants, qualified or not."[29]

Black contractors considered such practices as examples of racial discrimination and frequently protested that the industry perpetuated a double standard in which "the requirements for minority contractors are often twice as rigorous as those imposed on non-minority contractors under similar circumstances." In published articles and congressional committee testimonies, Debro and other minority contractors told of surety companies denying bonds to qualified minority contractors. They further charged that the U.S. Department of the Treasury, which was responsible for regulating surety companies, turned a blind eye toward these unfair practices. These protests notwithstanding, overt discrimination was difficult to prove because the majority of black contractors could not meet the capital requirements of most bonding companies.

Debro believed that the free market could neither solve the bonding problem nor the other obstacles that limited their opportunities. He maintained that "all these problems are aggravated by the inaction of city leaders in the unions, government, private business, and universities who should be devoting their time to mobilizing resources on a local level to cope with the exclusion of minorities from all phases of the construction industry."[30] Before black contractors could expect to receive external assistance, however, Debro felt that they needed to organize themselves on a larger scale. This posed a potential challenge because African Americans who became contractors in the 1940s and 1950s appeared hesitant to expand their operations. Many feared that doing so would "involve too much book work," create "more headaches," and risk "losing everything" when they were already making a "small profit."[31] Moreover, although black contractors had a history of mutual self-help, they typically avoided participating in formal trade and professional associations. Debro therefore anticipated that he might "have to drag, cajole, push and pull some people to get into the larger jobs."[32]

The political, economic, and social context of the 1960s ensured that Debro's search would not be as difficult as he expected. Perhaps more than any other industry, construction provided a venue where the demands of civil rights and community activists converged with government attempts to stimulate black business enterprise, strengthen equal employment laws, and to rebuild the nation's inner cities. As the authors in this volume demonstrate, civil rights and community activists picketed construction sites in cities across the country to protest the exclusion of African American workers from publicly funded projects. In the Bay Area, protesters targeted the construction of the Bay Area Rapid Transit system (BART), a billion-dollar project that was scheduled to take five years to complete. Much of BART's construction was located in some of the poorest neighborhoods in Oakland and San Francisco, and local residents, along with their allies in the NAACP and Congress of Racial Equality, made it clear that they would not stand by idly while white construction crews performed the work. Debro, who was serving as the executive director of the Oakland Small Business Development Center (OSBDC) at the time, considered these protests and the subsequent efforts of the federal government to secure black employment on construction projects such as BART as "the volatile issue needed to get people organized."[33] And it was in that tumultuous atmosphere that a black electrical contractor named Ray Dones walked into his office in pursuit of a loan in 1966.

Although Dones was not specifically seeking a contract on BART, he hoped that the OSBDC could help him obtain a loan so that he could bid on other government projects. Born in Marshall, Texas, he obtained his contracting license after learning the plumbing and electrical trades while working as a Pullman porter in Denver, Colorado. Dones moved to the Bay Area in 1950, and in 1953 he established Dones Electric (which later became Aladdin Electric) in Berkeley. Like many other black contractors in the Bay Area during this period, Aladdin procured steady employment on small residential buildings, and by the mid-1960s he had a workforce of six full-time electricians—all of whom were African American. Yet when the residential market slowed, Dones was unable to obtain the necessary surety bonds to bid on lucrative government-financed construction projects, and as a result he had to lay off two of his workers.[34] Hoping to avoid further cutbacks and to possibly expand his business, he visited the OSBDC.

Dones and Debro immediately hit it off, and instead of arranging a loan they discussed the possibility of forming an organization that could assist black contractors in making the transition from small residential construction to larger public-sector projects. Shortly thereafter, Dones met with fifteen other contractors in Oakland on August 13, 1966, "to discuss their problem and to attempt to develop plans to alleviate it."[35] With the assistance of Debro and the OSBDC, this meeting led to the formation of the General and Specialty Contractors Association (GSCA), which was among the first minority contractor associations to organize across craft lines in the United States. Over the next seven years, more than one hundred similar associations were established in cities across the country, including two across the bay in San Francisco and another just to the north of Oakland in Richmond, California.[36]

The founders of the GSCA hoped their organization would appeal to small-scale contractors by offering a variety of programs designed to provide the managerial and technical assistance needed to compete with more established firms on large and publicly financed projects. In essence, a major goal of the GSCA and its counterparts across the country was to teach black contractors to think more like businessmen and less like craftsmen. Toward that end, the association obtained a $75,000 grant from the Economic Development Administration (EDA), which was established within the Department of Commerce by the Public Works and Economic Development Act of 1965, and applied it toward enlisting a staff of management experts and "the more successful Bay Area contractors" to conduct monthly seminars that addressed topics such as "budgeting, preparing cash flow projections, estimating, contractors' overhead calculations, and job scheduling." In addition, in its first three years, the GSCA developed programs to provide information to minority contractors about publicly funded contracts to be let, to assist inexperienced members with preparing estimates, to assist members with business procedures on jobs in progress, and to serve as mediators in labor disputes and "help to negotiate a transition process into union-shop status as each firm moves into the mainstream of the industry."[37]

The GSCA programs appeared to have had the appeal that Debro and Dones desired. In its first three years, GSCA membership grew from its original size of sixteen to seventy-three.[38] Most of these contractors were African American, however the association's membership rolls included a few Mexican Americans, Japanese Americans, and two whites. Its advocacy on behalf of "minority contractors" distinguished it, along with its national successor, from the consortium of African American contractors that the NAACP formed in 1969. In 1968, six GSCA members further pooled their resources to form Trans-Bay Engineers and Builders, Inc., a general contracting firm that they hoped could compete with the larger white-owned general contracting companies in the area.

Managerial and technical training was just one component of the two-tiered GSCA program. Because of their need for skilled craftsmen, the GSCA contractors made training black and other minority workers an equally important part of its mission. "I've always looked at this from the overall view as a two-level thing," Lee Marsh, one of the two white GSCA members, stated. "It's always been my feeling that if you are able to get a big, strong, profitable contracting organization you have your best guarantee that there's going to be training of minority craftsmen," he continued. "Conversely, minority contractors cannot get strong if there is not a good source of minority craftsmen."[39]

The GSCA emphasis on training minority workers for the building trades served two political purposes as well. First, black contractors hoped to convince Labor Department (DOL) officials busy with developing affirmative action programs for the construction industry that they should include provisions that would help minority contractors obtain government building contracts. GSCA contractors stressed the historical link between minority contractors and construction workers and added that construction unions' history of discrimination caused young blacks to avoid union-administered apprenticeship programs. If black contractors had a more prominent role in state-sponsored affirmative action programs, they contended, more young African Americans would consider a career in construction. They further stressed that most skilled construction workers had not graduated from formal apprentice programs in the first place. Rather, GSCA leaders insisted, most construction workers learned the trade through on-the-job training—something black workers acquired while working for black contractors.

Second, GSCA contractors sought the trust and support of the community activists whose protests were among the primary causes of government action in the first place. As the historians Robert Self and Matthew Countryman have demonstrated, the campaigns for construction jobs in inner-city neighborhoods were part of broader "place-based" social movements designed to combat the demolition and displacement of homes and businesses that urban renewal often entailed.[40] Black contractors, some of whom did not reside in the poor and working-class neighborhoods where federal construction projects were taking place, understood the need to be conscious of how they positioned themselves within these communities.[41] After all, they were often fighting for the contracts to demolish the homes and businesses that residents were fighting to save. The GSCA, Debro explained, sought to "plug in the contractors in the communities" in order to "plug in people who live in these communities into the construction trade."[42] By making the training and employment of minority workers a major part of their mission, GSCA contractors hoped to improve their chances of gaining support from black communities as well as from the government agencies working to integrate the skilled building trades.

Black contractors sought a model for integrating the construction industry that also eliminated the barriers that limited their access to jobs. By summer 1967, the GSCA and OSBDC had drafted a "community action program" for Oakland that proposed to use minority contractors as the primary vehicle for integrating the skilled building trades. The plan called for an "On the Job Training Credit Bank" that would provide training and employment for approximately six hundred workers while creating "an economically viable group of building contractors who will be able to carry-on the training of minority workers and assist the less qualified associated in increasing their business skills." With proper funding, the Credit Bank would help cover the training costs for the upgrading of minority construction workers while simultaneously increasing the bonding capacity of minority contractors. For each worker that a contractor trained, $2,000 would be deposited in his account at the Credit Bank. These funds could then be applied toward meeting bonding requirements. As GSCA members obtained more contracts, they would also receive the technical and managerial assistance that the organization provided through its EDA grant. The GSCA proposal had the support of the Building and Construction Trades Council of Alameda County, which, noting that one-third of GSCA contractors already had union agreements, expected to use it "as a vehicle to sign others in the Association as well as to upgrade the presently non-union workmen and get them in the Union." By using minority contractors and cooperating with organized labor, the GSCA believed that "the most meaningful contribution that this project could make would be the establishment of a new Federal program modeled on its success."[43]

However, Dones and Debro quickly learned that convincing the federal government to take on a joint employment and business affirmative action program would be exceedingly difficult. Dones first brought the Credit Bank idea to the DOL—a logical move considering the department's involvement in eradicating racial discrimination in construction employment. The DOL, however, rejected the proposal because financing contractors fell beyond its jurisdiction.[44]

Private philanthropies went where the government feared to tread. The GSCA and OSBDC took their proposal to the Management Council for Bay Area Employment Opportunity, a group funded by the Ford Foundation.[45] This time the proposal was well-received, although the Council suggested that the contractor and apprenticeship components of the program be split so that the GSCA still might be able to obtain DOL funding on the latter.

By the time it received the GSCA proposal, the Ford Foundation had already developed an interest in minority contractors. In 1967, the foundation began to discuss the bonding problem with surety companies, and the Department of Housing and Urban Development (HUD) requested its assistance in helping minority contractors for its projects.[46] The Ford Foundation approved the proposal in 1968 and awarded the GSCA a three-year grant in the amount of

$300,000, which was used to establish a revolving fund that GSCA members could use to meet bonding requirements.[47] As a pioneering effort to assist black and minority-owned businesses, the Ford grant also generated interest at the national level. "This project could be done throughout the country," the executive director of the Lower Manhattan Small Business Development Corporation predicted, "and the association could be the vehicle whereby it could spread out throughout the different cities, and where the association feels it is important to work."[48]

The Oakland Bonding Assistance Program, as it was named, produced immediate results. Within a few months of operation, the program provided N. G. Tademy, a black general contractor based in Berkeley, with a $15,000 working capital loan. The loan enabled Tademy to secure a bond for a $255,000 contract on a University of California fraternity house, the largest contract that Tademy had ever won.[49] The program would go on to make thirty-five bond-related advances totaling $287,544. Trans-Bay Engineers and Builders was the program's biggest client. It was able to obtain an interest-free $50,000 loan from the revolving fund to secure a bond on the construction of the West Oakland Health Center, a contract that the company would otherwise have lost because the surety company had cancelled its bond at the eleventh hour. That job netted the company a $26,000 profit and quickly led to contracts on several other redevelopment projects worth $5 million.[50] Among them was the construction of three high-rise apartment buildings sponsored by More Oakland Residential Housing, Inc. (MORH), a nonprofit community sponsor comprising West Oakland community organizations. As the general contractor on this project, the *Oakland Post* reported, Trans-Bay became the first minority firm to build a high-rise in the western United States.[51]

The GSCA was also encouraged by the early attempts to implement the training component initially outlined in its Credit Bank proposal through two pilot programs: Project Upgrade and PREP (Property Rehabilitation Employment Project). Through them, the GSCA contractors hoped to demonstrate that minority contractors were capable of attracting minority workers who might otherwise be skeptical of traditional union-administered apprenticeship programs. Both programs were formed in cooperation with the Alameda County Building and Construction Trades Council and financed with grants from the DOL and the Ford Foundation.[52] Established in 1968, the mission of Project Upgrade was to help minority craftsmen with previous construction experience attain journeyman status.[53] Launched in summer 1969, PREP aimed to provide construction experience for minority youths who were unable to matriculate into union apprenticeship programs. The two training programs showed early signs of promise. By 1970, twenty-eight of the eighty-six trainees matriculating into

Project Upgrade had been initiated into craft unions, twelve were awaiting initiation, and thirty-seven were continuing their training. Similarly, in its first year PREP counted ninety-six recruits and had placed fifteen students on construction jobs and six as indentured apprentices.[54]

The success of these programs helped the GSCA become an integral component of the Oakland Redevelopment Agency's (ORA) attempts to maximize minority participation in its West Oakland projects. The GSCA helped minority contractors secure "turnkey" agreements with the Oakland Housing Authority, and in 1970 the ORA, under the leadership of John Williams, its African American director, awarded the association nonprofit sponsorship on low- and medium-income housing projects.[55] By the end of 1972, the ORA reported that 30 percent of its projects—totaling $10.4 million—had been allocated to minority contracting firms; another 28 percent worth $9.7 million had been awarded to joint ventures involving minority and white-owned firms.[56] This level of participation had a direct impact on minority employment on redevelopment projects. In 1970, Debro reported that 200 new jobs were generated, minority craftsmen work hours and wages roughly doubled, and "generated more non-white union journeymen in the high-wage crafts than in the entire history of the local hiring-hall process."[57] Between 1968 and 1972, the ORA later reported, 2,207 of 3,484 jobs on redevelopment projects had gone to minority workers. In recognition of the contribution of Trans-Bay to these results, the ORA awarded the firm a Certificate of Merit in Affirmative Action in December 1972.[58]

The GSCA's pilot projects in the Bay Area became a model for programs elsewhere, and helped Bay Area contractors take a lead role in the founding a national minority contractors association to build upon their success. Based on early returns in Oakland, the Ford Foundation helped launch similar programs in New York, Boston, and Cleveland.[59] Yet Ford Foundation officials and minority contractors felt that any long-term solution required a stronger commitment from federal, state, and local governments.[60] The task was to convince government officials that assisting black contractors was the most expedient way to integrate the construction industry.

By organizing themselves into collective associations and advancing their program in Oakland, black and other minority contractors injected an additional element into the simmering debates concerning the employment of minority workers in the construction industry. In a memorandum written approximately a month after issuing the Operational Plan for San Francisco Bay Area Construction Compliance in 1966 (which was the product of the DOL's intervention in BART construction), Director Edward Sylvester of the OFCC suggested that general contractors work with the GSCA to "encourage minority group subcontractors and subcontractors with minority representation among their employees to bid for subcontracting work."[61] In the summer of 1967, an EDA-funded construction project in Oakland adopted an affirmative action program that placed a "premium on equal opportunity actions with particular reference to the elimination of the practice of excluding minority group sub-contractors and employers."[62] As part of the agreement, the general contractor on the job pledged to "contact the General and Specialty Contractors Association, Inc., and arrange to notify them of jobs being bid requiring services of subcontractors."[63] When the U.S. Commission on Civil Rights held hearings on racism in the construction industry in San Francisco on May 2, 1967, it invited Ray Dones to testify on the problems that black contractors faced and how they could get more black workers employed on government jobs.[64] That same spring, the Urban League began working with the GSCA on developing a *Directory of Minority Journeymen* in the Bay Area, and in August, the San Francisco Human Rights Commission instructed the Housing Authority to include "the minority contractors group" in its invitations to bid on jobs on the city Hunters Point housing rehabilitation project.[65] In 1968, the Construction Industry Labor Management Committee on Equal Opportunity adopted a policy on affirmative action for the Bay Area that included a provision to use the GSCA for outreach to "minority group subcontractors."[66]

Meanwhile, the GSCA also heightened the NAACP's growing interest in the plight of black contractors. Herbert Hill, the NAACP labor director, had expressed concern for black contractors as early as 1963, when civil rights protesters picketed construction sites in New York, Philadelphia, and Cleveland.[67] Under his guidance, the national office closely followed the activities of the GSCA from its inception and came to view black contractors as key players in its fledgling campaign to integrate the building trades. By the end of 1967, the NAACP had concluded that "the issue of Negro contractors getting some of the government contracts is a very live issue that we are going to have to deal with," and the national office instructed its West Coast affiliates to "work very closely" with the GSCA and "attempt to involve them as well in the whole of the issues on public construction that we are seeking to take on."[68]

The NAACP officially added black contractors to its construction industry program in 1968, when Roy Wilkins announced a new initiative "to organize small Negro contractors into larger units so that their resources can be pooled and they can qualify for surety bonds, thus enabling them to bid on large construction contracts."[69] The idea for the program was likely an outgrowth of the NAACP's observations of the GSCA. In fact, the NAACP Labor Department cited the case of black contractors in the Bay Area when first explaining the concept for the plan in its 1967 annual report.[70] The NAACP-led venture, which it named the National Afro-American Builders Corporation (NAABC), was a for-profit consortium (participating contractors were also required to join the NAACP). The NAACP hired Robert Easley, a former labor organizer who oversaw the integration of Navy contractors for the Department of Defense from 1965–1967, to direct the program under the supervision of Herbert Hill.[71] Easley's plan was to target "cities with the best bonding potential and prospective government contracts," but he did not appear to spend much, if any, time organizing contractors in the West. As had been Debro's experience in Oakland in 1966, Easley found black contractors willing and ready to organize to bid on large projects in the cities he did visit.[72] In its first nine months, Easley reported, the program organized 24 working chapters in 21 states, including a national headquarters in Philadelphia and regional offices in Gary, Indiana and Newark, New Jersey. And although the corporation had "lost some of the bids because the time element (for bidding and estimating) was too short to secure the needed capital," its local chapters had secured housing contracts in Boston, South Bend, Gary, Flint, Dayton, Birmingham, Mobile, and High Point, New York.[73]

The NAACP's decision to organize black contractors marked a strategic and philosophical shift in its approach to employment discrimination in the construction industry. Although the association had previously recognized the problems that black contractors faced, its prime objective had been to integrate the skilled building trades unions. For instance, in a paper prepared for the NAACP's West Coast Asilomar Conference in 1967, David G. McConnell, Chairman of the Labor and Industry Committee of the association's Columbus, Ohio, branch, suggested that black contractors—being skilled in their respective trades—were ideal candidates for potential test cases against the unions. "Ferret these colored journeymen out," he advised his colleagues, warning them that these contractors might be reluctant to be "a guinea pig for integration" and "don't want to lose their men." In McConnell's assessment, which appeared to be representative of NAACP officials more generally, unionized black workers would then make it possible for contractors to bid on large closed-shop government contracts.[74]

The NAABC project of the NAACP partly turned this logic on its head by suggesting that black contracting firms could potentially facilitate the entry of black workers into the skilled trades. "The establishment of a national organization of Negro contractors would make possible the employment of large numbers of Negro construction workers who are denied access to union controlled hiring halls and also makes possible the establishment of independent apprenticeship programs directly operated by groups of Negro-owned contractors," Herbert Hill explained in a 1968 report, "thereby bypassing the traditional restrictive apprenticeship training system which excludes Negroes from skilled craft occupations in this industry."[75]

The NAACP grew increasingly forthright in its campaign to assist black contractors in the immediate lead-up and aftermath of the Philadelphia Plan. "Giving a preferential status to black contractors is the only realistic way of guaranteeing that a substantial number of black craftsmen will be employed on Model Cities and other publicly funded construction," Hill declared at 1969 hearing held in Boston.[76] In August 1970, he objected to a final draft of the New Orleans Plan, in part because "Negro-owned building contractors have no representation on the Administrative Committee and indeed, are excluded entirely from the scope of the plan." Hill added that "It is absolutely essential, that Negro and other non-white contractors have an opportunity to bid for both prime and sub-contracts on all public construction projects.... The total omission of this point in the plan is most significant."[77] The NAACP "Proposed Model Plan for Construction Industry Agreements" included a provision requiring that minority subcontractors receive contracts whose combined dollar value is equivalent to seventy percent of the total dollar value of all work subcontracted in any city covered by the agreement.[78]

Like the NAACP, GSCA leaders also mobilized to influence debates that engulfed the Philadelphia Plan. To help coordinate their efforts with contractors in other parts of the country and to exert greater influence among policymakers, the GSCA, together with black contractors in Los Angeles, spearheaded the formation of the National Association of Minority Contractors (NAMC) in July 1969. As the founding executive director and president, respectively, Joseph Debro and Ray Dones viewed the NAMC as the vehicle for taking the GSCA mission to the national level. Headquartered in San Francisco, the NAMC defined its aim as "to help a proportionate number of minorities enter the mainstream of American economic life through the key industry of construction." Like the GSCA, it outlined an economic program to help create opportunities, capital, and training for minority contractors. The NAMC also stressed minority contractors' commitment to training minority workers, which was significant given that the Nixon administration's official introduction of the Philadelphia Plan had come just one month earlier.

The NAMC went further to position its program within the politics of community control by promoting the idea that black business enterprise—particularly in construction—was crucial to the revitalization of U.S. inner cities. The association mission statement included rebuilding "the rotting, inner core of the cities"; providing "adequate, safe and sanitary housing"; constructing "sufficient health and educational facilities suitable to the needs of the inhabitants"; and fostering "greater minority participation in the planning of redevelopment area structures, and the management of new and rehabilitated facilities."[79]

In addition, Joseph Debro headed a congressional lobby organization whose name reflected the growing power of a community control movement. Called Contractors Organized to Lobby (CONTROL), it consisted of twelve prominent minority contractors from across the nation whose objective was to secure "economic control" of the construction process in U.S. inner cities. Debro explained:

> We have formed this organization because we are deeply troubled by the way in which public money has been consistently used to create private fortunes for white Americans. We are troubled and angered by the way the Federal Government has seen fit to rebuild the inner city ghetto: with white architects, white lawyers, white bankers, white planning consultants, white contractors, white suppliers, white craftsmen—in short, with white control over a process designed to provide housing and community facilities for minority people.[80]

Debro argued that opening up construction jobs to inner-city residents was not enough as long as white contractors continued to reap the financial benefits of public construction projects. "The minority contractor is one of the most important agents in rebuilding the inner city ghetto," he implored. "Not only does he provide jobs for community residents, but he also gives a measure of control over the rebuilding of the community to its residents....Jobs performed by minority contractors help to increase the dignity and self-reliance of the community."[81]

In their effort to place inner-city construction under community control, African American contractors also appealed to the Nixon administration's promotion of black capitalism. During his first term, in particular, the contractors who formed the NAMC appeared to offer an opportunity for Nixon to deliver on his pledge to foster black capitalism, which he hoped would stabilize the urban ghettos by giving black militants a "piece of the action" so that "black pride, black jobs, black opportunity, and...black power" would flow constructively from black ownership.[82]

Nixon's black capitalism generated intense debates among African American activists and intellectuals during Nixon's first term.[83] Contractors such as Debro were apprehensive yet willing to support any initiative that afforded them the opportunity to increase their economic power. Debro quipped that he was "not sure what Nixon means by black capitalism," however he welcomed government aid as a means to stimulate economic activity in the inner cities.[84] Because of the amount of money generated by the construction industry and the anticipated growth in publicly funded construction throughout the 1970s, Debro considered it "the last great opportunity for non-white Americans to move into the main economic system of the nation."[85] For Debro and other minority contractors, black capitalism in construction stood for black power as well as racial integration.

By fusing the politics of community control and black capitalism, African American contractors also sought to convince administration officials that they could help keep the peace in the inner cities. As Dean Kotlowski has argued, Richard Nixon "used affirmative action and minority enterprise as crisis management tools" to "promote minority economic development and thus allay urban unrest."[86] In the months following the unveiling by the Nixon administration of the Philadelphia Plan, a series of volatile protests and counterprotests erupted in Chicago, Seattle, and Pittsburgh as tensions between civil rights activists and construction unions intensified. In the Bay Area and in cities across the country, some black contractors played prominent roles in these protests. When the NAACP planned a series of Black Monday rallies in cities along the West Coast, demanding the expansion of the Philadelphia Plan in October 1969, GSCA members joined as cosponsors and employed militant rhetoric while sharing the rostrum at the San Francisco event. "If we don't rebuild it, we feel it won't be rebuilt," Emmet Scales, GSCA executive director, announced before a crowd of roughly one hundred protesters. "We ain't going to leave and we ain't going to disappear," added Charles Walker, a trucking contractor and GSCA member.[87] Several weeks later, Walker led a successful construction-site shutdown on a redevelopment project in the San Francisco Western Addition district that resulted in contracts for black trucking and demolition contractors.[88]

Movements for community control and construction site shutdowns were a double-edged sword for black contractors. On the one-hand, such protests were an important ingredient to the gains black contractors made in the 1960s. Although contractors actively participated in construction site shutdowns in several instances, according to Debro it was "typically the allies of the contractors who were militant, not the contractors themselves."[89] Debro himself relied more on the specter than the act of violence and confrontation when lobbying government officials. "In Seattle, Chicago, Pittsburgh, Newark, the community has clearly stated that the reconstruction of the inner city ghetto must take place with minority participation or it will not take place at all," he admonished a congressional committee in 1970. "We building contractors have come together as a last resort to try to use the formal legislative process to effect change."[90]

On the other hand, direct action movements for community control also posed potential problems for black contractors, particularly for those who sought jobs outside of their own districts. In Buffalo, for example, black residents picketed the Winston Burnett Construction Company, a Harlem-based firm, until the company was able to convince the protesters that it was committed to employing local residents on a local housing project.[91] Similarly, in Los Angeles, a group called the Community Council for Justice and Construction protested the awarding of a $1.7 million housing development contract to Curtis

Johnson, a black contractor based in Bakersfield, because he was not from the project area.[92] Because of the problems that they sometimes caused for black contractors, Robert Easley advised NAABC members to refrain from participating in community construction coalitions.[93]

The Nixon administration appeared to welcome the creation of the NAMC, and several of its top-ranking African American officials attended the association's founding conference in San Francisco. Among them were Arthur Fletcher, assistant secretary of labor, and Samuel Simmons and Samuel Jackson, both HUD assistant secretaries. Fletcher, who praised the contractors for "functioning within the system rather than trying to destroy it," predicted that the Philadelphia Plan would also help minority contractors because they were more likely than white contractors to employ minority workers on their regular work crews.[94] Samuel Simmons assured the NAMC that HUD would abide by Section 3 of the Housing and Redevelopment Act of 1968, which required it to provide jobs and business opportunities for individuals and businesses in HUD project areas.[95] He also told the NAMC of a pilot program—the Los Angeles Plan—in which a percentage of HUD contracts would be set aside for minority-owned firms.[96]

The Small Business Administration (SBA) also offered support through the creation of a National Construction Task Force in fall 1968. As part of the SBA's Project OWN, the task force proposed to "coordinate the previous fragmented efforts of the private sector, the government and other interested groups" to provide "capital assistance, management and technical training and market information to minority construction contractors at the municipal level; to develop a national strategy and organization for implementing a practical action program to assist in the growth and productive capability of minority entrepreneurs in the various fields of construction in the United States."[97]

But black contractors chafed at the limitations of various HUD and SBA programs, which proliferated a series of task forces that rarely solicited input from minority contractors and were often beset by interagency inertia. Although HUD helped some minority contractors win jobs on its projects in the early 1970s by waiving the bonding requirements, HUD secretary Samuel Simmons lamented that there was no single department of the federal government that "can relate to the minority contractors' total range of problems or a comprehensive program designed to meet their needs."[98]

Minority contractor dissatisfaction with the divorce between the promise of black capitalism and the reality of dysfunctional bureaucracy was accompanied by a sense of frustration about having been excluded or marginalized by early affirmative action plans in the construction industry modeled after the Philadelphia Plan. "The various job plans were created by a group consisting of one-third white contractors, one-third union representatives and one-third minority people, who don't know what they are doing in this industry and who are interested in civil rights, but who lack the knowledge of both the industry and bargaining methods," Joseph Debro exclaimed.[99] Eddie Camese, who headed a group of black contractors in Louisiana, protested that the New Orleans Plan should have included his group in the plan formulation.[100] After reviewing "hometown plans" in Seattle, Chicago, and Pittsburgh, the NAMC's Paul King (a Chicago-based painting contractor), explained that the association was not satisfied "because none of the plans yet provided are capable of satisfying our needs."[101]

Black contractors also worried that without provisions for minority contractors, that the plans would drive a wedge between them and black workers by depriving them of their workforces. "I fear there would be a raping of black contractors if all of a sudden white contractors and unions start looking for blacks, they would want the best trained men available," worried Herbert Williams, director of a black contractor association in Atlanta. "And these men are now working for black contractors."[102] Nor did this help black workers. "The problem," explained Boston contractor Jack Robinson, "is that they [white contractors] achieve their high visibility factor, but when the job is complete and the contractor moves on, he doesn't take the black tradesmen with him."[103]

Not content to let federal departments develop affirmative action programs for the construction industry, in 1969 CONTROL enlisted the support of William Moorhead, a Democrat Representative from Pennsylvania, and Birch Bayh, A Democrat Senator from Indiana. Behind Moorhead and Bayh, CONTROL sought legislation that would coordinate and fund federal programs to assist minority construction contractors and workers. To remedy the lack of technical management skills, they sought legislation that would require HUD and the SBA to fund technical assistance programs. To help compensate for minority contractors' lack of capital, they proposed that HUD and the SBA set up revolving funds that would be managed by local minority contractor organizations and that would provide working capital for minority contractors who could not obtain financing from private institutions. The revolving funds would also help minority contractors obtain bonds on large projects. They also proposed a host of other measures to help minority contractors overcome the bonding problem, including government-guaranteed bonds on all HUD projects, an SBA-issued "certificate of competency" in lieu of a bond on federally assisted projects, the division of large government construction projects into smaller units, the stricter regulation of surety companies by the U.S. Department of the Treasury, and legislation that would raise the ceiling on federally assisted projects not requiring bonds from $2,000 to $50,000.[104]

Taken together, the CONTROL proposals amounted to a federally funded and administered version of the program that the GSCA had implemented in

Oakland. CONTROL believed that these reforms give minority contractors control over the reconstruction of the inner cities as well as make it possible for them to obtain private contracts on jobs outside the urban ghettos. The legislative program, Bayh stated in 1969, represented "an important step toward bringing some sense of credibility to the rhetoric of minority economic development."[105]

Ultimately, the period surrounding the Philadelphia Plan and related debates about how best to integrate the construction industry produced mixed results for black contractors. For the most part, they were unable to persuade civil rights activists and liberal politicians that, in Robert Easley's words, "getting black contractors on the job is the solution" to getting blacks into the skilled trades.[106] Although HUD and the SBA experimented with programs to assist minority contractors throughout the 1970s, the CONTROL legislative agenda was never fully realized.[107]

Moreover, government programs often suffered from inadequate funding, lack of coordination, and corruption. The net result was a period of uneven development, in which some minority contractors found success while many others either went out of business or remained on the margins of the construction industry. "The future for minority contractors as a group looks bleak," Reginald Stuart wrote in 1971, when NAMC was just getting off the ground. "There is a diminishing shortage of young minority contractors, which threatens the future existence of minorities in the industry."[108]

The mixed legacy of black contractors' activism was evident in the Bay Area, where their national movement had originated. Without federal assistance, the gains made by the Ford Foundation–sponsored Oakland Bonding Assistance Program could not be expanded upon. The program did help Trans-Bay Engineers and Builders become a successful general contracting firm and launched the careers of Ray Dones and Joseph Debro, both of whom remained active as contractors into the twenty-first century. According to the 1970 *Registry of Minority Construction Contractors,* Trans-Bay had obtained the largest bonds and worked the largest jobs of any minority general contractor in the Bay Area.[109] Throughout the 1970s, Trans-Bay occupied a regular position on the *Black Enterprise* list of one hundred leading black-owned or managed businesses, and in 1974 Ray Dones earned the *Black Enterprise* Achievement Award in Construction for his work with the firm.[110] But the Oakland program was unable to help launch other minority firms. In 1984, Debro called the MORH housing project in West Oakland the only real victory in the fight to integrate the construction industry in Oakland.[111] Meanwhile, modest results from affirmative action plans prompted the Department of Labor to reconsider its support of Project Upgrade in 1970 and in 1976 the program folded altogether.[112] Throughout the 1970s and

1980s, minority contractor activists such as Joseph Debro continued to work at the local, state, and federal levels to break the cycle that continued to limit the horizons of black businesses. But they would do so in a context less conducive to meaningful change.

In recent years, historians of affirmative action and fair employment have taken a growing interest in the Philadelphia Plan. Although most agree that the plan, at a minimum, had the symbolic significance of constituting the first modern federal affirmative action program in employment, they also find much to debate. But scant mention is made in those debates of the African American contractors who sought to fuse affirmative action in employment with affirmative action in business.[113] Ultimately, the much-maligned minority set-aside programs emerged as the government answer to the problems of minority contractors. Yet, as the experience of the GSCA, NAMC, and CONTROL shows, black contractors in the late 1960s offered a much broader vision of how black entrepreneurs could help alleviate the problem of unemployment in the U.S. ghettos and integrate the national economy. Even if some contractors hoped to use the issue for personal gain, as Debro's critics charged in the 1995 dispute, as a group they still offered an alternative to the form that affirmative action ultimately took in the Philadelphia Plan.

COMMUNITY CONTROL OF CONSTRUCTION, INDEPENDENT UNIONISM, AND THE "SHORT BLACK POWER MOVEMENT" IN DETROIT

David Goldberg

In June 1968, nine black contractors in Detroit, Michigan, formed Allied Workers International Local 124, an independent, black-run, multitrades union. Seeking to fulfill the 1966 Model Cities mandate to hire black skilled tradesmen and train inner-city residents, Local 124 sought work on the $900 million worth of federally funded projects to rebuild postrebellion Detroit. "The black man lives in the inner city, and the black man must have equal opportunities for the many jobs now available and which will soon become available." "The ghetto development," argued Calvin Stubbs Jr., president of Local 124, "will be determined by the Blacks!"[1]

The formation of Local 124 signaled the rise of a much broader movement—the struggle for employment for inner-city residents and businesses, labor organizations responsive to the needs of black workers, and community control of redevelopment. Identifying "land as the basis of all wealth and power," black businessmen, intellectuals, militants, economic nationalists, community and tenants rights activists, and revolutionary nationalists involved in the Detroit Black Power movement began creating and supporting parallel institutions such as Local 124 to challenge racism within the construction industry and their communities. They sought to accomplish this by controlling the hiring, firing,

I thank Shawn Alexander, Beth Bates, Melba Joyce Boyd, Sundiata Cha-Jua, Trevor Griffey, Clarence Lang, Daniel McClure, and particularly Rhonda Y. Williams for sharing ideas or providing comments and criticisms on earlier drafts of this chapter.

training, contracting, and planning processes and thereby securing access to, as well as control of, the vast financial resources involved in inner-city reconstruction and federally funded urban renewal programs in postrebellion Detroit.[2]

As elsewhere, black workers in Detroit—neither willing nor trusting of others to address discrimination and institutional racism on the job, in the unions, or in society at large—increasingly connected Black Power and black nationalism to black working-class struggles and organizing. As Philip Foner explained, the Black Power unionism that resulted took "many forms," including "black caucuses, wildcat strikes in defiance of institutionalized union procedures, black unions organized outside the traditional AFL-CIO [American Federation of Labor–Congress of Industrial Organizations] structure, and even black revolutionary union movements."[3] Black workers and activists in Detroit were at the forefront of this movement, both ideologically and organizationally. Most well known are the Revolutionary Union Movements (RUMs), which began with the formation of the Dodge Revolutionary Union Movement (DRUM), soon spread to other plants and industries, and later coalesced under the umbrella of the League of Revolutionary Black Workers (LRBW). These formations helped redefine Black Power into a revolutionary black working-class movement that connected black workers' struggles to "community struggles around housing, welfare rights, and community control of school" while advocating "a revolutionary separatist politics that sought to break completely from the labor establishment and rejected integrated class struggle."[4]

The RUMs and the LRBW exemplified Black Power unionism locally and nationally, but they did not form in isolation. Independent unions or black caucuses consisting of workers from an array of ideological perspectives and occupations—UPS employees, police and firefighters, public utility workers, teachers, and black tradesmen—emerged across the country during this period, but created a particularly "strong alliance" in Detroit, the heart of labor movement and industrial production. While working in different areas and industries, Detroit Black Power unionists sought to create a means for black workers and communities to independently represent and pursue their own interests and agendas. In the process, they directly challenged the reformist, integrationist approach taken by civil rights leaders by joining together to gain control of the direction and leadership of black labor struggles and the freedom movement in Detroit.

Although nationalist and Black Power currents had a long and rich history in Detroit, the limits of liberalism, the rising disconnect between local civil rights leaders and inner-city residents, the 1967 rebellion, and the brutal state response to it all radicalized the black community and dramatically altered the tenor, direction, and leadership of the local freedom movement. Galvanized by this rising militancy, Black Power activists in Detroit attempted to supplant or bypass established liberal, civil rights and labor organizations as a means to establish community control during the postrebellion rebuilding process. By doing so, Black Power activists in Detroit took the struggle for economic and political self-determination to both the "house of labor" and to the land on which their communities rested.[5]

"Black Power," as Rhonda Y. Williams argues, "was a multifaceted, at times elusive, concept that eventually spurred new alliances as well as divisions and inflected the political context in which people lived and organized."[6] The Detroit community control of construction movement, although not as radical or as visible as DRUM or the LRBW, was an integral component of the distinctive brand of labor-based Black Power and the organizing tradition that it established in Detroit.[7] Unified by the urgency of the historical moment and weight of shared opposition, these and other organizations worked together, despite their differences, to create avenues for black self-determination and coordinated action outside the confines of white-controlled unions and liberal-labor politics. Although the process was often fraught with discrepancies regarding exactly what Black Power and community control entailed, Detroiters, by organizing institutionally and at the grassroots level, produced independent and radical alternatives to address building trades union discrimination and forced federal action and intervention on the issue before the movement died out in the early 1970s.[8]

Detroit's community control of construction movement ultimately fell victim not to its own excesses and contradictions—although these certainly existed—but to the inaccessibility to funding; coordinated intimidation campaigns by the building trades unions; the refusal of local and national authorities to enforce standing law; and collusion among the federal government, the Detroit Building Trades Council (DBTC), and the "old guard" civil rights unionists. These seemingly disparate groups worked together to remove Local 124 and the Ad Hoc Construction Coalition (AHCC)—a local construction coalition formed by Black Power activists, including members of Local 124 and the LRBW, from the very negotiations their activism and actions had inspired. The subsequent removal of these groups from the negotiation and implementation of the Detroit hometown plan allowed local civil rights leaders and members of the city liberal-labor coalition to thwart the challenge that Black Power and community control activists posed, but at a tremendous cost. By regaining control of the local freedom movement by willingly nullifying the more radical aspects of the movement's demands, the "long civil rights movement" effectively shortened the Black Power movement while simultaneously shaping the ascendancy of a liberal and symbolic form of Black Power that served to further institutionalize racism within the building trades, a legacy that continues to hamper black access to Detroit building trades unions to this day.[9]

Reconstructing Black Detroit

Prior to summer 1967, Detroit held a national reputation as a Model City and a glimmering example of the ability of liberalism and the Great Society to quell racial strife and solve the urban crisis. The economic boom that Detroit experienced during the mid-1960s, the support by the ruling liberal-labor coalition for civil rights and the implementation of Great Society programs, and black access to relatively good-paying industrial jobs had, in the eyes of many pundits, alleviated the rampant racial tensions and hatred that was boiling over on to the streets of other major cities during the 1960s. Detroit, many felt, was too progressive to riot.[10] When the largest urban uprising of the 1960s began in the early hours of July 23, 1967, Detroit city officials and civic leaders were left dumbstruck. Within a five-day period, 2,509 buildings were burned and looted, resulting in $50 million of property damage. To quell the uprising, municipal leaders, with help from state and federal officials, deployed "a combined force of nearly seventeen thousand law enforcement officers" to largely black inner-city neighborhoods—the epicenters of the rebellion. Calm was eventually restored, but only after thousands of arrests and forty-three deaths—thirty of which were attributed to law enforcement personnel.[11]

The rebellion revealed the discontent and anger long simmering beneath the surface. Black Detroiters, as Heather Thompson points out, were not only "lashing out at members of law enforcement, figures against whom they had obvious grievances, they were also raging against the strategies and politics of white administration liberals and the middle-class black leaders of the city's civil rights movement."[12] During and following the rebellion, the weakness of established civil rights leaders and their lack of a base within inner-city neighborhoods became clear. At the same time, grassroots support for militant leaders and programs committed to black self-determination rose in the aftermath of the uprising. For instance, during a citywide meeting held at the Detroit City-County building on August 9, 1967, "established Negro leaders" were jeered at and silenced by the crowd as "representatives from all the different groups and tendencies in the city" formed the Citywide Citizens Action Committee (CCAC) and selected Reverend Albert Cleage, a controversial and well-known black nationalist, to chair the organization. Upon accepting the post, Cleage remarked that a "New Black Establishment" had emerged, and from that point forward, "The Toms are out."[13]

CCAC formed to challenge the existing civil rights leadership as well as the recently formed New Detroit Committee (NDC), an agency of labor, civic, and business leaders created to oversee the pacification and rebuilding processes immediately following the rebellion. CCAC argued that the community should take control of, and redirect, the redevelopment efforts that often did little to improve black residents' lives but, instead, displaced them by gentrifying their neighborhoods. In one of its first actions, the group passed a resolution demanding that the NDC fund but cede control of all inner-city redevelopment programs. If the NDC refused, CCAC, Cleage warned, was "preparing for all kinds of conflict." When the city agency proceeded with its redevelopment plans despite the CCAC admonition, Cleage promised a fight, informing the press that "Black people are determined to control the black community and we are not going to let them forget this lesson."[14]

In response, CCAC leaders and other sympathetic community activists and intellectuals organized the Federation of Self-Determination (FSD), a multi-class "black united front," to fight for community control and economic self-determination. The FSD hoped to use Cleage's reputation as a militant and fears of further unrest as bargaining chips to secure NDC funding. More moderate civil rights and labor leaders, including FSD member Robert Tindal of the National Association for the Advancement of Colored People (NAACP) and the Trade Union Leadership Council (TULC), contested the subsequent request by the FSD for over $500,000 from the NDC. In response, these leaders formed a separate organization, the Detroit Council of Organizations (DCO), and sought funding on their own.[15] The NDC responded by offering both groups $100,000, but with a precondition that neither participate in political activities. The deal, in Cleage's estimation, constituted an attempt to buy off the black community "at 16 cents per black person in Detroit[,]...which with the best of intentions would be insufficient, but as offered, would set an example nationwide, mortgaging the freedom of black people and playing-havoc with their self-respect." Whereas the more moderate DCO took the money, the FSD, after identifying Mayor Jerome Cavanagh and Walter Reuther of the United Auto Workers (UAW) as the authors of this Faustian bargain, publicly severed its ties to the NDC on January 5, 1968.[16]

Unable to secure funding locally, Cleage; Karl Gregory, an economist; and Walter McMurtry and Donald Roberts, fellow FSD representatives, then turned to the Inter-religious Foundation of Community Organizations (IFCO) in New York, a charitable organization comprising representatives of Protestant denominations committed to the principles of minority self-determination. The FSD requested "10s of millions of dollars" from IFCO to form a black-owned bank to circulate urban renewal monies within the black community, to expand funding for a nonprofit small business association designed to create businesses and to create a development company that would rehabilitate housing and property, buy out slumlords, and develop housing cooperatives.[17] Although impressed with the FSD proposal, IFCO had limited money and simply could not afford to fully fund the project. FSD representatives, however, did secure a no-strings-attached $85,000 grant—a supportive gesture, but hardly the type of financial support needed for such a broad-based approach to urban reform, community control, and black economic development.[18]

As FSD efforts to control the rebuilding of inner-city Detroit languished, racial tensions mounted again. Although confrontations between blacks and police escalated in Detroit and across the nation, Detroit did not experience any of the 295 urban disorders that occurred in early 1968 and in the wake of the assassination of Martin Luther King Jr. Nonetheless, police repression did create an increased sense of unrest, urgency, and militancy within the Detroit Black Power movement. Many of the younger, and often more militant, segments of the Detroit Black Power movement, including a majority within the FSD, began seeking new, more effective, immediate, and independent means to fight against white control and aggression against black people and communities. On April 18, Black Power activists, disillusioned with Cleage—his frequent speeches to whites, his association with Edward Vaughn, and the ineffectiveness of the FSD approach—unanimously voted to disband the organization.[19]

Around the same time, federal money began pouring into Detroit to spur its reconstruction, much of it War on Poverty funds that required partnerships with community organizations. Consequently, Detroit politics was soon transformed by a wave of insurgent black radicals from various quarters who reorganized into new formations to control the postrebellion rebuilding process. For the most part, these radicals emerged from two different black community groups that had challenged the liberal–civil rights coalition in the early to mid-1960s: neighborhood and community control activists opposed to existing urban renewal schemes and labor radicals opposed to union racism. The convergence of these two groups reshaped and radicalized the community control of construction movement, a process that was expedited when white power in the building trades unions was put on full display a month after the FSD ceased to exist.

The Detroit Civil Rights Movement and the Building Trades

In fall 1967, the NDC Redevelopment Subcommittee and Task Force had estimated that an additional 5,000–7,000 skilled tradesmen were needed to complete the already scheduled Model Cities and urban renewal projects, let alone the rehabilitation of the 100,000 substandard dwelling units in Detroit. In May 1968, when a number of construction projects were slated to start, the building trade unions attempted to capitalize on the severe shortage of skilled labor by striking and demanding 30 percent annual wage increases. In an attempt to weaken union members' ability to supplement their incomes during the strike, contractors locked both union and nonunion workers out of work. As a result, during the more than two-month shutdown, black nonunion tradesmen were left without work. When work finally resumed, the union victories only increased the difference in the quality of work and pay available to white versus black workers.[20]

The economic gains secured by the largely white building trades during the 1968 strike rested on shared histories of exclusion. For nearly a century, the Detroit building trades unions had used apprenticeship programs as screening mechanisms to limit union membership and maintain an often nepotistic, lily-white job trust. After World War II, protest campaigns organized by the Detroit branch of the National Negro Congress and the Detroit Urban League helped increase black access to the construction trades for a few black workers. By the early 1960s, Detroit officials, touting the progressiveness of the city, claimed Detroit as a national leader in the integration of the construction trades. Blacks, however, accounted for only 11.6 percent of all construction workers in Detroit during the 1960s and were overwhelmingly concentrated in the "trowel trades" (bricklaying, cement finishing, plastering, etc.) and the Jim Crow laborers' union.[21]

The situation in Detroit was hardly distinctive. During summer 1963, civil rights groups in Newark, Cleveland, New York City, Philadelphia, and Brooklyn had waged direct action protests to oppose continued construction industry racism. The Detroit civil rights movement, however, pursued a slightly different approach. Led by Horace Sheffield, a TULC stalwart, Detroit civil rights and black labor activists instead placed their faith in the local liberal-labor coalition and the courts rather than in protest politics. The TULC, for example, filed a complaint with the Michigan Civil Rights Commission (MCRC) that charged the International Brotherhood of Electrical Workers (IBEW) Local 58 with running a discriminatory apprenticeship program in a publicly funded trade school. Realizing that the commission had the power to review but not remediate complaints, the TULC also filed a federal lawsuit. The court responded by issuing an injunction preventing Local 58 from continuing to conduct its all-white training program, thereby suspending its apprenticeship classes.[22]

The court injunction, however, did not resolve the underlying concern of the TULC—increasing black access to the building trades unions and jobs on construction projects. After spearheading the formation of an umbrella organization, Operation Negro Equality (ONE)—a coalition of thirty-two groups that included integrationist civil rights organizations such as the Detroit branches of the Congress of Racial Equality (CORE), the Student Nonviolent Coordinating Committee (SNCC), the NAACP, the Detroit Council of Human Rights (DCHR), and the Cotillion Club as well as more militant nationalist organizations such as UHURU and the Group on Advanced Leadership (GOAL)—the TULC and ONE threatened to picket job sites if employers and the unions failed to commit themselves to the immediate establishment of equal opportunity.[23] Fearing large-scale protests and negative publicity in the black press due to previous vigorous TULC support of his election, Mayor Jerome Cavanagh negotiated a settlement between the TULC and the DBTC that lifted the standing court injunction, mandated that six black trainees be placed in apprenticeship programs, and required local contractors and unions to "pledge" that they would eliminate discriminatory practices in the future. Little changed as a result of this voluntary approach. By 1966, blacks still constituted less than 2 percent of Detroit building trades apprentices.[24]

After two years of continued protest, in 1966 the TULC, in an effort to further increase the number of black apprentices and skilled tradesmen, became directly involved in the training process. As with the Urban League and Workers Defense Fund elsewhere, the TULC, in conjunction with the DBTC, was made a partner in a federally funded but locally administered, joint preapprenticeship program designed to recruit and train black youths for upcoming union-sponsored apprenticeship exams. Even though the number of black apprentices doubled between 1966 and 1968, black apprentices remained at less than 4 percent in a city rapidly approaching a black majority. Only a few blacks managed to pass the initial screening process, and even fewer survived the low-paying, three- to five-year apprenticeships required for journeymen status. In 1967 and 1968, to maintain the pretense of action rather than to actually attempt to desegregate the building trades, the federal Bureau of Apprenticeship Training (BAT) granted the TULC $178,000 to expand its preapprenticeship program despite its woeful results. Even Horace Sheffield, the man responsible for running the TULC program, recognized that it was "a sham." "It turns out to be a collusive kind of thing," Sheffield explained to Herbert Hill during a 1968 interview. "To have a program…that may get fifteen people in it for a year and a half—that's got to be a joke."[25]

Discrimination in apprenticeships programs contributed to this, but it was not the only factor. The types of skills covered and the varied pathways to securing journeyman status also shaped the racial demographics of membership. Excluding the trowel trades, in Detroit by late 1968 only 131 of 14,166 journeymen—or less than 1 percent—were black. And even though these select few had become card-carrying journeymen, they often faced difficulties finding steady or good job assignments from union hiring halls. Moreover, whereas black workers had to take the formal route to union membership, whites played by a different set of rules. Most white workers started "as laborers, and were upgraded to a skilled classification when their work was considered satisfactory"—an "informal" process that further served to lock black workers out of almost all of the building trades' unions.[26]

Black Power and Inner-City Construction

Despite his being recognized by the state of Michigan as a licensed plumber, Calvin Stubbs was one of many black tradesmen in Detroit never afforded the opportunity to partake in the informal journeyman process. Although he agreed with Sheffield's critique regarding the futility of the preapprenticeship program, Stubbs felt that the TULC, by helping maintain an ineffective program used by the building trades unions to show that they were making good faith efforts toward integration, was part of the problem. He further resented that the TULC, rather than black skilled tradesmen, was given control of a training program never intended to produce more than a token number of black apprentices and journeymen. "It should be evident," Stubbs told the *Michigan Chronicle*, "that every man trained at TULC, under the supervision of whoever it might be, and then turned down by the Building Trades Council has a definite problem." Rather than working inside a discriminatory labor movement, Stubbs, following the lead of DRUM (which had been formed a month prior) turned to independent labor organizing—or as the allies of the liberal-labor coalition in the black press referred to it, "outlaw unionism."[27]

During the 1968 building trades unions' strike, Stubbs, like other small black contractors and independent construction workers, had been locked out of work. At the same time, spiraling building trades union wages, which drove up the cost of construction, all but guaranteed that low-income residents would be priced out of most inner-city rehabilitation projects. The stoppages not only threatened black laborers' ability to secure wages and provide for themselves and their families; it also forestalled progress in addressing the conditions and control of their neighborhoods. Postrebellion urban renewal provided an opportunity for—or initiated hope in the possibility of—transforming substandard overcrowded conditions into rehabilitated neighborhoods that would ensure an affordable, better quality of life as well as community control of local institutions and development. To Detroit's Black Power and community control activists, racism within building trades unions, construction industry, and urban redevelopment increasingly were identified as key components behind black displacement and the maintenance of white power and internal colonization.

Frustrated with the unions' having ceased work at a critical time in the re-construction process and anxious to find avenues around building trades union leaders to steer urban reconstruction money, activists created new institutions meant to create Black Power in the construction industry. In June 1968 Karl Gregory, black economist and former FSD member, along with a small group of black intellectuals, business people, and white investors, formed a general con-tracting firm, Accord, Inc. Accord focused on purchasing run-down, absentee-owned apartment buildings in the inner city at a low price, rehabilitating them, organizing tenants into cooperatives, and gradually transferring ownership to the residents. Designed to finance rehabilitation projects and contract work to black building companies and subcontractors, Accord intended to accrue and reinvest mortgage monies in new projects to keep black workers working, black builders building, and Accord profitable. Although its black capitalist form of nation-building had detractors among more radical segments of the Detroit Black Power movement, Accord represented for many an opportunity to bypass the discriminatory white building trades unions and their exclusionary hiring halls by serving as a conduit for federally funded jobs governed by Model Cities and Federal Housing Act of 1968.[28]

Local 124 formed less than a week after the founding of Accord. Calvin Stubbs had quietly obtained a charter from the Allied Workers International Union of Hammond, Indiana, during the building trades union strike.[29] Local 124 was or-ganized to supply contractors such as Gregory with "local workers" and to supply inner-city residents with on-the-job training. Accord, as the financer of rehabili-tation projects, would hire the Urban Design and Development Group (UDDG), led by community control activist, tenants rights organizer, and architect Hank Rogers, to design projects and would then contract with Exquisite Construction, a black-owned building company. Exquisite would then "subcontract the labor to Local 124." According to DRUM organizer General Baker, who later became involved in these efforts and had working relationships with those involved, these organizations were formed independently, but were designed as a means to gain control of "everything from the top down."[30]

With roughly 4,000 different rehabilitation projects already in the pipeline, however, Local 124 did not wait for official union approval, black builders, or nonprofit housing corporations to receive contracts to start working. In August, a white contractor, seeking to use a black workforce on a fifty-two-unit renova-tion project in the heart of the near west side of Detroit, hired Stubbs and nine other Local 124 contractors to work side by side with members of AFL-CIO-affiliated unions. Ignoring its long history of racial exclusion, the DBTC attacked Local 124 for being antilabor and for practicing "dual unionism." The black men soon ran into resistance from a white AFL-CIO business agent on the job site who, according to Stubbs, "approached us and told us to get off the job because we were not union men." When they refused, the business agent insisted they get temporary permits to be allowed to continue to work and pay dues without the benefits of membership. The members of Local 124 refused. As Stubbs later explained, "We didn't accept tokenism, we didn't join the AFL, but we did finish the job." While continuing work on the project, Local 124 was registered with the U.S. Department of Labor, but pressure from the DBTC and its member unions took its toll. As the project neared completion, the general contractor informed Mildred Rollocks, the Local 124 attorney, that he would not hire Local 124 members again due to threats from the unions.[31]

The pressure intensified when Local 124 began work on the Hamilton Park Cooperative Apartments in November, sparking what NAACP Labor Secretary Herbert Hill, a long-time critic of building trades union racism, referred to at the time as "a confrontation of national significance." The $1.2 million federal rehabilitation project was located on Seward Street in the "heart of the riot area." The Goldfarb Building Co., the prime contractor on the ninety-two-unit job, hired fifty workers from Local 124 as well as workers from AFL-CIO Local 334, a predominantly black, unskilled laborers' union, to rehabilitate the property. After five conflict-free days, Local 334 requested that Goldfarb provide "a list of all subcontractors and their workers" and provoked a jurisdictional dispute by claiming that Goldfarb, as well as all other builders with agreements with DBTC, must hire AFL-CIO-affiliated workers exclusively. Local 124, on the other hand, argued that the federal mandates requiring resident labor superseded the exclusivity clause contained in the laborers' contract. If the clause was upheld, Rollocks explained, "then the Laborers would refuse to work with our black tradesmen, and that would kill" Local 124.[32]

Seeking to negate the DBTC attempt to drive them out, Local 124 staged a "one-day walkout aimed at focusing public attention on their situation." Local 334 responded by threatening to halt construction altogether following the walkout. Representative Charles Diggs (D-Mich.), an African American, then intervened in the "highly explosive" situation, chiding the DBTC for its discriminatory practices and for disrupting the much-needed rebuilding process. In the meantime, Tom Turner, "the newly elected Negro head of the Wayne County AFL-CIO," met with Stubbs and representatives of the Federal Housing Administration (FHA), offering to fold Local 124 into Local 334 laborers' union. Local 124 leaders quickly refused, reminding Turner and the DBTC that Local 124 was explicitly formed because black tradesmen "had become weary of trying to fight discriminating trade unions from within the AFL structure" and that Local 124 was a multi-trades, not a laborers', union. After Local 124 rejected Turner's overture, Local 334 began picketing on November 22, 1968, "to affect a boycott by members of other AFL-CIO skilled employees on the project until the independent union workers" were forced off the job. Local 124 walked off the site "in sympathy" with the black workers in Local 334, who they felt were "being used as a front for white tradesmen" and the DBTC, but promised to return to work the next day "by any means necessary." Fearing further delays and possible bloodshed, Representative John Conyers (D-Mich.) arranged a tenuous truce in which Local 334 agreed to return to work while he attempted to negotiate a settlement among the laborers' union, Local 124, and representatives from the Department of Labor. This brought the workers together at the workplace while their representative unions fought one another at the federal level. Local 334 filed charges against Goldfarb with the National Labor Relations Board (NLRB), and Local 124 continued to hire and train black workers while awaiting a resolution of the matter.[33]

Local 124 received firm support from black leaders across the political spectrum and claimed the truce as a victory that "set a precedent which may be followed by black trade unions all over the country." The issue, however, was hardly resolved. As work continued, the DBTC began pursuing a different tactic to break Local 124. The TULC, on behalf of the DBTC, approached the skilled members of Local 124 to offer them immediate inclusion in their respective trade unions. But "they were standoffish against going in," recalled Robert "Buddy" Battle of the TULC. "Their explanation was that they could make more money working on the street" than "going into the union and being saddled to just a job here and a job there." Rebuked, Battle went on the offensive, critiquing the independent unionism of Local 124 and its separatist approach in the black press, remarking that he "could not support 'the idea of an all black union.'"[34]

Battle's statements regarding Local 124 angered Mike Hamlin of DRUM, who along with General Baker had previously been criticized and physically threatened by TULC leaders for "working outside the system" and opposing the liberal-labor coalition and civil rights movement. DRUM was "not merely a labor organization, but an organization established 'for the liberation of black people' which [happened] to be working on the labor front." But there was, as Hamlin pointed out, "a strong alliance between DRUM and Local 124 and other dissident black labor organizations."[35]

This alliance grew organically from the shared local Black Power movement assault on business unionism and liberalism and on the mutual enemies that this struggle engendered, but it was also a working relationship. Although several of the DRUM leaders held reservations about the Local 124 community control agenda and its ultimate objectives, they also perceived the union as being part of a black worker–oriented "survival program" that could help improve living conditions, empower inner-city residents, and provide work for those who had lost their jobs fighting the auto companies and unions in the plants. Glanton

Dowdell, who worked with Local 124 and DRUM, served as the primary conduit between the two groups—a relationship that produced tangible benefits as both groups confronted management and the unions in their respective industries. A number of the twenty-six Eldon Gear and Axle Revolutionary Union Movement (ELRUM) members who participated in a wildcat strike at Chrysler Eldon Avenue Gear and Axel in late January 1969, found work through Local 124 as the UAW slowly processed their grievances. DRUM and ELRUM workers and activists, in turn, helped strengthen Local 124 by serving as workers and "business agents." General Baker, Chuck Wooten, Glanton Dowdell, and members of what Karl Gregory and others referred to as "Glanton's army" later protected Local 124 members from hostile union members. Their presence was later crucial in helping stave off pickets, construction shutdowns, and union sabotage.[36]

The confrontation over black control of inner-city construction and independent unionism came to a head during the rehabilitation of Selden Court Apartments, a forty-unit, four-story building on Magnolia Street. When construction began in March 1969, the truce between DBTC and Local 124 remained intact. Accord, hired by Reverend Nicolas Hood's nonprofit housing corporation, Modern American Living (MAL), was the prime contractor on the project. Exquisite Construction oversaw construction, and two of the six subcontractors that Exquisite had hired employed a total of fifteen workers form Local 124. Work on the apartments proceeded uninterrupted until April, when Jack Wood, the head of the DBTC and an NDC board member, learned about the Selden Court project when Reverend Hood requested more funding from the NDC Housing Subcommittee to support other MAL-sponsored low-income rehabilitation projects. "The very next day, [Wood] was on the phone screaming" about the use of NDC funds to employ non-AFL-affiliated labor. The event strained the already uneasy relationship between the DBTC and the community control of the construction movement, and portended a showdown.[37]

On May 12, the DBTC broke the truce, staging pickets in hopes of shutting down construction at Selden Court Apartments and breaking the backs of both Local 124 and the relatively undercapitalized black-run building companies, Accord and Exquisite. The initial picketers were predominantly white and included carpenters, painters, electricians, teamsters, laborers, and other members of the DBTC. Within several days, black workers from AFL-CIO-affiliated painters' and laborers' unions, paid $35 per day, replaced the white picketers. James Jackson of Exquisite, the project coordinator, reported that the picketers had prevented carpenters and plumbers from reporting to work and that the "delivery of supplies" had been restricted. After several delays, Local 124 plumbers managed to install new plumbing stacks in the structure, but these did not last long. "We came in one day," Karl Gregory recalled, "and someone had poured cement in the stacks."

"We never operated with a lot of cash," Gregory explained, and "that incident with the stacks really hurt us."[38]

Each delay had also placed James Jackson and Exquisite Construction under fiscal strains. During the picketing and shutdowns, Jackson joined with Local 124 to charge the DBTC with unfair labor practices and to ask the NLRB to conduct an expedited certification election. Wood and DBTC, however, vowed to ignore "any NLRB order," promising to fight until they were "down to the last dime of its 87 million dollar war chest." While Accord, Exquisite, and Local 124 waited for the NLRB to act, Local 124 business agents came to job sites daily to protect workers and to ensure that work continued. The daily atmosphere at the job site, as the *Detroit Free Press* reported, was tense. "Pistols have been seen, rocks thrown, epithets hurled and trucks turned away." "We had a couple of real battles there," General Baker recalled. "We had to carry arms to go to work because they weren't going to back up." Police were called to the scene twice, but no one was hurt and "an uneasy calm" prevailed. In the evenings, Glanton Dowdell and others slept in the buildings to prevent further sabotage.[39]

The tenseness of the situation was exacerbated further on June 4, 1969, when Robert Brown, Richard Nixon's special assistant, arrived in Detroit to discuss a pending funding proposal filed by Calvin Stubbs that sought to establish a $21 million, BAT-funded, independent apprenticeship training program.[40] Stubbs's proposal sought to enlarge the number of black apprentices in Detroit by lowering educational requirements and offering higher pay and benefits during the apprenticeship terms. It differed from the TULC preapprenticeship program in that it was neither preparatory nor affiliated with DBTC unions. Although Brown refused to "elaborate on the union problem," he intimated that there was "plenty of money available" for the program if it was approved by the Secretary of Labor. When asked by the press if the proposal and training program effectively signaled an impending "war with the AFL-CIO," Stubbs pointed out that the war had long been underway.[41]

The DBTC suffered another setback when all nineteen workers at the Magnolia site voted to remain in Local 124 during an NLRB union certification election held June 10, 1969. True to its word, the DBTC and its affiliates continued picketing throughout the summer until the courts compelled them to stop. On August 8, 1969, federal Judge Theodore Levin found that the primary reason for the DBTC picketing had been "to destroy Local 124" and ordered the AFL-CIO construction unions to "immediately stop." On September 17, 1969, the NLRB found Local 334 and the Carpenters District Council of Detroit guilty of unfair labor practices and awarded James Jackson and Exquisite Construction compensatory damages, seemingly clearing the way for Local 124 and Exquisite to proceed on other projects without further union interference.[42]

Although the NLRB victories and the Local 124 meeting with Robert Brown suggested that the independent union was making substantive progress, the protracted battles in the courts and on the job had taken a toll on community efforts to control local construction projects—as the DBTC had intended. Shortly after the plumbing stacks at Magnolia were filled with concrete, Accord, lacking the working capital to continue, left the project and soon after ceased to exist. Fearing costly conflicts with the building trades unions and potential reprisals, other inner-city contractors began falling in line, forming "joint ventures with established builders who have long-standing relationships" with the DBTC. The few small black development companies and nonprofit organizations still willing to do business with Exquisite and Local 124 lacked the capital needed to acquire bonding for large-scale projects. As a result, DBTC member unions continued to monopolize inner-city construction work, whereas Local 124 confronted increased federal scrutiny. In July 1969, the Department of Labor tabled the Local 124 apprenticeship proposal when Calvin Stubbs came under investigation by a federal grand jury for improperly dispersing of a $20,000 loan that the union had received from a wealthy suburban businessman earlier in the year—a charge Stubbs maintained that the DBTC had "prompted" in "attempt to smear him."[43]

The Ad Hoc Construction Coalition and Urban Reparations

By summer 1969, efforts to secure community control of postrebellion construction in Detroit were at a standstill. Union aggression and pressure on black contractors frustrated efforts to control inner-city rebuilding "from the top down" in the Motor City, but events elsewhere inspired new tactical approaches and opportunities locally and nationally. Direct action protests at federally funded construction sites during the summer and early fall of 1969, and the subsequently announced intention by the Department of Labor to extend the Philadelphia Plan to other cities—including Detroit—provided local activists with a new avenue to revive the movement for community control of the rebuilding process. In response to the growing national attention being given to construction industry discrimination, the Detroit NAACP called a meeting in September 1969 to build an organizational base in Detroit to negotiate for strong federally imposed guidelines and time tables to address racial discrimination in the Detroit building trades.[44]

Community control and Black Power activists, however, had serious reservations about the local branch of the NAACP and feared that its leaders might hijack their movement. The national NAACP, particularly Labor Secretary Herbert Hill, had consistently encouraged aggressive action and independent organizing among both black contractors and tradesmen, but the local Detroit NAACP branch was led by Tom Turner, the president of the metropolitan Detroit AFL-CIO Council, who was derisively referred to by many in the Detroit Black Power movement as "Uncle Tom" Turner. Perhaps due to his lack of support within the construction coalition movement, Turner sent Detroit NAACP Secretary William Penn to represent the organization at the meeting, and Penn was quickly outmaneuvered. Stacking the meeting with allies, Detroit Black Power activists called for the creation of the Ad Hoc Construction Coalition (AHCC) to represent the black community at the negotiating table. Henry "Hank" Rogers, an architect, UDDG board member, and long-time tenants' rights and community control activist, was elected to chair the organization.[45] The AHCC consisted of representatives from roughly fifty different civil rights, Black Power, and community-based organizations, including local chapters of the NAACP and Urban League; the West Central Organization (WCO); the W. E. B. Du Bois Institute of Black Studies at Wayne State; the League of Revolutionary Black Workers; the Detroit branch of the Black Panther Party; black contractors, designers, and planners; and Local 124. The TULC, however, left the coalition once it realized that it could not control it.[46]

The AHCC adapted tactics used elsewhere to fashion a strategy that directly tied the implementation of affirmative action to community control of labor, contracting, and the resources behind inner-city construction. The group went public in early October 1969 by presenting a series of unprecedented and audacious demands that half of all reconstruction monies go to black workers, businesses, and financial institutions. Its demands echoed James Foreman's call for reparations from religious institutions made during his reading of the "Black Manifesto" in Detroit in May. The demands addressed the vast institutional and financial inequities that stood in the way of community control of construction efforts and attempted to set the bar as high as possible in the impending negotiations. The AHCC presented the demands to the city of Detroit, the Department of Housing and Urban Development (HUD) FHA Detroit Insuring Office, the DBTC, Wayne State University, BAT, the Detroit Housing Commission, the Board of Education, the Associated General Contractors (AGC), and the Department of Labor.[47]

The AHCC demand for half of all funding included not just contracts and subcontracts. It required that half of AGC profits, union fees from pension funds to dues, and Department of Labor funds be placed in "black financial institutions." It also demanded that BAT fund and certify the Allied Trades Apprenticeship (ATA) program and "immediately decertify all construction trades apprenticeship programs in Detroit which are not 50% black," including the TULC preapprenticeship program. To be thorough, AHCC also demanded that Wayne State University stop all construction until 50 percent of the workforce and professionals associated with construction were black and that half of all funds earmarked for construction be deposited in black-owned financial institutions.

Similar stipulations were given to other local institutions, with the city of Detroit given the added task of guaranteeing a "$20,000,000 bond for the purpose of establishing a Black bonding company which would be Detroit-based."[48]

The AHCC demands, alongside the threat of violent confrontations and construction shutdowns, caused significant concern. Although largely rhetorical strategies—a means to ensure immediate and comprehensive good faith negotiations—such threats greatly concerned business leaders as well as local and federal officials. The DBTC, however, all but ignored the AHCC. Its leaders, for example, refused to attend an October 8, 1969, meeting at Representative John Conyers's office to discuss the AHCC demands and develop parameters for the negotiations. In the weeks that followed, coalition members in hard hats confronted white tradesmen across the city, trading racial invectives and threats. Tempers flared. The building trades unions "vowed to fight any close-down attempt" in the city, but now expressed a willingness to negotiate with anyone other than the AHCC.[49] The confrontations and the recalcitrance of the DBTC, however, provided the AHCC with exactly what it needed to negotiate from a position of strength—a level of tension that portended violence.

Within a week, HUD officials in Washington cobbled together a proposal for a ten-year plan. But the AHCC refused subsequent HUD offer of $16 million, which AHCC President Hank Rogers referred to as a paltry attempt to "appease the restless natives with trinkets, gadgets and a program."[50] A few days later, on October 17, 1969, AHCC representatives attended a summit in Pittsburgh, Pennsylvania, to discuss how "to make their attack on job discrimination in the construction industry more meaningful and effective" at the national level. The meeting, called by the Pittsburgh Black Construction Coalition, brought together black representatives from relatively isolated construction coalitions in Boston, San Francisco, New York, Newark, Chicago, Buffalo, Detroit, and Pittsburgh to exchange ideas, share strategies, and plot a future course. Aimed toward establishing a communications network between coalitions as federal negotiations commenced, the meeting also sought to provide a foundation for the creation of a larger black workers' movement. "What you see before you," Byrd Brown, Pittsburgh representative and an attorney, proclaimed to the *Pittsburgh Courier,* "is the first black convention of what is to become one of the greatest forces in this country...Organized black labor."[51]

The conference was held a month after the nationwide escalation of Black Monday protests and construction shutdowns in Chicago, Philadelphia, Pittsburgh, and Seattle. The initial purpose of the meeting was to unify the disparate local movements to form a Black United Front that could coordinate strategy and ensure that "individual actions" taken in one particular city during negotiations "would not inadvertently be detrimental to each others future gains."

Although leaders from the nationally known, battle-tested, Pittsburgh and Chicago construction coalitions were in attendance—including Michael Dismond of the Black Construction Coalition (BCC) and C. T. Vivian of the Coalition for United Community Action (CUCA)—the representatives of the Detroit AHCC, according to several press reports, set both the tone and agenda of the conference by introducing the groups gathered in Pittsburgh to the distinctive brand of Black Power politics and unionism in the Motor City.[52]

The Detroit representatives, Henry Hagood, a building contractor, and Ozell Bonds Jr., a Wayne State University instructor, insisted that coalitions "move beyond making jobs their primary goal" and, instead, seek solutions geared toward the "black community's total economic development." Bonds urged the coalitions to demand both jobs and "a fair share of construction contracts in the black community" and warned them to be leery of "good faith" promises or "solutions" that placed the fate of black workers and the black community in the hands of the very institutions responsible for the intractable nature of racial discrimination in inner-city construction—particularly the building trades unions and the Department of Labor.[53]

In a thinly veiled criticism of negotiations already underway in Chicago and Pittsburgh, where coalition leaders had begun capitulating during negotiations, Bonds chastised those willing to barter movement demands for piecemeal or personal gains, remarking, "If we ever want to stop being niggers…we have to stop making niggardly demands and settling for niggardly responses to our demands." Instead, he proposed that coalitions seize "control of their own labor supply" by "setting up their own apprenticeship training programs and…unions" rather than relying on compromise settlements and payoffs that were designed to fail. Bonds, according to the *Pittsburgh Courier*, was "met with continuous applause" when he revealed that Detroiters had already formed their own black-led union, United Construction Trades, Local 124. Although a proposal to pursue the formation of a national black construction union was approved, local coalitions soon found themselves embroiled in local negotiations, and nothing came of the idea.[54]

The Detroit Plan and "The Short Black Power Movement"

The national construction summit meeting marked the high point of AHCC influence both locally and nationally. The Department of Labor, capitulating to the building trades unions and following the precedent set during negotiations in Chicago, abandoned the federally imposed guidelines of the Philadelphia Plan and pushed for voluntary hometown plan settlements. Despite Bonds's admonitions in Pittsburgh, the abrasive tactics and audacious demands of the AHCC—although effective in attracting the attention of HUD—made the DBTC refusal to negotiate with the coalition during hometown plan defensible in the eyes of federal negotiators. In turn, HUD officials enabled the DBTC to subvert the bargaining process by bypassing the AHCC. At Jack Wood's prompting—and with the support of the DBTC, HUD, and several NDC members—Horace Sheffield of the TULC was named chairman of the Detroit Plan Board of Directors, the body responsible for negotiating the Detroit hometown plan.[55]

The willing betrayal by Sheffield and the TULC of the black construction coalition was a calculated move by the DBTC and the TULC to render the AHCC, Local 124, and other black nationalist challengers politically ineffective while also protecting the TULC preapprenticeship program. Although the AHCC call for "immediate decertification" of the TULC program was unlikely given the prior reluctance of BAT to enforce its own regulations, progress had been made on the proposed Local 124 training program. This turn of events posed a threat to TULC and DBTC control of the apprenticeship training and hiring apparatus in the construction industry. In 1970, Calvin Stubbs unsuccessfully applied for a Jobs '70 contract to help fund the Local 124 training programs (the Allied Trades Apprenticeship program), an application that met firm resistance from the head of the Detroit Bricklayers, Masons, and Plasterers Union, who wrote the Department of Labor in opposition to the proposal. Stubbs met with greater success later in the year when he applied for a $1,414,087 contract with the Model Cities–funded Model Neighborhood Program to develop a program to train plumbers, electricians, carpenters, painters and plasterers, and heavy equipment operators. The NDC, which had encouraged Stubbs to apply, agreed to consider supplementary funding if he received significant external support. In November, the Detroit Model Neighborhood Agency approved the grant, but awaited final approval from HUD, which was scheduled to occur some time in early 1971.[56]

Although the NDC (by then called New Detroit Incorporated, NDI) had steered Stubbs in the right direction, the relationship of the organization to Local 124 and its apprenticeship program was complicated. Stubbs had received $10,000 from the NDC in early 1970 when the union was struggling to find work and its training program remained but a dream. More substantive funding, however, had been denied. In an undated confidential internal memo, NDC members explained the economic reasons behind both the NDC interest in and its tepid support for Local 124:

> The continued spiral of wages and costs in the construction industry has removed residential building costs to the upward margin of attainable

goals for an increasing segment of the working population. An infusion of new workers into the field should at least alleviate some of the created shortages and may slow to a more acceptable rate the wage-cost sweepstakes....Although the particular basket of Local 124 may seem attractive to some at the moment, there is not a requirement that all the eggs be placed there.[57]

This was especially true in 1970. New contracts with the building trades unions had been reached during the summer after President Richard Nixon had cut federal construction projects by 75 percent, thereby increasing the availability of surplus labor.[58]

As Stubbs and James Jackson awaited word from the Detroit Model Neighborhood Program, members of the NDC privately discussed the future viability of both Local 124 and its ATA program. At an October 22, 1970, meeting, John Armstrong, a NDC board member and builder with firm ties to Jack Wood and the DBTC, met with the NDC President William Patrick and others to voice his opinions regarding the impending Detroit Plan, the Local 124 ATA program, and the NDC position on these issues. Armstrong, "in direct contradiction to comments normally made by the advocates for the Building Trades Council," acknowledged the competency and workmanship of Local 124 members, but firmly warned the NDC against taking actions that might hinder the DBTC plan for the Detroit Plan:[59] "A very strong point was made of the possibility that Jack Wood will withdraw all support not only from New Detroit—which he has threatened—but from the United Foundation should New Detroit provide any further funds to the 124-Allied Trades effort. Mr. Armstrong did not take this possibility lightly and raised the question of whether or not NDI or the United Foundation could or should take this risk."[60] Armstrong instead encouraged the NDC to support the TULC program, which in his estimation "could become an even more relevant [sic] operation" if "combined with the implementation of the Detroit Plan."[61]

This was because the Detroit Plan, crafted by Sheffield and Jack Wood, contained a specific clause precluding builders and workers "from dealing in any way with the Allied Apprenticeship Training School." More specifically, those who received "apprenticeship training and *pre-vocational* training through this facility would be ineligible for entrance into an AFL affiliate," and "any signator who hires these trainees would be in violation of the agreement and subject to some difficulty in obtaining other trainees from AFL-CIO unions." Manatee Smith from Model Cities had been added as a "coalition" signator, for example, a move "undoubtedly" made to attempt to block the ATA program from receiving Model Neighborhoods funds in the near future.[62]

While much time and care had been taken to ensure that the AHCC, Local 124, and ATA program were removed from the Detroit Plan negotiations as well as the plan "solution," Jack Wood and the DBTC member unions—with tacit support from HUD and Horace Sheffield—had also made sure that negotiations would stall and that the Detroit hometown plan would be weak, ineffectual, and unenforceable. In 1971, the year that the hometown plan became active, black Detroiters were on the verge of becoming a majority. The Detroit Plan, however, required only that the white-dominated unions "make a good faith effort" to raise the percentage of black and minority workers in each craft to 15–20 percent within a five-year period, and only "if economic conditions permit." William Gould, Wayne State professor of law, in sworn testimony before the MCRC in 1971, called the Detroit Plan "woefully deficient" because it did "not provide any binding obligation on anyone to do anything" and was inconsistent "with either the goals of equal employment opportunity or the requirements of federal and state law as well as the Constitution." MCRC Commissioner Milton Robinson concurred and flatly rejected a proviso that held that the plan as such satisfied all affirmative action requirements and therefore exempted contractors and unions from federal, state, and local antidiscrimination laws. Horace Sheffield, nonetheless, responded to his numerous critics by remarking, "We don't want to put" the Detroit Plan "into effect in spite of them, but we will if we have to."[63] And, with the backing of HUD, the DBTC, and Department of Labor, they did.

The machinations behind the Detroit Plan and its ultimate passage effectively thwarted the very movement that had given rise to the negotiations and took the community out of the coalition. Efforts to mobilize against the plan were further stunted in March 1971 by the untimely death (from a stroke) of Hank Rogers, the AHCC chairman. Rogers, a tireless advocate for community control of construction for over half a decade, died at the age of thirty-seven—just before the MCRC began challenging the validity of the plan. Rogers, in many respects, was the glue that held the organization together. Following his death, the AHCC quickly diminished in size and strength.[64]

Local 124 and Exquisite Construction, meanwhile, suffered financially while awaiting federal funding, with builders' being pressured to not use their services. The Department of Labor did certify the ATA program a year after the Detroit Plan had been finalized, but it quickly decertified the program the following year after President Nixon appointed Peter Brennan, New York building trades official and white hard hat leader, as Secretary of Labor. According to the Federal Bureau of Investigation (FBI), which had begun investigating Local 124 in April 1969 after the Department of Labor received a speculative embezzlement complaint just before DBTC member unions began picketing the Magnolia site, the decertification of the ATA program hinged on three related factors: (1) not enough of the "right kind of training," (2) pressure from the AFL-CIO, and (3) that "financial assistance from the Department of Labor did not materialize." Working members of Local 124, realizing that the union could not provide further training, upgrading, or job placement, began defecting in large numbers in hopes of securing union access via the Detroit Plan.[65]

While they were shut out of work, suffering attrition, and awaiting word on the pending funding proposals, Jackson, Stubbs, and several Local 124 board members turned to violence, intimidation, and extortion, acts for which they later served substantial prison sentences. Once a part of a larger "black united front" for community control and independent unionism, the Local 124 leaders began lashing out at those who had cowed to the building trades unions.[66] Furthermore, without a larger movement around them to ensure a commitment to larger principles, they began exploiting the nonprofit housing organizations attempting to build housing for low-income residents. Thus, whereas the threat of violence had previously created opportunities for Black Power and community control activists, actualized intra-racial violence now symbolized (but did not cause) the fall of the movement.

Stubbs, Jackson, and other Local 124 representatives went to prison for their transgressions during the 1970s, but the Detroit building trades unions and the DBTC—thanks in part to the TULC—escaped being held accountable for their numerous legal violations and retained control of the discriminatory government-certified and -funded apprenticeship programs. Not surprisingly, black inclusion in the building trades unions dragged at a snail's pace and everyone but the building trades unions panned the Detroit Plan as a failure.[67]

The fall of the Detroit community control of construction movement and the implementation of the Detroit Plan had particularly dire consequences. Black Power activists within the local freedom movement, after several years of intense repression, began shifting away from grassroots community control efforts, independent labor organizing, and economic self-determination to focus on securing black control of municipal power during the early 1970s. Although this shift helped facilitate the election of Coleman Young in 1973, the Detroit hometown plan had made sure that, even though a black man might run the "New Detroit" or "Next Detroit," black people would neither own nor build much of it. Detroit has since been led by a succession of black, pro-affirmative action mayors, yet the Detroit area continues to have one of the least racially representative construction workforces in the nation.[68]

"THE STONE WALL BEHIND"

The Chicago Coalition for United Community Action and Labor's Overseers, 1968–1973

Erik S. Gellman

Surveying Chicago in 1969, the Reverend Cordy Tindell (C. T.) Vivian declared, "A Revolution is in progress here." Vivian, a leader of the Southern Christian Leadership Conference (SCLC), had helped organize freedom marches from Nashville to Selma during the early 1960s: Reflecting on these events, he wrote that Dr. Martin Luther King Jr. had "removed the Black freedom struggle from the economic realm and placed it in a moral and spiritual context." Yet, he lamented, "America was unable to respond to love; and we were unable to succeed with loving appeal." Although this earlier movement had been vital to securing certain African American freedoms, Vivian concluded, "When we won a battle against segregation, it was like tearing down paper to expose the stone wall behind....In order to effect change," the Reverend contended, "we would have to create coalitions as massive as the institutions we opposed."[1]

Vivian's reflections came from his experience with just such an institution—the Coalition for United Community Action (CUCA). Formed in 1968 to attack those who built that concrete wall, the CUCA federation of sixty-one African American organizations sought to desegregate the Chicago construction industry by training and placing thousands of young black men in trades jobs. Chicago's African American neighborhoods, like those around the country, struggled with high structural unemployment that excluded most of their residents from the

I acknowledge the help of Charles Branham, Darlene Clark Hine, Nancy MacLean, Martha Biondi, Michael Sherry, Kerry Taylor, and Fernando Carbajal; I especially thank C. T. Vivian, Bob Taylor, Sally Johnson, and Paul King for their invaluable reflections on this chapter.

post–World War II U.S. boom. One economic study found that in Chicago, "Negro men stood just as far behind white men on the occupational ladder in 1960 as they did in 1910."[2] Automation, deindustrialization, and the flight of companies to the suburbs made African American job prospects scarce by the late 1960s. Between 1957 and 1966, Chicago lost 48,000 jobs while the suburbs gained 276,000. The group most affected was young black males, whose unemployment rate during summer 1969 was a staggering 31 percent, three times the national average.[3]

The history of CUCA remains unknown because Chicago has largely come to symbolize how whites in the urban North stymied civil rights activists when they tried to apply nonviolent activism above the Mason-Dixon line. The traditional narrative of civil rights in Chicago focuses on African American activists who organized boycotts against racial inequalities in the public schools and who then joined SCLC and Dr. King in a 1966 campaign to renew and integrate housing in the city. Although this Chicago freedom movement drew national attention to the virulent racism of whites in the Chicago southwest neighborhoods, a summit with Mayor Richard Daley ended with few concessions. Most historical accounts follow this trajectory, ending their studies when King retreated from Chicago.[4]

This elision of the history of the Black Power movement has reinforced the conclusion that social disorganization dominated Chicago's African American communities after 1967. In this telling of Chicago's African American history, the optimism of "We Shall Overcome" becomes the hopelessness of "Burn Baby Burn." Studies of the black "underclass," the poorest African Americans that civil rights and the new black middle class in the suburbs left behind, have thus explored how gangs, guns, and drugs replaced education and activism among young blacks in Chicago.[5] Black neighborhoods *did* deteriorate and dire poverty *did* breed new social problems; nevertheless, these studies of the underclass in Chicago imply a dangerous teleology. The formidable challenge to deep-seated institutional racism by CUCA required new ideas and tactics outside of the conventional framework of civil rights liberalism. Largely ignoring this activity as something other than civil rights, scholars of urban history often implicitly blame the victims for a pathological culture or conclude that Black Power signified an incoherent strategy of rage.[6]

The CUCA effort to unify black communities in Chicago to fight for jobs provided a cogent response to the urban crisis. CUCA activism exposed the racial discrimination of unions and contractors, but also, and just as important, made transparent the Chicago Democratic political machine that profited from a "plantation politics" formula of racial segregation that bred poverty. The effective challenge of CUCA to this iniquitous formula came from its unification of community groups, churches, and civil rights groups. "In the summer of 1969," one federal official remarked, "the black community in Chicago was better orga-nized than anywhere in the country."[7] John Sengstacke, *Chicago Defender* editor, agreed. There is "more compact unity behind [CUCA] on this issue," he opined, "than there was behind Martin Luther King in the struggle for integrated hous-ing in Chicago."[8]

The legion of organizations in CUCA made jobs into a salient issue, but it was its gang participation that drove its activism. The street gangs, one CUCA leader concluded, put the "troops in the field."[9] But most examinations of gangs in the United States are ill-equipped to explain this kind of political activity. Until recently, studies of gangs have relied on an anachronistic methodology of the University of Chicago School that sees gangs as monolithic outgrowths of poorly organized immigrant communities.[10] This framework ignores any possi-bility that there are contradictory tendencies within gangs, which merit the same treatment as other organizations rather than perceiving them solely through the lens of social deviance.[11] The history of CUCA thus provides an opportunity to describe how African American gangs in Chicago sought to transform themselves into agents of economic renewal for poor black neighborhoods—and how the Chicago police, with the support of its machine politicians and judges, sought to thwart this conversion. This retelling of Chicago history makes its deindus-trialization and the creation of an underclass a contested rather than inevitable process, informed by conscious political decisions among competing economic and government actors.

Black Chicagoans had long protested job discrimination, with some of their most long-standing grievances directed toward the unions that controlled ac-cess to the skilled construction jobs in the city. Demands for black worker access to construction trades work began as early as the 1910s, peaked during the 1930s–1940s labor-based civil rights movement, and declined by the 1950s into municipal-sponsored "race relations" organizations that had little power to place sanctions on employers.[12] The symbol of white supremacy in the trades was the racially exclusionary Washburne Trade School, the only apprentice training pro-gram in the city certified by the American Federation of Labor (AFL) unions.[13] Graduation from Washburne allowed job applicants to skip the complicated jour-neyman application process (and impossible tests given to minority applicants) because the craft unions granted them automatic membership.[14] Despite waves of protests, the formation of separate unions, lawsuits, petitions, and edicts from government fair employment committees, by the late 1950s Washburne and the construction industry remained lily-white.

Sparked by the escalation of the southern civil rights movement, black labor activists in Chicago renewed their own struggle for jobs. At the May 1960 found-ing conference of the Negro American Labor Council (NALC), over one hundred

Chicagoans gathered alongside nine hundred other delegates in Detroit to tell "disgusting tales of hypocrisy in high union circles" and "Jim Crow practices disguised as 'temporary' expedients." One member explained that her employer fired her for attending a Chicago NALC meeting and fellow Chicagoan Nahaz Rogers fumed about the timidity of many black middle-class leaders. During the next few years, the Chicago chapter of the NALC focused its efforts on access for blacks to the skilled trades, but to no avail. It issued a comprehensive report on racial discrimination at the Washburne Trade School in 1961 that found only 26 black apprentices of the 2,682 at the school, with seven of the twelve trades having no black apprentices at all.[15] Its subsequent desegregation campaign faced antagonism from the Daley machine. Daley worked a deal with Walter Reuther to have African-American United Auto Workers leader Willoughby Abner transferred to Detroit. Meanwhile, the Board of Education harassed NALC President Timuel Black, who worked as a public school teacher, effectively blocking him from a promotion. Within less than two years, the Chicago NALC campaign against Washburne was all but dead. At the request of the NALC, the National Association for the Advancement of Colored People (NAACP) filed a 1963 suit against the federal government over the lack of black employment on the building of a new federal courthouse in Chicago. By the time the case came to trial, however, a federal judge declared it moot because the building had already been completed.[16]

At roughly the same time, Nahaz Rogers and Lawrence Landry cofounded the Association of Community Teams (ACT), an organization designed to challenge employment discrimination. In 1964, ACT demonstrated against glazier and ironworker union racism at the construction site of an Illinois Bell Telephone office. But without more members and financial resources, it was underequipped to launch a citywide jobs campaign in the mid-1960s; instead, ACT restricted its activities to single-building rent strikes and school boycotts.[17] Due to the "iron clad grip" of the local Democratic machine and "white liberals" who purported to speak for black interests, Rogers lamented, "civil rights progress is going backwards in Chicago."[18]

Meanwhile, the Chicago Urban League (CUL) worked through business channels in the 1960s to integrate the building trades, but it proved no more successful than the militant groups. The CUL, in line with the national organization, began to consider the construction industry "a major responsibility" in the mid-1960s and developed a training program with the Illinois Bureau of Employment Services called Project 110. Because the CUL had an explicit policy against "direct action as pickets and boycotts," its members did not protest against discriminatory unions and contractors but rather focused on advertising its training programs.[19] Its own statistics claimed that its efforts placed 82, 169, and 179 men in programs between 1966 and 1969, which its staff members "were the first to point out...was not the achievement of equal opportunity."[20]

The arrival of the SCLC in Chicago in 1966 heightened expectations for economic justice. The Chicago Freedom Movement, a coordination of the national SCLC staff with the local activist network in the Coordinating Council of Community Organizations (CCCO), brought the national spotlight to Chicago for a nonviolent direct action campaign. The proposed goals of the Freedom Movement included fair employment, a minimum wage, training programs using government funds, and tax reductions for employers who expanded opportunities. By attacking "economic exploitation" as "crystallized in the SLUM," its leaders saw trades jobs as "opportunities which could easily be learned by persons with limited academic training" if they could remove the union "bar" on blacks.[21]

Yet, soon after arriving in Chicago, SCLC decided to direct most of its energy toward housing and not jobs. Martin Luther King's speech during the spring Chicago Freedom Festival hinted at the reason for this. Despite the continued migration of blacks "up and out of the Delta heartland of Dixie" to Chicago, King declared that the job market in Chicago had "Gone with the Wind" due to the automation of industry and having "doors slammed in their faces" by employers. "Our greatest need is economic security," King concluded, because "what does it profit a man to be able to send his children to an integrated school if the family income is insufficient [and] what will he gain by being permitted to move into an integrated neighborhood if he cannot afford to do so because he is unemployed?"[22] Stopping short of a call for action, King claimed that "the forces of good will" in "the labor movement have already come and pledged themselves in the struggle." But did they ever make such a pledge? Regardless, the Freedom Movement, perhaps fearing repercussions from attacking two of its traditional liberal allies—northern Democrats and labor unions—backed away from a jobs campaign. Instead, its housing campaign exposed (and perhaps even consolidated) white opposition to civil rights in Chicago, motivated no more than 3 percent of Black Chicagoans to participate, and resulted in only token concessions from Mayor Richard Daley.[23]

The experience of this campaign motivated community organizers to develop new tactics. In July 1969, residents of Lawndale watched as another Federal Housing Association broke ground in their West Side neighborhood without a single minority worker. Although the general contractor had promised positions on these projects to Paul King, a spokesman for the African American West Side Builders Association, these jobs never materialized. Indeed, Clayborn Jones, an Urban League staffer assigned by the City of Chicago to investigate this project, was transferred to another assignment during the same week that Pepper Construction won the contract.[24] Aggravated, blacks from the neighborhood decided to act. On Wednesday, July 23, they picketed the construction site and then marched alongside young black men wearing berets to the Building Trades Council office. They proceeded to stage a spontaneous sit-in by barricading themselves in the office before police knocked down the door and arrested seventeen protestors. Two days later, other black activists joined the fight by demanding that white construction workers cease all work on three West Douglas Boulevard sites. The somewhat confused workers obliged, and the activists posted signs that read, "This job closed by the community." By the end of the month, a group calling itself the Coalition had shut down four more sites in African American neighborhoods as the number of protestors swelled to several hundred.[25]

The people who formed the Coalition that emerged with such force during summer 1969 had begun their work on April 4, 1968. At a CCCO meeting at a local high school on that fateful day, Sally Johnson remembered, the "room went up" when someone came rushing in to announce that Dr. King had been killed. Thereafter, she remembered, "Hector Franco, myself, my girlfriend named Bill [Wilma Williams], and two other Hispanic people went off to the side and decided now we're going to call ourselves Allies for a Better Community." Allies for a Better Community (ABC), a West Side organization composed of Puerto Ricans and African Americans, became a member of CUCA in 1969, with Johnson as its representative. Yet Johnson did not decide to become a full-time activist in a single moment. Previously, she had gone alone, and against her husband's wishes, to march with Martin Luther King in Marquette Park. In her own neighborhood, she took a job at the Urban Progress Center, a city of Chicago agency created after a Puerto Rican "riot" in 1966.[26] While there, Johnson enrolled at the Urban Training Center for Christian Mission (UTC), an institution that later housed the CUCA offices.

Founded in 1963 by several local churches "transcending denominations," the UTC trained activists for urban mission work. With a five-year grant from the Ford Foundation to train African American organizers and the subsequent appointment of C. T. Vivian as director of fellowships and internships in 1965, UTC programs took an explicitly political direction. Vivian, a minister from western Illinois, had emerged as a civil rights leader during Nashville sit-in campaign in 1960; faced off with Sheriff Jim Clark in Selma, Alabama, over voting rights in 1965; and helped integrate the St. Augustine beaches before moving to Chicago to work with the UTC and the Chicago Freedom Movement.[27] By 1968, the Chicago Action Training (CAT) at the UTC embraced "a strategy of Black Power, Black identity, and Black unity" because "Black CATs are no longer hung-up on services; they see the taking of power from structures which affect their lives."[28]

In addition to Vivian and Johnson, local clergy such as David Reed, community organizers such as Meredith Gilbert of the Lawndale Union to End Slums, and black construction contractors such as Paul King joined, demonstrating the broad appeal of CUCA. Organizational representatives included the Kenwood-Oakland Community Organization, Black Liberation Alliance, Congress of Racial Equality, Valley Community Organization, and National Welfare Rights Organization. After the murder of Dr. King, they redoubled their efforts for co-ordination at the Urban Training Center, making CUCA (originally called the Black Consortium) into a well-organized network of African American men by 1969.[29]

C. T. Vivian, the head of the Coalition, believed that protests by men at build-ing sites in 1969 would lead not just to an amelioration of ghetto conditions but to reclaiming power. "Because culture has closed [young blacks] out," he stated, they needed "to find a way to get in, and all they're asking is to ... rebuild their own community and this is the way you cure the problem of the ghetto." A press release titled "It's Our Thang" outlined the Coalition objectives as "carrying on a fight to end racism in the trade unions, open up thousands of jobs to the Black community and increase the Black community's power of self-determination."[30] At an August 4 meeting at its headquarters, the Coalition issued its specific de-mands to the building trades: 10,000 total jobs, the immediate promotion of blacks with four years experience to foremen, the elimination of testing for on-the-job training, automatic union dues deduction, and abolition of the union hall referral system.[31]

These demands for community self-determination were also framed as a means for black men to reclaim their manhood. Although Sally Johnson came from a similar path of grassroots organizing, she was the only female representa-tive on the CUCA board. She largely kept quiet in meetings and "whispered" in C. T. Vivian's ear on matters of strategy. To many in CUCA, these jobs repre-sented the potential for "self-esteem of guys to put on a big belt with tools on it and go to work and earn an honest dollar" during a time when even black leaders such as Bill Berry of the Urban League termed discrimination against black men "cultural castration." Indeed, a letter from Aleta Styers of the National Organiza-tion for Women (NOW) requested that the Division of Contract Compliance also look into sex discrimination, charging contractors and unions with treating women's interest in apprenticeship as a "joke" and "publicity stunt." NOW sup-ported CUCA, but no evidence exists that the relationship went both ways; in 1969, black and white women marched for CUCA, but as supporters of their men and often in demonstrations designed as either exclusively male or female.[32]

Central to the Coalition project of empowering young black men was its choice to enlist the participation of the Chicago black street gangs as advocates, recruiters, and activists for the Coalition employment program. These younger men, CUCA believed, statistically and psychologically represented the "hard-core unemployed" of Chicago's West and South Side neighborhoods. A focus on their gender and youth did not seem to CUCA activists as exclusionary but rather an urgent necessity because, they thought, a lack of steady jobs led many young men to gang activity at the expense of stable marriages and families.[33] Provided with the opportunity to become part of CUCA, male gang members became the leading force in the Chicago construction campaign as an outgrowth of their own evolving politicization and empowerment.

During the 1960s, Chicago gangs went through three basic phases of development. They began as peer groups at local high schools and juvenile detention centers that often served as a means of protection against interracial incidents during a decade when many western and southern Chicago neighborhoods shifted from white to black.[34] Next, they increasingly competed against one another, often with their fists, for members and territory. Territorial fights, however, had diminished somewhat by the late 1960s because these black teenagers became drawn to the energy of the civil rights movement. In 1966, SCLC arranged for a busload of Chicago gang leaders to attend a march in Alabama, prompting the New Yorker to label Dr. King "an incomparable strategist."[35] As a result, key gang members in Chicago now also considered the civil rights movement as a source of pride and strength.

The engagement of the War on Poverty with these already politicized gangs proved transformative and controversial. In 1967, the Blackstone Rangers and Eastside Disciples, who had formerly competed over territory in the Chicago South Side, signed a truce to work with The Woodlawn Organization (TWO) in the creation of a War on Poverty job-training program. TWO and the staff at the First Presbyterian Church, with the collaboration of members of both gangs, launched an experimental program that received almost $1 million from the federal Office of Economic Opportunity (OEO). Previous programs in Chicago, controlled by the local political machine, had always demanded that gang members renounce their affiliations as a precondition for receiving services. This grant differed because Reverend John Fry and Reverend Arthur Brazier of TWO sought to engage the existing gangs in an attempt to adapt their tightly knit structure to more progressive applications.[36]

Bypassing the Daley machine, however, had political consequences—soon thereafter the Chicago Red Squad deemed the TWO program a new target. The Red Squad, the powerful intelligence unit of Daley's police department, had begun as an anticommunist unit following the Palmer Raids in the 1920s. By the 1960s, it had widened its scope to include extensive surveillance files on any opponents of the status quo or threats to the local Democratic machine.[37] When black street gangs in Chicago furthered their political development, the Red Squad reacted to this perceived threat by forming the Gang Intelligence Unit (GIU) in

1967 as a new vanguard division of its intelligence operation. After the TWO grant began, the GIU raided the First Presbyterian Church to unearth weapons (that they already knew lay dormant in the office safe due to the ceasefire). And from spring 1967 into 1968, the GIU harassed gang members who participated in the job program and gathered evidence of criminal behavior to expose the grant as a fraud.[38]

Local Chicago Democrats used evidence gathered by the GIU to make an unlikely national alliance with John McClellan, a southern segregationist Democrat. McClellan, as chair of the Permanent Subcommittee on Investigations, agreed to hold Senate hearings in July 1968 to look into TWO misappropriation of federal grant money. The GIU found three star witnesses for this Washington, D.C., spectacle: a former Disciple, a former Blackstone Ranger, and the mother of eight Rangers. During the hearings, they testified about the nefarious activities of the gangs, alleging that they used the money to buy drugs and guns as well as host "sex parties." All three witnesses testified in exchange for immunity from criminal charges for themselves and their families. For the defense, witnesses could only answer the questions of the committee and were not allowed to present their own version of the TWO job program. Therefore, Jeff Fort, the leader of the Main 21 of the Blackstone Rangers, only spoke his name to the committee before walking out of the hearings; he was later arrested in Chicago on charges of contempt of the U.S. Senate.[39] Following the hearings, highly publicized arrests of gang leaders for rape and murder scared off employers even though most never went to trial and few were ever found guilty.[40]

CUCA leaders in Chicago, however, dismissed the hearings as show trials in favor of the firsthand evidence of neighborhood work by the Chicago gangs. Despite harassment from the Democratic machine and police in Chicago, the TWO program still put 105 "hard core unemployable" young men to work. In addition, gangs such as the Rangers proved they could maintain order in their own neighborhoods. After the assassination of Dr. King, the West Side erupted in a riot, but the South Side, and especially Woodlawn, "stayed cool." The Blackstone Rangers posted signs in the windows of local businesses that read, "DO NOT TOUCH— MAIN 21," and 3,000 "Stones" and 300 Disciples marched through the streets of Woodlawn to demonstrate their power, which largely kept a riot from erupting on the South Side.[41]

CUCA leaders sought to channel this energy when they allied with the three dominant African American gangs in Chicago: the Conservative Vice Lords, an amalgam of West Side gangs; the Black P. Stone Nation, formerly the Blackstone Rangers of the South Side; and the Disciples, formerly the Devil's Disciples, also a South Side gang. Commonly referred to as the Lords, the Stones, and the D's, these three gangs began to refer to their coalition by the acronym LSD. With LSD as a point of departure, CUCA leaders hoped to reorient gang members, as well as the black ghettoes where they operated, through the experience of civil rights work. And gang members in turn found that the association with CUCA reaffirmed their claims to neighborhood power even if it made demands on them to change how they exercised that power.[42]

Coalition leaders such as C. T. Vivian and Meredith Gilbert of the Lawndale Union to End Slums played a vital role in the CUCA attempt to incorporate gangs into the civil rights movement. They worked with gang members in their neighborhood organizations and solicited the most sympathetic representatives to join CUCA meetings. Leonard Sengali of the Stones, for example, was not only one of the Main 21 in the gang structure but a transforming influence. As his name change from Dickerson to Sengali indicates, Sengali joined the growing black nationalist movement and began articulating a class analysis of oppression alongside pan-African solidarity and race pride. Although Jeff Fort, a Ranger leader, had earned the nickname "Black Prince," the Rangers' overall conception of racial solidarity had been abstract prior to Sengali's transformation. Bob Taylor, a member of the Coalition and director of the Chicago branch of the Welfare Rights Organization, had previously worked with Sengali. "He was smooth," Taylor recalled. "You knew Leonard had control over the people in his organization [and] you also...never saw Leonard get violent."[43] In the Vice Lords, Pat Patterson, described as a great thinker by other Coalition members, "reined his guys in"; and other inspired gang leaders represented the Disciples.[44]

The first CUCA job campaign in which gangs took a leading role took place in March 1969, when it disputed and subsequently changed the employment practices of the Red Rooster supermarket chain.[45] But the scale of that campaign was dwarfed by its campaign for jobs in the construction industry. With gang members providing many of its demonstrators, CUCA became the national vanguard of construction trades activism during summer 1969 when it shut down twenty-four federal construction sites in Chicago totaling more than $80 million in building contracts.[46] The CUCA leaders articulated the goals of the construction jobs campaign, but the protests themselves were led by the LSD, which claimed more than 50,000 members across the city. Wearing berets—red (for the Peace Stones), blue (for the Disciples), and tan (for the Vice Lords)—they became the shock troops of the movement to open the building trades during that summer, demonstrating at construction sites by the busload. Just as important as their numbers was their great discipline. Paul King, coalition leader, remembered gangs meeting from "seven in the morning until seven at night" and concluded that they were the most loyal Coalition participants.[47]

The opponents of CUCA often seized on its collaborations with the gangs as a reason to dismiss its call for affirmative action as criminal. The construction contractors, unions, and the white press argued that gang participation made CUCA an illegitimate civil rights group. "Once again, agitators are trying to correct one evil with a greater evil," the *Tribune* editorialized, as "roving gangs of young Negroes have turned to violence." Thomas Nayder, secretary-treasurer of the Chicago Building Trades Council, and Thomas Murray, the president of the council, derided the protestors. They claimed that sit-ins did not make "instant craftsmen" and that the demonstrators were "more eager to capture headlines than participate in the kind of activity which brings quiet results." They stated that they would continue to train blacks through the CUL, even though the league admitted that its 1969 program resulted in "pitifully few Black applicants."[48]

But the discipline of CUCA members at demonstrations left contractors and union workers watching in frustration as police stood aside while black activists shut down one construction site after another. When the Coalition moved to close the Mount Sinai hospital extension, for example, the executive vice president suddenly had his office "jammed full with about 30 black people" who demanded he shut down the project. Despite the militancy of the demand, the vice president admitted to the press, "We talked in a fairly pleasant vein."[49] "Some people might say that some of what we did was forceful," Bob Taylor stated, "but I prefer to think of it as gentle persuasion."[50] LSD members intimidated but remained nonviolent at construction sites.

The Chicago police changed its approach to the movement when the Coalition moved from sites in black neighborhoods to the University of Illinois Circle Campus (UIC) on August 13. There, officers aggressively confronted CUCA and arrested the leaders of the march. Reestablishing the composure of the crowd, LSD members led three hundred other Coalition members to the Civic Center to protest the arrests. A delegation met with Daley staffers as "gangs of youth stood in military formation" on the sidewalk. Meanwhile, two hundred other protestors gathered outside the police station on State Street while Chief John E. Harnett met with CUCA. Both meetings ended without resolution as CUCA vowed to expand its protests to more sites.[51] David Reed, a founding CUCA member and former member of Illinois Governor Richard Ogilvie's Human Resources Commission, said that the idling of construction work would continue unless authorities put "a national guardsman on each shovel."[52]

With their projects stalled by CUCA, building contractors increasingly claimed that they, not the African Americans, were the victims in this crisis. Backing these builders, the *Tribune* asked, "Why has one contractor after another caved in to the unofficial orders of roving bands of youngsters if not from fear?"[53] After one site had been closed by the Coalition, two dozen white construction workers drove to the federal building and confronted Thomas Foran, U.S. attorney, with demands for an investigation.[54] This call for punitive action by the *Tribune* and white workers ended up in court. A. L. "Jake" Spencer, the executive vice president of S. N. Nielsen Company, called the protests "anarchy," and an operator claimed he was "slightly hurt" when pulled off his tractor. Other workers claimed that black gangs "swarmed" and shouted at them and that their placards read "You Can't Stop Bullets" and "Burn Baby."[55] These complaints, coupled with legal pressure by both unions and contractors, resulted in a speedy injunction against the Coalition that limited demonstrations to five people at a site and forbade entrance to the property.[56]

The Coalition decided to defy the injunction. Speaking for the Coalition, Meredith Gilbert said, "We are not going to honor any court injunction since the issue is much more important and deals with the survival of black people."[57] Learning of the injunction at its national conference in Charleston, South Carolina, SCLC moved its national meeting to Chicago to "dramatize the need for more jobs for blacks." After previously opposing gang collaborations, Jesse Jackson, leader of Operation Breadbasket, also offered his support to the Coalition, claiming he would join the group in protest "not [to] fight this legally" but to "fight it morally."[58]

These new allies helped build momentum but also caused tension within CUCA. After having dozens of nonviolent demonstrations composed of rival gang members, CUCA was surprised when members of Operation Breadbasket threw "bricks [and] beer cans" at a UIC rally. Realizing that their success came from disciplined demonstrations, CUCA leaders concluded that "we don't need *this* kind of participation again," which led them to redouble the activist training of newcomers.[59] Although this lack of discipline and Jesse Jackson's focus on publicity created some resentment, the presence of Breadbasket put more headlines in the Chicago papers about the jobs campaign and expanded the CUCA base of supporters. On August 21, a five-hour meeting in a "steaming hot church" showed a newfound solidarity around the jobs campaign never seen before in Chicago. The Coalition convened at Mt. Pisgah to a packed house of 2,000 people that included at least 300 gang members, who sat alongside churchgoers and a delegation of mothers from a local school. Swept up in the enthusiasm, one reporter in attendance wrote, "The songs were about freedom, and pride. The mood was expectant. The issue was construction jobs."[60]

As the CUCA protests spread, Chicago representatives of a dozen federal agencies responded to the "crisis" of protests by forming the Federal Ad Hoc Committee Concerning the Building Trades (FAHC) to bridge bureaucratic governmental boundaries in discussing how to "enforce the executive orders as they are now written." During their meetings, several representatives expressed sympathy for the Coalition. Andrew Corcoran of the Department of Housing and Urban Development (HUD) believed that all funds should be cut off until the contractors and unions complied.[61] Studies commissioned by the FAHC confirmed blatant exclusion in every trade union in Chicago except three. Even more revealing, the FAHC found that nine of the unionized industries had 25–50 percent labor shortages but continued to racially discriminate.[62]

Using this and other reports to induce negotiations between the CUCA and building trades, the FAHC also validated the role of the gangs in demanding justice. When Robert Tucker, the acting chair of the FAHC, attended a CUCA meeting to outline the position of the federal agencies, he reported back that the CUCA "accepted my statement with a surprising degree of pleasure."[63] Edwin Berry of the Urban League, despite facing the possibility of losing financial support for the program of his own organization, endorsed the CUCA demands and warned that "refusal to recognize it as a responsible element of the black community will prolong negotiations and increase…conflict."[64] The Midwest director of the U.S. Department of Justice concurred. After surveying other federal administrators about whether CUCA represented a "responsible" organization because its "adversaries refer to the Coalition as 'hoodlums' and 'thugs,'" he concluded that the "Coalition is representative of a broad segment of Chicago's Negro community," its members "are genuinely interested in increasing employment opportunities," and its "leaders have done all within their power to negotiate a settlement and to respond to the current crisis in a nonviolent manner."[65]

As protests at federal construction sites spread to cities around the country in late August and September, Chicago became a bellwether for affirmative action.[66] The sincere, sustained actions of the Coalition caused Secretary George Romney of HUD to file a suit in U.S. District Court to freeze $38 million in federal funds of the Chicago Model Cities Program.[67] These federal government actions, combined with the street-level protests, caused representatives of the unions and contractors to expect federal sanctions unless they negotiated. Michael Shane, a Disciples representative in the Coalition, captured the mood in Chicago when he concluded, "We [have] the overseers of labor in utter fear."[68]

Fear brought all parties to the negotiating table. The first three discussions in August among the Coalition, builders, and unions "were unproductive." In early September, the Coalition sent the Building Trades Council and Building Employers Association a list of demands; several days later, the two building groups responded with a counterproposal; and at a subsequent meeting, CUCA walked out. A key point of contention was that the Coalition wanted to control its own apprenticeship programs due to the racist record of the Washburne Trade School; both groups also stood miles apart on the number of jobs and the pace to achieve training and placement. "You are playing games…with the Black Community," Vivian thundered at union and contractor representatives, because your proposal "does not deal with the reality of the people who need work."[69]

After these unproductive meetings, CUCA again resumed its protests. At UIC, as summer turned to autumn in 1969, demonstrators found new allies waiting for them on campus. White allies from the New Left on the UIC campus, including Local 1627 of the American Federation of Teachers, the Students for a Democratic Society John Brown chapter, the Young Socialist Alliance, and University Christian Movement came out in support of CUCA. These UIC student activist groups joined demonstrations and held their own rallies (including a march led by three hundred black women) to demand that the president of the university stop all construction and for UIC to expand its minority enrollment. In October, 150 students cheered as 240 faculty members passed a resolution to stop all construction. In this and other battles, although the Coalition remained an all-black organization, it allied with white New Left groups that supported its goals.[70]

Unlike these UIC students and faculty, white workers reacted with indignation. These protests put the northern white working-class backlash on full display when, after nearly two months of CUCA protests, Undersecretary of Labor Arthur Fletcher came to Chicago in late September to hold hearings on whether to extend the revised Philadelphia Plan to cities across the country. Fletcher, the coauthor of the plan and outspoken advocate of affirmative action, intended to use the hearings as a publicity vehicle for breaking the back of national union resistance to desegregation.[71] But it was probably not lost on Chicago union and political leaders that Fletcher, a Republican in the Nixon administration, was making this move against the stalwart supporters of the same Daley political machine that many believed had deprived Nixon of the presidency in 1960.

When he arrived in town, Fletcher faced massive resistance that rivaled, if not exceeded, the ferocity of the anger that had greeted Dr. King three years earlier. On September 24, at least 3,500 "angry white workers, in work clothes and helmets" disrupted the hearing by filling the meeting room and demonstrating outside. Fletcher convened the hearings for about twenty minutes as white workers in the audience subjected him to a torrent of abuse. Pressured by the hotel management to vacate this "two ring circus" and concerned that the "Chicago police were behaving very gently toward the pickets," Fletcher recessed the hearings, "shoulder[ing] our way past some catcalling construction workers." Fletcher described the attempt to find an alternate meeting space in the city with adequate police protection a "crucial challenge" to the fate of the Philadelphia Plan. "The federal government," he recalled, "had to demonstrate that it could function in Chicago. The full hearing had to be held, if there was to be anything left of the federal anti-discrimination program."[72]

With an assurance from the White House that the military would airlift troops into Chicago if necessary, Fletcher and members of the FAHC reconvened the hearings at the U.S. Customs House on Canal Street in early October. With an estimated 5,000 white workers "ringed [around] the building," restrained by 200 helmeted Chicago policemen and federal marshals, the scene dramatized the desperation of white workers. Their anger led to the assault of a black man that they mistook for Art Fletcher; Fletcher himself had to take the precaution of entering the back door with armed guards. Eliding what C. T. Vivian described inside the Customs House as "400 years of past racism" and the "economic survival of black people in this city," white workers inside held signs reading, "Keep Quality in Jobs," "No Giveaways, No Bums," and "Why Should They Get Our Jobs?" In the street, the white workers grumbled that "we're tax payers; they're tax eaters" and "nobody here has anything against the colored—when they can act like a white man." They confronted C. T. Vivian and Jesse Jackson as the two entered the Customs House to testify. Jackson pleaded that this "horizontal fight between the have-nots must shift into a vertical fight," but Jackson's audience reacted with hostility, and, fortunately for him, Buzz Palmer and other members of the Afro-American Police League led him safely inside.[73]

The spectacle of a potential race war in the Chicago downtown Loop, combined with the possibility that the federal government would respond by withholding of millions of dollars in federal funds, spurred Mayor Daley to try to control the negotiations with the Department of Labor.[74] Claiming he represented an "impartial" third party, Daley called the groups together in early October for negotiations in City Hall. CUCA had unprecedented leverage in the negotiations because it had shut down millions of dollars of federally subsidized housing projects and the FAHC backed their demands as within affirmative actions statutes.[75] After three months of negotiations, CUCA felt optimistic; in December, it hosted a holiday celebration and benefit featuring the music of B. B. King and Oscar Brown Jr., the comedy of Dick Gregory, and the dancing of Jean Pace at the Auditorium Theatre of Roosevelt University, where its leaders predicted signing an agreement after the New Year.[76]

Eleven CUCA representatives, including members of all three gangs and the representatives of the Building Trades Council and Building Construction Employers Association, signed the Chicago Plan in early January 1970. The plan called for 1,000 qualified minority journeymen to go to work immediately and become members of their respective trade unions, the training of 1,000 minority 17- to 24-year-olds (the age group of the three gangs), and 1,000 on-the-job trainees who would not be required to take tests to enter their chosen trade. An Administrative Committee and an Operations Committee (representing all the parties involved) would implement the agreement on a craft by craft basis.[77]

All parties publicly hailed the Chicago Plan as a milestone. Arthur O'Neil of the Building Construction Employers said it "will prove to be a model for the nation." Arthur Fletcher concurred, but also had private reservations, warning that if "it is just a show, then we can and must move in to see that there is no discrimination." Fletcher further hoped that local "solutions" could now be brokered elsewhere to make affirmative action a federal policy by bringing unions, contractors, and applicants together without creating an inefficient federal bureaucracy that would impose sanctions on hostile parties. The Chicago Plan thus provided the boilerplate language and process that the Department of Labor used to broker similar hometown solutions around the country. And, perhaps most important, as Michael Shane of the Disciples declared, "This showed that three youth nations could come together peacefully and at last do something constructive" and "this will alleviate much of the gang warfare."[78]

But, although the Chicago Plan was publicly hailed a success, its implementation triggered a wave of hometown plan failures across the nation. CUCA had significant leverage going into the Chicago Plan negotiations to demand better enforcement provisions. But stiff union resistance, conciliatory federal negotiators, and a joint Federal Bureau of Investigation (FBI)–Chicago police crackdown on gangs undermined the CUCA position just as it reached the apex of its power. As a result, behind-the-scenes political pressure from the Daley machine ensured that the Chicago Plan, and plans modeled on it, had weak federal enforcement provisions based on presumptions of good faith that left the power of building trades patronage networks largely unchallenged.

The negotiation of the Chicago Plan coincided with the height of the GIU and FBI harassment of the gang members who formed CUCA base. After the injunction against Coalition-led job closures took effect, police officials pleaded that the "way the courts have stripped [us] of any power, [we] are helpless against [gangs]." Mayor Daley agreed and called a meeting with Attorney General Ed Hanrahan, Circuit Court Judge Eugene Wachowski, and other civic officials to establish a special judicial branch, approvingly deemed a "terrorist" court by the *Chicago Tribune*. The city of Chicago, with a fivefold increase in GIU officers from 38 to 200 between 1967 and 1969, effectively declared a full-scale war on gangs.[79]

Throughout summer and fall 1969, Coalition representatives charged police with the nighttime assault of gang members who participated in demonstrations; the arrest without cause of scores of gang members in Washington Park; and the arrest and imprisonment of Leonard Sengali, the lynchpin between the P. Stones and the Coalition, on a trumped-up murder charge. Although fabricated FBI rumors (disseminated through its covert action program, COINTELPRO) failed in their goal to turn the Black Panther Party, the Rangers, and the Disciples against one another, the FBI raid and subsequent killing of Fred Hampton and Mark Clark, Panther leaders, just one month before the signing of the Chicago Plan demonstrated the lengths that the federal and city police would go to in their war on gangs.[80] Members of the Coalition had reason to fear for their safety.

CUCA documented sixteen cases between June 1969 and May 1970 in which "black youths [were] murdered by the police." Reverend Vivian received information that his own life was in danger, prompting gang members to stand guard outside his house.[81]

Thus, a local and federal police crackdown compromised the coherence of CUCA during negotiations about the Chicago Plan and produced a hasty settlement. In jail and awaiting trail, Sengali was visited by the attorney general. According to Sengali, Hanrahan offered to dismiss the charges if he would denounce the CUCA leaders as being under the influence of communists. He refused. But when the office of the Mayor added the release of a few key gang members, such as Sengali, as a secret reward for signing the Chicago Plan, the Black P. Stone Rangers urged the Coalition sign without delay.[82]

With CUCA weakened, it proved easy for unions with extraordinary inside knowledge of the construction industry to outmaneuver the Chicago Plan. Robert Tucker, the HUD equal employment officer, and Rutgers University Professor Alfred Blumrosen, Fletcher's fair employment law consultant, might have been able to counter the union attempts to water down the Chicago Plan, but HUD pulled both men from the meetings early on.[83] The meeting minutes during the negotiations among CUCA, the construction industry, and the mayor thus portended the problems that would develop in its implementation. Vivian worried that, without a strong agreement, "We would end up fighting the battle with 19 different locals." The subsequent agreement floundered precisely because the individual unions made little effort to enforce it and the administrative committee, paralyzed by its own bureaucracy, had little power to sanction the unions.[84]

In the wake of the signing of the Chicago Plan, the decimation of the Coalition became more and more apparent. To Bob Taylor, the pivotal moment occurred when members of Black P. Stone Rangers who he did not remember being involved in the Coalition paid a visit to his office at the newly founded Black Street Academy, an educational offshoot of the Coalition. Taylor recalled, "They took out a .38 and emptied all the bullets except one...and they started spinning it and shooting it up in the air. [They said,] "Bob, we want all fifty of these slots.' [And] I said, 'Man, listen, there's no way on earth that I can do that.' And after [this discussion] I went into my office and packed up everything that I had and put it in the trunk of the car...and I never went back."[85] Taylor left Chicago to direct the Street Academy program in Washington, D.C., and did not return for two years. Caught in the middle of escalating violence by police, union thugs, and gangs, many key Coalition leaders similarly fled Chicago or became less active in the organization by the early 1970s.[86]

By summer 1970, CUCA, joined by the newly founded Black Strategy Center of C. T. Vivian, ran out of patience with the Chicago Plan. The plan had managed to place only about one hundred blacks in training programs and subsequent jobs. The Coalition, noting that only one of the nineteen unions had met the goals for the training of minority workers, sent a telegram to the Department of Labor urging it to freeze all federal funding for local building contracts. By September, an independent investigation of the Chicago Plan by Herbert Hill confirmed its failure, while the Reverend Dunlap of the Coalition noted that gangs are "frustrated because of the standstill." Meanwhile, the Nixon administration began a slow retreat from affirmative action. Federal officials hesitated to impose sanctions when the hometown plans failed, and the president initiated massive budget cuts in federal construction contracts, thereby making it more difficult to meet the hiring targets of the plan.[87]

The only person who remained optimistic about the Chicago Plan during 1970 was Alderman Fred Hubbard, the appointed plan chair. CUCA had accepted his appointment but also resented the African American alderman because of his lack of previous involvement in the issue. During the summer and fall, Hubbard kept asking both sides for more patience to allow the plan to work. Although this request seemed reasonable at the time (most of the federal money for the plan did not arrive until the early summer), it became clear that Hubbard had never thought the plan would work when, a year later, he disappeared after embezzling over $100,000 from its coffers. CUCA blamed Hubbard for wrecking the Chicago Plan, saying that a machine politician should never have been put in charge.[88]

But even with a better administrator, CUCA leaders lamented, a lack of good faith would still have left the Chicago Plan stillborn. Once the CUCA street heat had been effectively bogged down in battles for survival against an army of machine-funded GIU officers, the unions were able to subvert the Chicago Plan with impunity. Just one month after the agreement, Peter Stahl, a sympathetic administrator in the Department of Justice, concluded that the Chicago Plan "is a very bad agreement as far as the black community is concerned." He believed that the two plan committees needed too many votes to pass anything "substantive," and with blacks as 0.7 percent carpenters, 0.1 percent sheet metal workers, and 3.8 percent electricians, "there is very little likelihood of a white man acting in good faith." In conclusion, Stahl wrote that $600 million in federal contracts in Chicago had to make "the stomach of a black man" "regurgitate" when reading that the plan would only be implemented "if general business conditions permit."[89] Over the next year, Stahl's assessment proved accurate. The individual trade unions dragged their feet by disqualifying many applicants, and the Nixon administration budget cuts allowed builders to claim that business conditions prevented its implementation.[90] The Chicago Plan template, once heralded as a model for the nation, quickly became a national embarrassment for Fletcher and the Department of Labor, dealing a blow to the national campaign for the desegregation of the construction industry.

Following the collapse of the first Chicago Plan, "new" iterations of it proved only marginally better, and CUCA began its steady decline. Although periodic protests continued, the mass pressure that had brought concessions and enforcement dramatically dissipated as community groups turned on one another in the wake of the failure of the federal government to negotiate or enforce a stronger affirmative action plan. Coupled with federal budget cuts and the mismanagement of HUD and other programs in the late 1970s and into the Ronald Reagan years, the affirmative action promise of "Build Baby Build" to provide jobs and resources to low-income people of color collapsed.

In spring 1972, with a New Chicago Plan sponsored by the federal government in the works, the remaining members of CUCA renewed their struggle and attempted to learn from past mistakes. The New Chicago Plan promised 10,000 jobs by 1976 and put the Urban League in charge with help from both CUCA and the Latin American Task Force. With $1.7 million from the Department of Labor and endorsed by fifteen unions and nine contractors associations, the plan, CUCA representatives hoped, would not flounder again by forcing individual unions to endorse the initial agreement. "We are entering into this agreement," Carl Latimer, the new CUCA leader, said, "with the hope we shall never have to hit the streets again."[91]

By the following year, however, Labor Department officials, now working under Peter Brennan, the former head of the New York City Building Trades Council, cut off information and reduced the regional contract compliance staff to two people. This lack of government information obfuscated how many actual jobs minorities had attained, putting the Urban League, according to one reporter, "in a fog" that made enforcement impossible. Street protests resumed in 1973, and Labor Department officials pledged support in September for the 2,000 men that CUCA had recruited over the last eleven months. But, yet again, these promises came without results.[92] Without federal support, and with the unions refusing to provide on-the-job training, the CUL and CUCA resigned from the program, prompting the Department of Labor to pull the plug in October 1974.[93]

As the New Chicago Plan floundered, allies increasingly engaged in bitter battles that by 1973 destroyed the CUCA federation. In 1972, the Coalition had boasted a board of directors that included black aldermen, businessmen, and officials from Jesse Jackson's Operation PUSH (People United to Serve Humanity). But while meeting in Washington, D.C., in late September 1973, the CUCA leadership splintered. While members negotiated in Washington, the Board of Directors, apparently at the urging of Noah Robinson, who headed the Breadbasket

Commercial Association, voted to oust the entire staff. On their return to Chicago, Latimer and the other Coalition leaders refused to vacate the CUCA offices in favor of the newly appointed leader, Reverend A. I. Dunlap. Robinson subsequently called for another "new" Chicago Plan in May 1973, fought with Jesse Jackson and Operation PUSH over the contracting of the Carter Woodson Public library project, and held a benefit dinner that one Urban League staffer complained had "poor content" and a "large number of empty tables." The Urban League charged CUCA with "serious infractions…of record keeping standards" and feared the organization would face an audit by the federal government that could expose financial malfeasance in the New Chicago Plan.[94]

This infighting and the poor performance of the New Chicago Plan also alienated the newfound Coalition allies in the Puerto Rican and Mexican communities. These communities had been eager to join the movement for jobs in the construction industry in the early 1970s. But, only a few years later, Jose Ovalle, the Latin American Task Force (LATF) leader, bitterly complained that the Urban League had shut the LATF out as an equal partner and referred to the CUL leaders as "house niggers" who did not want "to make social changes." The Spanish Coalition for Jobs, a coalition of twenty-three Latino neighborhood groups modeled after CUCA and the LATF, followed suit, accusing the Coalition of treating their concerns as secondary, making the potential citywide coalition of Latinos and blacks an opportunity lost amid the failure of the New Chicago Plan.[95]

Despite the dedication of CUCA members, the good faith of the Chicago Plan never translated into access to jobs, so Coalition members had to use other creative methods to integrate the trades. The unions backed away; the Washburne Trade School remained practically all white; and when forced to take minorities, the school relocated to the suburbs. As a silver lining, Paul King applied the tactics of CUCA from the perspective of a contractor. If black contractors got a foothold in the industry, he reasoned, they would supply the "good faith" jobs for African-American workers. In the 1970s, the National Association of Minority Contractors, with directors in two-dozen cities, supported the shut down of more sites across the country and then "educated" congressmen like Parren Mitchell of Michigan to write affirmative action statutes for contractors into federally funded projects.[96] For Chicago-based workers, it took an Executive Order from Harold Washington, the city's first African American mayor, who had previously attended CUCA protests and rallies as a state representative, to create set-aside jobs in the 1980s for minorities and contractors in the building trades.[97] Since the 1990s, however, even this modest program has been under legal attack and hampered by the creation of false-front minority businesses by unions and builders.[98]

Meanwhile, by waging war on CUCA's "troops" (the politicized gangs), the Chicago building trades unions, police, and politicians helped make their policies self-fulfilling for African American youth. Treated like "thugs and criminals," according to one federal memorandum, gangs struggling to survive such repression had little choice but to respond as such.[99] Their experience within the Coalition temporarily changed the direction of the gangs from violence to community improvement. Through the Coalition, many young black men came to share with civil rights leaders the desire to rebuild the black communities. But, with their job programs thwarted and under intense police pressure, they chose to restructure themselves for survival by seeking other, illicit means to earn a living.

When C. T. Vivian declared, "We can no longer fence with straw men in our battle for survival," he and other CUCA members defined Black Power as a means of destroying the "stone wall" of institutional racism.[100] Despite the attempts of CUCA to batter down that wall, it held together because its structure comprised the interwoven constituencies of labor unions, employers, and one of the strongest Democratic Party political machines in the country. The CUCA street actions worked in part because Lyndon Johnson's Great Society had put federal affirmative action statutes in place that activists were able to wield as weapons in local struggles. The freezing of government housing construction loans and other sanctions seemed for a time, even to those who worked in Nixon's Department of Labor and other federal agencies, potentially hard-hitting and transformative.

Yet the intransigence of local officials and the acquiescence to the Chicago hometown plan model, much to Nixon's delight and Art Fletcher's dismay, created a wedge between labor and civil rights activists in the Democratic Party. The damage inflicted, the Nixon administration then pulled back from affirmative action enforcement. As a result, many white union households in the building trades gravitated to Nixon in the 1972 presidential election while concomitantly increasing their support for Mayor Daley's democratic machine locally (these white working-class voters replacing the growing number of disaffected black voters who had previously provided Daley with the margin of victory between 1955 and 1963). It is no wonder then that Nixon expressed admiration for Daley in 1972 because "he's playing our game right now and they run a good show."[101]

The story of CUCA thus suggests the need for an expansion of what we consider the trajectory and scope of the twentieth-century civil rights movement in the United States. The interplay between disparate historical actors, such as a Republican president with a Democratic mayor, unions with employers, and street gang members with federal bureaucrats, suggests alliances that both cross and reconfigure racial, class, and regional categories. A wider field of vision allows us to see how the CUCA version of Black Power defies the typical explanations of the decline of the West and South Sides of black Chicago. Rather than stemming from the cultural pathology, gangbanging, or passivity of black Chicago residents, the decline resulted from the actions of Chicago police, unions, and employers who parried the full-scale CUCA assault to protect the wall of racial inequality. This aggressive assault, combined with the federal withdrawal from enforcing affirmative action, prevented the Chicago Plan from translating into the bricks and mortar necessary for African Americans to rebuild the West and South Sides of Chicago. Instead, the good faith of the Chicago Plan became a war against inner-city blacks as civic outlaws rather than constructive citizens, and that legacy has cast a shadow of amnesia over remedies for race and class oppression in our contemporary urban environment.

"THE BLACKS SHOULD NOT BE ADMINISTERING THE PHILADELPHIA PLAN"

Nixon, the Hard Hats, and "Voluntary" Affirmative Action

Trevor Griffey

The conventional history of the rise of affirmative action in the late 1960s and early 1970s tends toward a too simple dialectic. The early creation and extension of affirmative action law is often described as an extension of the civil rights movement, whereas organized opposition to affirmative action is described as something that occurred later, as a backlash or reaction that did not fully take hold until Ronald Reagan was elected president in 1980.[1]

In this chapter, I tell a different story. I describe the role that labor union resistance to affirmative action played in limiting the ability of the federal government to enforce new civil rights laws well before the more overt backlash against affirmative action became ascendant in U.S. political culture in the 1980s and 1990s. There was no heyday for attempts by federal regulatory agencies to impose affirmative action on U.S. industry. There was no pristine origin against which a backlash could define itself, because enforcement of affirmative action had accommodated its opponents from the beginning.

Affirmative action law emerged out of and in response to civil rights movement protests against the racism of federal construction contractors, whose discriminatory hiring policies were defended and often administered by the powerful building trades unions.[2] But the resistance of those unions to the 1969 Revised Philadelphia Plan—the first government-imposed affirmative action plan—severely curtailed the ability of the federal government to enforce affirmative action in all industries. By undermining the capacity of the U.S. Department of Labor's Office of Contract Compliance (OFCC) to enforce executive orders against racial discrimination by federal contractors, unions played a crucial role

134

in shifting the enforcement of equal employment law to the courts, which lacked the administrative capacity to effectively oversee complex workplace desegregation orders.

The fact that the building trades unions were not able to completely stop affirmative action has caused historians to overlook the effect that union resistance had on the evolution of public policy. The building trades unions believed that the intervention of the Philadelphia Plan in the construction industry would compromise their hiring halls and their apprenticeship programs, and violate the prohibition against racial quotas in Title VII of the 1964 Civil Rights Act. Convinced that they were the targets of a Republican Party conspiracy against organized labor, they lobbied their Democratic Party allies in Congress and the Department of Labor in 1969 to stop the plan. Rather than acceding to the desegregation orders of the state and federal government fair employment agencies, the unions used aggressive litigation throughout the 1960s and early 1970s to forestall their regulation. Both their legal and legislative resistance failed in the short term. In addition, the union rallies against the Philadelphia Plan in 1969 undermined their cause by producing media images of white workers whose rage against "forced integration" crossed over into over antiblack racism.

Yet, even though they failed to completely stop affirmative action, the building trades unions were neither innocent victims nor passive objects of reform. Considering their labor rights inalienable, many white workers responded to the implementation of the Philadelphia Plan in 1969 and 1970 by walking off the job. When forced to return, hostile union journeymen hazed new black journeymen off jobs with impunity, and others simply refused to teach black apprentices. Lacking the resources and political will to overcome union resistance, the Department of Labor backed off from enforcing the Philadelphia Plan by promoting voluntary desegregation plans for the construction industry over government-imposed plans, local "hometown plans" over a single national one, and conciliation over punishment when "goals and timetables" were not met. Rather than securing everyone's cooperation, the return of the Department of Labor to voluntarism allowed unions (and contractors) to openly violate the plans. By 1971, the resulting chaos pressured the Richard Nixon White House to either redouble its efforts or abandon workplace desegregation, as it had school and housing desegregation, as too politically costly.[3]

The choice facing Nixon of whether to enforce the Philadelphia Plan was not as simple as it may appear in retrospect. Nixon believed that affirmative action was necessary, although he was wary of its political costs. Because the building trades unions were solidly enmeshed in Democratic Party politics, he originally felt little allegiance to them. But when construction workers organized a wave of pro–Vietnam War demonstrations across the country in support of Nixon's foreign policy in May and June 1970, they transformed Nixon's political calculus. Branding themselves instant spokesmen for Nixon's previously abstract and rhetorical "silent majority," New York City building trades union leaders disavowed ulterior motives for their patriotic rallies. Their new hard hat cultural politics promoted a shared commitment to masculinity, law and order, and anticommunism that supposedly transcended partisan politics. Nixon was extremely grateful—indeed desperate—for their support. Reaching out to the unions, he and union leaders cocreated a hard hat movement whose media representations staged the racial reconciliation between the white working class and the Republican Party. Presenting this movement as a restoration of white men's moral authority against liberal permissiveness, both union and Nixon officials used the media icon of the hard hat to shore up their power against critics on the left.

Although the hard hat movement did not explicitly evoke the politics of race, the subversion of the Philadelphia Plan was the essential precondition that made it possible for the unions to ally themselves with Nixon. The New York building trades unions made their support for Nixon's reelection in 1972 contingent on his backing off from enforcing the desegregation of the construction industry. Forced to choose between the Philadelphia Plan and an alliance with the building trades unions on support for his foreign policy, Nixon chose the unions. It was this choice, forced by union pressure and not the inevitable result of a coherent domestic political program against the unions or the civil rights movement, that finalized Nixon's decision to court the support of the unions instead of trying to smash them.

Thus, less than two years after creating the Philadelphia Plan, Nixon gave the green light to reversing his always tentative support for affirmative action. While his staff hollowed out the substance of the Department of Labor's affirmative action enforcement within and outside the construction industry, Nixon declared himself to be against "quotas" and removed Art Fletcher, the architect of the Philadelphia Plan, from the Department of Labor. The busting of the building trades unions, which he had briefly flirted with, would be, Nixon quipped, "somebody else's problem."[4]

The Nixon–hard hat alliance had two profound effects on the politics of the 1970s. First, it shaped the evolution of government power over the workplace. The building trades unions had lost control of the Department of Labor when Nixon took office in 1969. But their resistance to its affirmative action decrees stalled its plans, while the aggressive courting of Nixon by the New York unions effectively stymied its capacity to adapt. The union pressure paid off. The building trades unions effectively recaptured the Department of Labor when, as an expression of gratitude for their support, Nixon made Peter Brennan, the head of the New York Building Trades Council, the U.S. secretary of labor in 1973.

Brennan, in turn, did not abolish affirmative action as much as he shifted its enforcement to the courts. Without a cabinet-level agency such as the Department of Labor to enforce equal employment law, employers adopted new affirmative action guidelines largely to defend themselves against the threat of litigation. The retreat from the Philadelphia Plan thus contributed to the transformation of affirmative action, as Kevin Yuill puts it, from a "civil rights demand to a watered-down bureaucratic program."[5]

Second, the building trades union leaders' creation of a hard hat movement played a key role in developing Nixon's outreach to white ethnic and blue-collar voters in the urban North through "social" rather than economic issues. This movement helped delink the cultural symbols of an implicitly male white working-class consciousness from Democratic Party politics outside the South.

The broad outlines of Nixon's attempt to reach out to so-called white ethnics and his "romancing [of] the new right worker" are well known.[6] But most histories of the strategy describe Nixon's alliance with conservative unions as only tangentially related to the politics of the Philadelphia Plan. Numerous works have contributed to our understanding of how the hard hats came to be seen as "the shock troops for the emerging New Right" in the 1970s.[7] Previously overlooked conversations in the Nixon tapes and recently disclosed documents in the Nixon papers reconnect these studies to the development of affirmative action as public policy. These sources shine a light on a part of labor history that union leaders have never wanted to acknowledge—that some conservative labor leaders, rather than being the victims of identity politics, cultivated and benefited from a class consciousness that was exclusively white and male. Although the hard hat alliance collapsed in the wake of the Watergate scandal, the heroic quality that Nixon imparted to the defection of white working-class men from the Democratic Party allowed Nixon and the unions to reconnect opposition to the civil rights movement with mainstream discourses of U.S. liberalism that persist to this day. They did this not by opposing civil rights laws per se but by finding common cause in making the law unenforceable.

Subverting the Revised Philadelphia Plan

The Philadelphia Plan fused the politics of civil rights and union-busting rather than treating the former as a smokescreen for the latter. Although acting in response to African American protest movements, Nixon's Department of Labor had its own multiple and independent motivations for taking the unprecedented step of imposing involuntary affirmative action requirements on the construction industry in 1969. Republicans had a long-standing hostility to the powerful building trades unions and the Democratic Party machine politics they helped prop up in cities across the country. Labor Secretary George Shultz believed that bypassing the construction industry apprenticeship programs would increase the labor supply and put downward pressure on wages that could spur new construction, create more jobs, and curb government spending. And Shultz had a complementary commitment to make jobs available to racial minorities in a civil rights program that would supposedly reduce the need for welfare.[8]

Nixon tentatively embraced the revival of the Philadelphia Plan by the Department of Labor for these reasons, as well as to reduce inflation.[9] It was not until a few months after the Department of Labor had initiated the revival of the Philadelphia Plan, when union resistance became fierce, that Nixon became interested in its potential to exacerbate conflict between two of the key constituencies of the Democratic Party—white union members and African Americans.[10] But from late 1969 through early 1971, even that idea was tentative, contested, and not well thought out.

As the Nixon administration charted this uncertain course, it created what Hugh Davis Graham, an historian of affirmative action policy, has described as policy "incoherence," or contradictory tendencies. Only in retrospect were these contradictions clearly resolved into what we might call classic Nixonian politics: preempt your enemies' agendas to confound their expectations, divide their loyalties, defer follow-through to a divided electorate, and then gain new followers by blaming the policy for its own failure to produce a compromise. With the federal government moving in multiple directions at once, local struggles informed the creation of new political blocs. And battles within the Nixon administration over the enforcement of the Philadelphia Plan became increasingly heated as interest groups—particularly within organized labor—began to pressure the administration.[11]

Nixon did not have a preconceived plan to impose affirmative action when he was first elected president. But when he tapped Arthur Fletcher to be his undersecretary of labor for wage and labor standards in spring 1969, he inadvertently set change in motion. Fletcher, a black Republican who had run a strong but unsuccessful race for lieutenant governor of Washington state in 1968, was one of few black Republicans whose career seemed to be on the rise at the time. Fletcher had served in leadership roles in Kansas and California Republican Party politics in the 1950s and 1960s, including a stint on Nixon's presidential campaign in California in 1960. He had moved to the Tri-Cities, Washington, in 1965, where he promoted fair employment at the Hanford Nuclear Power Reservation, administered a War on Poverty job-training program, and was elected to the Pasco City Council. Signaling his commitment to take leadership of Nixon's fair employment politics, Fletcher attached two conditions to his appointment:

(1) that equal employment be considered a "labor standard" (implicitly within the purview of his job title), and (2) that, because the OFCC would be reporting directly to him and not to the Secretary of Labor as it had previously, he be given the power to appoint the new OFCC director.[12]

The OFCC had a credibility problem among civil rights organizations when Fletcher arrived. The National Association for the Advancement of Colored People (NAACP) had recently accused the small and ineffectual OFCC of being captive to "bigoted labor unions" because, under the Lyndon Johnson administration, it had drafted but then refused to implement the Philadelphia Plan. In addition, nearly two decades of aggressive criticism of racism in the building trades unions by NAACP Labor Relations Director Herbert Hill, along with open and steadfast refusal by the unions to compromise, had made these unions, according to Fletcher, "the central symbol for our time of the quest for equality in employment opportunity."[13]

Having set out to change the image of the OFCC, Fletcher quickly rose to become the most outspoken advocate of the Philadelphia Plan. In that role, he became, according to the *Washington Post*, "the go between for any black, Chicano, or Indian who tries to deal with the Nixon administration." Fletcher personally announced the issuance of the Revised Philadelphia Plan during a press conference in Philadelphia on June 27, 1969. The Revised Plan took effect in the city of Philadelphia immediately, but Fletcher also claimed that the plan "will be put into effect in all the major cities across the Nation as soon as possible."[14]

According to William Gould, professor of fair employment law, between late June and September 1969, during the comment period before the Philadelphia Plan could be expanded to other cities, "the winds of Philadelphia were being felt throughout the land." Mass protests by African Americans in cities around the country demanded the immediate expansion of the Philadelphia Plan, forcing both Democratic and Republican elected officials at the local level to reach out to the Department of Labor for help with "crisis management." Fletcher then positioned himself to reinforce support for the Philadelphia Plan as the only way to resolve the urban crisis.[15]

The resistance of the building trades unions to the Philadelphia Plan and its expansion was immediate and intense. Union leaders marshaled their allies in the Department of Labor and Congress in an attempt to quash the plan. They also organized massive counterdemonstrations against the extension of the plan to other cities, at which they demanded compensation for wages lost during the protests and called on politicians to use the police to protect their workplaces. When contractors and freedom movement activists negotiated ad hoc affirmative action deals across the country in anticipation of federal intervention, union members raised the specter of hate strikes by walking off the job. In all these activities, union leaders claimed to be color-blind, championed the token and often ineffectual minority preapprenticeship plans they had adopted to deflect criticism, and stated that they opposed the Philadelphia Plan's bypassing of government-certified apprenticeship programs and collective bargaining rights.

The union criticism of freedom movement activists as the misguided tools of corporate interests revived old stereotypes of black workers as union-busters and enabled overt racism to come to the fore during union-led counterdemonstrations. Protests by the building trades unions in Pittsburgh in August and September 1969 were especially hostile. In Pittsburgh, after a protest by a few hundred the day before, over 4,000 white construction workers demonstrated on August 29, 1969. They invoked labor politics by wearing hard hats and demanding wages lost during the protests. But many carried signs and chanted slogans supporting arch-segregationist George Wallace for president in 1972, putting on display what one commentator called "labor's double standard" in conflating union rights with racial privilege. Similar protests of thousands of workers—with a pageantry of U.S. flags and inverted black freedom movement slogans such as "equal rights for whites" and "we build not burn"—took place in Chicago in September, in Seattle in October, and elsewhere on a smaller scale during fall 1969.[16]

It was in Chicago where the confluence of the national politics of the Philadelphia Plan and local resistance from the building trades unions was most intense. Fletcher convened public hearings in Chicago in September 1969 to provide a legal foundation for the expansion of the Philadelphia Plan to other cities. Yet his first attempt to hold a hearing was stifled when hundreds of construction workers, seemingly with the assent of the Chicago police, filled the hotel conference room where the meeting was being held, causing the meeting to be canceled. Afterward, according to Fletcher, "the management of the hotel asked us not to hold the hearing and, in effect, told us to get out, because of the trouble." Workers' angry catcalls and jostling of his entourage portended violence. Fletcher later learned that the Federal Bureau of Investigation (FBI) had picked up rumors of a contract put out on his life. "Here in Chicago," he recalled, "the apparent helplessness of the federal government would destroy not only the EEO [Equal Employment Opportunity] program but many other programs as well. It could not be that a mass of hard hats could stop the federal government from functioning." Fletcher successfully reconvened the hearings under federal guard on federal property, but he and black activists required police escorts to keep from being assaulted. Fighting later broke out outside among blacks, union members, and police.[17]

The firestorm that Fletcher weathered in Chicago had a transformative effect on him. He described his experience as a moment when he "faced the elementary forces of life, racism and fear of loss of jobs," resulting in a battle of "naked power."[18] With his illusions thus stripped from him about what would be required to overcome resistance to affirmative action, he became an unabashed opponent of the building trades unions. Removed from the context of his experience in Chicago, Fletcher's criticism of labor-union racism has often been misconstrued as evidence that he was antiunion; actual evidence for such accusations is sketchy.[19] Believing that Chicago presented a northern form of massive resistance, Fletcher viewed the hearings there as a historic breakthrough for racial equality and as a confirmation of his belief that only the Republican Party could help blacks achieve equal economic opportunity.

Yet Nixon's commitment to the Philadelphia Plan, as Fletcher probably knew but did not admit, was uneven. Nixon was well aware that he had received little support from black voters during his campaign and that George Wallace's strong showing in 1968 demonstrated a growing backlash against the enforcement of civil rights law. Having been elected president of the United States with 43 percent of the popular vote, Nixon spent his first term in office obsessed with creating a "new majority" for the Republican Party.[20]

Invoking presidential privilege to enforce executive orders, the White House effectively beat back the opposition to the Philadelphia Plan in Congress before the 1969 Christmas holiday. But it did not take long before Nixon reconsidered his actions. During and after the 1968 election, Kevin Phillips, Republican Party strategist, had advised Nixon to pursue a "Southern strategy" by appealing to segregationist Democrats to switch their party allegiance to the Republican Party, popularizing the idea after the election in his book, *The Emerging Republican Majority*. During the winter holiday, Nixon read Phillips's book, and in early January he told his aide H. R. Haldeman to "use Phillips as an analyst—study his strategy—don't think in terms of old-time ethnics, go for Poles, Italians, Irish, must learn to understand Silent Majority....don't go for Jews and Blacks."[21]

As pressure from the construction unions grew, the White House showed signs of retreat on the Philadelphia Plan, even though it had successfully divided liberal Democrats. On January 11, 1970, George Meany, the executive secretary of the American Federation of Labor–Congress of Industrial Organizations (AFL-CIO) and a plumber from New York City, held a press conference at which he dismissed the Philadelphia Plan as "bunk" and as an attempt to win "brownie points" from civil rights groups. On January 13, Nixon, reading a news summary of Meany's remarks, uncomfortably noted, "this hurts us. With our constituency we gained little on the play." On January 28, Nixon met with Richard Scammon, coauthor of *The Real Majority*, to discuss how "the social issue" (which Phillips summarized as concern about "law and order, permissiveness, campus anarchy, [and] racial engineering") could be tapped to galvanize the "silent majority."

During the meeting, Nixon praised Meany for his "guts and courage." Two months later, in a meeting with prominent academics from around the country at Harvard University, Nixon complained, according to the *Washington Post,* that "there is little political gain" in civil rights advocacy and that the Philadelphia Plan "was giving him no credit among Negroes." The day after the meeting, a January 1970 memo from Daniel Patrick Moynihan, a Nixon advisor, recommending that the president pursue a policy of "benign neglect" toward African Americans was leaked to the press. By April, Nixon had become even more cynical, telling Haldeman that the only blacks who would work with him were "Uncle Toms, and we should work on them and forget militants."[22]

It was in this context of fierce union resistance, Nixon's cynicism about civil rights, and his desire to reach out to a "silent majority," that the Department of Labor quietly subverted the Philadelphia Plan. In late September 1969, Fletcher had announced that the Department of Labor sought to extend the Philadelphia Plan to nine other cities: New York, Chicago, Pittsburgh, Detroit, Boston, St. Louis, San Francisco, Los Angeles, and Seattle. But the OFCC at the time had only twelve contract compliance officers for a decentralized industry with thousands of employers and millions of seasonal employees.[23] In the face of massive resistance in the North, Secretary of Labor George Shultz lacked the administrative capacity and political will to impose affirmative action orders across the country. So he used the threat of an imposed plan to inspire the negotiation of voluntary, local, hometown solutions on a city-by-city basis.

Whether Shultz shifted the expansion of the Philadelphia Plan from imposed plans to voluntary ones at the behest of the White House is unclear. As early as August 11, 1969, Fletcher himself acknowledged, "the federal government simply cannot involve itself in manpower planning in every city in the country. It cannot even develop the framework—a Philadelphia Plan—for every city in the country. It doesn't have the resources, and basically it's not the right level of government anyway." What affirmative action had thus initiated was a fierce debate over what constituted the "right level of government." By March 1970, Nixon began providing an answer by defending hometown plans to building trades union leaders as the kind of "voluntary approach" to affirmative action he stood for.[24]

The capitulation by the Department of Labor to Mayor Daley's political machine in Chicago months after the September hearings showed just how ineffective the voluntarism of the Nixon administration would be. The Department of Labor certified the Chicago hometown plan—the second such plan after Boston—on January 12, 1970. The plan was a success in principle because it included "minority community" representatives in construction industry labor negotiations, extended OFCC power to regulate private industry as well as federal contracts, and enabled the Department of Labor's Manpower Administration to fund the plan. But the blueprint for negotiating hometown plans was fatally weakened by the certification of the Chicago Plan. Fletcher himself was at pains to explain to reporters why the voluntary Chicago Plan lacked the craft-specific hiring goals of the Philadelphia Plan and lacked its penalties for not meeting these vague goals.[25] With Chicago minority community representatives rendered ineffective by Daley machine pressure, the Department of Labor certified a plan that subverted the whole point of affirmative action—to set measurable goals so as to punish noncompliance when voluntary desegregation failed.

Just as it was watering down the Philadelphia Plan, the Department of Labor also weakened the broader affirmative action decree modeled after it. Less than two weeks after issuing Order No. 4, the Department of Labor qualified its requirement that all federal contractors meet statistical benchmarks for hiring nonwhite workers to, according to the *New York Times*, "take into account the availability and eligibility of minority group workers."[26] The order still inspired the adoption of contract compliance programs by local and state governments across the country, but the enforcement of those programs could now be subject to further bias, debate, equivocation, and delay.

The Nixon administration had thus established the legal foundation for affirmative action while simultaneously backing away from its enforcement. This set the stage for chaotic battles that fused the emerging culture war with debates over the limits of federal government authority. When Secretary Shultz announced the extension of the Philadelphia Plan to nineteen more cities on February 9, 1970, the threat remained heavily, although not totally, symbolic.[27] Local building trades unions, although publicly howling against racial quotas, still had the ability to hollow out the substance of those plans, using their negotiating savvy to make the plans weak and unenforceable. Or, because the hometown plans required the assent of all parties, the unions or contractors could simply drag the negotiations on interminably. By refusing even basic concessions as violations of collective bargaining agreements or employer prerogatives, they pushed the meaning of voluntary cooperation to its limit and challenged the Department of Labor to impose a plan that it could not enforce. Both forms of resistance were especially prevalent before October of 1971, when legal challenges to the Philadelphia Plan were exhausted when the Supreme Court declined to rule the plan unconstitutional.[28]

This resistance to the Philadelphia Plan sapped the energy from the direct action campaigns of 1969 by initiating interminable negotiations that produced few immediate concessions. When the plans failed to meet their weak goals or when negotiations stalled, internal divisions within the local civil rights coalitions often became more intense, as groups wanting to administer the plans (usually allied with organized labor or the Urban League) found themselves at odds with more insurgent and activist voices in the black community. Multiracial coalitions of nonwhite men seeking access to the trades were also strained in places such as Chicago and New York as differences over how confrontational they should be inflamed preexisting tensions between minority communities.

The Department of Labor had set itself up for failure. It was reticent to impose the plans or void federal contracts in the face of rampant noncompliance, but it was too understaffed and ill-equipped to impose more specific penalties on unions or contractors who openly violated its plans. "We were soldiers fighting a lost cause," Fletcher reflected four years later. "The result was two years lost, a long series of futile and fruitless negotiations, no really successful Plans, and a new and deeper level of bitterness in the black community."[29]

Despite Fletcher's frustration, the existence of the Philadelphia Plan and the threat of imposed plans still provided activists around the country with some leverage to force moderate concessions through the hometown plan process. In addition, the Philadelphia Plan and Order No. 4 pushed state, county, and local government agencies—as the major recipients of federal funds—to set up their own nondiscrimination laws and contract compliance programs, some of which were stronger than federal law. This, in turn, provided minority and also some women activists another means to gain entry to professions historically reserved for white men. Even if none of the plans could be considered a success, they produced hundreds of new fronts in the war against the politics of whiteness and masculinity that had long rationalized economic inequality in the United States.

Absent aggressive government support and without full employment programs to lessen the stakes of desegregation, activists seeking to transform the U.S. workplace during the 1970s faced poor odds. As the economy entered a recession in 1970, the Nixon administration added to the woes of the construction industry by cutting federal construction spending by 75 percent.[30] The Department of Labor hometown plan "goals" for minority hiring—focused largely on federal contracts, based on the percentage of nonwhite people in the population, and independent of the variable cycles of the construction industry—further increased unemployment for white construction workers while providing remarkably few jobs for nonwhite workers.

It was in this context that, during 1970 and 1971, local on-the-job resistance by white workers to affirmative action in the construction industry spread like wildfire while the federal government proved either unwilling or unable to stop it. As in Seattle (Griffey, chap. 7 in this volume), white workers hazed nonwhite workers until they left the job or simply gave nonwhite workers nothing to do and refused to teach them the trade. Contractors, meanwhile, moved nonwhite workers from job to job to keep multiple sites in what was cynically referred to as "paper compliance." Because hell came to those who fought, graft and mismanagement (most spectacularly in Chicago and Pittsburgh) became the paths of least resistance in the face of open resistance to new, nonwhite, non-union labor entering the construction workplace through affirmative action. The hometown plan system made it easy for nonwhite workers who showed up to jobs but made no effort to learn, and it rewarded administrators who certified such dishonesty as "affirmative action." But with the goals met only on paper and corruption rampant, no one was satisfied. As a result, a shared disillusionment in government grew as the law was flouted on all sides. Animosity over this state of affairs on the job provides a crucial context for understanding the significance of the hard hat revolt of the early 1970s.

Naming the Backlash: The Invention of the Hard Hat

John Ehrlichman, Nixon's aide in charge of his domestic policy, later recalled the enthusiasm with which the White House saw white and black workers fighting over the Philadelphia Plan.[31] But how open to be about setting these two major Democratic Party constituents against one another, and how far to pursue it, was never agreed on.[32] Beginning in spring 1970, books such as *The Emerging Republican Majority* and *The Real Majority* and a Department of Labor report titled "The Problem of the Blue-Collar Worker" provoked a spirited debate within the Nixon administration about whether and how to appeal to organized labor—a debate that continued through the rest of 1970 and was not resolved until mid-1971.

This debate over Nixon's relationship to the white working class became increasingly urgent on May 8, 1970. That day, hundreds of New York City construction workers descended from the buildings they were working on to viciously attack anti–Vietnam War protesters. The protesters were marching through Wall Street to protest Nixon's invasion of Cambodia and the shooting of four student protesters at Kent State on May 4. Wielding construction tools and wearing hard hats, the construction workers violently dispersed the protest and then marched on City Hall to demand that city leaders fully hoist the flag (it was at half mast for the Kent State victims). More construction workers, seemingly coordinated, arrived in waves to join the attacks, swelling the mob's ranks to as many as five hundred as they shouted patriotic chants and assaulted long-haired people whom they assumed were opposed to the Vietnam war. After leaving City Hall, the mob attacked students at Pace College and chased bloodied and beaten victims of the melee into Trinity Church, where they ripped down the church Red Cross banner and twice tried to break through its gates. The unprovoked rampage lasted four hours and left over seventy people injured, some very seriously—including a twenty-nine-year-old Democratic candidate for State Senate, who was rushed to the hospital with "his right eye completely closed, a large welt on his head, and five boot marks were imprinted on his back where he had been stomped after he was down."[33]

The riot had clearly been planned, but by whom and to what degree have never been proven. A seemingly more spontaneous event had occurred the day before, when several dozen construction workers reportedly threw debris at antiwar protesters on Wall Street. But on May 8, according to *The Nation*, workers had been paid during their time off work (some reports claimed they were paid as much as double a regular day's wage). The police knew the attack was coming ahead of time, but did not intervene or make any arrests. Workers had U.S. flags at the ready for their violent march. And "agents of a small, right-wing sheet, the New York *Graphic*" were immediately on the scene distributing handbills and giving orders and speeches through megaphones. The *Wall Street Journal* reported that one worker "who said his life would be in danger if he was identified, claimed the attack was organized by shop stewards with the support of some contractors. He said one contractor offered his men cash bonuses to join the fray."[34]

White House outreach to the union leaders following the riot was extremely swift. The day after the Kent State shootings, Charles "Chuck" Colson, the special counsel to the president tasked with cultivating interest group support for Nixon, went to work. Colson met with Jay Lovestone, the head of the AFL-CIO International Affairs Division and an ardent anticommunist whom Colson later described as "too hard-line [about détente] for reason." At the meeting, the two discussed a plan to get the formal endorsement of the AFL-CIO for the Vietnam War. As Colson sought labor movement support, the president avoided Washington, D.C., and worried those close to him by engaging in erratic behavior as waves of student strikes against the war closed universities and gripped the nation.[35]

Conservative members of the AFL-CIO, concerned by the growing radicalization of the labor movement, began reaching out to the White House to offer their support. As Philip Foner documented, Nixon's escalation of the war to Cambodia "brought into the antiwar movement huge sections of the trade unions never before involved in such protests." In the San Francisco Bay Area, even building trades union leaders and Teamsters joined the regional labor movement to demand an immediate cease-fire in Vietnam. The death on May 9 of the potentially most prominent labor movement spokesperson against the war, United Auto Workers (UAW) President Walter Reuther, reduced the visibility of the growing antiwar sentiment in the labor movement, but the AFL-CIO still felt it had to respond to the antiwar activism within labor. As a result, on May 13 the AFL-CIO Executive Council officially endorsed the Vietnam War.[36]

Although the AFL-CIO presented its endorsement as a nonpartisan patriotic act, Nixon's advisers treated it and the construction worker riot as a potentially historic breakthrough for the Republican Party. Tom Huston, White House deputy counsel, captured this feeling with impassioned memos calling for the aggressive courting of organized labor because the hard hat violence provided the only real evidence of grassroots support for Nixon. On May 12, Huston wrote to the president's aides demanding that they block any Department of Justice inquiry into the riot. On May 13, he explained, "what we saw in New York on Friday was the first manifestation of a willingness to fight for the America the blue-collar American loves," adding that "the greatest bulwark against revolution in America is the working class" and "we need to quit talking about the great Silent Majority and start talking to it."[37]

Meanwhile, New York building trades union leaders, stigmatized by accusations of racism and under pressure from Mayor John Lindsay and the Department of Labor to desegregate, were emboldened by their new celebrity status. In the week following the riot, Peter Brennan, head of the New York City Building and Construction Trades Council, accelerated his pro-war organizing among the 200,000 council members and over 110 union locals. On May 11 and 12, thousands of construction workers "roamed through Lower Manhattan in organized bands," occasionally assaulting passersby, as some downtown workers cheered. On May 15, the crowds became more diverse as between 2,500 and 5,000 "construction workers, longshoremen, and white-collar workers" marched together through the New York financial district. The *New York Times* later reported that the workers' march received a "'Hero' Welcome": "There was applause, confetti and data tape from the Wall street canyons at times, as if the hard hats were hero astronauts."[38]

Meanwhile, Brennan announced plans for a massive march in New York on May 20 and worked with other building trades leaders to encourage similar demonstrations elsewhere to "set an example to the rest of the country and be a source of inspiration to our men overseas." The White House, which had already been considering Reverend Billy Graham's advice that Nixon stage a "pro-America rally" to counter the antiwar protests, supported the march, with Lovestone serving as liaison between Brennan and Colson during the lead-up. But the organizing came mainly from the New York Building Trades Council, with support from Thomas "Teddy" Gleason, head of the International Longshoremen Association (ILA).[39]

The resulting demonstration on May 20 was massive, mobilizing over 100,000 construction workers (who were encouraged by their unions to wear hard hats) and their allies. The pageantry of the march combined the celebration of militaristic patriotism, masculine toughness, and working-class populism. It marshaled a striking imagery that, whether viewed as creeping fascism or a restoration of moral order, most observers saw as a portentous rupture with 1960s liberalism. Heeding New York leaders' call for solidarity, thousands of construction workers in Buffalo, Pittsburgh, and San Diego organized similar marches, some of which were marred by violence against antiwar counterdemonstrators.[40]

The New York march deeply impressed White House officials, with Colson later referring to it as "a seminal event." Steven Bull, Nixon White House staffer, wrote to Charles Colson afterward, speculating that "Obviously, more of these will be occurring throughout the Nation, perhaps partially as a result of your clandestine activity." He added approvingly, "This display of emotional activity from the 'hard hats' provides an opportunity, if under the proper leadership, to forge a new alliance and perhaps result in the emergence of a 'new right.'"[41]

It was an opportunity soon seized, with Colson anointing himself the "custodian of our Hard Hat constituency"—a position through which he gained increasing power within the White House. At Colson's suggestion, the president personally thanked Brennan for organizing the May 20 march. Colson then set a meeting between Nixon and New York City building trade union leaders "to present a hard hat to the President...as the symbol of freedom." This was done, Colson later recalled, over the "almost a unanimous opposition" of White House staff, who saw the move as crass "pandering." Before the meeting, Colson advised the president to not mention the riot because "The construction workers, while a symbol to most Americans of loyalty and patriotism, are also a symbol to some of repression and anti-intellectualism." Instead, Colson counseled Nixon to "express your appreciation for their demonstration of loyalty to the country (I would recommend emphasizing country rather than this Administration since many of these men feel that the Secretary of Labor has not been friendly and they disagree with some of our labor policies)."[42]

Nixon's meeting with New York construction union leaders provided the presidential imprimatur to the hard hat movement. By seizing on the hard hat iconography, he disassociated the movement from its vigilante origins to make construction workers the representatives of a "silent majority" that had previously been a political abstraction. With this encouragement, and probably behind-the-scenes coordination, hard hat marches (and violence) soon spread to other cities, many with the sponsorship of the AFL-CIO Building and Construction Trades Council. On May 31 in Tempe, Arizona, approximately 300 construction workers violently waded into an antiwar rally of 2,000, requiring more than 100 police to break up the resulting fistfights. On June 8, 45,000 construction workers paraded through the streets of St. Louis to show their support for the war and assaulted antiwar protesters who dared display dissent. On June 11, building trades union leaders in Seattle staged a Civil Responsibility Rally, bringing together 2,500 construction workers, police officers, and their families to protest "a complete breakdown of law enforcement" in the supposed coddling of antiwar protesters and black militants (they failed to get the 14,000 they had hoped would attend). On June 15, roughly 75 percent of Baltimore's construction trade union members marched along with firemen in a parade of 15,000 people to honor the flag, support the war, and oppose both the New Left and hippie counterculture. On June 25, Nixon staff sought to finally add his presence to these movements by organizing a massive pro-Nixon parade and rally of tens of thousands of people in St. Louis to celebrate "what is right about America." The event, meant to stage Nixon's supposed popularity in "Middle America," relied in part on Ironworker Union President John Lyons's "building a crowd" at the last minute.[43]

By the end of June, the cumulative effect of one month of aggressive pro-police, pro–Vietnam War events took hold. Throughout the rest of 1970, the term *hard hat* spread like wildfire through the popular culture to become what the *Washington Post* described as a "new political catch-all label" to describe a structure of feeling for the New Right. Hard hats became symbols of opposition to the New Left and support for the Vietnam War, reframing a broader cultural war already underway. Although Merle Haggard had released his antihippie anthem "Okie from Muskogee" in 1969, it was not until after the events of May 1970 that the press began to refer to Haggard as the "poet laureate of the hard hats." Innumerable newspaper pieces about everything from hard hat hairstyles to film characters proliferated in the months and years that followed. Through them, working-class conservatives—and often the whole white working class—were celebrated or stigmatized for supposedly having a hard hat aesthetic. So when the TV sitcom *All in the Family* launched in January of 1971, featuring a bigoted white male character named Archie Bunker, the immediate popularity of the show rested on its controversial portrayal of Bunker's "stereotyped, hard hat interpretation of modern morality."[44]

The power of the hard hat image came partly from its ideological flexibility but also from its expression of an explicitly male sensibility. Its populist anti-elitism evoked New Deal sensibilities, but its celebration of masculine force against the supposed excesses of liberal tolerance was distinctly reactionary. Brennan personally helped the White House understand the fundamentally emotive, gendered, and nonpartisan nature of the movement. Colson later wrote to Nixon describing Brennan's explanation "for the 'hard hat' support of you more perceptively than I think we have analyzed it."

> He said that the "hard hats" wave the flag and cheer the President but that, in and of itself, does not translate into votes. Moreover most of the "hard hats" don't like our economic policies and feel that we are pushing

them too hard in the civil rights area. What is winning their political loyalty is their admiration for your masculinity. The "hard hats", who are a tough breed, have come to respect you as a tough, courageous, man's man. Brennan's thesis is that this image of you will win their votes more than the patriotism theme.[45]

While the cultural politics of the hard hat movement took on a life of its own in popular culture, the first test of its political possibilities came during the 1970 mid-term elections. Following the hard hat march, some of the most powerful New York labor leaders began to offer their clandestine support for the Conservative Party campaign of James Buckley for U.S. Senate in 1970. Toward the end of June, Haldeman ordered Pat Buchanan, Nixon speech writer and adviser on outreach to Catholic voters, to "put someone on to the New York senate race…who can counsel Buckley on strategy and planning" by "going for the Catholic Democrats and the Nixon Republicans and really playing this up." By September, Colson was secretly organizing what he called "hardhat support for Buckley," facilitated by Brennan; Mike Maye, New York firefighter union leader; and others who were also engaged in what Colson cryptically called "political chicanery."[46]

Buckley's election as a pro-war third-party candidate and the willingness of the unions to organize their communities to break ranks with the Democratic Party deeply impressed Colson. Soon after, he began to obsessively follow internal discussions in the AFL-CIO in the hopes that he could facilitate the unlikely defection of the unions to Nixon in 1972. Lovestone nurtured Colson's hopes by providing him with information during biweekly meetings. Meanwhile, Colson became closer to conservative New York union leaders following Buckley's election. Colson was soon referring to Brennan as one of his union "spies" and listed Thomas Gleason, ILA president; Jesse Calhoun, Marine Engineers leader; and Harry Van Arsdale, Central Labor Council leader and former president of the International Brotherhood of Electrical Workers (IBEW) Local 3, as his other "lines of communication in New York." Politically speaking, this group of labor leaders, and especially Brennan, determined the shape of hard hat politics and Nixon's outreach to organized labor in the years that followed.[47]

Affirmative Action and the "Social Issue"

Despite Colson's union allies in New York, Nixon's support from organized labor decreased rather than increased during late 1970 and early 1971, mainly because of the worsening economy. The poor performance of Republicans in the 1970 elections, and the fewer-than-anticipated union votes for Republican Party candidates, inspired some White House officials to argue that the hard hat alliance had produced only marginal results and that it was time to "take the gloves off." As organized labor continued to criticize Nixon's economic policies during the first few months of 1971, these debates raged within the White House, and Nixon's domestic programs evolved in ways that were often at odds with one another.[48]

Nixon's choice in late February to suspend the Davis-Bacon guidelines, which required the federal government to pay prevailing (i.e., union) wages in the construction industry, brought the debate to a head.[49] Nixon's economic advisers worried about the control that the construction unions wielded to force high wage settlements (thereby driving up the cost of construction), which many felt contributed to inflation. But attacking one of the bedrocks of building trades union power drew open and intense criticism from George Meany of the AFL-CIO as well as other union leaders.

When Nixon sought to recoup his image by retreating to the "heartland" to stage a pro-Nixon rally in Des Moines, similar to St. Louis rally a year earlier, he confronted an ad hoc alliance that threatened to undermine his use of cultural politics to shield his economic policies from criticism. "An unusual joint protest of hard-hat construction men, antiwar students and angry farmers" organized itself in response to the President's visit, and subjected him to a barrage of boos, catcalls and even snowballs. The *Wall Street Journal* took note, reporting that "on recent trips around the country, Mr. Nixon has been picketed by angry groups of construction workers. Suspension of Davis-Bacon seemed to have undone all the administration's careful cultivation of the blue collar vote."[50]

The negative publicity spurred Colson to desperately reaffirm his connection with Brennan (who had publicly denounced the suspension of Davis-Bacon as "union busting" but had stopped short of personally criticizing the president).[51] Colson could not comprehend what he called the "Des Moines disaster," preferring instead to believe his union contacts, who reassured him that "many of the 'hard hats' were not, in fact, 'hard hats' but students posing as 'hard hats.'" Regardless, Colson pushed officials in the Nixon administration to schedule a meeting with New York building trades leaders in an attempt to "avoid a demonstration" there.[52] He also continued to work behind the scenes in an unsuccessful bid to have Brennan replace C. J. Haggerty as the head of the AFL-CIO Building and Construction Trades Council while also pushing for the president to meet directly with Brennan for the first time since the previous May.[53] The president held off for a few months, but Colson justified the importance of the meeting by explaining:

> Brennan has 250,000 building tradesmen under him in New York. He exercises tight, tough control; he can swing a large block of them politically as demonstrated in 1970: he strongly backed Rockefeller and

Buckley; even in a 3-way race Buckley got almost 50% of the blue collar vote in New York and heavily carried wards that Brennan "controls." [In January] Brennan told me that he would do for you in New York what he did for Rockefeller and Buckley.[54]

Just as Colson was seeking to salvage his union outreach, the negotiations in New York City over its prospective hometown plan broke down. A plan had been finalized in December 1970, but had a number of weaknesses as a result of the unions, contractors, and politicians locking civil rights groups out of the negotiations. The plan caused immediate outrage among freedom movement activists, who labeled it a fraud. Mayor Lindsay, swayed by the pressure, opposed the plan in January and requested that the Department of Labor not certify it. The New York negotiations descended into chaos as the unions refused to budge and the Lindsay administration blocked tens of millions of dollars of government construction contracts as the economy worsened.[55]

Art Fletcher and his staff refused to override Lindsay and certify the original affirmative action plan of the New York unions. OFCC Director John Wilks rejected the New York Plan as inadequate, citing it as a potentially bad precedent for other plans. Fletcher, meanwhile, decided that he needed to take action to salvage the entire Philadelphia Plan and hometown plan process—which meant not certifying any more unenforceable plans. "In the spring of 1971," Fletcher recalled, "the delay [in implementing hometown plans] had become intolerable to me." To boost enforcement, he oversaw a "stem-to-stern reorganization" of the OFCC, and increased the OFCC staff from twenty-six to ninety-six to enforce its hometown plans. He also expanded the scope of the Philadelphia Plan hiring goals to cover all projects—public or private—overseen by federal contractors. "I could say that we were ready, not only in the field of construction, but also in the rest of our area of responsibility, to become an effective law enforcement agency."[56]

But Fletcher was dispirited to see his entire program, not just the Philadelphia Plan, languish. At least ten federal government agencies and departments either willfully ignored OFCC mandates or refused to take remedial action when they were found to be in violation of rules requiring federal construction contractors to engage in affirmative action. "We were becoming another typically inactive agency," Fletcher recalled, "more concerned about our internal affairs, because we suffered the frustration of not being able to implement our program."[57]

So, Fletcher fired off a memo to the secretary and undersecretary of labor in February proposing a last-ditch effort to save the Philadelphia Plan and rescue the OFCC from irrelevance. In it he recommended the immediate imposition (rather than negotiation) of areawide plans in Chicago, St. Louis, and San

Francisco to put pressure on other cities to negotiate. He also argued for the development of a hometown plan for Atlanta to be used as a template for other southern cities (none of which had adopted voluntary plans).[58]

When Fletcher, at a March 12, 1971, conference of minority construction contractors, announced this push for a new round of imposed plans, he confirmed the worst fears of the building trades unions. "The era of union domination of the employment pattern in the construction industry is over," he told the audience and gloated, "the unions were whipped" when "the union movement was not able to kill off the Philadelphia Plan." With the attempts to get cities to voluntarily adopt the Philadelphia Plan struggling, Fletcher announced, "We shall impose plan after plan in cities where the hometown solution doesn't work, until we move toward the concept of a nationwide plan....And the craft unions no longer have the power—in Court, in Congress, or with the President—to stop such a plan."[59]

News of Fletcher's speech spread quickly, with newspapers announcing that a Nixon administration official had declared open war on the powerful building trades unions.[60] Union leaders were outraged and began circulating copies of the speech to building trades locals throughout the country as evidence of what they had long claimed—that the Philadelphia Plan was a Trojan horse for union-busting. In March and April, union leaders began openly calling for Nixon to fire Fletcher.[61] Behind the scenes, Donald Rodgers, New York construction union leader and Brennan protégé, sent an urgent letter to Nixon staff demanding a meeting. By the end of the month, Rodgers delivered the message that the New York building trades unions were now calling in their favors. They wanted the New York Plan—which Fletcher and his staff had refused to approve—certified by the Department of Labor. They demanded "a 'yes' or 'no' answer" and wanted it now.[62]

When Fletcher then announced that new plans would be imposed in San Francisco, St. Louis, Chicago, Atlanta, Detroit, Buffalo, Houston, and Miami in time for the 1972 election, he gave Colson the pretense he needed to fire him. "I think I understand basic arithmetic," Colson bitterly complained to Haldeman.

> We got less than 10% of the black vote last time and I do not think we will get any more next time. We had close to 40% of the labor vote (higher among construction workers) last time and we could do better, except that we appear to be trying not to....
>
> I don't want to argue the merits. I am sure that the Department and Mr. Fletcher are absolutely right. I am equally convinced that this is political dynamite especially when one recognizes that George Meany is a hard-hat and regards the building trades as the heart of organized labor. We must deal with this.[63]

On May 7, 1971, Colson took his message to the president. In a phone call, ostensibly to prepare Nixon for a meeting later that day with Meany, Colson attempted to sway Nixon to rein in Fletcher. "Of course, the building trades need...some modification," Nixon responded. "They are ingrown and so forth. But hell. Why fight that battle? That's somebody else's problem. There's no votes in it for us." With the Philadelphia Plan, Colson added, "we turn off the Italian carpenters in Pittsburgh and the Irish in New York. San Francisco, Chicago. Everywhere where they're strong, and they've been for us. And they are for us." During his meeting with Meany later in the day, Nixon promised "that this administration is not going to be a party to anything which is detrimental to the building trades," although Meany had expressed only passing interest in the issue, focusing his attention on foreign policy and the economy.[64]

Soon after Nixon's meeting with Meany, Fletcher found his plan to redeem affirmative action mired in roadblocks and delays. He followed through on his threat and imposed an affirmative action plan on the San Francisco Bay Area; he also resisted pressure to certify the New York Plan. But "within the Labor Department," Fletcher recalled, "bureaucratic maneuvers continued to attempt to restrict my authority. The pressures from unions in the construction industry continued to mount."[65]

Colson was the key conduit of such pressure. On May 14, one week after he had failed to convince Ehrlichman to force Fletcher to certify the New York Plan, Colson sent him an almost hysterical follow-up memo. Colson demanded that the White House kill Fletcher's plan to rejuvenate the Philadelphia Plan, calling it "the most critical political question that we face with respect to our relationship with the building trades unions." Colson, later that month, complained, "we are on the verge of being irreparably damaged with the 'hard hats' even though 6 months ago this represented one of our most fertile fields for political gain." By June, he became desperate, complaining in an "eyes only" memo to Ehrlichman on June 7 that White House efforts to certify the New York Plan "are being sabotaged."[66]

Colson's constant lobbying and his emphasis on the damage done by Fletcher's attack of the icons of the new majority as racist finally won Nixon over. By the end of June, the question was not whether to get rid of Fletcher but how. In a conversation during which Colson was prepping Nixon for a meeting with Brennan on July 2, 1971, Colson and Nixon talked about the plan to remove Fletcher from the Department of Labor and put him in a powerless advisory committee on urban affairs. Nixon added that before Fletcher left Colson had to "get the New York Plan approved. Get something approved before the meeting [with Brennan] if you can." Colson responded by saying, "The Fletcher news is probably the biggest thing we could do for them. When that happens, they'll understand it." Nixon concluded the conversation about Fletcher's firing by noting approvingly, "that will be so we can produce something for Brennan."[67]

When Brennan met with Nixon later that day for an "off the record private talk," he handed Nixon a frank, one-page memo that described Nixon's affirmative action program as the single largest barrier preventing craft unions and the Republican Party from joining forces to oppose the New Left.[68] The memo, which the president wrote on as he read it, described the U.S. labor movement as "one of the strongest bulwarks against communism....were it not for the Building Trades it is safe to assume that American Labor would be on the extreme left and highly politically oriented." Next to Brennan's claim that "The political forces on the left (both within and without the labor movement) must cripple the Building Trades and reduce their influence in the whole of the Labor Movement in order to dominate that Labor Movement (and eventually the government of the U.S.)," Nixon wrote "Absolutely *true.*" Where Brennan wrote that the hard hat riot had "scared hell out of the leftists," Nixon wrote "correct," although Brennan's sentence continued: "and pointed up the need for the dismemberment of the Building Trades as a force in America!...The attack plan has been to use the racial issue to put the Building Trades 'out of business.'" "Unfortunately," Brennan wrote, "it's working."

> The Building Trades are being persecuted, prosecuted and murdered—and it's all being done in the name of Richard Nixon....If the picture is not immediately reversed, Richard Nixon *inadvertently* must be credited with crushing the Building Trades, destroying a free Labor Movement (economically motivated) and bringing about a politically motivated (European) *non-American* Labor Movement.[69]

But Brennan had no need to worry. During their conversation, Nixon explained his decision to fire Fletcher and certify the New York Plan in roundabout fashion, disavowing a quid pro quo and thanking Brennan for his support for Nixon's foreign policy. "You fellas came to our need when frankly, the business community did not, the education community did not, and the great newspapers did not, except for a few...and I am aware of that."[70]

Brennan's cultural politics—which, in the name of fighting communism at home and abroad, invoked economic populism to repress rather than join forces with the antiwar left and black freedom movement—shaped Nixon's outreach to organized labor as a whole. Three weeks after meeting with Brennan, the president and his top aides met to finally resolve the debate within the White House over his blue-collar strategy. Confirming where Nixon stood on the labor question after over a year of debate and two years of going in multiple directions at once, the president, according to Colson's notes, "said that the farmers and the hard hats represent 'whatever is left of the character of this country.' . . . Regardless of the politics, he held it vital that we continue to recognize and work with this group and that we not attack unions which represent the organized structure of the working man."[71]

The subsequent retreat from affirmative action was swift. The Department of Labor certified the New York Plan on August 11, 1971. In September, Fletcher was transferred out of the Department of Labor and became the U.S. alternative representative to the United Nations—a position he quit less than three months later, joining the exodus of high-profile black appointees from Nixon's first-term administration. When Labor Secretary Hodgson nominated Lowell Perry, an auto industry executive from Detroit, to replace Fletcher, Colson successfully blocked Perry's appointment solely because he was black. As Ehrlichman explained to Nixon, Colson "is just adamant . . . [that] the blacks should not be administering the Philadelphia Plan at least for a while until we get well with the unions."[72]

"Getting well with the unions" took far more than firing Arthur Fletcher and putting the kibosh on the administration's enforcement of affirmative action, however. In Fall 1971, James Suffridge, head of the Retail Clerks Union and a Nixon supporter, advised the White House that, because of outreach blunders and heavy-handed economic regulations, "our relationship with labor leadership has steadily deteriorated and is now at an all time low." Colson responded by working clandestinely to shore up support among organized labor while employing "dirty tricks" against Democratic Party presidential candidates. Colson also worried that George Meany wanted the Teamsters Union to rejoin the labor movement. Fearing that the ability of the Teamsters to "quietly work very hard for us, with money and organizational support" would be compromised if it rejoined the AFL-CIO, Colson successfully negotiated Nixon's pardon of former Teamsters President Jimmy Hoffa in December 1971.[73]

In spring 1972, Colson hired Donald Rodgers, who had negotiated the New York Plan with Brennan, to organize a Labor Committee for the Nixon reelection campaign. Colson hired Rodgers for his contacts with "building trades leaders in New York, New Jersey, Pennsylvania, Ohio and Illinois, the very labor constituencies that we need to make our major efforts with." But Colson also had Rodgers do favors for Nixon allies in the labor movement, including stifling a Department of Justice investigation into Jesse Calhoun's Marine Employees union; blocking a Department of Labor investigation into the election of Paul Hall, Seafarer union president; granting exemptions to wage freezes for Gleason's longshoremen; and providing assorted favors to Teamsters President Frank Fitzsimmons.[74]

How much Colson and Nixon knew about corruption in the unions they courted is unclear. When a small publication called *Scanlan's Monthly* documented the criminal backgrounds of the union leaders who met with President

Nixon after the hard hat riot, Colson, instead of refuting the charges or cut-ting ties with these labor leaders, teamed up with Brennan to drive *Scanlan's* out of business. In the New York construction industry, corruption became so pervasive in the 1970s and 1980s that James Jacobs, a law professor, labeled the city building trades unions a "cosa nostra fiefdom." State and federal govern-ment investigations during the 1980s documented the extent of labor racketeer-ing and mob ties—including Cosa Nostra control of some laborer union locals for half a century and the Genovese crime family's effective control of the Car-penters Union New York District Council. These facts lend credence to Larry Summers's difficult-to-verify claim that the New York Building Trades Council "was mob-linked, and Brennan routinely carried a loaded gun and traveled with bodyguards."[75]

But, regardless of what he knew, Nixon's bending of the law for the conser-vative unions raised the question of whether the labor support for Nixon was ultimately less about the "social issue" and more about seeking protection from the enforcement of the federal civil rights, labor, and racketeering laws. Playing hardball with the enemies of labor certainly emboldened Colson, who soon de-veloped a public swagger as Nixon's "hatchet-man." So when the OFCC director resigned in protest over the retreat of the Department of Labor from affirmative action in mid-1972, Colson, rather than suppressing the story, played it up. "The reason this guy is quitting," Colson told Rodgers,

> is because we are suppressing his minority hiring practices program. We are doing this because of your goddamn Building Trades. At least if we are going to have the Blacks up in arms at us, we ought to be getting some brownie points from the Pete Brennans of this world and oth-ers....we do have the Labor Department under control and it is now [John] Mitchell's job to get Justice under control. Can't you get some-one to write an article that Rodgers is hired, he's here a month and the head of OFCC resigns?[76]

With inside knowledge about the labor movement and contacts with con-servative union leaders in the building trades, Rodgers and Brennan proved in-valuable to the Nixon campaign. Together, they helped ensure that the AFL-CIO Building Trades Council remained neutral in the presidential election, built a coalition within the AFL-CIO to do the same, and helped secure individual en-dorsements from union locals and their leaders across the country.[77]

The success of Nixon's labor strategy should not be overstated. It would have been impossible to ensure union neutrality in the election had the Democratic Party presidential nominee supported the Vietnam War. Busing proved to be a much more charged issue than affirmative action during the 1972 election, with Dick Scammon, author of *The Real Majority,* secretly advising Colson to "exploit" the issue in "15 to 20 critical cities across the country" (which Colson often did by spreading false rumors to stir racial anxieties). And many white workers supported local Democrats while voting for Nixon in 1972. Yet Nixon's labor outreach still helped mold and give voice to dissidence among Democratic Party stalwarts. And his victory lent credence to his strategy of building a new Republican Party majority through cultural rather than economic politics. As the president watched the results come in on election night, he toasted Colson, reportedly saying, "Here's to you, Chuck. Those are your votes that are pouring in, the Catholics, the union members, the blue-collars, *your* votes, boy. It was your strategy and it's a landslide!"[78]

Nixon's Cultivation of Labor: Institutional and Cultural Legacies

Colson, exhausted by the campaign and worn down by questions regarding his role in the Watergate burglaries, nonetheless felt a sense of triumph. "I believe," he wrote the president immediately after the election, "we are on the threshold of one of the most significant realignments in American political history....We have cracked the solid foundation of the Democratic Party; its traditional base of labor, blue-collar, white ethnics have now become part of the Nixon Majority....Our challenge, it seems to me, is to convert the Nixon personal New Majority into a permanent institutional majority."[79]

The Department of Labor, he believed, could be a "magnificent vehicle for making the New Majority permanent." But, Colson believed, its nonpartisan reporting of the worsening state of the economy, its employment programs for minorities, and its prosecution of union corruption had supposedly made it a "disaster."[80]

Yet Nixon's celebration of Colson was overblown and fleeting. Colson wanted Nixon to appoint him secretary of labor "to direct more effort into 'our' constituents...not the deadbeat minority worker who cannot be helped by any amount of federal money and who will never be part of the Nixon Majority." But Nixon, wanting someone from the labor movement, opted instead to appoint Brennan. At the same time, Don Rodgers, the other major hard hat in the administration, stayed on in the White House as the consultant to the president for labor, drawing up a plan for transforming the Labor for Nixon committee into what Colson hoped would become a "permanent, continuing organization."[81]

From their new positions of power, the New York building trades union leaders deepened the institutional foundation of the backlash against affirmative action. As secretary of labor, Brennan shifted from departmental enforcement of fair employment executive orders to increased voluntarism and localism and overruled local affirmative action plans that had strict standards. He then decentralized OFCC functions throughout the Department of Labor. These institutional changes, and the cultural politics that Nixon used to rationalize them, had a lasting effect on U.S. politics despite the fact that neither Fletcher's, Brennan's, nor Colson's visions for the future survived Nixon's resignation and the aftershocks of the Watergate scandal.[82]

Absent support from the Department of Labor, the 1970s activist campaigns to the desegregate the U.S. workplace became increasingly dependent on (1) Title VII litigation, mediated by a court system that lacked the administrative capacity to enforce wide-ranging affirmative action decrees; (2) discrimination complaints submitted to the Equal Employment Opportunity Commission (EEOC), a weak and underfunded federal agency whose backlog of unresolved cases swelled into the hundreds of thousands by the mid-1970s; and (3) the enforcement of local fair employment laws to desegregate the U.S. workplace on a piecemeal rather than industrywide basis.[83]

Nixon, under pressure from Haldeman and Ehrlichman (who had long resented Colson's power and who sought to make him a scapegoat for the Watergate burglaries), pushed Colson out of the White House after the 1972 election. Betrayed, Colson returned to his law firm, where he was put on retainer by the Teamsters before being convicted for his role in the Watergate coverup. Colson's collapse mirrored the fate of his plans for a new majority. The electoral alliances that Nixon sought to solidify were discredited and disassembled by the Watergate scandal. President Gerald Ford responded by distancing himself from Nixon's allies in organized labor, and both he and Jimmy Carter purged the federal government of tainted Nixon appointees, including Brennan. A few prominent union members of Democrats for Nixon had been prosecuted for corruption during the 1972 election, but that trickle became a flood after Nixon resigned and the Departments of Justice and Labor resumed their prosecution of organized crime in the labor movement.[84]

Nixon's failure to create a new majority was still productive, however. His choice to adopt the union opposition to affirmative action contributed to a new language for U.S. politics that persisted well beyond his own political career. The hard hat–inspired alliance between white workers and the Nixon administration reframed the solidarities of whiteness around a coded rhetoric of color-blindness that had a national appeal. Framed as a backlash against the supposed excesses of Black Power and affirmative action, hard hat politics conveniently erased the history of the grassroots movements against open housing, school desegregation, fair employment, and police accountability. Framed as a working-class, white ethnic phenomenon, it downplayed the role that middle- and upper-class people of all ethnicities played in the supposed backlash against civil rights. Although not leading in any simplistic way to the creation of the Reagan Democrats or the culture wars of the 1980s and 1990s, hard hat politics provided a language for expressing the trauma of economic dislocation, blaming affirmative action instead of neoliberalism or deindustrialization for the decline of the middle class in the 1970s.

Perhaps one of the most bitter ironies of this new, post–civil rights cultural politics was how paltry its "wages of whiteness" were, how little the conservative unions and their members benefited from their defection from the Democratic Party. Workers who felt common cause with the Republican Party on the "social issue" were hardly prepared for the antiunion campaigns of the 1970s and 1980s. In the construction industry, business leaders and politicians—while paying lip service to hard hats in electoral politics—pushed to replace union journeymen with narrowly specialized and lower-paid nonunion workers throughout the construction industry from the late 1960s to the early 1980s. The long, bitter campaigns against affirmative action drew the resources and energy of the building trades unions away from effective responses to these challenges. And, as the economy worsened, many construction workers further hastened the erosion of the power of their unions by working nonunion jobs to make ends meet. The building trades unions have never recovered from these defeats, nor have they fully reckoned with the costs they incurred as defenders of a narrow vision of craft unionism.[85]

Yet, no matter how misleading hard hat stereotypes were or how little white men stood to gain from them, real construction workers and their unions helped create the hard hat image and were partly responsible for its effects. The unions and their leaders were not merely the victims of stereotypes in the media or of Nixon's cynical ambitions. Nixon's embrace of the hard hats was reactive and profoundly shaped by union leaders' protests and guidance. Nixon's betrayal of Fletcher and retreat from the Philadelphia Plan came at the request of union leaders. This retreat silently facilitated the coordinated appeals of the unions and the Republican Party to a patriotic white working class rather than a multiracial working class. Similar divisive campaigns for a supposedly color-blind economic populism continue to pit calls for equal opportunity against affirmative action, and class against racial justice, while giving us neither.

FROM JOBS TO POWER

The United Construction Workers
Association and Title VII Community
Organizing in the 1970s

Trevor Griffey

"We don't just want the jobs," Tyree Scott, the leader of the United Construction Workers Association (UCWA), announced in June 1972 to a group of one hundred black construction workers and their allies in Seattle, Washington. "We want some control over them."[1]

Scott's announcement, borne of two years of frustration with the way that on-the-job resistance had undermined affirmative action, marked a dramatic shift in the Seattle campaign for community control of the construction industry. It had been three years since Scott had led direct action protests in Seattle that inspired the U.S. Department of Justice to file suit against the four elite Seattle building trades unions. In 1970, federal Judge William Lindberg found the racially exclusive union hiring halls and apprenticeship programs in violation of Title VII of the 1964 Civil Rights Act. Because previous attempts to negotiate voluntary affirmative action had failed, Lindberg ordered the unions to desegregate through an ambitious affirmative action plan to train a total of roughly one hundred black "special apprentices" per year.[2] But during 1970–1972, the Seattle construction industry failed to meet the court-ordered affirmative action goals, and their noncompliance went largely unpunished. The unions and employers blamed the terrible economy, complaining that the region's affirmative action goals and timetables had not changed to reflect the recession in the construction industry. The UCWA, formed in 1970 to represent black workers who entered the Seattle construction industry under the court order, had a different explanation. It questioned the very structure of affirmative action plans that relied on white journeymen and employers to train people whose presence on the job they deeply resented. The original sin of affirmative action, the UCWA argued, was that it put racists in control of the desegregation process. Or, as Tyree Scott put it, "you can't leave those who created the problem in charge of the solution."[3]

The UCWA responded to the failure by the unions and employers to comply with the court order by demanding that black workers be made the subjects and not merely the objects of antidiscrimination law. It issued its demands through a series of direct action protests that brought to a halt construction on $50 million in private and government construction projects in the Seattle area during the first week of June 1972. The UCWA partly sought to redeem the integrity of the law by demanding the immediate hiring of black apprentices and the active enforcement of the original affirmative action goals of the court. But, more important, the UCWA demanded to join the lawsuit and be granted traditional union and employer powers to screen, hire, and dispatch black apprentices. Scott explained the UCWA position to Judge Lindberg, stating that the UCWA would not allow work to continue until the court granted black workers "control and self-determination."[4] The judge, Scott later explained to supporters, "thinks we want to integrate and become white. We've changed our minds and want integration with recognition that we are different. We want to control our own destiny."[5]

The UCWA shift from demanding jobs to seeking power represented a radical response to the failure of the Philadelphia Plan approach to affirmative action. President Nixon's defunding of War on Poverty employment programs and his slashing of federal construction spending had eliminated many of the jobs that black radicals thought would be made available to them. As a result, both government imposed and voluntary affirmative action plans pitted white and black workers against one another for increasingly scarce jobs. The economic cost of compliance with the federal plans increased dramatically as unemployment in the construction industry skyrocketed. Meanwhile, the economic cost of non-compliance decreased as building trades unions successfully convinced President Nixon to promote "voluntary" affirmative action plans, hollowing out the enforcement of fair employment law by the Department of Labor (see Griffey, chap. 6 in this volume).

The lack of political will by the federal government to enforce the goals and timetables of affirmative action plans forced the largely ad hoc Black Power campaigns of the late 1960s to reinvent themselves. Because many movements to desegregate the building trades in the 1960s were led by people who lacked experience in the construction industry and spoke for black workers without including them, they were often ill-equipped to monitor the implementation of affirmative action plans. Some were compromised by the role they were given administering weak plans; others struggled to adapt to the early failures of affirmative action. In many cities, to the degree that affirmative action in the construction industry persisted at all, it was largely through pre-apprenticeship programs (sponsored primarily by the Urban League and funded by the Department of Labor) that left the unions in control of apprenticeship and dispatch programs. Pre-apprenticeship programs increased the visibility of the Urban League in promoting affirmative action, but they did so at the cost of emphasizing social service over community organizing and emphasizing individual black self-help over collective action. They were institutions that operated on the premise that unions and employers would implement affirmative action plans in good faith, when often they did not.[6]

In a few cities, black construction worker organizations evolved in the early 1970s to challenge the inability of pre-apprenticeship programs to enforce affirmative action requirements, and to challenge the ongoing control that unions retained over their apprenticeship programs and hiring halls. The three most sophisticated black construction worker organizations to emerge in the 1970s as watchdogs of government affirmative action plans were the UCWA in Seattle, Harlem Fight Back in New York, and the United Community Construction Workers (UCCW) in Boston. As community organizations, they represented predominantly black inner-city residents who demanded jobs and urban reconstruction during an era of federal abandonment, white flight, and deindustrialization. As worker organizations, they promoted a community-centered labor politics that connected minority caucuses within the unions to broader social-movement organizing. By using fair employment law and affirmative action plans to organize for political and economic power, they produced and occupied a hybrid political space between labor unions and social service agencies. Their contribution to black urban politics in the 1970s helped translate Black Power at work into community-controlled hiring halls and apprenticeship programs for inner-city residents. These campaigns were part of a broader movement that transformed the black community control campaigns of the 1960s into community-based minority worker organizations and "poor workers' unions" during the 1970s.[7]

This chapter presents the history of the UCWA as a case study for understanding the origins, organizational structure, and legacy of black construction worker radicalism in the 1970s. (Similar histories still need to be written about Harlem Fight Back and UCCW.) It describes a form of labor radicalism forged through the "hellfire of hostility" that black workers faced in the workplace when they entered the construction industry via affirmative action.[8]

The history of the UCWA provides an opportunity to extend the civil rights movement history well into the 1970s instead of portraying the era as one of mere cooptation and declension. The UCWA organizing model gave organizational voice and political power to minority workers entering hostile workplaces through affirmative action plans. It used class action Title VII lawsuits to organize an affected class of minority workers into community-based labor organizations that could oversee the implementation of court-ordered affirmative action plans. The UCWA then used this model to organize Filipino cannery workers in Alaska; black construction workers in Denver and Portland; black truck drivers in Oakland; and the Southwest Workers Federation, an eight-city black worker organization in southern cities largely untouched by the economic gains produced by the black freedom movement.

The UCWA's insistence that minority workers oversee the implementation of affirmative action presented a direct challenge to the trend that has received more attention from civil rights movement historians: the emergence of middle-class professions, inside and outside government, to manage the enforcement of civil rights laws passed in the 1960s and early 1970s. Title VII of the 1964 Civil Rights Act outlawed both racial and gender discrimination in hiring by employers and unions, but it did not explicitly describe the process for desegregation for those found guilty of violating the law. As National Association for the Advancement of Colored People (NAACP) Labor Director Herbert Hill pointed out during the 1960s, "Title VII is not self-enforcing." It offered a legal sanction for workers to challenge discrimination on the job, but provided little guidance for whether and how the government would support worker claims. For middle-class bureaucrats who fought over how to enforce the law, the 1970s may have been an era "when the marching stopped" and black politics shifted from the streets to the state, "from protest to politics," or "*From* Direct Action *to* Affirmative Action." But many workplace pioneers had a different experience, and the history of the UCWA shows that new black worker organizations emerged and direct action protests persisted as part of workplace battles for both power and inclusion in the 1970s.[9]

Workplace Culture as a Site of Resistance to Affirmative Action

The refusal by the Seattle building trades unions to negotiate even token affirmative action plans provided the crucial context in which the UCWA created its innovative community-organizing model. As documented throughout this volume, the exclusionary practices of the building trades unions blended with the politics of whiteness to deny union membership to nonwhite workers through informal means. Unions then refused to dispatch or apprentice nonwhite workers, ostensibly because they were not union members.

In Seattle, as early as 1949, after local building trades had largely jettisoned their most explicitly racist membership policies, the Seattle Urban League records detail "numerous reports of Negroes and other minority people who had not been admitted into building unions that were members of the Building Trade Council." Letters to the council, however, were ignored, and meetings with council leaders produced no changes in apprenticeship hiring practices.[10]

The unions acknowledged that they had been openly racist before the 1950s, but were hard-pressed to explain why segregation persisted for decades afterward. By 1969, only 29 of the 14,821 members of the Seattle building trades were nonwhite. The most pervasive discrimination occurred in Ironworkers, Local 86. In 1969, the Washington State Board Against Discrimination found that "except for a rodman who worked for a day or two in 1939 no person who was clearly a Negro has ever been a member of or been referred by the Union to employment." With "300 to 400 Negroes working as welders in Seattle manufacturing plants, shipyards, and even in construction work as sheetmetal workers," the Local 86 discrimination appeared blatant even to outsiders.[11]

To insiders, the racism within Local 86 was an open secret. Donald Kelly, a white apprentice in Local 86, recalled that his apprenticeship coordinator reportedly told him, "we have no Negro apprentices, and we will never have no Negro apprentices.…When they file their application—we have a stack of applications. We will just keep pulling from the bottom just constantly." Kelly later goaded the Local 86 business agent into telling him, "No black son-of-a-bitch bastard will ever work out of this union as long as I am business agent." When Kelly challenged him by saying that blacks' entry into the trade was "inevitable," the business agent elaborated: "if they force me into it, I will take one of the black sons-of-bitches, and if I put him out on a beam at two or three hundred feet in the air, either he will walk it or he will fall off." Kelly was later kicked out of the apprenticeship program and told that he "was not fit to be an Iron Worker" because he was a "hippie." After first coming forward in 1967 with stories of union racism he had witnessed, Kelly "got the hell beat out of me" by people he had never seen before. During the melee, his assailants accused him of being "a nigger lover" and "the one who is trying to bring the black bastards in the iron workers."[12]

The discrimination practiced by Local 86 was hardly unique. Federal Bureau of Investigation (FBI) interviews of black workers and white union leaders in Seattle conducted in late 1969 and early 1970 document how International Brotherhood of Electrical Workers (IBEW) Local 46, Operating Engineers Local 302, Sheet Metal Workers Local 99, and Plumbers and Pipefitters Local 32 all used control of their hiring halls and apprenticeship programs in racially exclusive ways. White workers with personal connections to union contractors or union leaders found it easy to receive dispatch or entry into apprenticeship programs even if they had no previous experience. But experienced black workers (from the Seattle shipyards and from the aerospace industry, from the military, and from War on Poverty job-training programs) faced an altogether different process. If they were told about an out-of-work list at all, they were often put on a separate list so that the union could appear to be in compliance with the law. Many sat all day in hiring halls wondering why their names were not being called until finally they gave up and went back to industrial jobs. When Junior Lee, who had learned to drive heavy trucks in a federal Job Corps program, applied for dispatch from Operating Engineers Local 302, he was told that the only job available was over a hundred miles away in Yakima. When Lee said he was willing to find his own transportation out to the job, the dispatcher, according to Lee, "didn't refer me to a job. He asked me, 'Have you ever operated a yo-yo?' I says, 'No.' He says, 'Have you ever seen one?' I says, 'Yes.' That was that."[13]

When black workers applied for work directly to employers, going around the union hiring halls, employers were still bound to hire only workers referred by a union hiring hall dispatcher. This, in turn, gave unions far more control over hiring than they usually acknowledged. When Robert Lucas, the white owner of Lewis Refrigeration, called Local 32 in 1963 and specifically asked for a black plumber to be dispatched to his job, the dispatcher reportedly laughed and said "I can just picture my wife going to the back door and seeing a big black man there and he says 'I came to fix your refrigerator.'" After about a year of trying to hire a black worker, Lucas finally gave up.[14]

From 1965 to 1968, leaders from various local War on Poverty agencies, the Urban League, the NAACP, and the Congress of Racial Equality all sought, but failed, to negotiate voluntary outreach and recruitment plans to desegregate the Seattle-area building trades unions. When the State Board Against Discrimination ruled in March 1969 that Local 86 had refused to accept a welder who had passed as white into its membership after he told his coworkers that he was black, the mainstream civil rights movement in Seattle publicly broke with the labor movement over building trades union discrimination and began seeking ways to hire non-union black workers on War on Poverty construction projects. Faced with the absolute refusal by unions to admit black workers or apprentices to their ranks, a coalition of civil rights organizations complained in March, 1969 to the American Federation of Labor–Congress of Industrial Organizations (AFL-CIO) that Austin St. Laurent, head of the Seattle–King County Building and Construction Trades Council, was a "bigoted racist.... Every proposition, every plan, every program designed to assist minority youth into apprenticeship in the trades has been rebuked, opposed and stymied by him." Meanwhile, St. Laurent refused to acknowledge racial bias within the labor movement and remained convinced that affirmative action was a scam for contractors to use civil rights groups to "break the back of the building trades unions."[15]

This was the context in which Tyree Scott, a black electrician and head of a black contractors association seeking to gain access to Model Cities construction projects in Seattle, finally got fed up with trying to figure out how to hire black workers without running afoul of the unions. Inspired by similar protests in Chicago, Philadelphia, and Pittsburgh, Scott led a series of direct-action protests against building trades union racism during late August and early September 1969. The protests—which made decades of private grievances public—culminated when Black Power activists drove trucks into open pits at the University of Washington and briefly shut down air traffic at Sea-Tac Airport by marching on to the tarmac. These actions, which local media observers considered "riots," inspired fear and immediate conciliation by local government officials and contractors.[16]

The unions were much less swayed by the Black Power protests, however. If union leaders showed up to negotiations during the job closures, it was usually to protest the negotiations as violations of their collective bargaining agreements. When employers and government officials created a unilateral affirmative action plan to stop the protests and black workers began to appear on government construction projects in early September 1969, union members went on strike. When the courts forced union members back to work, they took to the streets. Austin St. Laurent organized the ad hoc Voice of Irate Construction Employees (VOICE) in early October 1969. Through it, he staged two marches of thousands of workers against King County Executive John Spellman and Washington Governor Dan Evans (both of them Republicans) for participating in negotiations with freedom movement activists. The VOICE marches were similar to the raucous construction worker counterdemonstrations seen in August and September 1969 in cities such as Philadelphia, Pittsburgh, and Chicago. In Seattle, they were led by men wearing hard hats and carrying U.S. flags and signs filled with righteous anger about "reverse discrimination," including a prominent one that read "Equal Rights for Whites."[17]

The hostility of the Seattle-area unions to the Philadelphia Plan was so absolute that it brought a higher level of federal intervention in Seattle politics than in most other cities. When the U.S. Department of Labor briefly investigated the issue in Seattle at the request of Governor Evans, it "concluded that a voluntary agreement was unlikely to be obtained" because of the refusal of the unions to compromise, so it "referred the matter to the Department of Justice." On October 31, 1969, the U.S. Department of Justice announced that it would file a lawsuit—*U.S. v. Local 86*—against the elite five of the Seattle Building Trades unions for systematically denying black workers entry into union and apprenticeship programs.[18]

Even then, union resistance ensured that the case went to trial and was not settled. After six months of fruitless negotiations to bring the trades not named in the lawsuit into compliance with new federal affirmative action guidelines, both Seattle-area unions and contractors announced that they would implement their own affirmative action plans. The unions promised training but did not promise to dispatch workers to jobs, and the contractors promised to hire new black workers only if the government would pay for it. Both sides claimed to be in compliance with the law, but the Department of Labor refused to fund either plan because voluntary affirmative action required a consensus of all parties.

Although successfully marginalizing the civil rights activists and holding the Department of Labor and contractors at bay, the failure of the unions to negotiate a voluntary affirmative action plan with contractors and civil rights activists had the opposite effect of what unions intended. Judge Lindberg might have deferred to a tripartite hometown plan as sufficient redress for past discrimination if he had found the unions guilty. But without such a plan, unions appeared to be operating in bad faith, and this invited more substantial forms of intervention. Believing affirmative action to be unconstitutional, they refused to settle the lawsuit, despite most observers believing that the Philadelphia Plan had changed the political landscape.[19]

The force that courts brought to bear on the Seattle building trades unions thus ended up being far beyond anything that would have come from the Department of Labor. Judge Lindberg, a Democrat from the New Deal era who had served as the secretary of the Washington State Senate in 1933 and had been appointed to the federal judiciary by President Harry Truman in 1951, heard *U.S. v Ironworkers, Local 86* a year before he retired. He issued his affirmative action decrees on June 16, 1970. The relief that Lindberg prescribed in the case was, according to William Gould, a fair employment attorney, "at the time of its issuance…more comprehensive and detailed than that set forth by any other judge in any employment discrimination case in the United States." Lindberg called for the immediate hiring of forty-one black workers whose individual experiences the prosecution had used to prove a pattern of racial discrimination in the four trades. In addition, he ordered the creation of a special apprentice program with fewer restrictions to fasttrack black workers into journeymen status in two years instead of the regular four; loosened the age and education requirements for incoming apprentices; and set 1:4 minimum ratios of black apprentices to white journeymen at job sites and in training programs. Finally, to rearrange labor relations within an industry that employed tens of thousands of people, Lindberg created the Court Order Advisory Committee (COAC), a quasi-governmental institution, directly accountable to him, to bring all parties together to enforce his order.[20]

Putting Unions in Charge of Their Desegregation

Because their long-standing resistance to affirmative action had played a significant role in the Seattle building trades unions' being placed under court order, it would have been surprising if they had *not* resisted Lindberg's affirmative action plan. But Lindberg's order, modeled on other 1960s-era government manpower programs, did not take the possibility of such resistance into account. Instead, it focused its attention on breaking down the barriers to work without considering the relationship between exclusive hiring practices and social hierarchies on the job.

The intellectual foundation for these manpower programs—which came from industrial relations literature pioneered by business economists and lawyers—relied on social psychology that treated the racially exclusive workplace as normative and the excluded worker as deficient in human capital and in need of remedial support to be successfully integrated into skilled trades.[21] Affirmative action programs based on these well-meaning studies left union journeymen in charge of the construction workplace, thereby granting them substantial power over desegregation. Affirmative action, in this context, meant forcing unions to dispatch black workers to jobs and union journeymen to train black workers in their trade without explaining exactly what union members' good-faith participation in affirmative action would entail.

The difference between good faith and resistance was especially difficult to establish in the largely informal workplace environment of the construction industry. According to a study of the construction industry in the early 1970s by Jacob Riemer, a sociologist and construction worker, construction work is inherently difficult to monitor because it uses a variety of specialized trades whose skilled craftsmen are spread across a construction site. This made "a tight organizational structure difficult to achieve and in many respects impractical." Instead, high-skilled craftsmen worked with relative autonomy on job sites and coordinated their activities through a distinct masculine subculture that was as social as it was professional and whose mores were often at odds with bureaucratic and bourgeois norms. The physical and dangerous nature of the work was frequently linked to demonstrations of physical prowess that were saturated with sexual references. These physical displays of achievement and acts of bravado easily crossed over into fights and physical pranks that asserted forms of ritual dominance over others on the crew.[22]

The initiation of others into the trades was an important way to assert one's individual male prowess and the fraternal identity of the group. Socialization into the construction workers' subculture often came through physical and character hazing that both allowed journeymen to demonstrate their skills and tested apprentices' fitness to work in dangerous situations. Learning a trade was synonymous with being integrated into the social life of the construction site, and formal evaluations of apprentices emphasized "explicit mastery of skills and techniques particular to the work" with "an acceptable adoption of a related set of implicit qualities." These "qualities" were based on individual fitness for work and the ability to work on a team, defined vaguely as "character," which became synonymous with manhood—and, given the restrictions on entry into the trade, whiteness.

The hazing of new recruits, in this context, was an integral part of the construction workplace. As Riemer notes, "the work culture of the building trades dictates that new apprentices should be teased, ridiculed, and generally pushed to their limits. As part of their initiation into the fraternity of tradesmen and as a test of their acceptability, apprentices must continually prove themselves 'under fire.'" Examples of such initiations for white men could include sending apprentices for tools that did not exist, scaring them by performing risky feats meant to discourage them, sending them to undesirable workplaces, or giving them demeaning jobs.[23]

In Seattle and across the country, resentful journeymen responded to the imposition of the mandates that they train black workers by making their usual ritual hazing of apprentices punitive instead of redemptive. The pushing of black apprentices to their limits, rather than initiating them into the trade, thereby served to reassert white men's exclusive claims to work, to union membership, and to workplace authority.

Union resistance to affirmative action was at its most overt during the first couple of years of the program. During September 1969, in response to ad hoc affirmative action plans meant to quell street protests, union members simply walked off the job. When the courts forced them back to work, journeymen ignored their apprentices. Calvin Amerson, one of the first black apprentices to enter the Seattle construction industry, told a local reporter, "The first six days, we didn't do any work. Just sit around. Then today, they had me working out for a little while, for about a half an hour. It's just out there, you know, people have a funny attitude, you know. They look like they hate you or something when you walk into their jobs. They don't want you out there."[24]

In fall 1969, union journeymen developed a series of other tactics for refusing to train unskilled black workers. The Seattle chapter of the American Friends Service Committee (AFSC) found that black workers experienced "a range [of tactics,] from a hands-off treatment, where they are virtually ignored and given no training, or at best given routine, dead-end jobs, to harassment, name-calling, intimidation, and 'accidents.'"[25]

These strategies threatened to turn civil rights law into a dead letter. If black apprentices contested the treatment that they received at the hands of white journeymen, they could be accused of insubordination or even be fired if goaded into a fistfight. If they did not contest their hazing, the chances that they would learn a trade were low. Some of those who stayed tried to get paid for doing no work—which white workers cynically used as evidence of the folly of affirmative action. In the end, all sixty-five of the first black apprentices who entered the Seattle construction industry in fall 1969 ended up quitting within a few months. They were not replaced because the plans required only that a certain number be hired, not retained on jobs or as union members eligible for dispatch.[26]

As a result, even before the court order was issued in Seattle, union journeymen found a way to meet the statistical goals of affirmative action plans on paper while hollowing out their substance. Unions could cycle through black apprentices instead of training them and discourage black workers from staying or learning a trade. When workers quit, unions disavowed any responsibility and blamed the black workers for the high attrition rates, often implying that nonwhite workers were too lazy or unintelligent for skilled work and that affirmative action was impossibly utopian social engineering.[27]

Union resistance strategies expanded as the economy worsened during the early 1970s and Lindberg's court order imposed a much stricter regime of goals and timetables for minority hiring. A simultaneous decline in commercial and military airplane contracts during the late 1960s and early 1970s drove Boeing to lay off much of its workforce, devastating the Seattle-area in the process. The company reduced its workforce from 100,000 in July 1968 to 48,000 people in the Seattle area by the end of 1970, and would cut one third of those remaining jobs by summer 1971. A growing housing recession both locally and nationally, magnified by the Nixon administration's choice to cut federal construction spending, also produced substantial layoffs in the region's construction and logging industries. The state's resulting unemployment rate of 12 percent was double the national average, and Seattle's unemployment rate of nearly 16 percent was the highest of any major metropolitan region in the United States. While Nixon aide John D. Ehrlichman took a special interest in the city's plight, his hands were tied by the free market ideology of Nixon's economic advisers. It wasn't until a decade later that the region even began to recover from its decline and deindustrialization with the growth of the region's computer and biotech industries.[28]

The economic crisis deepened social conflict over racial discrimination in the Seattle construction industry. Union leaders did not seem to direct white worker resistance to affirmative action. But their steadfast opposition certainly encouraged workers to believe that affirmative action was illegal and antiunion, and was a means by which to take away "their" jobs. The specialized nature of the trades and idiosyncratic quality of the construction industry subculture in turn made it easy for individual workers who were resentful about their precarious class and racial status to take advantage of new black trainees in ways that had systematic effects. Michael Fox, who represented the UCWA beginning in 1971, described the work conditions that grew out of the Seattle court order as "a hellfire of hostility towards the presence of these black apprentices, who were referred to on many occasions as Lindberg Journeymen." Henry Andes, an IBEW business agent, concurred, albeit vaguely. Describing the tenor of the work environment following Lindberg's order, he noted, "There was [pause] a lot of turmoil, a lot of resistance and a lot of hate and dissension."[29]

Todd Hawkins, an Ironworker apprentice and UCWA activist, recalled that as the court order began to be implemented, "industry racism really began to flourish in insurmountable numbers, incidents on jobs, journeymen or white workers didn't want to relate to the old black journeyman or the apprentices, did [not] want to teach him, did not want him in his shop." A journeyman might, for instance, tell a trainee to polish pipe, but he "doesn't really tell you why the pipe needs to be polished, why the oxidation needs to be taken off, how the oxidation will affect the solder once the heat has been put to it. He doesn't take time to explain. He just pigeonholed him" by giving him what appeared to be useful work without teaching him.[30]

White journeymen might also put their apprentices in situations in which they were likely to be injured. Hawkins explained:

> If you look at someone arc-welding, you can burn your eyes very seriously. And this journeyman thought it was a big joke to have this apprentice watch him weld. And you know, it injured his eyes very seriously. The next day it feels like sand. And if you watch it for any period of time, it just gets worse. This kid was messed up for more than a week, and they wanted to cancel him out of the program [for missing work].[31]

Or white workers might send an apprentice to get the prized tools of a master craftsman, only to be immediately accused of theft because he had not been told that these particular tools were off-limits. Others were sent for tools that do not exist to intentionally provoke the apprentices' anger in a way that could earn them bad reviews or start fights that would get them kicked out of the program. Acts such as these added a toxic dimension to the pranks and hazing that had been a regular feature of construction workplace culture before the entry of the nonwhite trainees. They also allowed racism to be masked as redemptive and the pioneers' angry responses as an indication of their inability to "take a joke" or get along with the team.[32]

The subversion of the dispatch system by union dispatchers and contractors further undermined the affirmative action plans from within. According to Northwest AFSC Director Arthur Dye, during the first couple of years of the court order,

> Some [black] workers appeared at the hiring hall day after day for several months and were never dispatched. If they began to ask questions

why they were not dispatched they would be sent out to jobs in Port Angeles or Yakima, both a hundred miles or so away, only to find out that when they arrived at their destination there wasn't a job. Or they would be dispatched to a job where there was considerable possibility for physical intimidation.[33]

Even when there were jobs in such far-flung places, it placed an extra expense on black apprentices' participation in affirmative action plans. A number of apprentices did not have cars or had cars that were not in proper condition to make long commutes, and carpooling with white workers was out of the question. Moreover, some employers moved black apprentices from job to job to have them counted by government compliance agencies more than once—a practice that both increased apprentices' transportation costs and reduced their ability to learn a trade.[34]

The government was largely impotent to counteract the subversion of affirmative action by unions and employers. Three of the four unions subject to the court order filed an appeal (the Ironworkers chose not to) that removed the case from Judge Lindberg's jurisdiction and prevented him from substantively changing his order. And although the Ninth Circuit Court of Appeals upheld Lindberg's ruling on May 17, 1971, the subsequent union appeal of that ruling to the Supreme Court was not denied until December of that year. According to Luvern Rieke, a University of Washington law professor who chaired COAC, "during the time that the appeal was pending, nobody was giving anything.…So there was a year and a half or two years during the appeal period in which the district court couldn't make changes and obviously changes are necessary."[35]

By exploiting their control of workplace culture and maintaining social hierarchies at work, on-the-job resistance turned affirmative action into more or less a dead letter while union appeals were pending in the courts. According to a Seattle Urban League report, "Union representation on the committee rarely [attended] the meetings and, excluding Electrical Workers Local 46, Union efforts to implement the Special Apprentice Program were token. The Unions argued that the economy was too poor to provide work for the total number of Special Apprentices required by the order."[36]

Contractors, especially small ones, made similar economic arguments. In December 1971, some contractors openly refused to hire black trainees even when their contracts required it. When the matter was referred to COAC, it found itself powerless to tell contractors or unions to hire staff they claimed they could not pay. According to a report by the Seattle chapter of the Associated General Contractors (AGC), "It is extremely difficult for any of the [COAC] staff to get other than a courteous reply when there is no authority back of their request other than the burdensome, difficult process of requesting a court order." Seeking legal redress through the courts was made more difficult because the Department of Justice lawyers tasked with enforcing the court order were located in Washington, D.C., and black workers lacked formal representation in the lawsuit.[37]

The United Construction Workers Association and Black Construction Worker Radicalism

The UCWA emerged from the black community control movement as a vehicle for black workers to challenge the on-the-job subversion of affirmative action. But the idea to form a new organization to represent black construction workers in Seattle came from an unlikely place—the Northwest Chapter of the AFSC.

The AFSC began consulting with Tyree Scott and other black contractors after white workers drove black apprentices off the job during fall 1969. Scott had come to the attention of the AFSC while leading the Central Contractors Association (CCA)—an organization of black contractors brought together in spring 1969 by the Seattle Model Cities program to get federal construction contracts and train black construction workers. Scott grew up in a small segregated town in Texas in the 1940s and 1950s; he dropped out of high school to enter the Marine Corps to support his family when his girlfriend became pregnant. He served in the Marines for nine years, where he learned to be an electrician, but decided against reenlisting after serving in the Vietnam War and seeing white soldiers' racist treatment of the Vietnamese. After his discharge, Scott moved to Seattle with his family to work for his father's electrical business, which meant working on nonunion jobs at the margins of the industry because of local building trades union racism. Scott soon became friends with a number of other black workers in Seattle with experiences similar to his own: skilled veterans, primarily from the South, who had migrated to Seattle for work after being stationed in one of the military bases in the area, only to find Seattle housing and employment completely segregated. It was through this social network of black contractors that Scott became a founding member and leader of the CCA. And as the CCA began staging direct action protests during August and September 1969, Scott consciously expanded his organizing beyond black contractors to include black welders and other industrial workers from the Seattle shipyards.[38]

In early 1970, the AFSC chose to bankroll the UCWA—hiring a community organizer to be its director, providing it with office space and a secretary, and working with it to seek fund-raising from church and progressive philanthropies—while deferring to its leadership and membership on its ultimate course of action. The AFSC report announcing the formation of the

UCWA to potential donors and supporters claimed that the group intended to recruit "minority building tradesmen and potential trainees" to "exert pressure to enforce the laws already in existence." No matter how that worked in practice, according to the report, "the important thing, we feel, is to facilitate some community organization among the people most affected by discrimination in employment in the construction industry."[39]

After three months investigating the issue and interviewing dozens of people, the Seattle AFSC hired Scott to lead the new organization. The AFSC consciously chose not to dictate the direction that the UCWA would take once formed, although its various ideas highlighted the experimental and hybrid quality of the organization. The AFSC at once imagined that the UCWA might evolve into an industrial union of black workers excluded from the craft unions, a caucus of black workers in the unions, a service organization for apprentices, a watchdog group for affirmative action enforcement, an ally for black contractors, or a combination of all these things. Once hired in June, Scott chose to reject both the dual-union and caucus options that the AFSC had considered. Instead, he linked the organization to the *U.S. v. Local 86* lawsuit by making the UCWA a vehicle for black workers to demand vigorous enforcement of the court order. This meant enlisting black workers to study the law, determine their rights, and decide how best to assert them. Reflecting on this use of affirmative action litigation as basis for community organizing, in 1975 Scott recalled that "the UCWA is built around the Title VII case and other cases brought since then. I spent a lot of time learning the use of Title VII, what [it] actually meant."[40]

Scott held the first meeting of the UCWA on July 14, 1970, to bring together the workers found to have been illegally denied employment in *U.S. v. Local 86*, and whom the court had ordered the unions to hire. Twenty-five of the forty-one individuals attended. "They discussed the personal experiences with discrimination on the job and," according to a UCWA report, "determined that they would work together to fight this discrimination, beginning by going over the new court order to inform themselves of their new rights under it." Starting with these workers, and then the dozens of other special apprentices that Lindberg had ordered the unions to hire, the UCWA set out to facilitate communication and provide legal and political advocacy on behalf of all black workers whose experiences would determine the fate of Lindberg's affirmative action plan. Within a month, its workers-only meetings were drawing as many as one hundred attendees. At the meetings, workers received updates on the enforcement of the court order, pooled information about their dispatch from union hiring halls, discussed tactics for responding (and not responding) to on-the-job racism, and coordinated transportation to work and other activities meant to overcome barriers faced on and off the job.[41]

The UCWA advocacy, which was central to the early life of the organization, provided a powerful contrast to the black worker recruitment and training done by the Urban League and AFL-CIO affiliates around the country in the 1960s and 1970s. Most affirmative action plans in the construction industry trained new workers without educating them about their rights. Without an advocacy arm through which workers could demand redress when confronted with on-the-job union or contractor racism, these training programs effectively depoliticized the civil rights struggles.

The bypassing of the Seattle Urban League by the UCWA was delicate and facilitated indirectly by unions' refusal to differentiate between the managerial approach to civil rights politics of the Urban League and the radical democratic politics of the UCWA. In fall 1969, the Seattle Urban League hired Cecil Collins as a full-time staff person to support black contractors, anticipating that this would set the Urban League up to administer any forthcoming affirmative action plan. In December 1969, Collins tried to convince the Seattle AFSC to limit its advocacy in the construction industry to "attitude changing, such as the sensitivity training conducted within some big businesses." Collins reportedly told the AFSC in spring 1970 that a black workers' organization might needlessly inflame tensions and told the AFSC that, as a predominantly white organization, it should not get directly involved in the building trades dispute. But with unions and employers unable to find common ground, the hopes of the Urban League to administer a local hometown plan were dashed. By September 1970, just two months after the founding of the UCWA, the Seattle Urban League realized that the Department of Labor would not fund its proposal to recruit black apprentices and withdrew its request, essentially ceding responsibility to the UCWA and the courts. The UCWA seized on its new role by trying to link the enforcement of Title VII to local community control politics and the radical democratic ethos of the New Left. "'Power to the People' becomes a fact, not a slogan," the AFSC announced, "when a black construction workers' organization is assisting a court appointed committee to carry out the court's orders regarding equal employment."[42]

But with unemployment skyrocketing, union resistance rampant, and the COAC resistant to providing the UCWA any official power, the UCWA struggled to support the workers that it advocated for. "We spent a great deal of that [first] year," Scott recalled, "just replacing guys that had dropped off the program." Part of the reason for the high black apprentice attrition was that slow economic times provided both a legitimate reason and an excuse for union dispatchers to slow the employment of black trainees. In this context, Scott said, "[A] Black apprentice might be out of work for a period of two or three months, while he is required to go to school…and of course his position was 'why should I go to school when

I'm not working?' And he hadn't stockpiled a bank account or anything. That was a cause for a lot of the attrition: the inability to work regularly."[43]

The UCWA responded to the economic crisis by scrambling to find contractors willing to employ black workers. "With all the jobs gone," an AFSC report noted, "placement has been limited to finding occasional jobs by pegging individual contractors who are either sympathetic, working in strategic Central Area locations, or who had been told by contract compliance officers to take on additional minority workers." In a number of cases, contractors accommodated affirmative action mandates by reducing the number of white journeymen on the job, further exacerbating tensions between white and black workers.[44]

Once on the job, black workers developed both individual and organizational responses to their conflicts with white workers. Each act of resistance was fraught with complex calculations about whether it was safe to speak out at a dangerous and hierarchical workplace. Individually, trainees did everything from disobeying orders to bringing guns to work to quitting. According to Tyree Scott, differences in white and black working-class cultures exacerbated workplace conflicts over affirmative action: "The Black worker might be 25, 30-years old. This [blank in transcript] has never had no job, ain't got no tools, coming to work in his high heeled shoes, and doesn't fit in, and also alienated from his white counterpart, who is hostile to him. So as a result, he shows up late, don't show up at all, gets into an argument with him."[45]

As black trainees asserted themselves at work, a workplace already prone to "physical horseplay" became increasingly tense and dangerous. As Michael Woo, a UCWA organizer, recalled,

> it was not the kind of work culture environment that would be tolerated in any way today.... It was an environment where these workers weren't feeling safe. We could visibly see the handguns, they would come from their job sites right to these [UCWA] meetings with their handguns because they were not feeling safe on these jobs. And I'm sure likewise a lot of the white workers were armed as well.[46]

UCWA meetings generally advocated preventive measures for deescalating situations on the job, teaching apprentices to not be baited into reacting to racist taunts in ways that could get them kicked off the job or out of the program. At meetings attended by dozens and sometimes as many as a hundred workers, UCWA leaders collected workers' stories from their jobs, kept track of union and contractor resistance, received updates from their attorneys, and strategized about the direction of the organization for the following days and weeks.[47]

When all else failed, UCWA activists selectively used construction site closures—a kind of strike by a community union—to resolve specific grievances.

As a dramatic example, Scott recalled that, when a black worker told a UCWA meeting that he had been given menial work by a journeyman in his trade only to be told by a member of another union that such work was outside his jurisdiction, "everyone thought that was absurd, what the hell, we have the right to work." The following morning, nearly one hundred black workers skipped their jobs, brought sticks and pipes to the construction site where the black trainee had been refused work, kicked all the plumbers off the job while allowing other workers from nonoffending unions to keep working, and forced the journeyman plumber to give the black trainee a meaningful job.[48] Taken together, these strategies that UCWA members developed for learning a trade in a hostile workplace environment highlight a new labor radicalism that emerged outside and sometimes in opposition to organized labor to enforce affirmative action plans in the 1970s.

From Jobs to Power

The escalating conflict between black and white workers on the job sent shock waves through the ineffectual structures meant to oversee their collaboration. By the time the U.S. Supreme Court denied the last appeal of the Seattle unions on December 7, 1971, the Seattle court order had been failing for some time. High attrition rates, the poor progress of the special apprentices in their accelerated two-year programs, and the open resistance of contractors and unions to the order had demoralized the COAC staff and committee members. Judge Lindberg solicited proposals to amend the court order for at least six months prior to the time he met with the COAC to discuss them. The unions, however, boycotted the meeting. Rieke, who chaired the meeting, recalled Lindberg's frustration that the goals of the court order continued to go unmet despite the fact that "the goals set in the Court Order are so modest that even in a weak economy they should be accomplished." In response to the looming sense of failure, the minority members of the COAC called for a higher ratio of nonwhite apprentices to be hired, but their "recommendation was opposed by Union and Management representation on the committee and no action was taken by the court."[49]

By early 1972, UCWA activists surveyed the political and economic landscape created by high attrition rates at the workplace. Noting that there were at least ninety fewer black apprentices in the trades than were required by Lindberg's order, a sense of despair mixed with outrage began setting in. White union power, solidarity, and experience had largely trumped the courageous but underfunded attempts of outside groups such as the UCWA to create an atmosphere on construction sites that could prevent black trainees from being driven out.

Despite acknowledging the failure to meet court-ordered requirements, neither the COAC nor Judge Lindberg had laid out an enforcement plan that would put the implementation of the order back on track toward meeting its hiring goals. "We were outraged about it," Scott recalled, "and all we were doing was going through that legal mumbo-jumbo."[50]

"We thought about closing the whole thing (the UCWA) down," Scott told one reporter in 1972. "It was becoming just another central area social-service agency. I didn't think that was a proper role."

> We had gotten to the point that we said, "to hell with it, we haven't done any good, all this effort … [19]69, 70, 71—all we have to show for it is 30–35 people in the industry." So we decided to go for broke.…We sat down and we planned it from day one that we were going to either win or lose, we would take them on one more time in the streets. And just show them that they were violating the court's orders.[51]

The campaign was a make or break movement to demand full and immediate implementation of the court order that quickly evolved into call for something that no court or government had heretofore granted minority workers or their representatives—inclusion as formal parties in the litigation that had imposed affirmative action on their behalf.

The subsequent construction site closures led by UCWA activists brought the informal conflict between white and black workers to a new level of crisis that barely avoided becoming an all-out gunfight. On June 1, 1972, UCWA leaders broke into the control room of the floating bridge on Interstate 90 (I-90) and jammed the bridge open to block the Seattle Police Department Tactical Squad from getting to the other side of Lake Washington. In the meantime, forty UCWA activists "shut down all I-90 projects [on a five-mile stretch] between Bellevue and Issaquah," doing at least $5,000 in damage to construction equipment in the process. Construction resumed on I-90 the following day, but UCWA activists continued their campaign by shutting down construction at two privately funded skyscrapers: Safeco Tower in the University District and the Financial Center building downtown. They also skipped a scheduled meeting with George Andrews, the head of the Washington State Highway Department, thumbing their nose at further participation in what they considered to be pointless negotiations. By June 5, when they closed seven different University of Washington job sites, the UCWA had disrupted more than $50 million in construction projects in less than a week.[52]

At an emergency COAC meeting held on June 5, thirty UCWA members presented non-negotiable demands and left without entertaining any discussion. The demands included full and immediate implementation of the court order to meet its hiring goals; "Complete control over all minority dispatches to construction work in Seattle"; and no work on any area construction projects until the court order was implemented in full. St. Laurent, the Labor Council head, boycotted the meeting. Glen Arnold, union representative, walked out as soon as the UCWA members arrived en masse. Dan Ruthford, the contractors' representative, warned that the unions were fed up and workers at some sites had voted to physically resist any further job closures.[53]

That same day, at the request of the AGC, Superior Court Judge David Hunter issued a restraining order against further UCWA job closures. The UCWA, disenchanted with what they considered to be the hypocrisy of the law, ignored the order. When served with the order the following morning, Tyree Scott publicly burned it, saying it should be ignored "just as the court order is not being followed." Todd Hawkins later explained that it "was a symbolic burning. The paper wasn't no good to us. We thought the paper meant something too, and every time we tried to play the game with the paper, we always got better results when we went to direct action."[54]

After burning the restraining order, Scott led a march of black workers and their supporters through the black neighborhood of Seattle, stopping jobs along the way and finally arriving at Seattle Central Community College (SCCC). The following three days of protest became the climax of three years of direct action by black construction workers in Seattle. When protesters arrived to shut down construction at the community college, the fifty workers on the job refused to stop working. The job supervisor and a protester got in a fistfight that had to be broken up. Following this altercation, white workers gathered on the second floor of the building, shouted epithets, and dumped water on protesters. In response, a number of black protesters scaled the building ladders and beat the white workers. Austin St. Laurent, who was with the workers who refused to quit work, was hit across the back, knocked to the ground, and had his glasses broken. Another union representative was knocked unconscious, while a third, Henry Andes, after stepping up to defend St. Laurent, was hit across the face with a rebar pipe and knocked unconscious while his head was repeatedly beaten into the ground (he was taken to the hospital to have his jaw reset). Instead of arresting the perpetrators, the police, who had done little to intervene until fighting broke out, arrested Tyree Scott, Todd Hawkins, and three prominent UCWA allies.[55]

The next day, Scott joined over 175 UCWA protesters and allies at the college and found the school ringed with police and filled with armed construction workers, many of whom were former veterans. Andes recalled that "the construction workers on the job were about the most heavily armed civilian personnel I've ever seen: 44 magnums, handguns all the way down to sawed off shotguns were there." Scott and other UCWA activists, clandestinely listening to the police radio, had learned about the situation that faced them and decided that trying to occupy the construction site would be suicidal. Instead, the protesters raided and badly vandalized an unprotected working building that was part of the college campus. With as many as nine hundred people in the building, protesters broke 110 windows and caused over $15,000 in damage in less than seven minutes. Exiting from the back of the building to avoid the police in front, nearly one hundred protesters encountered only a dozen police who tried to stop them. Photos of the pitched street battle between police and half a dozen of black activists wearing hard hats and wielding two-by-fours made it into the local newspapers and put the ineffectiveness of the court order on display better than any statistic could.[56]

That afternoon, Lindberg issued a supplement to his court order that (1) mandated a 1:5 minority apprentice-to-journeyman ratio, (2) required the enrollment of a minimum of 180 special apprentices by July 7 to meet the requirements of the court order (there were only 86 enrolled when he issued his order), and (3) granted the COAC authority to directly petition the court instead of using Department of Justice lawyers as intermediaries. He did not grant the UCWA dispatch authority or make it a party to the lawsuit, although he promised that a decision on these issues was forthcoming.[57]

June 8 brought the third day of protests at the college as well as a change of tactics by the protesters that was meant to deescalate what had become an extremely dangerous situation. It was, according to Scott, "the biggest demonstration we ever had. Everybody was there, the middle class people, priests, all sorts of folks, women and children. So we had a responsibility at that point, not to get people's heads beat." Scott, Hawkins, and two other UCWA allies chose to be voluntarily arrested to stop the street fighting and return the battle for Black Power to the courts. "We're not getting moderate. We just don't want to get killed," Scott claimed. "If we continue now they're going to kill some of us because we're so-called violent." They planned to use their time in jail to fast and dramatize the hypocrisy of black workers' being in jail while court-ordered hiring requirements continued to go unmet. But, instead, the district court judge waived bail after they refused to pay it, releasing them despite the fact that they refused to sign their own release papers. "This is embarrassing," Scott told the *Seattle Times,* now thoroughly disillusioned with what he considered the arbitrary enforcement of the law. "Getting thrown out of jail. This is as low as you can get."[58]

Following his ejection from jail, Scott led a series of community rallies to press for the UCWA to be granted dispatch power over minority workers. At a June 11 rally at Garfield High School, he linked the UCWA struggle to that of the black community more generally, saying, "What we want is the right for community control. That's what it means, the right to have minority workers dispatch out minority workers."[59]

Lindberg made the UCWA party to the *Local 86* lawsuit and official members of the COAC on June 12, 1972, but he again delayed a decision on dispatching power. When the COAC reconvened, union leaders boycotted it and contractors refused to endorse Scott's proposal to give the UCWA dispatching authority. But, because the contractors abstained from voting, a unanimous vote granted the UCWA dispatch power anyway. The vote, although only symbolic, once again threw the COAC into crisis.[60]

In response to Lindberg's new order, St. Laurent claimed that Judge was senile and called for his resignation. He announced his own resignation from the COAC in an open letter that claimed, "by giving [UCWA] dispatch or any other semblance of recognition, the judge would be, in effect, creating a new, separate, all-black union, which is what we don't want. We want everyone together in the present unions."[61] He complained that "it appears that every action of the Court in this case has been in reaction to illegal acts of violence and threats of such violence." And he seemed to threaten white worker violence by warning, "we are presently unable to continue to control our membership (both black and white) because of their belief that the Department of Justice and the Court is using the United Construction Workers Association (UCWA) and Tyree Scott to attempt to destroy the construction unions."[62]

The day that St. Laurent resigned from the COAC and called for Lindberg to be removed from his job, the UCWA organized a fifty-hour vigil outside the federal courthouse supported by members of the Church Council of Greater Seattle, who brought food and sleeping bags. But June 15 came and went with Lindberg again delaying his decision on how to reconstitute the COAC or on how black workers would be dispatched to construction sites. On June 16, the UCWA led a march that, in addition to black radicals, included Asian, Chicano, and white left activists. Together, they closed down three large and three small construction sites.[63]

The pressure eventually paid off. In July 1972, Judge Lindberg added the UCWA to the suit, gave it representation in the COAC, formalized its role as a counselor for and screener of all black apprentices prior to union dispatch, and issued a permanent injunction against the UCWA's shutting down another construction site. By making black workers' private grievances public and by taking the ongoing crisis within the construction industry from the workplace back into the streets, the UCWA had successfully linked affirmative action enforcement to black worker empowerment.[64]

The events of June 1972 thus broke the back of union resistance to affirmative action in the Seattle construction industry. Judge Lindberg's order, produced in response to over a month of militant direct-action protests, stood as a model for government activism at a time when the Department of Labor was retreating from affirmative action in an attempt to woo conservative working-class white ethnics to vote for Nixon in 1972. St. Laurent, outraged, canceled the parallel union affirmative action program and abandoned his claims that unions could oversee desegregation without cooperation from African American community organizations. In the time between Lindberg's temporary supplemental order in June and when it was made permanent in July 1972, seventy-five special apprentices were added to the previous ninety-two of the program, showing the power of community action to bring about a quick change of structures that had claimed to be hamstrung by political and economic constraints.[65]

The UCWA victory contrasted sharply with the experiences of black workers in cities across the country, for whom the failure of affirmative action plans brought further marginalization rather than empowerment. UCWA got more jobs for black workers in June 1972 than many affirmative action plans operating for two years in cities that were significantly larger and more racially diverse than Seattle. The more than one hundred voluntary plans across the country were unable to deal with high black attrition and low union compliance. In Chicago, the city that had the first voluntary plan for its construction industry and that was used as a model for hometown plans in other cities, the call to hire 4,000 new black apprentices in one year was met with only 75 new recruits. In addition, a city alderman who oversaw the finances of the program embezzled large amounts of Department of Labor money, and the plan collapsed in rancor. In Philadelphia, the original test case for affirmative action in the construction industry, plans for 1,000 new jobs for black workers in the first year brought only 60 hires. In Pittsburgh, the second city with a voluntary hometown plan, two years and $500,000 (some of it embezzled) produced only ten successful graduates of a black apprenticeship program. From Boston to San Francisco, Detroit to Atlanta, the statistics invariably told the same story: widespread failure to even come close to meeting the desegregation goals. By the end of 1972, the *New York Times* reported that "the Nixon administration has reportedly all but abandoned efforts to force Federal contractors to hire more blacks," and quoted a federal compliance officer as saying that "morale around here has hit the floor."[66]

In this context, NAACP Labor Director Herbert Hill and law professor William Gould began to tout the Seattle court order as an alternative means for making affirmative action work in the 1970s. A few years later, even Ray Marshall, President Carter's secretary of labor, coauthored a book that singled out the UCWA community action model of enforcing affirmative action as something for other cities to emulate.[67]

Yet UCWA activists did not kid themselves about the immediate effect of their victory in 1972. Despite the Lindberg order requirement to train 270 black workers in its first three years, only six workers had actually finished their training and become journeymen by summer 1972. The inclusion of the UCWA in the court order did not promise that it would be able to overcome the substantial barriers to training, placing, and making black workers full members in their respective unions. But it did give UCWA activists new means and new inspiration to promote a model of community organizing through Title VII law that gave black workers power to regulate workplace culture without placing the onus for change entirely on their shoulders.[68]

Title VII Community Organizing

Heady from their inclusion in the *U.S. v. Local 86* case, UCWA leaders branched out in numerous directions with the hope of planting the seeds of a national movement of minority worker radicalism based on the UCWA model. Between 1971 and 1974, the UCWA used its AFSC contacts in other cities to try to develop chapters outside Seattle—organizing black construction workers in Portland and Denver and hiring a former Black Panther to organize black truck drivers in Oakland, California. These efforts, however, quickly fizzled: local community activists proved wary of outsiders, and aggressive litigation strategies did not always fit with the desires of the communities to which the UCWA tried to expand.

But, in 1973, the UCWA secured a contract from the U.S. Equal Employment Opportunity Commission (EEOC) to host workshops on workers' rights under the 1972 Civil Rights Act in eight mid-size cities in Oklahoma, Texas, Louisiana, and Arkansas. Instead of hosting workshops, Scott, Hawkins, and Michael Simmons, an AFSC activist, decided to use the EEOC grant to do community organizing. They traveled from city to city—attending churches, visiting local Urban League and NAACP offices, hanging out in pool halls and barber shops, and attending barbeques—all the time asking about workplace discrimination and talking about what they had accomplished in Seattle.[69]

After gathering stories and making connections, Scott and Hawkins started small community organizations of blue-collar workers, trained workers to collect testimony for Title VII lawsuits, and connected workers with attorneys from Seattle, Stanford, and New York to assist with their legal strategy. In December 1973, as the EEOC grant expired, the UCWA held a conference in Waco, Texas, that brought together three hundred people from the eight cities to found a federation for their worker-led community organizations to sustain their aggressive campaigns to desegregate local industries. The umbrella organization they created, the Southwest Workers Federation (SWF), filed five Title VII lawsuits in seven months and at least 25 EEOC complaints in each city challenging racism in major industries throughout the region (the Little Rock chapter produced over 100 EEOC complaints alone). The SWF continued for roughly five years as black workers took advantage of the legal training they received to organize activist community groups that addressed everything from employment discrimination to police accountability to antiapartheid activism. In cities such as Tulsa and Shreveport, where white supremacy had been so entrenched that the civil rights movements there had rarely used nonviolent direct action, these new worker organizations became the most vocal and outspoken Black Power organizations the cities had.[70]

Meanwhile, in Seattle, the UCWA success in 1972 played an important role in the development of a worker-centered U.S. Third World Left in the mid-1970s. The distinguishing features of this emergent left were (1) multiracial solidarity; (2) a language of *third world,* rather than *minority* or *people of color,* to describe the communities that activists sought to unite in common cause; and (3) a labor radicalism whose campaigns for "self-determination" at home were framed in solidarity with "third world" independence movements abroad.[71]

The UCWA influence on Asian American radicalism in the Pacific Northwest was especially significant. In 1972, the UCWA provided seed money to Michael Woo, its Chinese American staff person, and a group of young Filipino activists to use the UCWA organizational model to combat racism in the Alaska cannery industry. These activists created the Alaska Cannery Workers Association (ACWA), filed a number of Title VII lawsuits, and used these lawsuits (which prohibit retaliatory firing) to protect themselves against International Longshore and Warehouse Union (ILWU) Local 37 and employer attempts to blacklist them. ACWA activists then created the Seattle chapter of the Filipino communist organization, the Katipunan ng mga Demokratikong Pilipino (KDP, or Union of Democratic Filipinos). This group, the only pan-Asian chapter of the KDP, played a large role in organizing grassroots pressure to preserve Seattle's International District. These same activists also formed a Local 37 Rank and File Committee, and began connecting their union reform politics to solidarity campaigns against the Ferdinand Marcos dictatorship (the corrupt union dispatch system rewarded allies of Marcos).[72]

Although growing in different directions, the ACWA and UCWA continued to collaborate through the Northwest Labor and Employment Law Office (LELO), which they cofounded in 1974. A law office for worker-led movements that was separate from the War on Poverty lawyers they had previously relied on, LELO hired lawyers to oversee the various lawsuits filed by the Washington state United Farm Workers (UFW), the ACWA, and the UCWA. The LELO Board of Directors originally consisted of three Filipino cannery workers, three Mexican farm workers, and three black construction workers.[73]

The experience of international travel played an important role in UCWA members' analytical shift from antiracist to anti-imperialist organizing in the mid-1970s. In 1971, UCWA leaders cofounded, along with AFSC-related groups across the country, the AFSC Third World Coalition (TWC). The TWC demanded affirmative action *within* the AFSC; the involvement of nonwhite people in the AFSC international peace work; and a rethinking of the AFSC mission from promoting peace abroad through charity work to promoting peace and justice through the support of anticolonial struggles. Milton Jefferson, UCWA activist, became the first TWC president, and Tyree Scott helped involve other Seattle-area activists by forming a northwestern TWC chapter that played an active role in national TWC affairs. Roberto Maestas, a Seattle Chicano activist, served as TWC president a couple of years after Jefferson. Under both men's leadership, the TWC provided an umbrella through which radical organizations around the country networked with one another and accessed resources from the AFSC that few other such radical organizations had. They used this money to travel around the world to meet anticolonial third world nationalist and communist revolutionary leaders, and to bring revolutionaries to the United States. During this time, Tyree Scott went on a workers delegation to China, and Todd Hawkins went to Mozambique. A large delegation of UCWA activists also started regularly participating in Venceremos Brigade trips to Cuba.[74]

International travel helped UCWA members rethink their local struggles in an international context. In 1976 when Tyree Scott became cochair of the TWC with Michael Simmons, fellow SWF organizer and AFSC staffer, the two spun off its affirmative action advocacy to the AFSC human resources department. They then focused the TWC on international solidarity work for the next three years. During the late 1970s, Simmons and Scott sponsored trips of AFSC organizers of color around the world and brought third world revolutionaries to visit the United States. They dovetailed their leadership of the TWC with the a new communist group that they were active in, the Organizing Committee for an Ideological Center (OCIC). Although separate from the AFSC, Scott and Simmons moved between the TWC and OCIC seamlessly as they coordinated a network of a dozen city-based revolutionary worker cadres across the country. Their organizing borrowed from the worker organizing they had done in the Southwest and even included a few activists from Tulsa who had moved to Seattle to be a part of its workers' group. Simmons's work, in particular, played an important early role in laying the groundwork for anti-apartheid activism in the United States in the 1970s.[75]

In Seattle, the international turn in the outlook of UCWA leaders influenced their decision to focus more on consciousness raising and power building than on desegregation per se. During the late 1970s, they published *No Separate Peace*, a periodical written by and about workers of color who framed their workplace and neighborhood campaigns for justice in Seattle as part of an international struggle against U.S. capitalism, white supremacy, and imperialism.[76]

The UCWA remained unable, however, to overcome the growing barriers that the institutionalization of affirmative action erected against ongoing community organizing. Once the UCWA had finally gained power in the COAC, its role shifted toward black caucus work within the individual building trades unions. But the recession in the construction industry and the decline of union power in the 1970s made it difficult to secure additional jobs. Most union members remained suspicious of, if not hostile to, UCWA members who showed up to union meetings demanding new and more inclusive forms of organizing. Scott himself was stretched thin by the ambitiousness of the UCWA expansion, and so were a few other UCWA leaders. As a result of his work, Scott was blacklisted, and other UCWA members found themselves struggling to get work or sent to do jobs that others did not want. The UCWA, along with the SWF, also found it easier to gain support from black apprentices and workers who needed to be politically active to gain access to jobs. But once jobs were opened up, many workers' political activity became uneven even before Scott and his allies became more focused on building worker cadres than building mass protest or social service organizations.[77]

The dissolution of the COAC proved a turning point for the UCWA. In 1978, employers, unions, and COAC staff argued that the construction industry had finally met Judge Lindberg's affirmative action goals. Tyree Scott and the UCWA, however, complained that the goals had been met only on paper and that racism persisted unimpeded. Black apprentices, they argued, had graduated but lacked the skills to compete and ended up working in the same shipyard jobs they had always been relegated to. Scott also claimed that the union dispatch procedures continued to be discriminatory. In response, Rieke, the COAC chair, took a narrow view of the court order. He argued that it required the indenture of a certain number of workers but never claimed to promise steady employment after they had learned a trade. Rieke thus concluded that racism in dispatch procedures or on the job was "an issue outside of this particular decree." After 1978, the responsibility of COAC to recruit black apprentices was thus spun off to a powerless social service agency while its oversight of the hiring and training of workers was returned to the labor unions, which were weaker than when the desegregation battles had begun.[78]

Without the COAC, UCWA lacked the institutional power that had made it distinct from other radical black worker organizations in the 1970s. Attempts to expand the UCWA model proved even more difficult. The EEOC backlog of discrimination complaints reached the hundreds of thousands by the mid-1970s, and Title VII lawsuits swelled the dockets of federal district courts around the country. With the EEOC badly underfunded and the courts ill-equipped to oversee wide-ranging decrees, the institutions established to enforce affirmative action became increasingly bureaucratic and reduced the opportunities for community organizing. Similarly, as the sense of urgency in response to black urban rebellion faded, Title VII case law evolved in a way that made litigation increasingly time-consuming, with some cases initiated by LELO taking between ten and fifteen years to resolve. These delays made it more difficult for activists to gain the cash settlements that the UCWA had hoped would fund the movement, while also making the litigation itself more costly.[79]

As it became more difficult to use affirmative action law for radical organizing, the UCWA disbanded, and its leaders folded their community-organizing activities into LELO, which they transformed from a law office to a multiracial community-based labor organization in Seattle. During the 1990s, LELO facilitated the organization of caucuses of workers of color and women within the unions; demanded jobs for people of color on public works and urban redevelopment projects; and played a prominent role in promoting police accountability. It organized local workers of color to protest at the 1999 World Trade Organization (WTO) meeting in Seattle and worked with other groups around the world to develop workers' proposals to restructure the global economy. LELO followed up on these activities in 2001 to connect the themes of global trade and local jobs by creating a Port Profits for Human Needs Campaign—inspired by a similar successful campaign in Los Angeles in the early 1990s. Tyree Scott's passing in 2003 slowed that campaign and LELO organizing. But the alternative labor movement that Tyree Scott led, and the generation of multiracial labor radicals and antiracist activists that he mentored, continue to organize two-pronged battles for both jobs and power.[80]

Conclusion

WHITE MALE IDENTITY POLITICS, THE BUILDING TRADES, AND THE FUTURE OF AMERICAN LABOR

David Goldberg and Trevor Griffey

On January 9, 2009, Robert Reich, Secretary of Labor during President Bill Clinton's first term, appeared before the House Democratic Caucus Steering and Policy Committee Forum to provide testimony regarding President Barack Obama's stimulus plan and its potential impact on the construction industry. At first, Reich reiterated a key axiom of liberal economic policy since the New Deal. "It seems to me," he explained, "that infrastructure spending is a very important and good way of stimulating the economy. The challenge will be to do it quickly, to find projects that can be done that have a high social return that also can be done with the greatest speed possible." But Reich went on to express "concern...that these jobs not simply go to high skilled people who are already in professions or to white male construction workers." Reich said that he had "nothing against white male construction workers," but added that if "jobs go mainly to white males who already dominate the construction trades, many people who need jobs the most—women, minorities, and the poor and long-term unemployed— will be shut out."[1]

Reich's testimony set off a firestorm of criticism from right-wing critics, who suggested that any race- or gender-conscious employment program would inherently discriminate against white men. Rush Limbaugh, conservative radio talk show host, for example, butchered Reich's comments while repeating the age-old justifications for white male privilege, telling his audience, "he doesn't want it to go to white construction workers; he wants it to go to inexperienced minorities and single women."[2]

It was not hard to grasp the political motivation for Limbaugh's dishonest description of Reich's comments. For the past forty years, Republicans have sought to organize white working-class men to oppose the New Deal state in general and federal employment programs in particular by exploiting workers' economic anxiety in racial and gendered terms. Ever since Nixon's blue-collar strategy and embrace of the hard hats, Republicans have insinuated that federal employment programs that focus on the poor—who are disproportionately nonwhite and nonmale—are a form of "reverse discrimination" against white men. This electoral strategy has discouraged white working-class men from thinking of themselves as part of the "deserving poor" and encouraged them to instead oppose federal spending even when it promises to stimulate the economy during a recession. The new rhetorical figure of "Joe the Plumber" during the 2008 presidential election was just the latest variant of this old icon of the new right—white working-class men who blamed their economic insecurity not on the retreat from full-employment programs but on government spending, taxes, and affirmative action.[3]

Barack Obama's election in November 2008 has at least temporarily shown the limits of these divisive cultural politics. We now have a historic opportunity, which may not last long, to move beyond unproductive culture wars and create a viable politics for full employment for the first time in over forty years. Only a new, multiracial movement of working-class men and women can move this political agenda forward. It is in the spirit of imagining what that movement might look like, as well as the challenges it faces, that we have brought together the studies in this book—because, although a great deal has changed in the forty years since the struggles discussed in this book took place, the racial segregation of U.S. cities and the need to rebuild them have become more extreme. Revisiting the economic agenda of the Black Power movement—its ambitious goal of community-controlled urban redevelopment and its more humble legacy of community-centered labor organizing—provides an opportunity for us to reflect on the kind of future that we want. It helps us imagine the kind of jobs programs needed to employ low-income, minority, and women workers while staving off the Great Recession and transitioning to a "new economy," as well as to consider the type of labor movement needed to put this nation on the path to social justice.

But, to imagine a way forward, we must first revisit the legacies and effects of the struggles for community control of the construction industry in the 1960s and 1970s. Here we provide an overview of those legacies before ending with a consideration of how social-justice unionism in the construction industry could, and should, play an important part in revitalizing the labor movement.

Black Power, White Wealth

The strategies that the black community control activists advanced to gain the badly needed money for urban redevelopment came with trade-offs. During the 1970s, black neighborhood activists—from small business owners to contractors to arts organizations to social service providers—increasingly turned to black electoral politics to promote locally controlled community-development agencies. But federal disinvestment, economic recession, and tax revolts made black elected officials better at dispensing political patronage than rebuilding the inner cities or substantially redistributing wealth. President Richard Nixon set this process in motion when he dramatically told his aides in the early 1970s to quietly "flush Model Cities and the Great Society."[4]

With racism still strong enough that U.S. politicians could appear credible by blaming nonwhites and the unemployed for the economic consequences of federal disinvestment and the urban crisis, mainstream U.S. political culture descended into what Cornel West aptly called a forty-year "political, moral and spiritual ice age."[5] Black workers—the vast majority of whom worked in blue-collar or service industry jobs—had fewer resources to adapt to deindustrialization. Black urban politicians who sought to address this disadvantage faced profound barriers to using local taxing authority to sustain or expand the inner-city projects that Nixon had abandoned. Rising operating costs, white flight, capital flight, and grassroots movements to limit county and state property taxes on suburban homeowners drove urban governments to the brink of bankruptcy during the 1970s, leaving black politicians with few tools to promote the social justice agendas that they had promised voters.

Nixon aided this process by fragmenting the already loosely defined Black Power movement, appealing to its more conservative and business-oriented elements through his advocacy of black capitalism, a trend reinforced through the dispersal of block grant funding.[6] This focus on black business growth for community development, in conjunction with the implementation of home-town plans sponsored by the American Federation of Labor–Congress of Industrial Organizations (AFL-CIO), created fissures between black contractors and construction coalitions by focusing more on providing set-aside contracts to minority-led businesses than on securing training and jobs for black tradesmen. As a result, some local construction coalitions devolved into "semi-official employment agencies" and "junior partners in a struggle to get more contracts for non-white contractors." As Gregory Butler, New York tradesman and author laments, "The minority worker Coalitions we built ended up decaying into class collaborationist institutions, servile to the contractors and dominated by the gangster....basically, they became mirror images of the very building trades unions they had risen up in opposition to."[7]

Black Power movement campaigns for community control of the construction industry during the 1960s and early 1970s fit within the broader movement for black economic development through their demands for jobs. Like many other aspects of the Black Power movement, the campaigns for self-determination were ironically dependent on government funding and aggressive federal enforcement. Without this support, community control campaigns were able to break open the racially segregated trade unions but failed to desegregate them.[8] They provided thousands of jobs that enabled blue-collar black workers to enter the middle class, but fell far short of making a meaningful dent in the rising black poverty and unemployment rates. They popularized the notion that the economic redevelopment of inner-city neighborhoods should benefit the residents of those neighborhoods. And they put the needs of everyday workers at the center of their alternative vision to deindustrialization and the displacement of unskilled workers by automation and capital flight. But it proved easier for black politicians and developers to adopt that rhetoric than to put it into practice.

As a result, well after the passage of the 1960s civil rights laws, a system of "American apartheid" persists to the present day. Despite the growth of a black middle class, most blacks remain disproportionately poor and segregated into spaces where their access to health care, education, employment, and a healthy environment is far below that of other groups in the United States. The emergence of black-market economies and the explosive growth in the incarceration of young unemployed men of color as part of the War on Drugs has hidden the deeper structural crisis produced in U.S. cities "when work disappears."[9]

When private investment finally began to flow into parts of the inner cities closest to downtown retail and business districts, two decades of recession left the residents of historically black neighborhoods with little leverage to demand more than symbolic concessions from developers. As Roger Waldinger and Thomas Bailey note, despite the effects of automation and deindustrialization, "there are still some very well-paying goods-producing jobs to be had in the postindustrial city. They can be found in construction, the one urban blue collar sector that has thrived during the years of manufacturing decline."[10] But the failure to gain community control of the construction industry has kept most of these jobs out of reach.

Because few community institutions were strong enough to demand that the flow of new investment benefit the inner-city residents, the revitalization of U.S. cities became synonymous with gentrification—the displacement of working people from their homes and neighborhoods by rising property values. A few black middle-class residents may have profited from the selling of their homes or businesses as increasingly affluent residents moved in and property values increased, but low-income renters, who make up the majority of inner-city residents, have not been so fortunate. In the absence of community control of urban redevelopment, investment in the inner cities increased rents without providing jobs for the unemployed or higher wages for low-wage workers. The resulting displacement of a predominantly nonwhite working class from the inner cities to exurbs with cheaper rent in cities such as New York, Boston, and Seattle has separated the working poor and working classes from basic services such as public transportation and social services. Unhelpful debates about gentrification have mystified this process, putting the focus on whether reinvestment should take place at all rather than on who controls and benefits from the redevelopment of inner-city neighborhoods.

Reactionary Unionism and the Paltry Wages of Whiteness

The building trades unions have not benefited nearly as much as they could have from the rampant real estate speculation in cities at the center of the U.S. "knowledge economy." Construction workers' control over local labor markets after World War II provided enormous dividends that accrued through the cultivation of racial privilege. But the ongoing union defense of that control along narrow craft-oriented lines proved reactionary. By *reactionary,* we mean backward-looking, trying to preserve gains from the past in a changing society rather than wrestling with the new organizing demands of the present.

The seeds of this backwardness were laid by the response of the building trades unions to the post–World War II migration of black workers to the urban North. The United States of the 1960s and 1970s was not the same place as the United States of the 1930s and 1940s. Craft unions in the AFL may have been able to prevent racial discrimination from being prohibited as an unfair labor practice in federal labor law, but Title VII of the 1964 Civil Rights Act included union racism as a form of employment discrimination, making it illegal. The Title VII prohibition of racial quotas, however, forestalled an immediate requirement that the building trades unions desegregate.[11] But fear of black urban violence and of Black Power protests, along with the assassination of Martin Luther King Jr., cleared the way for racial liberals in the government to set more rigorous standards of compliance with civil rights law. The union's refusal to compromise in good faith with these racial liberals or to adhere to the standing law undermined their ability to incorporate or represent the interests of the new working class and weakened the labor movement as a whole.

By treating affirmative action as antiunion while refusing to reform union locals' abuse of their hiring hall and apprenticeship programs, the unions all but ensured that racial desegregation would require challenging their collective bargaining rights. The unions, some of which had been controlled by organized crime, originally had organized through the sabotage of construction sites and threats of violence, but now hypocritically viewed Black Power disruptions of the construction industry as both criminal and antiunion. Although they had consolidated their power and wealth through the New Deal, the unions now portrayed government regulations that they disagreed with as infringements on their freedoms rather than disruptions of their privileges. Union's defensive embrace of law and order politics proved especially ironic given that the police and military had a long history of being used by the U.S. government to break strikes by organized labor. And their embrace of Nixon for cultural and racial rather than economic reasons highlighted the ways in which masculinity and race informed the boundaries of white men's solidarity among the so-called barons of labor.[12]

Once the building trades unions were able to blunt the enforcement of affirmative action by reducing it to being localized and voluntary, they could more or less maintain the informal hiring and training practices that had preserved their racial exclusivity. Indeed, resentment about having ever been subjected to affirmative action mandates—no matter how briefly or poorly enforced—provided the unions with a new rationale for perpetuating the informal practices that favored white workers. But the resulting "wages of whiteness" have impaired the standing of the unions in the industry and retarded their ability to organize the twenty-first-century workplace.

The reaction of many white tradesmen to the gradual inclusion of black workers in the industry blamed affirmative action for something it had nothing to do with—the extremely high rates of unemployment that devastated the entire construction industry during the 1970s. There is no doubt that there were a few years in the early 1970s when the hometown plans prevented the unions from providing jobs or apprenticeships to white workers. And in the mid- to late 1970s, the court-ordered desegregation of unions that resisted the hometown plans resulted in some white workers not having access to the jobs and apprenticeships they felt entitled to. But these losses were minor compared to the massive injuries inflicted on *all* construction workers during the 1970s by a recession that left more than three-quarters of tradesmen in some cities regularly out of work. The tacit acceptance of the normalcy of economic downturns in a capitalist system minimized this understanding, however. And the growing threat of nonunion labor made new construction workers—first nonwhite men, then nonwhite women, and then white women—easy scapegoats for white men during prolonged periods of unemployment.

Chronic unemployment during the 1970s and 1980s dealt a devastating blow to the power of the building trades unions. Between 1973 and 1984, the union share of total construction volume in the United States decreased from 50 to 30 percent. The inroads by "open shop" construction into the residential construction industry had begun in the mid-1960s but accelerated so quickly that, by the early 1980s, union contractors controlled 10 percent of residential construction nationally, at best.[13] During that same time, unions went from representing 40 to just 23 percent of the construction workforce, and many of those who remained in the unions began "double-vesting," working nonunion as well as union jobs, to make ends meet.[14]

There were multiple causes for the deunionization and deskilling of the construction industry in the 1970s and 1980s, but affirmative action was not one of them. Faced with joblessness rates as high as 90 percent for some skilled trades in northeastern cities, the building trades unions resisted the renegotiation of their collective bargaining agreements, and many union workers and union contractors began doing lower-paying nonunion jobs on the side. Nonunion contractors did not just pay the journeymen less; they also refused to adhere to journeyman-to-apprentice ratios that prevented the hiring of low-skill workers to do journeyman labor. New job categories such as "sub-journeyman" and "helper" proliferated in nonunion firms, as contractors came to rely on a few skilled journeymen to do specialized jobs while employing semiskilled workers to do the mundane, repetitive tasks that first- and second-year apprentices once did.[15] But, whereas apprentices were groomed to learn a trade and eventually move up into the ranks of skilled labor, "helpers" and "sub-journeymen" effectively deskilled part of the labor force.

Despite the fact that nonunion contractors claimed that these new positions provided minority workers more jobs, it was white workers who did the majority of nonunion work in the 1970s.[16] In the Southwest, Latinos were disproportionately relegated to the new lower-skilled, lower-paying jobs in the construction industry (a trend that has accelerated nationally since the 1970s).[17] Nonwhite workers elsewhere presumably would have jumped at the chance for nonunion work as well, but nonunion firms grew far more in the suburbs than in the inner cities, leaving workers of color more dependent on the urban economies in which the unions still held significant sway.[18]

The downward pressure that nonunion contractors placed on wages and working conditions motivated union contractors to demand major concessions from the unions as a matter of survival—a demand with which most unions complied. So, even though the construction industry finally revived in the 1990s, deunionization continues to this day. Only 15 percent of construction trades workers were union members or covered by union contracts in 2006, and many of those worked on federal construction projects.[19] The cultural politics of the construction workplace, however, continues to retard the ability of the unions to respond to this catastrophic loss of power.

To this day, many white workers in the building trades are more likely to view affirmative action as a greater threat to their employment prospects than the lack of a full-employment program. A study of construction industry apprentices in Baltimore in the early 1990s, for instance, found an ideology of reverse discrimination widespread among white apprentices. Believing that affirmative action had made it harder for white men to get jobs, even though few if any had ever personally experienced an act of antiwhite discrimination, white apprentices justified the special favors that they received from employers, teachers, and relatives in the trades as *necessary* to their success. The fact that black apprentices rarely, if ever, received such favors was not seen as discriminatory. Whites' defensive maintenance of discriminatory hiring policies thus "served to create disincentives for including blacks and replaced the old black-inferiority rationale for exclusion with a new black-ascendancy rationale." And although many youth have adopted more flexible approaches to race, apprentices' dependence on older white men for employment and support still creates a "strong disincentive against making any proactive attempts to include black men within predominantly white networks." As a result, black workers who attended the same trade school and earned grades that were just as good as, if not better than, their white counterparts still ended up being less likely to find gainful employment in the construction trades. Because of their frequent experiences with racism, even those black apprentices in Baltimore who did succeed sometimes expressed a preference for self-employment or for working in lower-pay, lower-skill jobs in order to be in environments in which they would not supervised by white workers.[20]

According to Kris Paap, a sociologist and former tradeswoman, when she entered the construction industry, she found that "the most significant elements of the social structure—that of the class inequality between the men in construction—appeared to be virtually unrecognized."[21] Instead, she found many union journeymen "identifying up the chain of command" and believing that they had more in common with white contractors than with their fellow nonwhite or women workers. When "well-intentioned individuals are able to participate comfortably in the subordination and exclusion of others," Paap argues, even traditionally exclusive skilled craft unions become weaker.[22] She found that a macho workplace culture encouraged work speedups, unsafe work habits, and cut-throat competition instead of solidarity and teamwork among workers. When journeymen shop stewards felt a greater kinship with their employers than their fellow workers, union contracts that might have provided workers with a means to avoid unnecessarily high injuries or protected workers from arbitrary firings often went un-enforced. Or they were renegotiated without complaint. Or they were simply "dismantled little by little by individuals" on the job who were more likely to blame one another than management for their economic insecurity and to blame themselves for avoidable workplace accidents.[23]

Women in the Construction Industry

Some of the most searing indictments of the effects of white male cultural politics in the construction workplace, and some of the best organizing to push the construction unions to represent all workers, have come from the tradeswomen movement that emerged in the 1970s and continues to this day. The tradeswomen movement was inspired by black workers' campaigns to desegregate the construction industry in the 1960s, but it received little support from the black community control campaigns, except in those cities where black construction workers formed their own independent organizations. And even then support was uneven.

White and nonwhite men's competition for jobs in the construction industry has often been over the limits of the rights and privileges associated with manhood. Even as they debated masculine fitness for blue-collar labor and the standards of high-skilled labor, most actors in the civil rights and labor movements still largely shared an unspoken belief that *only* men belonged in blue-collar industries. Although racial and gender discrimination often relied on the same dehumanizing arguments, and the same laws that prohibited racial discrimination prohibited gender discrimination, the two were treated completely differently by male employers, unions, and civil rights activists in the 1960s. Legal breakthroughs secured through the black freedom movement set precedents for equal opportunity that made women's exclusion from blue-collar industries seem unjustifiable. Yet the barriers to employment that civil rights and Black Power activists delegitimized for black men during the 1960s proved more enduring when women began challenging them. Government enforcement agencies for antidiscrimination law proved wary of extending women the same legal rights to employment as men. When they did, it usually occurred years after black men had been granted similar rights and mainly in response to independent women's organizing.

During the 1960s, the federal government's enforcement of nondiscrimination law focused almost exclusively on men's rights to earn a living. Title VII of the 1964 Civil Rights Act prohibited employment discrimination on the basis of sex as well as race, but the enforcement of the law by the Department of Justice during the 1960s focused on developing remedies for racial discrimination against men. Various presidential orders issued between 1942 and 1965 prohibited employment discrimination based on race, but they were not amended to include sex discrimination until President Lyndon Johnson issued Executive Order 11375 in 1967.

Federal agencies were totally unprepared for, and uninterested in, the more than 2,500 sex discrimination complaints (nearly 30 percent of all Title VII complaints) filed with the Equal Employment Opportunity Commission (EEOC) during the first year after Title VII went into effect. Unlike race-based struggles against employment discrimination, these complaints *preceded* the development of any sustained push by advocacy organizations calling on women to challenge employment discrimination at work. In many ways, the complaints drove the creation of new organizations seeking to catch up with individual women's growing radicalism and rights consciousness.[24] New political promises of equal opportunity resulting from prior black freedom movement pressure thus created new opportunities and showed that change was possible. At the same time, they locked women out of that change.

Women's activism emerged to push federal agencies to enforce these laws. The negligence of the EEOC in enforcing nondiscrimination law based on sex during the 1960s provided the main inspiration for the founding of the National Organization for Women (NOW) in 1966. Inspired by the example of the civil rights movement, NOW billed itself as the "N.A.A.C.P. of women's rights." Still, it was not until July 1970 that the Department of Justice filed its first Title VII sex discrimination case. And the Department of Labor did not make a serious effort to enforce Executive Order 11375 until organized pressure from NOW and the Women's Equality Action League (WEAL) shamed them into it in 1970.

In the construction industry and other skilled trades historically dominated by men, the enforcement of equal employment law by the Department of Labor gave priority to ending racial discrimination, not sex discrimination, even though the Department of Labor was ostensibly enforcing executive orders that promised both. Although the Department of Labor's Office of Federal Contract Compliance (OFCC) developed programs during the mid-1960s to enforce prohibitions against racial discrimination, the Department of Labor's Women's Bureau remained separate from this process and was essentially powerless.[25] The revival by the Department of Labor of the Philadelphia Plan in 1969 and its issuance of Order No. 4 in early 1970 promised more rigorous enforcement of federal antidiscrimination law by invoking the threat of imposed affirmative action plans on U.S. industries. But neither one explicitly mentioned sex discrimination. The Department of Labor thus treated women's and nonwhite men's claims differently, using affirmative action to attack stereotypes about lack of competency and interest that barred nonwhite men from skilled trades while invoking the same stereotypes to deny women similar access.

Although the Philadelphia Plan's focus on men has gone almost entirely un-mentioned by historians of affirmative action,[26] women's groups at the time were highly critical of their own exclusion from the Philadelphia Plan. As Arthur Fletcher moved to implement the Philadelphia Plan, NOW claimed that 1,300 federal contractors were openly violating Executive Order 11375 and teamed up with other women's organizations to lobby members of Congress to put pressure on the Department of Labor to take action. In response, the Department of Labor issued guidelines on sex discrimination on June 9, 1970; but these guidelines fell short of the more rigorous requirements of Order No. 4 that federal contractors conduct reviews of statistical workplace disparities to impose goals and timetables for eliminating those disparities.[27] NOW responded by conducting protests and demanding more aggressive federal action.[28] Secretary of Labor James Hodgson promised the following month to eventually "use goals and timetables to achieve equal job opportunity for women in Federal contract work," but hedged on when he would take action. Women's claims were complicated, he explained, by the lack of "availability" of women as well as a low degree of "interest."[29]

Additional pressure from women's organizations finally prompted the Labor Department to issue a Revised Order No. 4 in late 1971 "in the dead hours, elud-ing all but the most cursory notice."[30] Dean Kotlowski, Nixon historian, has de-scribed the Revised Order No. 4 as "the Magna Carta of female employment" because it was the first federal rule to actually specify that women were an af-fected class that federal contractors were required to hire through affirmative action plans.[31] But, in reality, the revisions to Order No. 4 accomplished little. Order No. 4 retained qualifications about women's availability that shaped the extremely low estimates used to determine affirmative action plan "goals." These qualifications gave compliance officers enforcing the order "wide discretion," which in practice meant that the order was not taken seriously.[32] This neglect was reflected by the Department of Labor 1972 Guidelines for Apprenticeship Train-ing, which added goals and timetables for racial minorities but not women.

As a result, women's entry into jobs in the skilled trades was minimal between 1972 and 1977—except, that is, when assertive women (often nonwhite women who entered the industry through their race and not gender) took it upon them-selves to enter this male-dominated world. During the mid-1970s, feminist orga-nizations in the San Francisco Bay Area, New York, Boston, Seattle, Madison, and elsewhere became the watchdogs of local government affirmative action plans to support workplace pioneers in blue-collar industries—including the construc-tion industry. Tradeswomen activism was heavily funded by the Department of Labor new manpower training program, the Comprehensive Employment and Training Act (CETA), inspiring Nancy MacLean to claim, "the federal govern-ment underwrote the movement."[33]

The efforts of pioneering tradeswomen groups in the mid-1970s allowed them to document the rampant sexual harassment in the industry and sex discrimination in hiring. Their lawsuit, which eventually became *Advocates for Women et al. v. Ray Marshall,* criticized the Department of Labor for refusing to set specific goals and timetables for women's entry into the construction industry years after Secretary Hodgson had promised to do so. Tradeswomen demanded something close to equity in the market, pushing for 40 percent of all construction jobs. The out-of-court settlement of the lawsuit in 1978 set much more modest goals. Contractors on federally funded projects had a goal for women of 3 percent that would rise to 6.9 percent in 1980, and the unions had a goal of 25 percent women for their apprenticeships.[34] But the enforcement mechanisms were never based on women's proportion in the workforce, and were always low and even easier to undermine than the goals and timetables set for nonwhite men. Thus, they were not difficult for contractors and unions to evade with impunity.

The literature on the tradeswomen movement, produced mainly by tradeswomen themselves, focuses less on the politics of statistical hiring goals than on the lived experiences of women on the job. Women pioneers in the construction industry—both feminist activists and working-class women in search of living-wage jobs—were met with near-universal hostility, contempt, or passive disregard. Numerous oral histories with tradeswomen document the fierce resistance they faced on entering the construction industry: the vicious hazing, the sexual harassment, and, most of all, the isolation. Providing inspiring stories of personal heroism and the role of tradeswomen organizations as support groups, many of the stories also provide scathing indictments of the "brotherhoods" that could not—and still largely cannot—view women as workers with equal rights to earn a living.

The building trades unions continue to hold the tradeswomen movement at arms' length and allow sexual discrimination and sexual harassment at work to go largely unchallenged. Also, by reserving living wage jobs for white men while excluding the working poor (the majority of whom are women), they have weakened their bargaining position, the unions, and the labor movement as a whole.[35]

No Worker Left Behind? Stimulus Spending, Green Jobs, and the Future of the U.S. Labor Movement

The construction industry remains an important site of social struggle for two reasons. First, construction remains a centerpiece of the U.S. economy and continues to have the capacity to produce good-paying jobs. Second, and even more important, the industry will play a large role in attempts to replace dishonest real estate speculation and derivatives trading with a more stable form of U.S. capitalism.

Employment rates in the construction industry have always remained extremely variable, but the significance of the industry to the U.S. economy remains profound. In 2003, the industry accounted for 8 percent of the U.S. GDP and produced $250 billion in payroll. Prior to the current recession, the construction industry accounted for 7.7 million wage and salary jobs, 64 percent of which were in the specialty trades—primarily plumbing, heating, and air conditioning; electrical; and masonry. Unlike more top-heavy industries, two-thirds of all jobs in the construction industry go to construction workers, with an additional 12 percent going to blue-collar workers in maintenance, installation, hauling, and production.[36]

Yet, even though new housing and construction starts remain key economic indicators, the racial and gender stratification of those indicators rarely receives mention. Women of all backgrounds and African American men remain grossly underrepresented in the industry since gaining their access following the implementation of affirmative action in the 1960s and 1970s. This has remained true even in good times. According to a study conducted just prior to the current recession, "if blacks were employed in construction at the same rate that they are employed in the overall work force," 42,700 more blacks would need to be employed in construction to achieve parity in the eighteen metropolitan areas covered in the study. Women fared far worse, "making up only 2–6 percent of the [construction] workforce in most cities." At the time, the federal government estimated "that the construction industry will need to recruit and train 245,900 new workers each year to meet labor demands."[37] Demand must return for the economy to turn around, but whether women, minorities, the poor, and long-term unemployed can gain access to those jobs remains in doubt.

The significance of the construction industry to economic opportunity becomes even larger when we consider the shaky financial foundation of the U.S. economy. Unemployment in U.S. inner cities had been extremely high for decades, especially in the "rust belt" cities of the Midwest and Northeast. But the current economic crisis has expanded the unemployment woes associated with U.S. deindustrialization well beyond any particular group of workers or region. Michigan, because of the auto industry collapse, is ground zero for the current unemployment crisis. Official unemployment, for example, was well above 15 percent during the summer of 2009, while the official unemployment rate in Detroit approached 30 percent, a figure the *Detroit News* later estimated was actually closer to 50 percent.[38]

White male hard hats, and white workers in general, tend to champion calls for regional unity and control when they are beneficial to them, but they adamantly oppose similar efforts for "outsiders." Take, for example, recent events in Michigan. In 2008, Michigan Governor Jennifer Granholm introduced local tax incentives for the film industry in an attempt to diversify the state economy and attract new, good-paying jobs. After receiving additional locally funded infrastructure improvements and county-funded tax subsidies, California-based Unity Studios agreed to build a $146 million "state-of the art production studio" in Allen Park, Michigan, an industrial suburb located a few miles from the western-most border of Detroit. Allen Park, in conjunction with the studio, passed an ordinance giving local residents and then laid-off autoworkers in the region priority in receiving training and access to the roughly 3,000 skilled positions created by the development project, including hundreds of jobs in construction. The plan, lauded by the mayor of Allen Park as "an economic development win-win-win for Allen Park residents," received backing from the governor and county commissioner and nearly universal praise from state residents.[39]

Yet a similar form of regional and statewide cooperation for community-based solutions to the economic woes of the region was not forthcoming when the city of Detroit sought state and regional funding to expand and renovate its rapidly deteriorating convention center, Cobo Hall. Lacking the revenue needed to begin the $288 billion project, Detroit, following the passage of state legislation authorizing the formation of a regional authority, entered negotiations to finance the project and to set parameters for the authority. Suburban officials, echoing a stance taken long before the current economic crisis set in, agreed to help fund the project, but only if "city residents and Detroit companies no longer would get first choice for jobs and contracts." The executive of the wealthiest Michigan county, for example, threatened to either withdraw from the regional authority or build a new suburban convention center unless "equal opportunity for suppliers and contractors in Oakland [County]" became part of the regional authority plan for Cobo Center. Suburbanites and the press, claiming that unemployment and economic instability were regional problems requiring regionwide solutions, roundly supported these stipulations while chiding the Detroit City Council for "playing the race card." These provisions were added to the final bill authorizing the expansion of Cobo Center, which Governor Granholm signed two months after the passage of the Allen Park jobs initiative.[40] As this situation in Michigan makes clear, the political will and desire to steer construction jobs and training toward those hit hardest by the recession remain weak, despite the fact that the current economic crisis is historic and unavoidable.

The question now facing the United States is not *if* it needs to restructure its economy, but *how*. So far, the economic policy of the Obama administration has been to shore up the financial sector while providing a temporary stimulus that was largely consumed by state and local government budget cuts. Obama has postponed the day of reckoning over which kind of economic investments can provide more sustainable economic growth. Until that happens, most commentators believe that, if there is an economic "recovery" at all, it will probably be more or less "jobless."[41]

The prospects of an oxymoronic jobless recovery are bleak for everyone— but the costs will be borne disproportionately by the urban poor. One estimate suggests that if current economic trends continue, "40 percent of African Americans will have experienced unemployment or underemployment by 2010, and this will increase child poverty from one-third of African-American children to slightly over half."[42] And, although it is well beyond the scope of this book to offer a roadmap for change, it is worth directing our attention to contemporary movements for justice whose answer to this economic crisis relates to, or is informed by, the history documented in this book.

The labor movement—particularly segments hit hard by deindustrialization, such as the steelworkers—environmental groups, Democratic Party officials, and inner-city community organizers have for the past few years been flirting with finding common cause in an emergent "green jobs" movement. The foundation of this movement, as described by Van Jones, a community organizer from the Ella Baker Center for Human Rights, is putting forward a positive, alternative vision to neoliberalism. "The dominant economic model of the past 30 years," Jones recently remarked, "has utterly failed not only the world's poor but now, apparently, the world's rich. And we've created a world economy that is driven by U.S. consumption, not U.S. production. By U.S. debt, not by the smart savings....And finally, based on environmental destruction, not environmental restoration."[43] The answer of the green jobs movement is to demand a "green New Deal"—a massive federal government reinvestment in repairing the crumbling infrastructure of U.S. cities while upgrading buildings' energy efficiency to meet the environmental challenges of the twenty-first century. Because suburban development has proved to be environmentally unsustainable, Jones advocates in *The Green Collar Economy* that the investment go to making our urban infrastructure more sustainable and to employing inner-city residents, lest it simply go toward shoring up lifestyle environmentalism and the production of a new "eco-apartheid."[44]

Following on Jones's analysis, Green for All, an organization that he founded, currently advocates "greening the ghetto" by training and "genuinely engaging" communities of color in "the struggle over our nation's energy and economic future." Seeking to "build an inclusive green economy strong enough to lift people out of poverty," Green for All is currently lobbying to increase funding for the Green Jobs Act, which already is set to provide roughly $860 million for training and support. The organization is also lobbying to have the Green Construction Careers Demonstration Project, which allows "the Secretaries of Labor and

Energy to target employment and training opportunities in green construction to workers and communities who traditionally have had little access to career-track jobs with high-road contractors in the building trades," included in the American Clean Energy and Security Act (ACES).[45]

The green jobs movement faces innumerable hurdles. The first is that there seems to be little political support for the scale of federal spending that its advocates call for. Legislation such as the Green Jobs Act makes steps in that direction, but its scale falls far short of the kind of programs that Jones and others advocate "to retrofit, reboot, re-power the whole U.S. economy."[46] Second, coalitions forming to promote green jobs—including numerous local "Blue-Green Alliances" and "sustainable jobs" coalitions—have shown more interest in accepting what little funding is available to shore up Democratic Party patronage networks in organized labor and the environmental nonprofit community than in providing jobs to unskilled inner-city residents.[47] Third, Jones, the most eloquent spokesperson for the need to include the voices of people of color and the poor in the movement, accepted a job as "a special White House advisor for 'green' jobs, enterprise and innovation," but was forced to step down after conservatives rallied against his prior activities as a leftist organizer.[48]

Regardless of whether labor or the United States promotes a stimulus that is "green," there are a number of policy ideas that have been put forward to ensure that stimulus dollars provide job training and jobs for those currently living in poverty. Robert Reich, for example, has suggested that contractors be required to set aside 20 percent of all stimulus-funded jobs—be they federal, state, or local—for "people with incomes at or below 200 percent of the federal poverty level," including women, minorities, and the long-term unemployed. He also recommends allocating 2 percent of all project funds for job-training programs that include inclusive apprenticeship training as well as up to six months of income assistance.[49]

While Green for All and Reich seek to create or expand legislation improving training and placement opportunities, an existing federal law with similar requirements is already being tested. In 2005, JOBS NOW worked with then U.S. Senator Barack Obama, Richard Costello, and Kit Bond "to get a 'Sense of Congress' amendment, which stated that local residents receive 30 percent of the jobs on highway projects, inserted into the Safe Accountable Flexible and Efficient Transportation Equity Act—A Legacy for Users (SAFETEA-LU)." The amendment requires that the hundreds of billions of dollars of federal spending on construction should "leverage scarce training and community resources to help ensure local participation in the building of transportation projects."[50] The JOBS NOW campaign, created by the Transportation Equity Network (TEN) and the Gamaliel Foundation, seeks to "get thousands of high paying jobs for low-income people, minorities, women and ex-offenders through workforce development agreements and policies." As the 2007 TEN study of the construction industry points out, "Every one billion spent on highways creates almost 48,000 jobs. If just 15% of these jobs were filled by to low-income minorities, women, and ex-offenders, 7,050 construction jobs per $1 billion spent could go directly to the needy. The effect of SAFETEA-LU can be enormous because as many as two million jobs could be generated for low-income communities over the life of this $286 billion bill."[51]

Seeking to build on the Sense of Congress amendment, JOBS NOW is currently working to make mandatory a "little known" U.S. Department of Transportation (USDOT) regulation that encourages states to use 0.5 percent of federal highway funds "to promote workforce development and job training." Local affiliates in the JOBS NOW campaign have succeeded in enforcing this provision, securing community benefit agreements that include a percentage of work hours and funding for training programs on highway projects in St. Louis, Kansas City, and Cincinnati, as well as a statewide commitment in Michigan that dedicates $15 million for job training in Michigan over a four-year period. Perhaps most important, activists in Kansas City have secured a local "ordinance that requires construction firms to employ 10% minorities and 4% women throughout their entire construction payroll in an 11 county area in order to bid on public works or tax abatement construction projects," a distinctive approach that circumvents ineffective good faith pledges and that can be applied in metropolitan regions across the country.[52]

As the history of black community control movements show, neither a vision for the future nor laws promising to deliver it are of much use without community organizations working as watchdogs to enforce the law. Both TEN and the JOBS NOW drew inspiration from the organizing successes of the Alameda Corridor Jobs Coalition (ACJC) in the Los Angeles area in the late 1990s. The ACJC formed in 1997 to demand that the $2 billion Alameda Corridor rail construction project between Los Angeles and Long Beach provide jobs to the low-income neighborhoods that the project was slated to go through. After it "mobilized thousands of people and a wide range of community organizations," it was able to secure "a commitment to ensure that community residents would perform at least thirty percent of the work hours and the project," funding for 1,000 preapprenticeship training slots, and a requirement forcing prime contractors to "specify how they would comply with hiring and training requirements" during the bidding process.[53] The coalition also began working with the Carpenters Education Training Institute, which taught basic math and education skills and provided wages during training as well as stipends for child care and transportation. With contractors obligated to prove their compliance with the training requirements before receiving bids, other unions became increasingly involved and began marketing training programs to individual contractors. As a result, contractors paid for preapprenticeship training conducted by the unions while "the coalition and its allied community based organizations" were "responsible for recruitment and candidate assessment."[54]

The story of the Alameda Corridor Jobs Coalition shows what *can* happen when community-based labor organizations and labor unions work in common cause as part of a broader movement toward economic justice. And it suggests that the collaboration of organized labor with community-centered labor organizations *could* provide a path to a new social justice unionism anchored in the demand for both jobs and urban redevelopment. Two trends of the last few decades have facilitated such union-community collaborations: (1) the proliferation of community-based labor organizations connected to immigrant-rights struggles and (2) progressive labor organizers' collaborations with community economic justice campaigns through Jobs with Justice coalitions. The challenge facing such coalitions is to demand jobs programs that are substantial enough to lift a significant number of people out of poverty rather than placing a few community organizers in charge of programs that train people for jobs that do not exist.

Unlike many of movements in the 1960s and early 1970s chronicled in this book, these recent campaigns are purposefully more inclusive and bring together women, low-income people, and communities of color in common cause. Yet, even though such recent instances of union cooperation exist, the histories chronicled in this book show that increased access to union-sponsored preapprenticeship and apprenticeship training programs often produced meager results. Programs seeking to train and place low-income people in middle-class jobs in the new economy are certainly laudable, but years of racism, economic deprivation, and prior access to decent-paying jobs with minimal education make worker retraining difficult. In Michigan, which has instituted a No Worker Left Behind program to retrain underemployed and unemployed workers, "one out of three working-age adults, or 1.7 million people, do not read well enough to be hired for a job that will support a family." According to the Michigan director of lifelong learning for the Bureau of Workforce Transformation, "it would take billions of dollars" to remediate these workers, "yet the state is currently servicing only 48,000 people with a budget of $33 million."[55] The point, then, is that job training for low-income workers of all backgrounds can be effective only if the unions and the public are committed to providing the training and funding needed to produce prepared workers as well as the jobs for them to enter.

The labor movement must come to see the recruitment, training, and employment of the unemployed as key to the advancement of its own cause. And, to do that, it must demand not just jobs for its members but also a robust jobs program for the unemployed. As Robert Pitts notes, "the labor movement represented 32.5% of the workforce in 1953. Since then, the union density has declined to the point where in 2003, unions represent just 9.0% of private sector workers."[56] Nostalgia for the past, or even a hope to revive old labor politics, will not help the labor movement adapt to the conditions of the twenty-first century. As Bill Fletcher Jr. and Fernando Gapasin have lamented, "the United States has never had a true labor movement. Only a segmented struggle of workers."[57]

The decline and exclusivity of the labor movement are not unrelated. Both the labor movement and the working class in the United States have suffered mightily from the dual effects of deindustrialization and deunionization during the last three decades. Now, facing the threat of a "jobless recovery," we have briefly been liberated from a world in which the building trades unions and unemployed inner-city residents have jobs to fight over. They will need to find greater common cause by forging a revitalized labor movement that can secure the jobs that both need and deserve.

Yet, if building trades unions receive funding for preapprenticeship training programs but then restrict access to apprenticeships and jobs placements, as they have in the past, little change will occur. And although present-day activists are organizing across the county, they are not attached to larger social movements like activists in the 1960s and 1970s. The most likely scenario in this instance is that the fortunes of both groups will continue to decline.

Avoiding this fate depends largely on the building trades unions and on the labor movement as a whole. If the unions continue to isolate and undercut themselves by restricting access to jobs and the unions, they will be responsible for maintaining an outdated form of identity politics that is detrimental to all workers as well as to the rebuilding of a viable labor movement in this country. By actively incorporating and seeking common ground with women, low-income workers, and communities of color, the building trades unions could greatly enhance the cause of social justice unionism while redefining and reinvigorating the labor movement in the United States.

Notes

INTRODUCTION

1. Melvin Oliver and Thomas Shapiro, *Black Wealth/White Wealth: A New Perspective on Racial Equality* (New York: Routledge, 1995); Douglas Massey and Nancy Denton, *American Apartheid: Segregation and the Making of the Underclass* (Cambridge, Mass.: Harvard University Press, 1993).

2. William Haber and Harold Levison, *Labor Relations and Productivity in the Building Trades* (Ann Arbor: University of Michigan, 1956), 3.

3. Vanessa Tait, *Poor Workers' Unions: Rebuilding Labor from Below* (Cambridge, Mass.: South End Press, 2005), 2, 11–13. See also Ira Katzelson, *When Affirmative Action Was White: An Untold History of Racial Inequality in the Twentieth Century* (New York: W. W. Norton, 2005).

4. David Schwartzman, *Black Unemployment: Part of Unskilled Unemployment* (Westport, Conn.: Greenwood Press, 1997).

5. Thomas Sugrue, "Affirmative Action from Below: Civil Rights, the Building Trades and the Politics of Racial Equality in the Urban North, 1945–1969," *Journal of American History* 91 (June 2004): 145–73, esp. 155; Sugrue, *Sweet Land of Liberty: The Forgotten Struggle for Civil Rights in the North* (New York: Random House, 2008), 292. For the rise of black nationalism during the Cold War, see Martha Biondi, *To Stand and Fight: The Struggle for Civil Rights in Postwar New York City* (Cambridge, Mass.: Harvard University Press, 2003), esp. 250–63; Matthew Countryman, *Up South: Civil Rights and Black Power in Philadelphia* (Philadelphia: University of Pennsylvania Press, 2007), 83–119.

6. Sugrue, "Affirmative Action from Below"; Sugrue, *Sweet Land of Liberty,* 289, 306, 314.

7. August Meier and Elliot Rudwick, *CORE: A Study in the Civil Rights Movement* (Urbana: University of Illinois Press, 1975), 304. Meier and Rudwick, as Matthew Countryman points out, wrongly interpret this shift along the same lines as the standard declension narrative (a belief that the movement declined once the halcyon days of the modern Civil Rights Movement had been supplanted by Black Power), *Up South,* 333 n. 14.

8. Sugrue, "Affirmative Action from Below," 173; Anthony Chen, *The Fifth Freedom: Jobs, Politics, and Civil Rights in the United States, 1941–1972* (Princeton: Princeton University Press, 2009).

9. Black Power contained many different, and often competing, tactical and ideological tendencies that make the movement difficult to define. We, however, use the term to refer to the broad spectrum of approaches that constituted the movement—from the relatively conservative black capitalist model advanced by many black contractors and the racial and ethnic pluralism of Stokely Carmichael and Charles V. Hamilton to the revolutionary nationalist approach of groups like the Revolutionary Action Movement and Black Liberation Army. While fundamentally different in how they defined Black Power or proposed to seek it, the various tendencies within the movement shared common objectives: black control of institutions that impacted black communities and black self-determination.

10. There are a number of scholars who have already worked in this area, albeit with various degrees of emphasis on the campaigns to desegregate the building trades and their connection to shifts in the civil rights and Black Power movements. See Nancy Banks, "'The Last Bastion of Discrimination': The New York Building Trades and the Struggle over Affirmative Action," PhD diss., Columbia University, 2006; Joseph Rodriguez, "Transit and Community Power: West Oakland Residents Confront BART," *Antipode* 31, no. 2 (1999): 229–42; Deborah Henry, "Structures of Exclusion: Black Labor and the Building Trades in St. Louis, 1917–1966," PhD diss., University of Minnesota, 2002; Brian Purnell, "A Movement Grows in Brooklyn: The Brooklyn Chapter of the Congress of Racial Equality (CORE) and the Northern Civil Rights Movements during the Early 1960s," PhD diss., New York University, 2006; Clarence Lang, "Between Civil Rights and Black Power in the Gateway City: The Action Committee to Improve Opportunities for Negroes (ACTION) 1964–75," *Journal of Social History* 37, no. 3 (2004): 725–54; Robert Self, *American Babylon: Race and the Struggle for Postwar Oakland* (Princeton: Princeton University Press, 2003), esp. 191–98; Countryman, *Up South,* esp. 120–47.

11. In 1971, the U.S. Department of Labor, recognizing that no version of the Philadelphia Plan had been adopted in the South, sought to impose a plan in Atlanta as an example for other southern cities. This was motivated less by grassroots action than by Arthur Fletcher's desire to create the foundation for a national plan to desegregate the construction industry; see Trevor Griffey, chap. 7 in this volume.

12. Jeanne Theoharis and Komozi Woodard, eds., *Freedom North: Black Freedom Struggles outside the South, 1940–1980* (New York: Palgrave Macmillan, 2003); Theoharis and Woodard, eds., *Groundwork: Local Black Freedom Movements in America* (New York: New York University Press, 2005); Theoharis, "Black Freedom Studies: Re-imagining and Redefining Fundamentals," *History Compass* 4 (2006): 348–67.

13. For exemplars of this approach, see Charles Payne, *I've Got the Light of Freedom: The Organizing Tradition and the Mississippi Freedom Struggle* (Berkeley: University of California Press, 1995); John Dittmer, *Local People: The Struggle for Civil Rights in Mississippi* (Urbana: University of Illinois Press, 1994); Theoharis and Woodard, *Groundwork;* Theoharis and Woodard, *Freedom North;* William Chafe, *Civilities and Civil Rights: Greensboro, North Carolina, and the Black Struggle for Freedom* (New York: Oxford University Press, 1980).

14. Sugrue, "Affirmative Action from Below," 173.

15. See Nancy MacLean, *Freedom Is Not Enough: The Opening of the American Workplace* (Cambridge, Mass.: Harvard University Press, 2006), 76–113. For declension narratives, see Clayborn Carson, *In Struggle: SNCC and the Black Awakening of the 1960s* (Cambridge, Mass.: Harvard University Press, 1981); Doug McAdam, *Political Process and the Development of Black Political Insurgency* (Chicago: University of Chicago Press, [1982] reprinted 1999); Payne, *I've Got the Light of Freedom;* William Van Deburg, *New Day in Babylon: The Black Power Movement and American Culture, 1965–75* (Chicago: University of Chicago Press, 1992.

16. For the implementation of racial quotas for federal contractors during the 1930s and 1940s, see Marc Kruman, "Quotas for Blacks: The Public Works Administration and the Black Construction Worker," *Labor History* 16, no. 1 (1975): 40–49; Robert Weaver, *Negro Labor: A National Problem* (Port Washington, N.Y.: Kennikat Press, [1946] 1969), 10–12; Herbert Hill, *Black Labor and the American Legal System: Race, Work and the Law* (Madison: University of Wisconsin Press, 1985), 241–243; F. Ray Marshall, *The Negro and Organized Labor* (New York: John Wiley & Sons, 1965); Wendell Pritchett, *Robert Clifton Weaver and the American City: The Life and Times of an Urban Reformer* (Chicago: University of Chicago Press, 2008), 55–57, 59–60, 80–84. For the postwar shift from hiring requirements to fair employment practices legislation, see Chen, *Fifth Freedom.* For postwar attempts to secure proportional hiring in New York, see Biondi, *To Stand and Fight,* 22–24, 105–11, 259–77.

17. Sugrue, "Affirmative Action from Below"; Sugrue, *Sweet Land of Liberty,* 306, 314.

18. Meier and Rudwick, *CORE,* 304.

19. "Negroes May Form Labor Unions," *Chicago Tribune,* December 28, 1964, 14; "CORE Hints at Plan For Negro Unions," *New York Times,* November 30, 1964; "Rights Leaders Hail Labor Bias Indictment," *New York Amsterdam News,* December 5, 1964; "New Builders Group Hailed," *COREspondent,* November 29, 1964, 1, 3, and Boston CORE to NAACP, April 2, 1965, both in the Papers of the Congress of Racial Equality, 1941–1967 [hereafter CORE Papers], Reel 21, Folder 50; "CORE's Position vis a vis Discriminatory Unions," CORE Secretary Eric Mann to James Farmer, Lou Smith, and Marv Rich, December 1, 1964, CORE Papers, Reel 27, Folder 152; Michael Flug, "Organized Labor and the Civil Rights Movement of the 1960s: The Case of the Maryland Freedom Union," *Labor History* 31, no. 3 (1990), 326, 336. We thank Michael Flug for sharing these important sources from the CORE papers.

20. Meier and Rudwick, *CORE,* 304; Self, *American Babylon,* 193, 195. We thank an anonymous reviewer for help contextualizing and historicizing community-centered and community control movements in the early and mid-1960s.

21. See Self, *American Babylon;* Robert Self, "The Black Panther Party and the Long Civil Rights Era," in *In Search of the Black Panther Party: New Perspectives on a Revolutionary Movement,* ed. Jama Lazerow and Yohuru Williams, 15–55 (Durham: Duke University Press, 2006); "'Negro Leadership and Negro Money': African American Political Organizing in Oakland before the Panthers," in *Freedom North,* ed. Theoharis and Woodard, 93–124; Biondi, *To Stand and Fight;* Countryman, *Up South;* Sugrue, *Sweet Land of Liberty;* Theoharis and Woodard, *Freedom North;* Nikhil P. Singh, *Black Is a Country: Race and the Unfinished Struggle for Democracy* (Cambridge, Mass.: Harvard University Press, 2004); Peniel Joseph, *Waiting 'Til the Midnight Hour: A Narrative History of Black Power in America* (New York: Henry Holt, 2006), 9–44; Peniel Joseph, ed., *The Black Power Movement: Rethinking the Civil Rights-Black Power Era* (New York: Routledge, 2006), 1–26; Timothy Tyson, *Radio Free Dixie: Robert Williams and the Roots of Black Power* (Chapel Hill: University of North Carolina Press, 2001).

22. John H. Bracey Jr., quoted in John H. Bracey, August Meier, and Elliot Rudwick, eds., *Black Nationalism in America* (New York: Bobbs-Merrill, 1970), lix.

23. Sundiata Keita Cha-Jua and Clarence Lang, "The Long Movement as a Vampire: Temporal and Spatial Fallacies in Recent Black Freedom Studies," *Journal of African American History* 92 (2007), 270–71.

24. This is articulated best in Rhonda Y. Williams, *The Politics of Public Housing: Black Women's Struggles against Urban Inequality* (Oxford: Oxford University Press, 2004); Matthew Countryman, *Up South;* Angela D. Dillard, *Faith in the City: Preaching Radical Social Change in Detroit* (Ann Arbor: University of Michigan Press, 2007); Laurie B. Green, *Memphis and the Black Freedom Struggle* (Chapel Hill: North Carolina Press, 2007). We thank an anonymous reviewer for helping us think through these complicated issues and helping us clarify the significance of the early articles in the volume.

25. Self, "'Negro Leadership and Negro Money,'" 99. Although Randolph did not run the institute, "the organization symbolized his economic approach to the racial problem, his support of a liberal coalition for social change, and his long campaign for a democratic and integrated labor movement." Not surprisingly, Randolph "strongly" endorsed "its activities and purposes." Jervis Anderson, *A. Philip Randolph: A Biographical Portrait* (Berkeley: University of California Press, 1986), 314.

26. Sugrue, *Sweet Land of Liberty,* 355.

27. See Glen Eskew, *But for Birmingham: The Local and National Movements in the Civil Rights Movement* (Chapel Hill: University of North Carolina Press, 1997); Michael Flamm, *Law and Order: Street Crime, Civil Unrest, and the Crisis of Liberalism in the 1960s* (New York: Columbia University Press, 2005); U.S. Kerner Commission, *Report of the*

National Advisory Commission on Civil Disorders (New York: New York Times, 1968); Angus Campbell, Robert M. Fogelson, and the U.S. Kerner Commission, "Supplemental Studies for the National Advisory Commission on Civil Disorders," U.S. Printing Office, Washington D.C., 1968; U.S. Senate Committee on Government Operations, "Riots, Civil and Criminal Disorders," Ninetieth Congress, Pt. 1, U.S. Government Printing Office, Washington D.C., 1967.

28. "3,100 Open Discussions at Black Power Parley," *New York Times,* August 31, 1968, 48. "3rd Black Power Conference to be Held," *Chicago Daily Defender,* July 15, 1968; "Philadelphia Parley to Focus on Battle for Black Power," *New York Times,* August 29, 1968; "Black Power Conferees Aim at Ghetto Controls," *Washington Post,* August 31, 1968.

29. "Third International Conference on Black Power: Economics, Minutes," Black Power Movement, Part 3, Papers of the Revolutionary Action Movement, 1962–1966, Reel 11, LexusNexus, Bethesda, 2002. For varying articulations and approaches to the "second ghetto thesis," see Thomas Sugrue, *The Origins of Urban Crisis: Race and Inequality in Postwar Detroit* (Princeton: Princeton University Press, 2005); Arnold Hirsch, *Making the Second Ghetto: Race & Housing in Chicago, 1940–1960* (Chicago: Chicago University Press, 1998); Countryman, *Up South;* Williams, *Politics of Public Housing;* Kenneth Jackson, *Crabgrass Frontier: The Suburbanization of the United States* (New York: Oxford University Press, 1987); June Manning Thomas, *Redevelopment and Race: Planning a Finer City in Postwar Detroit* (Baltimore: Johns Hopkins University Press, 1997); Adam Bickford and Douglass Massey, "Segregation in the Second Ghetto: Racial and Ethnic Segregation in American Public Housing," *Social Forces* 69, no. 4 (1991): 1011–36.

30. "Third International Conference on Black Power: Economics, Minutes."

31. Ibid.

32. The term *Black Monday* and the movement that followed gained traction after a well-publicized protest using the name took place in Pittsburgh on September 15, 1969. See "Demonstrations Set Monday, Sept 15th, Mass March, Boycott Slated," *Pittsburgh Courier* (city ed.), September 13, 1969; "Pittsburgh Coalition Sets 'Black Monday,'" *Chicago Defender,* September 11, 1969; "4,000 Renew Pittsburgh Job Protest," *New York Times,* September 16, 1969; "Black Monday and White Friday," *Newsweek,* October 6, 1969, 105–6; "Bucking Big Labor: Negro Drive for Jobs in Construction Unions Is Gaining Momentum," *Wall Street Journal,* September 26, 1969. A week after the first Black Monday protest, Rev. C. T. Vivian of Coalition for United Community Action (CUCA) in Chicago made an explicit call for national protests. See "Nationwide Black Walkout Urged to Back Job Demand," *New York Times,* September 22, 1969; "Pittsburgh Blacks Call for a 'Summit' on Building Jobs," *Washington Post,* September 20, 1969. For clashes among protestors, police, and tradesmen, see "Negro Groups Step Up Militancy in Drive to Join Building Trades Unions, *New York Times,* August 28, 1969; "'Hot Summer' Rips Pittsburgh," *New York Amsterdam News,* August 30, 1969; "Jobs Protest Spurs Pittsburgh Clash," *New York Times,* August 27, 1969.

33. Hugh Davis Graham, *The Civil Rights Era: Origins and Development of National Policy* (New York: Oxford University Press, 1990), 334–35; John D. Skrentny, *The Ironies of Affirmative Action: Politics, Culture, and Justice in America* (Chicago: University of Chicago Press, 1996), 100–103.

34. Skrentny argues that the 1969 protest wave "made room for a discourse of affirmative action which avoided the tricky [i.e., politically charged] issue of African American moral worthiness. To maintain order and control, justice could now institutionalize the 'reality' of race" by imposing affirmative action as a form of "crisis management." Skrentny, *Ironies of Affirmative Action,* 67–110. On affirmative action as managing a "legitimization crisis" for liberalism produced in part by the urban rebellions, see Kevin Yuill, *Richard Nixon and the Rise of Affirmative Action: The Pursuit of Racial Equality in an Era of Limits* (New York: Rowman and Littlefield, 2006). On the Philadelphia Plan as a civil rights

policy alternative to the War on Poverty, see Graham, *Civil Rights Era,* 278–300, 322–45; Skrentny, *Ironies of Affirmative Action,* 135–58; Jill Quadagno, *The Color of Welfare: How Racism Undermined the War on Poverty* (New York: Oxford University Press, 1994), 79–87; Dean J. Kotlowski, *Nixon's Civil Rights: Politics, Principle, and Policy* (Cambridge, Mass.: Harvard University Press, 2001), 109–15; Judith Stein, "Affirmative Action and the Conservative Agenda: President Richard Nixon's Philadelphia Plan of 1969," in *Labor in the Modern South,* ed. Glenn T. Eskew, 182–206 (Athens: University of Georgia Press, 2001); Nicholas Pedriana and Robin Stryker, "Political Culture Wars 1960s Style: Equal Employment Opportunity—Affirmative Action Law and the Philadelphia Plan," *American Journal of Sociology* 103, no. 3 (1997): 633–91; J. Larry Hood, "The Nixon Administration and The Revised Philadelphia Plan for Affirmative Action: A Study in Expanding Presidential Power and Divided Government," *Presidential Studies Quarterly* 23 (1993): 145–67.

35. Stein, "Affirmative Action and the Conservative Agenda," 186–90; Marc Linder, *Wars of Attrition: Vietnam, the Business Roundtable, and the Decline of Construction Unions* (Iowa City: Fanpihua Press, 1999), 241–63.

36. Yuill's history of affirmative action nonchalantly notes that he "does not discuss in any detail the race relations or civil rights movement though they formed the essential background of the story of affirmative action." Yuill, *Richard Nixon and the Rise of Affirmative Action,* 5. Skrentny goes further, suggesting that after 1969 "the images of the minority rights revolution are mostly of mainstream Euro-American males and minority advocates, wearing suits, sitting at desks, firing off memos, and meeting in government to discuss new policy directions." John D. Skrentny, *The Minority Rights Revolution* (Cambridge, Mass.: Harvard University Press, 2002), 5.

37. A small sample of works that refute the "culture of poverty" thesis, but from different approaches, includes Sugrue, *Origins of Urban Crisis;* Williams, *Politics of Public Housing;* Self, *American Babylon;* Countryman, *Up South;* Yohuru Williams, *Black Politics/ White Power: Civil Rights, Black Power, and the Black Panthers in New Haven* (New York: John Wiley & Sons, 2000); Felicia Kornbluh, *The Battle for Welfare Rights: Politics and Poverty in Modern America* (Philadelphia: University of Pennsylvania Press, 2007); Premilla Nadasen, *Welfare Warriors: The Welfare Rights Movement in the United States* (New York: Routledge, 2005); George Lipsitz, *A Life in Struggle: Ivory Perry and the Culture of Opposition* (Philadelphia: Temple University Press, 1995), 117–44; Quadagno, *Color of Welfare;* Annelise Orleck, *Storming Caesars Palace: How Black Mothers Fought Their Own War on Poverty* (Boston: Beacon Press, 2005).

38. Theoharis and Woodard, *Groundwork;* Joseph, *Waiting 'Til the Midnight Hour;* Jeffery Ogbar, *Black Power: Radical Politics and African American Identity* (Baltimore: Johns Hopkins University Press, 2004); Joseph, *Black Power Movement;* Judson L. Jeffries, ed., *Black Power in the Belly of the Beast* (Urbana: University of Illinois Press, 2006).

39. With the exceptions of Peter Levy, *The New Left and Labor in the 1960s* (Urbana: University of Illinois Press, 1994); Ruth Needleman, *Black Freedom Fighters in Steel: The Struggle for Democratic Unionism* (Ithaca: Cornell University Press, 2003); and Bruce Nelson, *Divided We Stand: American Workers and the Struggle for Black Equality* (Princeton: Princeton University Press, 2001), the majority of recent works that discuss Black Power and Black Power unionism have largely dealt with the League of Revolutionary Black Workers. See Muhammad Ahmad, *We Return in the Whirlwind: Black Radical Organizations, 1960–1975* (Chicago: Kerr Publishing, 2007), 237–306; Dan Georgakas and Marvin Surkin, *Detroit: I Do Mind Dying: A Study in Urban Revolution* (Cambridge, Mass.: South End Press, 1999); Heather Thompson, *Whose Detroit?: Politics, Labor, Race in an American City* (Ithaca: Cornell University Press, 2002); David Lewis-Coleman, *Race against Liberalism: Black Workers and the UAW in Detroit* (Urbana: University of Illinois Press, 2008); James Geschwender, *Race, Class, and Worker Insurgency: The League of Revolutionary Black Workers* (Cambridge, UK: Cambridge University Press, 1977); James Geschwender

and Judson Jeffries, "The League of Revolutionary Black Workers," in *Black Power in the Belly of the Beast,* ed. Jeffries, 135–62; Kieran Taylor, "Turn to the Working Class: The New Left, Black Liberation, and the U.S. Labor Movement (1967–1981)," 19–58; Joseph, *Waiting 'Til the Midnight Hour;* Jeffery Ogbar, *Black Power.* William Van Deburg, *New Day in Babylon: The Black Power Movement and American Culture, 1965–1975* (Chicago: University of Chicago Press, 1992), has a section on Black Power and labor, but it is only five pages long (92–96).

40. Levy, *The New Left and Labor in the 1960s,* 75–76.

41. Studies focusing on the struggle "for jobs and freedom" either downplay or ignore the influence of the Black Power movement on black labor struggles. See Jacqueline Dowd Hall, "The Long Civil Rights Movement and the Political Uses of the Past," *Journal of American History* 91, no. 4 (2005): 1233–63; MacLean, *Freedom Is Not Enough;* Timothy Minchin, *The Color of Work: The Struggle for Civil Rights in the Southern Paper Industry, 1945–1980* (Chapel Hill, University of North Carolina Press, 2001); Minchin, *Hiring the Black Worker: The Racial Integration of the Southern Textile Industry, 1960–1980* (Chapel Hill: University of North Carolina Press, 1999); Horace Huntley and David Montgomery, eds., *Black Workers Struggle for Equality in Birmingham* (Urbana: University of Illinois Press, 2004); Robert Zieger, *For Jobs and Freedom: Race and Labor in America since 1865* (Lexington: University of Kentucky Press, 2007); Dona Cooper Hamilton and Charles V. Hamilton, *The Dual Agenda: The African American Struggle for Civil and Economic Equality* (New York: Columbia University Press, 1997); Leon Fink and Brian Greenberg, *Upheaval in the Quiet Zone: A History of Hospital Workers' Union, Local 1199* (Urbana: University of Illinois Press, 1989); Venus Green, *Race on the Line: Gender, Labor & Technology in the Bell System, 1880–1980* (Raleigh: Duke University Press, 2001). Michael Honey's recent study of the Memphis sanitation workers' strike engages Black Power but not its impact on the sanitation workers themselves or on those, other than the "the Invaders," who supported them; Honey, *Going down Jericho Road: The Memphis Strike, Martin Luther King's Last Campaign* (New York: W. W. Norton, 2007).

42. For early black activism in the trades, see Herbert Hill, *Black Labor and the American Legal System: Race, Work and the Law* (Madison: University of Wisconsin Press, 1985), 237–40; Sterling Spero and Abram Harris, *The Black Worker: The Negro and the Labor Movement* (New York: Antheneum, [1931] reprinted 1969), 120–21; Philip S. Foner, *Organized Labor and the Black Worker, 1619–1981 (New York: International Publishers, 1982),* 147; Weaver, *Negro Labor,* 28–32; "Ask for Probe of AFL Hold on Trades Jobs," *Chicago Defender,* October 18, 1941; "Hillman Supports Job Drive," *Pittsburgh Courier,* April 26, 1941; "Steps Taken to Force Unions to Drop Race Ban," *Chicago Defender,* March 18, 1939; "St. Louis Tells Congress Committee Housing Ills," *Chicago Defender,* November 1, 1947; Detroit Coordinating Council on Human Relations Papers, Folder 22, Box 74, Archives of Labor History and Urban Affairs (ALUA), Wayne State University, Detroit.

43. Paul Frymer, *Black and Blue: African Americans, the Labor Movement, and the Decline of the Democratic Party* (Princeton: Princeton University Press, 2008), 27, 29.

44. For implementation of racial quotas during the 1930s and 1940s, see Kruman, "Quotas for Blacks," 40–49; Weaver, *Negro Labor,* 40–42; Hill, *Black Labor and the American Legal System,* 241–242; Marshall, *Negro and Organized Labor.*

45. Marshall, *Negro and Organized Labor,* 70, 85.

46. Herbert Hill to Boris Shishkin, Director, AFL-CIO CRC, 3/16/56, Unprocessed Papers, George Meany Memorial Archives, College Park, Md.

47. F. Ray Marshall, *The Negro Worker* (New York: Random House, 1967), 67.

48. Gilbert Jonas, *Freedom's Sword: The NAACP and the Struggle against Racism in America, 1909–1969* (New York: Taylor & Francis, 2004), 251. See also, 251–52.

49. Ibid., 255; "Unions Charged with Race Bias in Work on US Capitol," *New York Amsterdam News,* October 1959; "Must Hire Race on Capitol Wing," *Pittsburgh Courier,* October 31, 1959; Herbert Hill, "Racism within Organized Labor: A Report of Five Years of the AFL-CIO, 1955–1960," *Journal of Negro Education* 30, no. 2 (1961): 109–18.

50. Frymer, *Black and Blue,* 44–69.

51. It is remarkable, given the significance of CORE, that the organization has not received a book-length appraisal of its contributions to the civil rights movement in over thirty years. The chapters in this volume suggest that we need to rethink its relationship to the Black Power movement.

52. Paul D. Moreno, *From Direct Action to Affirmative Action* (Baton Rouge: Louisiana State University Press, 1999), 145–53; Roger Waldinger, *Still the Promised City?: African Americans and New Immigrants in Postindustrial New York* (Cambridge, Mass.: Harvard University Press, 1996), 174–97; Meier and Rudwick, *CORE,* 200–201, 304; Ahmad, *We Will Return in the Whirlwind,* 107; Brian Purnell, "'Drive Awhile for Freedom': Brooklyn CORE's 1964 Stall-In and Public Discourses on Protest Violence," in *Groundwork,* ed. Theoharis and Woodard, 45–76.

53. Komozi Woodard, *A Nation within a Nation: Amiri Baraka (Leroi Jones) & Black Power Politics* (Chapel Hill: University of North Carolina Press, 1999).

54. For an assessment of the various, largely failed experiments in incorporating nonwhite youth into apprenticeship training for skilled construction trades, see F. Ray Marshall and Vernon M. Briggs Jr., *The Negro and Apprenticeship* (Baltimore: Johns Hopkins Press, 1967).

55. Sugrue, "Affirmative Action from Below," 169.

56. Hill had been documenting and filing complaints about discrimination in the St. Louis building trades for almost a decade before the Justice Department decided to initiate its first Title VII lawsuit against them. For information on that lawsuit, see Robert J. Moore Jr. "Showdown under the Arch: The Construction Trades and the First 'Pattern or Practice' Equal Employment Opportunity Suit, 1966," *Gateway Heritage* (Winter 1994–1995): 30–43.

57. "NAACP Schedules Cleveland Protest, *New York Times,* April 23, 1965; "NAACP Renews Demands for Building Jobs, *New York Times,* January 19, 1965, 21; "Cleveland Pact Sought," *New York Times,* January 8, 1965; "24 Seized in Sit-in at US Office Site," *New York Times,* April 27, 1965; "Union Hiring Bar on Construction Jobs Feeds Race Crisis in Cities," *New York Times,* September 11, 1965.

58. Hill's campaigns to desegregate the building trades have never received the documentation they deserve, even though, as Nancy MacLean notes, he was "best known for his attacks on the building trades unions for excluding African Americans." Nancy MacLean, "Achieving the Promise of the Civil Rights Act: Herbert Hill and the NAACP's Fight for Jobs and Justice," *Labor: Studies in Working-Class History of the Americas* 3, no. 2 (2006): 15. See also, 16–19. For Hill's support for independent black worker and contractor organizations, see Herbert Hill, "Black Protest and the Struggle for Union Democracy," *Issues in Industrial Society* 1, no. 19 (1969): 19–29; "NAACP Is Forming Consortiums to Bid On Construction Jobs," *Wall Street Journal,* June 27, 1968.

59. Sugrue, "Affirmative Action from Below," 169; "Pickets Blockade Plumbers' Office," *New York Times,* May 13, 1964; "Court Restrains Rights Sit-In," *New York Times,* August 12, 1965; "NAACP Schedules Cleveland Protest, *New York Times,* April 23, 1965, 71; "NAACP Renews Demands for Building Jobs, *New York Times,* January 19, 1965, 21; "Cleveland Pact Sought," *New York Times,* January 8, 1965, 32; Moore, "Showdown under the Arch," 30–34; Lang, "Between Civil Rights and Black Power."

60. Quotation from Skrentny, *Ironies of Affirmative Action,* 136. The Revolutionary Action Movement was active in Cleveland, Philadelphia, and Oakland during this period,

as were the various Black Panther parties that emerged from it. See Ahmad, *We Will Return in the Whirlwind*. For the rise of Black Power and racial unrest in St. Louis, see Lang, "Between Civil Rights and Black Power"; "Negroes Renew St. Louis Protest," *New York Times*, September 30, 1966.

61. This paragraph draws heavily on Skrentny, *Ironies of Affirmative Action*, 133–38; Sugrue, "Affirmative Action from Below," 169–70.

62. Skrentny, *Ironies of Affirmative Action*, 137.

63. Sugrue, "Affirmative Action from Below," 170.

64. Self, *American Babylon*, 196–97; Rodriguez, "Transit and Community Power."

65. For a heavily influential articulation of this approach that gained heavy traction in black nationalist and radical circles during the 1960s, see Harold Cruse, "Revolutionary Nationalism and the Afro-American," *Studies on the Left* 2, no. 3 (1962): 12–25. For a domestic interpretation of this approach and its meaning to segments of the Black Power movement during the mid- to late 1960s, see Grace Boggs and James Boggs, "The City Is the Black Man's Land," *Monthly Review* 17, no. 11 (1966): 35–46.

66. For a history of the Washington Plan, see Richard L. Rowan and Lester Rubin, *Opening the Skilled Construction Trades to Blacks: A Study of the Washington and Indianapolis Plans for Minority Employment* (Philadelphia: University of Pennsylvania Press, 1972), 19–112.

67. Quadagno, *Color of Welfare*, 69.

68. William B. Gould, *Black Workers in White Unions: Job Discrimination in the United States* (Ithaca: Cornell University Press, 1977), 56.

69. Irwin Dubinsky, *Reform in Trade Union Discrimination in the Construction Industry: Operation Dig and Its Legacy* (New York: Praeger, 1973).

70. For information about the relationship of these two programs to the civil rights movement beyond the struggle to desegregate the building trades, see John Fry, *Locked-Out Americans: A Memoir* (Evanston: Harper and Row, 1973); Fry, *Fire and Blackstone* (New York: J. B. Lippincott Company, 1969); Arthur M. Brazier, *Black Self-Determination: The Story of the Woodlawn Organization* (Grand Rapids, Mich.: William B. Eerdman, 1969); John Hall Fish, *Black Power/White Control: The Struggle of the Woodlawn Organization in Chicago* (Princeton: Princeton University Press, 1973).

71. "Black Coalitions Organizing in More Big Cities," *Wall Street Journal*, September 26, 1969; "BCC Formulate Plans for All Black Union," *New Pittsburgh Courier*, October 25, 1969, 1; "Pittsburgh Blacks Call for a 'Summit' On Building Jobs," *Washington Post*, September 20, 1969, A6; "Negroes Plan Talks on Demand for Jobs," *New York Times*, September 20, 1969, 26. For the proposed expansion of the Philadelphia Plan by the Department of Labor, see "U.S. Will Extend Minority Job Aid," *New York Times*, September 30, 1969, 1.

72. Quoted in David Brewster, "Solidarity Forever!: Black Demands for Construction Jobs Have Revived Labor's Old Fighting Spirit—Not on Behalf of All Workers, but *White* Workers," *Seattle Magazine* (December 1969): 35–36.

73. Telephone conversation with Charles Colson, 7/2/71, Conversation 6-93, Nixon White House Tapes, Nixon Library, National Archives and Records Administration, College Park, Md.

74. MacLean, *Freedom Is Not Enough*.

75. For a survey of Title VII race and labor history, see Robert H. Zieger, "Recent Historical Scholarship on Public Policy in Relation to Race and Labor in the Post-Title-VII Period," *Labor History* 46, no. 1 (2005): 3–14. Recent studies of working class women's activism and Title VII law include Carrie N. Baker, *The Women's Movement against Sexual Harassment* (New York: Cambridge University Press, 2007); Kathleen M. Berry, *Femininity in Flight: A History of Flight Attendants* (Durham: Duke University Press, 2007), 144–73; Dennis A. Deslippe, *Rights, not Roses: Unions and the Rise of Working-Class Feminism,*

1945–80 (Urbana: University of Illinois Press, 2000), 146–65. The majority of studies of Title VII law, however, are from political science and sociology researchers focused more on state capacity than on sociolegal mobil,zations. See, for instance, Nicholas Pedriana and Robin Stryker, "The Strength of a Weak Agency: Enforcement of Title VII of the 1964 Civil Rights Act and the Expansion of State Capacity, 1965–1971," *American Journal of Sociology* 110, no. 3 (2004): 709–60.

76. The prototypical example of this approach is Judith Stein, *Running Steel, Running America: Race, Economic Policy, and the Decline of Liberalism* (Chapel Hill: University of North Carolina Press, 1998). For opposing perspectives, see Ruth Needleman, *Black Freedom Fighters in Steel: The Struggle for Democratic Unionism* (Ithaca: Cornell University Press, 2003); Ruth Needleman, "Union Coalition Building and the Role of Black Organizations: A Study in Steel," *Labor Studies Journal* 25, no. 1 (2000): 79–103; Herbert Hill, "Race and the Steelworkers' Union: White Privilege and Black Struggle, a Review of Judith Stein's *Running Steel, Running America,*" *New Politics* 8, no. 4 (2002): 147–207; David Roediger, "White Workers, New Democrats, and Affirmative Action," in *Colored White: Transcending the Racial Past* (Berkeley: University of California Press, 2002), 55–67.

77. Lewis-Coleman, *Race against Liberalism,* 116.

1. "REVOLUTION HAS COME TO BROOKLYN"

1. On the Birmingham demonstrations, see Juan Williams, *Eyes on the Prize: America's Civil Rights Years, 1954–1965* (New York: Viking Penguin, 1987), 179–95, quotation from King's letter is on 188. On the Birmingham movement generally, see Glenn Askew, *But for Birmingham: The Local and National Movements in the Civil Rights Struggles* (Chapel Hill: University of North Carolina Press, 1997). On the March on Washington and the bombing of the Sixteenth Street Baptist Church, see Williams, *Eyes on the Prize,* 197–205. On Kennedy's death and Johnson's leadership, see Williams, *Eyes on the Prize,* 226, 232. On Johnson, see Steven F. Lawson, *Civil Rights Crossroads* (Lexington: University Press of Kentucky, 2003), 31–94.

2. On demonstrations against racial discrimination in the construction unions, see Thomas J. Sugrue, "Affirmative Action from Below: Civil Rights, the Building Trades, and the Politics of Racial Equality in the Urban North, 1945–1969," *Journal of American History* 91 (June 2004), 145–73; Sugrue, *Sweet Land of Liberty: The Forgotten Struggle for Civil Rights in the North* (New York: Random House, 2008), 276–77, 291–97, 301–2, 362–64. On the history of discrimination in the New York City building trades industry, see Nancy Banks, "'The Last Bastion of Discrimination': The New York City Building Trades and the Struggle over Affirmative Action, 1961–1976," PhD diss., Columbia University, 2006, esp. chaps. 2–3; Clarence Taylor, *The Black Churches of Brooklyn* (New York: Columbia University Press, 1994), chap. 5; Clarence Taylor, *Knocking at Our Own Door: Milton A. Galamison and the Struggle to Integrate New York City Schools* (New York: Lexington Books, 1997), 117, 119, 124. During summer 1964, similar demonstrations broke out in St. Louis, Missouri. See Clarence Lang, "Between Civil Rights and Black Power in the Gateway City: The Action Committee to Improve Opportunities for Negroes (ACTION), 1964–75," *Journal of Social History* 37, no. 3 (2004): 725–54. For an overview of the efforts of the civil rights movement to create employment opportunities for people of color, see Nancy MacLean, *Freedom Is Not Enough: The Opening of the American Workplace* (Cambridge, Mass.: Harvard University Press, 2006).

3. On racial discrimination in the building trades industry, see George Straus and Sidney Ingerman, "Public Policy and Discrimination in Apprenticeship," in *Negroes and Jobs: A Book of Readings,* ed. Louis A. Ferman, Joyce L. Kornbluh, and Joe A. Miller (Ann Arbor: University of Michigan Press, 1968); Roger Waldinger, "The Continuing Significance of

Race: Racial Conflict and Racial Discrimination in Construction," *Politics & Society* 19, no. 3 (1991): 291–324; Roger Waldinger, *Still the Promised City?: African Americans and New Immigrants in Postindustrial New York* (Cambridge, Mass.: Harvard University Press, 1996), 174–205; F. Ray Marshall, *The Negro and Organized Labor* (New York: John Wiley & Sons, 1965); F. Ray Marshall, *The Negro and Apprenticeship* (Baltimore: Johns Hopkins University Press, 1967); F. Ray Marshall, *Equal Apprenticeship Opportunities: The Nature of the Issue and the New York Experience* (Washington, D.C.: Institute of Labor and Industrial Relations, University of Michigan, Wayne State University, and National Manpower Policy Task Force, 1968).

4. Herbert Hill, quoted in *Amsterdam News,* June 8, 1963, 20.

5. "Race Relations in Crisis," *The Open Mind,* June 12, 1963, transcript courtesy of Richard Heffner (in author's possession).

6. "State's Construction Outlays to Rise to Record 345 Million," *New York Times,* February 2, 1961; Marshall, *Negro and Apprenticeship,* 47, 50; Marshall, *Negro and Organized Labor,* 123. See also the New York City Commission on Human Rights, "Bias in the Building Industry: An Updated Report, 1963–1967," New York, 1967; Straus and Ingerman, "Public Policy and Discrimination in Apprenticeship"; Sugrue, "Affirmative Action from Below"; Waldinger, "Continuing Significance of Race"; Waldinger, *Still the Promised City.*

7. Waldinger, *Still the Promised City,* 178–82. See also "Not Racism, But Nepotism," *Time,* August 9, 1963; Gregory Butler, *Disunited Brotherhoods: Race, Racketeering and the Fall of the New York Construction Unions* (New York: iUniverse, 2006); Banks, "'Last Bastion of Discrimination'"; Joshua Freeman, "Hardhats: Construction Workers, Manliness, and the 1970 Pro-War Demonstrations," *Journal of Social History* 26, no. 4 (1993): 725–44; Marshall, *Negro and Apprenticeship,* 47–82.

8. Waldinger, *Still the Promised City,* 183; Banks, "'Last Bastion of Discrimination'"; Marshall, *Negro and Apprenticeship.*

9. Gilbert Banks's account is drawn from my oral history interviews with him, April 1–2, 2000, Bronx, New York, and from an interview with Gilbert Banks conducted by Debra Bernhardt, New Yorkers at Work Oral History Project, Wagner Labor Archives, New York University, October 22, 1980. The quotation is from the interview by Bernhardt.

10. "Wagner Directs Agencies to Push Minority Rights," *New York Times,* June 5, 1963, 1, 31; "Building Unions Pledge Bias Fight," *New York Times,* June 7, 1963; "Mayor Moves on Bias," *Amsterdam News,* June 8, 1963.

11. "Promise Mass Action on Building Trade Unions," *Amsterdam News,* June 8, 1963, 20; "Unions Here Get Warning on Bias," *New York Times,* June 13, 1963; "300 Cops Present: Pickets Clash at Hospital Site," *Amsterdam News,* June 15, 1963; "City Halts Work at Site in Harlem," *New York Times,* June 14, 1963; "The Time Is Now," *Amsterdam News,* June 29, 1963.

12. "State University Sets Vast Growth," *New York Times,* January 8, 1960.

13. Much of the following account comes from the following: interview with Oliver Leeds conducted by Howard August, August 9, 1983, New Yorkers at Work Oral History Collection, Wagner Labor Archives, Tamiment Collection, New York University; interview with Oliver and Marjorie Leeds conducted by Clarence Taylor, August 11, 1988 (in author's possession); interview with Oliver Leeds conducted by Dianne Esses, December 15, 1988 (in author's possession).

14. Interview with Oliver Leeds by Esses.

15. Taylor, *Black Churches of Brooklyn,* 143; interview with Oliver Leeds by Esses.

16. Taylor, *Black Churches of Brooklyn,* 118, 144, 145–46. On Milton Galamison's political activism, see Taylor, *Knocking at Our Own Door.* On Brooklyn CORE, see Brian Purnell, "A Movement Grows in Brooklyn: The Brooklyn Chapter of the Congress of Racial

Equality (CORE) and the Northern Civil Rights Movement during the Early 1960s," Ph.D. diss., New York University, 2006.

17. Interview with Oliver and Marjorie Leeds by Taylor.

18. Ibid.

19. Taylor, *Black Churches of Brooklyn,* 144, 146–47.

20. Elaine Bibuld recounted the same story on three different occasions. The most detailed version, from which this quotation is taken, is my interview with Elaine Bibuld, Rioghan Kirchner, Mary Phifer Kirton, and Msemaji and Nandi Weusi, April 7, 2000. See also my interview with Elaine Bibuld, February 18, 2001; interview with Elaine Bibuld conducted by Sheila Michaels, May 23, 2000, part of the Non-Violent Oral History Project, Columbia University Oral History Office. Jerome Bibuld also makes mention of the arrest. See my interview with Jerome Bibuld, January 2, 2003.

21. My interview with Elaine Bibuld; "Governor's Office Here Is Besieged as Sit-Ins Spread," *New York Times,* July 11, 1963; "Work Stop Looms at Hospital Site," *Amsterdam News,* July 13, 1963.

22. Clarence Taylor, *Black Churches of Brooklyn,* 151.

23. Interview with Oliver Leeds by August; interview with Oliver and Marjorie Leeds by Taylor; interview with Oliver Leeds by Esses; interviews with Arnold Goldwag conducted by Shelia Michaels, April 23, 1999, May 5, 1999, and March 9, 2001.

24. Interview with Oliver Leeds by August.

25. Ibid.

26. Interview with Oliver and Marjorie Leeds by Taylor; interview with Oliver Leeds by Esses.

27. "42 Rights Pickets Arrested by City," *New York Times,* July 16, 1963, 1, 15; quote on 1.

28. Ibid., quotes on 15.

29. Ibid.

30. Interview with Oliver and Marjorie Leeds by Taylor.

31. Ibid.

32. "Arrested Ministers Vow Fight," *Amsterdam News,* July 20, 1963, pp. 1, 42; "Race Protest Set at Hospital Site," *New York Times,* July 22, 1963, 44; "200 Racial Pickets Seized at Building Projects Here," *New York Times,* July 23, 1963, 1, 18; "Ministers Give Call to Fight," *Amsterdam News,* July 27, 1963, 25, 45; Taylor, *Black Churches of Brooklyn,* 150–52.

33. "143 More Seized in Protests Here," *New York Times,* July 24, 1963; "Rockefeller Bars Negro Job Quota; Hails Union Plan," *New York Times,* July 26, 1963; "Wagner Extends Civil Rights Talks on Job Practices," *New York Times,* July 31, 1963.

34. "27 Pickets Seized with 17 Children in Street Blockade," *New York Times,* July 20, 1963. After Brooklyn CORE organized the first children's arrest, eighteen more were arrested on July 30; see *New York Times,* July 31, 1963.

35. "Police Cut Chains to Seize Pickets," *New York Times,* July 26, 1963; for a picture of Goldwag and others on the crane, see *New York Times,* July 31, 1963, 14. See also Rioghan Kirchner misc. newspaper clippings, Brooklyn Collection, Brooklyn Public Library, Grand Army Plaza Branch; my e-mail interview with Shelley Spector Ipiotis, March 24, 2005; interview with Maurice Fredericks conducted by Deborah Burnhardt, April 28, 1981, New Yorkers at Work, Oral History Project, Wagner Labor Archives, Tamiment Collection, New York University.

36. My interview with Elaine Bibuld, Rioghan Kirchner, Mary Phifer Kirton, and Msemaji and Nandi Weusi.

37. Interview with Maurice Fredericks by Burnhardt; ibid.

38. My interview with Elaine Bibuld, Rioghan Kirchner, Mary Phifer Kirton, and Msemaji and Nandi Weusi.

39. My interview with Sonny Carson, November 13, 2000. See also Mwlina Imiri Abu-badika (Sonny Carson), *The Education of Sonny Carson* (New York: W. W. Norton, 1972).

40. My interview with Arnold Goldwag, October 13, 2000; Kochiyama quoted in Diane C. Fujino, *Heartbeat of Struggle: The Revolutionary Life of Yuri Kochiyama* (Minneapolis: University of Minnesota Press, 2005), 116, 119–20.

41. My interview with Frances Phipps Crayton, November 28, 2003.

42. Ibid.

43. Taylor, *Black Churches of Brooklyn,* 153–55.

44. "Near-Riot Flares in Race Protest at Project Here," *New York Times,* August 1, 1963; ibid., 155.

45. Interview with Oliver Leeds by August.

46. "Investigation of Activities of Procept Members in Connection with Brooklyn Chapter of Congress of Racial Equality," August 14, 1963, Vincent Young Papers, Bureau Special Services File, #334-M (in author's possession).

47. Ibid.; interview with Oliver Leeds by Esses. Leeds recounted this conversation, with subtle variations, in each of his interviews. See interviews with Oliver and Marjorie Leeds by Taylor and interview with Oliver Leeds by August; interview with Oliver Leeds by August Meier in Brooklyn, New York, April 28, 1971, in the August Meier Papers, Schomburg Center.

48. Taylor, *Black Churches of Brooklyn,* 155.

49. Interviews with Oliver and Marjorie Leeds by Taylor; interviews with Oliver Leeds by August and Esses.

50. Ibid.

51. Interview with Oliver and Marjorie Leeds by Taylor; Taylor, *Black Churches of Brooklyn,* 156.

52. My interview with Gilbert Banks.

53. Fujino, *Heartbeat of Struggle.*

54. My interview with Crayton.

55. Obituary, *New York Times,* December 23, 2002.

2. "THE LABORATORY OF DEMOCRACY"

1. "Racial Job Clash Erupts in Jersey," *New York Times,* July 4, 1963.

2. "Clash Brings Request to Halt Barringer Job: Mayor Asks Study of Bias," *Newark Evening News,* July 3, 1963, 1.

3. "Hearings before the United States Commission on Civil Rights: Newark, New Jersey, September 11–12, 1962," U.S. Government Printing Office, Washington, D.C., 1963.

4. Ibid., 18, 52, 58. Union leaders and state officials estimated that of the nearly 4,000 apprentices enrolled in federally registered programs throughout New Jersey only 14 were African American. "Racial Discrimination in the Nation's Apprenticeship Training Programs," *Phylon* 23 (fall 1962): 215–23, offers strikingly similar statistics for other cities.

5. "Hearings," 5–6.

6. "Building Trades Unions Include Few Negroes Here," *Newark Evening News,* September 11, 1962.

7. For more on urban renewal in Newark, see David Gerwin, "The End of Coalition: The Failure of Community Organizing in Newark in the 1960s," PhD diss., Columbia University, 1998; Michael Immerso, *Newark's Little Italy: The Vanished First Ward* (New Brunswick, N.J.: Rutgers University Press, 1997); Adele Oltman, "'A Diabolical Scheme': Urban Renewal and the Civil Rights Movement in Newark in the early 1960s," unpublished paper presented at Conference on "The Long Hot Summers in Retrospect: Urban Unrest in 1960s New Jersey," New Jersey Historical Society, November 13, 2004; David Levitus,

"Planning, Slum Clearance, and the Road to Crisis in Newark," *Newark Metro,* September 2005, available at: http://www.newarkmetro.rutgers.edu/reports/display.php?id=173 (accessed November 1, 2007).

8. Imamu Amiri Baraka [Leroi Jones], "The Practice of the New Nationalism," in *Kawaida Studies, the New Nationalism* (Chicago: Third World Press, 1972), excerpted in Clement Price, *Freedom Not Far Distant: A Documentary of Afro-Americans in New Jersey* (Newark: New Jersey Historical Society, 1980), 286–87.

9. See Julia Rabig, "The Fixers: Devolution, Development, and Civil Society in Newark, New Jersey, 1960–1996," PhD diss., University of Pennsylvania, 2007, chap. 3.

10. "Newark: A City in Transition," Vol. 1, tables 24–25, Mayor's Commission on Group Relations, Newark, 1959, Charles E. Cummings New Jersey Information Center, Newark Public Library [hereafter CCCNPL].

11. "Labor Force and Business Establishments," Newark, New Jersey, County and City Databooks, historic ed., available at: http://fisher.lib.virginia.edu/collections/stats/ccdb/ (accessed August 16, 2007).

12. "Contractors Fear Wage Boosts May Brake Construction Growth," *Newark Evening News,* September 30, 1962; "Hearings"; Advisory Committees to the United States Commission on Civil Rights, "Reports on Apprenticeship," U.S. Commission on Civil Rights, Washington, D.C., January 1964, 91–92.

13. Amiri Baraka, *The Autobiography of Leroi Jones* (Chicago: Lawrence Hill Books, 1997), 41–51; my interview with David Barrett, Columbia, Md., January 29, 2005.

14. Newarkers joined a national wave of protests against employment discrimination in the construction trades in 1963, the most prominent occurring in Philadelphia, Pennsylvania; Thomas J. Sugrue, "Affirmative Action from Below: Civil Rights, the Building Trades, and the Politics of Racial Equality in the Urban North, 1945–1969," *Journal of American History* 91 (June 2004), 146–50, 170–73; "Building Trades Unions Include Few Negroes Here."

15. Robert Curvin, "The Persistent Minority: The Black Political Experience in Newark," PhD diss., Princeton University, 1975, 14.

16. Mayor's Commission on Group Relations (later called the Human Rights Commission), "Newark Points the Way," 1957 pamphlet, CCCNPL. Chairman David M. Litwin's testimony in support of S. 692, U.S. Senate Subcommittee on Civil Rights, Committee on Labor and Public Welfare, March 6, 1954.

17. Points the Way"; "DAD Church Program on Religion & Human Relations," *Human Relations News,* February 1957, CCCNPL.

18. *Human Relations News* 1 (August 1956); *Human Relations News* 2 (March 1958). By the mid-1960s activists criticized Daniel Anthony, then the commission director, for his ineffectiveness. Anthony also clashed with the mayor and police over his support for a civilian review board to address police brutality. Memo, Ad-Hoc Committee for Improving the Operations of the Newark Commission on Human Rights to Mayor Hugh J. Addonizio, March 5, 1963, Daniel S. Anthony Papers [hereafter DSA Papers], Container 10, CCCNPL. When Anthony resigned that summer, he praised the Barringer protesters for energizing the city civil rights movement and voiced his long-standing frustration with the municipal government: "For ten years, I have witnessed cynical politicians make cheap political hay out of civil rights." "Anthony Resigns Rights Post," *Newark Evening News,* July 14, 1963.

19. The New Jersey Urban Colored Population Commission investigated discrimination complaints and referred job seekers to Urban League offices in the 1940s. Investigation, September 9, 1947, Investigative files office report, box 1, Urban Colored Population Commission Records, New Jersey Department of State, Trenton, N.J.; my interview with Lydia Davis Barrett, Montclair, N.J., April 2005; "Hearings," 11, 18.

20. My interview with Robert Curvin, Newark, N.J., September 2004. Curvin's Youth Council friends included William Payne and Stanley Aronowitz. Payne was active in the United Essex Civic Association and the NCC during the Barringer protest and was later elected to the New Jersey State Senate. Aronowitz became a Students for a Democratic Society (SDS) activist and radical sociologist. For more on earlier civil rights protests, see Kevin Mumford, *Newark: A History of Race, Rights, and Riots* (New York: New York University Press, 2007), 45–47.

21. "CORE Leaders Call for Store Boycott," *Newark Sunday News,* September 9, 1962.

22. My interview with Curvin, 2004; "2 Protests by CORE: White Castle Diners in Newark, Orange Are Picketed," *Newark Evening News,* July 22, 1963; "Police Picketed by Newark CORE," *New York Times,* August 4, 1963; "Police Brutality and Bias Charged a Newark Rally," *New York Times,* September 9, 1962.

23. "2 Protests by CORE," 5.

24. My interview with Robert Curvin, South Orange, N.J., August 8, 2007.

25. "Truce Is Reached in Barringer Job," *Newark Evening News,* August 14, 1963; "New Talks Start on Barringer Dispute" *Newark Evening News,* August 16, 1963.

26. For more on the scope of earlier civil rights activism, see Mumford, *Newark,* 76–85.

27. For African American support of Addonizio during both his 1962 and 1966 campaigns, see Luther Carter, "Newark: Negroes Demand and Get Voice in Medical School Plans," *Science* n.s. 160, no. 3825 (1968), 291; Curvin earned a doctorate in political science at Princeton University and wrote his dissertation on the development of black political leadership in Newark. He called the NAACP leaders of the 1950s and early 1960s "literal token representatives" and argued that those who held jobs in the Addonizio administration were expected to secure the mayor's support among African Americans. My interview with Curvin, 2004. For more on this dynamic as it pertained to NCC, see Curvin, "Persistent Minority," 51–54. A flyer circulated in the early 1960s called for a "courageous and militant NAACP Branch in Newark." Pointing to four NAACP officials who worked for the city, the author of the flyer argued that the Addonizio administration had bought the quiescence of the organization for the price of their combined salaries. Undated flier, Container 3, DSA Papers, CCCNPL. Similar claims were debated in the *New Jersey Afro American;* see Lee Johnson, "Inside Newark," *New Jersey Afro American,* May 9, 1964.

28. "Rights Board Finds Bias at School Job," *Newark Evening News,* July 10, 1963.

29. My interview with Curvin, 2007.

30. Ibid.

31. "Some Go to Work," *Newark Evening News,* July 8, 1963.

32. My interview with Curvin, 2007.

33. "Rights Board Finds Bias."

34. "School Officials Meet with Contractors, Stop Work," *Newark Evening News,* July 5, 1963; "Barringer Pot Boils Union May Refuse All School Jobs," *Newark Evening News,* July 7, 1963; "Union Men Balk," *Newark Evening News,* July 9, 1963.

35. "Rights Board Finds Bias."

36. "To Plan Project Hiring," *Newark Evening News,* July 11, 1963, 1.

37. "Barringer Pot Boils."

38. "Bias Panel Adds CORE," *Newark Evening News,* July 16, 1963; "Truce Called: Barringer Dispute Up to Negotiators," *Newark Evening News,* August 15, 1963.

39. "Building Trades Reject Demands," *Newark Evening News,* July 24, 1963, 1.

40. Quoted in "Pickets to Return to Barringer Site" *Newark Evening News,* July 25, 1963, 8.

41. Quoted in "2nd Showdown Due on Barringer Jobs," *Newark Evening News,* July 28, 1963, 6.

42. *U.S. v. United Association of Journeymen,* 1973 U.S. Dist. Lexis 14881.

43. "Hearings," 59. For trade union nepotism and its origins, see Jill Quadagno, "Social Movements and State Transformation: Labor Unions and Racial Conflict in the War on Poverty," *American Sociological Review* 57, no. 5 (1992), 624.

44. "Job Goes On Despite Barringer Pickets," *Newark Evening News,* July 29, 1963.

45. "2nd Showdown Due on Barringer Jobs"; "President of State NAACP to Seek Rights Unity Here," *Newark Evening News,* August 5, 1963.

46. "2nd Showdown Due on Barringer Jobs." 6.

47. "Building Unions Refuse Job Data Asked by Pfaus," *Newark Evening News,* August 9, 1963; "Pledge to End Job Bias," *Newark Evening News,* August 9, 1963; "Chief Asks Joint Rights Unit," *Newark Evening News,* September 17, 1963.

48. "Job Picketing Will Resume at Barringer," *Newark Evening News,* August 13, 1963.

49. "Truce Called."

50. "Beyond Demonstrations Negro Groups Seen Gaining in Projects to Get Jobs," *Newark Evening News,* August 18, 1963, 12.

51. My interview with Francis Warren, Philadelphia, PA, March 21, 2006.

52. "Attack on Job Bias Shows Some Gains," *Newark Evening News,* September 17, 1963; "Job Rights Group Bids Others Join," *Newark Evening News,* September 20, 1963. Twenty-two businesses had identified 125 vacancies, of which African American workers had filled 41.

53. For more on the philosophy of equal employment policies before affirmative action, see Stacy Kinlock Sewell, "'The Best Man for the Job': Corporate Responsibility and Racial Integration in the Workplace, 1945–1960," *Historian* 65, no. 5 (2003): 1125–46.

54. Plans for Progress Blue Program biographies, Plans for Progress folder, Box 8, Entry 4, Office of Chairman, Stephen Shulman (1966–1968), Records of the Equal Employment Opportunity Commission (EEOC), National Archives and Records Administration (NARA), College Park, Md. State officials identified BICC as a model for other cities. "Committee Report on Building Trades, Printing Trades, and other 'Closed Shop' Industries," Employment Committee, Bi-Partisan Conference on Civil Rights, folder 3, box 4, Ernest Thompson Papers [hereafter Thompson Papers], Rutgers University Special Collections, New Brunswick, N.J.

55. Rabig, "Fixers," chap. 3.

56. My interview with Curvin, 2007. At the time, CORE was negotiating with Pabst, Charles Bessler Company, Public Service, RCA, Tung Sol, and Western Electric. Notes, N.J. Bell Telephone, February 12, 1964; "Agreement Reached with A&P," set a goal of hiring two hundred black and Puerto Rican clerks from Newark in 1964, December 15, 1963; and "CORE Employment Committee Projects and Personnel," September 1, 1963; these three citations are from private papers of Robert Curvin [hereafter Curvin Papers].

57. "Addonizio Voices Hope for Pact on Negro Jobs," *Newark Evening News,* August 27, 1963; "Board Acts on Job Bias," *Newark Evening News,* August 28, 1963.

58. "Rights Unit Study Essex Job Pact," *Newark Evening News,* September 1, 1963.

59. The exact number of minority workers employed as a result of the Barringer protest is difficult to ascertain. Of the forty-two job seekers NCC referred, only one, an electrician, was actually employed through the unions; "Addonizio Voices Hope." Prior to the formal agreement, the Newark Board of Education responded to the protest by requiring unions to dispatch integrated crews to all school jobs (including Barringer). This new policy yielded only five African American hires—three painters, one carpenter, and one laborer; "5 Negroes Hired for School Jobs," *Newark Evening News,* August 9, 1963.

60. "Elizabeth Plan, Hughes Tells Job Bias Pact," *Newark Evening News,* September 19, 1963.

61. Ibid. See also "Pastor New Head of Local NAACP," *Newark Evening News,* September 18, 1963. For more on James Cantrell's leadership, see Curvin, "Persistent Minority," 55–57.

62. Ernest Thompson and Mindy Thompson, *Homeboy Came to Orange: A Story of People's Power* (New Jersey: Bridgebuilder Press, 1976), 158.

63. My interview with Rebecca Doggett, Newark, N.J., April 7, 2005.

64. "A Report on the Current Status of the Negotiations between the Greater Newark Coordinating Council and Rutgers University and Newark College of Engineering," folder 3, box 4, Thompson Papers.

65. Thompson and Thompson, *Homeboy Came to Orange*, 159.

66. In May 1964, Rutgers University announced that it would require contractors to submit information on the composition of the proposed workforce for analysis before construction began; "Contractors Asked to Give Racial Forecast for Project," *New York Times*, May 5, 1964, 37.

67. Thompson and Thompson, *Homeboy Came to Orange*, 159.

68. Ibid., 162–63.

69. "Rutgers to Crack Down on Unions," *New Jersey Afro American*, February 6, 1965.

70. "Hail Jersey Gov's Racial Bias Search," *Amsterdam News*, February 6, 1965, 24.

71. "Rights Groups Plan for New Rutgers Job Demonstrations," *Newark Evening News*, October 7, 1965; Thompson and Thompson, *Homeboy Came to Orange*, 165.

72. "Hearings," 382–416.

73. "A Report on the Current Status of the Negotiations."

74. My interview with Doggett. During the CORE negotiations with Newark corporations in 1963 and 1964, employers expected CORE to supplement the work of the Urban League by providing the names of black job seekers to fill positions. CORE insisted that its role was to pressure for redress of inequality, not to act as a placement service. Meeting notes concerning N.J. Bell Telephone, February 12, 1964 and Undated NCC "white paper" on Rutgers Law School and Newark College of Engineering Campaigns, Curvin Papers.

75. "Rights Groups."

76. "Danzig Tells Rights Groups, Keep Up Bid for Building Jobs," *Newark Evening News*, October 15, 1965.

77. Thompson and Thompson, *Homeboy Came to Orange*, 165.

78. Cyril DeGrasse Tyson, *2 Years before the Riot!: Newark, New Jersey and the United Community Corporation, 1964–1966* (New York: Jay Street Publishers, 2000); Leila Meier Rice, "In the Trenches in the War on Poverty: The Local Implementation of the Community Action Program, 1964–1969," PhD diss., Vanderbilt University, 1997; Rabig, "Fixers," chap. 2.

79. Carter, "Newark," 291–92.

80. "Organizations Win in Newark Wards," *Newark Evening News*, April 22, 1964.

81. Michael Parenti, "Power and Pluralism: A View from the Bottom," *Journal of Politics* 32, no. 3 (1970): 501–30, esp. 513–16, 514. Parenti used Newark voters' failed attempts to challenge established Democratic Party candidates and achieve greater representation for African Americans in the mid-1960s to expose the weakness of pluralism as a theory of how political power functions in U.S. cities.

82. Curvin, "Persistent Minority," 49.

83. Parenti, "Power and Pluralism," 513–16.

84. Komozi Woodard, "Amiri Baraka and the Black Power Experiment," in *Freedom North: Black Freedom Struggles outside of the South, 1940–1980* (New York: Palgrave MacMillan, 2003), 300–301; my interview with David Barrett.

85. "Newark College to Help Negroes," *New York Times*, August 4, 1967.

86. Leonard J. Duhl and Mary Jo Steetle, "Newark: Community or Chaos: A Case Study of the Medical School Controversy," undated, Newark, N.J., folder, box 380, Subject Corres (1942–1969), Housing and Urban Development (HUD), NARA. The City Hospital ratio of two nurses to thirty-nine patients wildly violated the 1:6–8 ratio prescribed by the state.

87. Ibid., 15.

88. Duhl notes that by 1967 Newark had received $325 million in federal funds for an urban renewal program that was the fifth largest in the United States. Shortly after Addonizio's 1962 election, the NHA received $350,000 to prepare a Community Renewal Plan that would integrate residents' concerns into the existing city urban renewal agenda, but Louis Danzig, NHA executive director, never delivered; ibid., 12–13.

89. John T. Cunningham, *Newark* (Newark: New Jersey Historical Society, 1988), 317.

90. Some observers and scholars argue that two riots, in fact, took place during the week of July 11. Residents' opposition to the arrest and treatment of Smith by police constituted the first riot. The second riot was instigated by the arrival of the National Guard, at which point the burning and looting of the downtown accelerated under the guise of searching for snipers.

91. Baraka, *Autobiography of Leroi Jones;* Cunningham, *Newark;* Tom Hayden, *Rebellion in Newark: Official Violence and Ghetto Response* (New York: Vintage Books, 1967); Ron Perambo, *No Cause for Indictment: An Autopsy of Newark* (New York: Holt, Rinehart and Winston, 1971).

92. "U.S. Court Says Jersey Unions Must Drop All Racial Barriers," *New Jersey Afro American,* January 30, 1971. "Development of the plan came about as a result of the July 1967 Newark riots, which erupted when unions and contractors refused to hire experienced blacks for jobs on the medical project." Although this statement drastically oversimplifies the causes of the riot, it represents a common belief that the medical school dispute was a significant proximate cause. Aide Memoir for the Undersecretary from Joseph Freitas Jr., December 29, 1967, Subject Correspondence (1942–1969), Newark, N.J., folder, box 380, HUD.

93. "Hughes Disputed on Newark Plan," *New York Times,* January 16, 1968; Duhl and Steetle, "Newark," 9, 14, 21–25.

94. Duhl and Steetle, "Newark," 18–20; *Essex County and Vicinity District Council of Carpenters and Millwrights of United Brotherhood of Carpenters and Joiners of America v. Conforti and Eisele, Inc. et al.,* 1971 U.S. Dist. Lexis 10915; Carter, "Newark," 291.

95. Walter H. Waggoner, "Newark Outline Plan for Medical Campus," *New York Times,* September 29, 1968.

96. See footnote 8.

97. Duhl and Steetle, "Newark," 51.

98. Carter, 292.

99. Subsequent to the Barringer High School demonstrations, activists targeted construction at the Rutgers Law School and Essex County Community College, among others. "Rights Groups"; my interview with Doggett.

100. Quoted in Carter, "Newark," 292.

101. "U.S. Court Says."

102. "Report of the Meeting of the Business and Industrial Coordinating Council," August 1969, Newark Q file [hereafter Q Files], CCCNPL.

103. "Hearings Asked on Bias in Building Trades Jobs," *Newark Sunday News,* March 1, 1970, 23.

104. "Hughes Threatens Suit to Put Blacks in College Site Job," *New York Times,* January 19, 1969.

105. My interview with Gustav Heningburg, Newark, N.J., December 6, 2006; "Report of the Meeting of the Business and Industrial Coordinating Council," July 1969, Q Files.

106. My interview with Heningburg.

107. *Joyce v. McCrane, Bricklayers, et. al.,* 1970 U.S. Dist. Lexis 9004.

3. "WORK FOR ME ALSO MEANS WORK FOR THE COMMUNITY I COME FROM"

1. "Oakland Fans Cheer Their Raiders as Jilted L.A. Fans Blast Al Davis," *St. Petersburg Times,* June 24, 1995.

2. "Contractor Is Behind Move to Put Raider Deal on Ballot," *Contra Costa Times*, July 22, 1995, A16; *San Francisco Chronicle*, July 21, 1995.

3. "Motives of Raiders Foe Questioned—Bankruptcy Papers List Contractor's Money Woes," *San Francisco Chronicle*, August 3, 1995, A13.

4. "Contractor Is Behind Move to Put Raider Dearl on Ballot," *Contra Costa Times*, July 22, 1995, A16.

5. E. Franklin Frazier, *Black Bourgeoisie: The Rise of a New Middle Class* (New York: Free Press, 1957), Chapter 7.

6. Most of the work on the integration of the building trades has centered on the Philadelphia Plan, which was the first federally imposed affirmative action program. On the origins of the Philadelphia Plan, see Hugh Davis Graham, *The Civil Rights Era: Origins and Development of National Policy 1960–1972* (New York: Oxford University Press, 1990); Dean J. Kotlowski, "Richard Nixon and the Origins of Affirmative Action," *Historian* 60, no. 3 (1998): 223–41; John D. Skrentny, *The Minority Rights Revolution* (Cambridge, Mass.: Harvard University Press, 2002); Kevin Yuill, *Richard Nixon and the Rise of Affirmative Action: The Pursuit of Racial Equality in an Era of Limits* (Lanham, Md.: Rowman & Littlefield, 2006); Thomas J. Sugrue, "Affirmative Action from Below: Civil Rights, the Building Trades, and the Politics of Racial Equality in the Urban North, 1945–1969," *Journal of American History* 91, no. 1 (2004): 145–73.

7. W. Avon Drake and Robert D. Holsworth, *Affirmative Action and the Stalled Quest for Black Progress* (Urbana: University of Illinois Press, 1996); Thomas Sowell, *Civil Rights: Rhetoric or Reality* (New York: William Morrow, 1984); George R. LaNoue, "Social Science and Minority 'Set-Asides,'" *Public Interest* 110 (winter 1993): 49–62; Thomas Edsall, *Chain Reaction: The Impact of Race, Rights, and Taxes on American Politics* (New York: W. W. Norton, 1991); Terry H. Anderson, *The Pursuit of Fairness: A History of Affirmative Action* (New York: Oxford University Press, 1994); Terry Eastland, *Ending Affirmative Action: The Case for Colorblind Justice* (New York: Basic Books, 1996).

8. James Gregory, *The Southern Diaspora: How the Great Migrations of Black and White Southerners Transformed America* (Chapel Hill: University of North Carolina Press, 2005).

9. Compliance Checks, Kingman's Report, September 30, 1944, reel 75, Records of the Fair Employment Practices Committee; Council for Civic Unity, Civil Rights Inventory, 1956, reel 9, folder 6, box 20, Homeland Ministry Archives.

10. Wilmer Joseph Leon, "The Negro Contractor in Oakland, California, and Adjacent Cities," MA thesis, University of California at Berkeley, 1954, 22–25.

11. Finding information on these contractors is difficult, but thanks to thirty-two interviews conducted by Wilmer Joseph Leon, a graduate student in sociology at the University of California at Berkeley, for his 1954 MA thesis, it is possible to gain insight into their experiences and attitudes toward the industry in the middle of the twentieth century. The following analysis draws heavily on interview excerpts that appear in Leon's study; ibid.

12. Ibid., 10, 22, 32, 25.

13. Ibid., 10, 52.

14. Juliet E. K. Walker, *The History of Black Business in America: Capitalism, Race, Entrepreneurship* (New York: Macmillan, 1998), xxii.

15. Leon, "Negro Contractor," 14, 26–27.

16. Reginald Stuart, "Black Contractors' Dilemma," Special Report for the Race Relations Information Center, Nashville, Tenn., August 1971, 9.

17. "A Survey of Minority Construction Contractors," published by the Office of the Assistant Secretary for Equal Opportunity, U.S. Department of Housing and Urban Development, 1970, 1.

18. Ibid., 13; Glover, *Minority Enterprise in Construction* (New York: Praeger Publishers, 1977), 23.

19. California Department of Employment, "The Construction Industry: Training Opportunities for the Minority Worker," October 1, 1965, Jobart Information Kit, folder 21, box 20, NAACP Region I Records, Bancroft Library, University of California at Berkeley.

20. Grace Palladino, *Skilled Hands, Strong Spirits: A Century of Building Trades History* (Ithaca, NY: Cornell University Press, 2005), 157.

21. Thomas O'Hanlon, "The Unchecked Power of the Building Trades," *Fortune,* December 1968, 102.

22. Cabinet Committee on Construction, "A Federal Program to Increase the Manpower Supply of the Construction Industry," General Records of the Department of Labor, Record Group 174, Office of the Secretary, Records of the Secretary of Labor George P. Schultz, 1969-1970, Box 58, Councils, Cabinet Committee on Construction Folder, National Archives (College Park, MD).

23. Joseph Debro, "Financing Minority Contractors," *Bankers Magazine* 154, no. 1 (1971), n.p.

24. Gilbert B. Friedman, "The Unbondable," *New Republic,* July 6, 1968, 28.

25. My interview with Joseph Debro, August 10, 2007, Oakland, California.

26. "Hearings before the Subcommittee on Housing of the Committee on Banking and Currency, House of Representatives, June 2, 3, 4, and 5, 1970," 91st Congress, Second Session, pt. I (Washington, D.C.: U.S. Government Printing Office, 1970), 400.

27. "Hearings before the Subcommittee on Small Business of the Committee of Banking and Currency, United States Senate, 91st Congress, Second Session, June 15, 16, and 17, 1970," 91st Congress, Second Session (Washington, D.C.: U.S. Government Printing Office, Washington, D.C., 1970), 128.

28. Stuart, "Black Contractors' Dilemma," 10.

29. G. Douglas Pugh, "Bonding Minority Contractors," in *Black Economic Development,* ed. William F. Haddad and G. Douglas Pugh (Englewood Cliffs: Prentice-Hall, 1969), 141.

30. Joseph Debro, "The Minority Builder," *Labor Law Journal* 21, no. 5 (May 1970), 302.

31. Leon, "Negro Contractor," 64.

32. Joseph Debro, quoted in "Grant Promotes Minority Builders," *Engineering News-Record,* July 11, 1968, 29.

33. Debro, "Grant Promotes Minority Builders," 27.

34. *Oakland Post,* February 5, 1970; "Ray Dones: Pioneer Builder Still Active," *Oakland Post,* February 22–28, 2006; Gilbert B. Friedman, "Unbondable," 27.

35. "A Brief History of the Origin and Purpose of the General and Specialty Contractors Association," folder 24, carton 23, NAACP Region I Records.

36. Robert W. Glover, *Minority Enterprise in Construction,* 106; "Minority Contractor Associations," *Minority Builder* 4 (July–Aug., 1974): 24–28.

37. "GSCA," Published by the General and Specialty Contractors Association, in author's possession.

38. "Fair Employment Report," 7, no. 22, October 27, 1969, 130, folder 15, box 41, Wharton Industrial Unit Records (UPB 5.9IR), University of Pennsylvania Archives, Philadelphia.

39. "Have We Been to the Mountain Top?" *Minority Builder* 3 (Sept.–Oct. 1973), 17.

40. See Robert O. Self, *American Babylon: Race and the Struggle for Postwar Oakland* (Princeton: Princeton University Press, 2003), 191–98, quotation on 193; Joseph A. Rodriguez, "Rapid Transit and Community Power: West Oakland Residents Confront BART," *Antipode* 31, no. 2 (1999): 212–28; Matthew Countryman, *Up South: Civil Rights and Black Power in Philadelphia* (Philadelphia: University of Pennsylvania Press, 2006), 135–49.

41. My interview with Debro.

42. Appendix I, Conference—Small Business Development Corporation, January 29, 1968, "Economic Development Opportunity," Hearings before the Select Committee on Small Business, United States Senate, Ninetieth Congress, Second Session, Newark, N.J., May 24, 1968, New York, N.Y., June 17, 1968.

43. Letter, J. L. Childers to C. J. Haggerty, August 24, 1967, and Joseph Debro, Jack Brown, and R. F. Gully, "On the Job Training Bank of Oakland," Civil Rights Division, RG 009-1, Apprenticeship Series, unprocessed records at the George Meany Memorial Archives. I thank Trevor Griffey for providing this source.

44. "Grant Promotes Minority Builders," *Engineering News-Record,* July 11, 1968, 28.

45. Ibid.

46. Pugh, "Bonding Minority Contractors," 140.

47. "Grant Promotes Minority Builders," 28.

48. Hearings before the Select Committee on Small Business, United States Senate, 90th Congress, Second Session, May 24, 1968 and June 17, 1968, Newark, N.J., New York, N.Y. (Washington, D.C.: U.S. Government Printing Office, 1968), Appendix I, 204.

49. "Grant Promotes Minority Builders."

50. "GSCA"; Debro, "Minority Builder," 304.

51. "Minorities Building Highrises in West Oakland," *Oakland Post,* August 17, 1972.

52. My interview with Debro; "Upgrade Oakland 1970," Project Upgrade, Inc., Oakland, Calif., 1970 (in author's possession).

53. "Ford Grant to Oakland Project," *Oakland Post,* November 13, 1968.

54. "GSCA"; "Upgrade Oakland 1970."

55. In 1966, the Oakland Public Housing Authority decided to construct 2,500 public housing units by the "turnkey" method, in which the housing was "planned and built by private enterprise, under supervision and contract with the Authority. At the completion of construction the Authority buys it and the contractor then 'turns the keys' over." *Oakland Post,* February 26, 1970, 8. "GSCA"; my interview with Debro; *Oakland Post,* January 13, 1972.

56. "ORA Reports on Minority Participation," *Oakland Post,* December 31, 1972.

57. Debro, "Minority Builder," 303.

58. "Honored for Minority Hiring," *Oakland Post,* December 27 and 31, 1972.

59. Pugh, "Bonding Minority Contractors," 145.

60. Ibid., 147.

61. Memorandum, Edward C. Sylvester to William W. Layton et al., February 6, 1967, folder 55, box 44, NAACP Region I Records.

62. "Equal Opportunity Activity Under Executive Order 11246 and Title VI Relating to Industrial Park Site "B", Oakland California, Records of the Economic Development Administration, Record Group 378, Records of the Office of the Executive Secretariat, Office of Administration, Subject Files, 1965-1969, Box 9, National Archives (College Park, Md.).

63. John T. Heafey to Port of Oakland, July 25, 1967, ibid.

64. Testimony of Ray Dones, U.S. Commission on Civil Rights, Contract Compliance Examiner, San Francisco Region, May 2, 1967, folder 36, box 104, NAACP Region I Records.

65. Newsletter of the Bay Area Urban League, Inc., Apr.–May 1967, folder 28, box 20, NAACP Region I Records; Human Rights Commission of San Francisco, minutes of meeting of August 24, 1967, folder 44, box 23, NAACP Region I Records.

66. Memorandum, William E. Riker to Members of the Construction Industry Labor Management Committee on Equal Opportunity, January 30, 1968, Civil Rights Division, RG 009-1, Apprenticeship Series, unprocessed records at the George Meany Memorial Archives. I thank Trevor Griffey for providing this source.

67. "Negro Builders Encounter Bias," *New York Times,* July 20, 1963; "N.A.A.C.P. Offers a Pact to Builders to Calm Protests," *New York Times,* August 9, 1963.

68. Letter, Robert L. Carter to Leonard Carter, December 20, 1967, folder 24, carton, 23, NAACP Region I Records.

69. "Wilkins Outlines Major NAACP Goals for 1968," *Los Angeles Sentinel,* January 18, 1968, B5.

70. NAACP Labor Department, "1967 Annual Report," Papers of the NAACP, Part 28, Series B, Reel 10.

71. "NAACP Expands Its Labor Unit," *New York Amsterdam News,* November 9, 1968.

72. Memorandum, Robert Easley to John Morsell, January 3, 1968, and Memorandum, Robert Easley to Roy Wilkins, August 20, 1968, Papers of the NAACP, Part 28, Series A, Reel 17.

73. Robert W. Easley, "The National Afro-American Builders Corp," Report for the NAACP 60th Annual Convention, June 29–July 5, 1969, Jackson, MS, Papers of the NAACP, Supplement to Part I, 1966–1970, Reel 9.

74. David G. McConnell, "Methods for Developing Complaints of Job Discrimination in the Columbus, Ohio NAACP, West Coast Asilomar Conference Workshop on Employment Discrimination, September 1, 1967, Papers of the NAACP, Part 29, Series C, Reel 10.

75. NAACP Labor Department, "1968 Annual Report," 3–4, Papers of the NAACP, Part 28, Series B, Reel 10.

76. "Contract Compliance and Equal Employment Opportunity in the Construction Industry," Open Meeting before the Massachusetts State Advisory Committee to the United States Commission on Civil Rights, Boston, Mass., June 25–26, 1969, U.S. Government Printing Office, Washington, D.C., 1969, 45.

77. Herbert Hill to Arthur J. Chapital Sr., August 4, 1970, folder, 34, carton, 13, NAACP Region I Records.

78. Memorandum, Herbert Hill to all NAACP Branches, State Conferences and Field Staff, August 4, 1970, folder 34, carton 13, NAACP Region I Records.

79. "What Is NAMC?" *Minority Builder* 2 (Oct. 1972).

80. Housing and Urban Development Legislation—1970, "Hearings before the Subcommittee on Housing," 398.

81. Ibid.

82. Richard Nixon, quoted in Robert E. Weems Jr. and Lewis A. Randolph, "The Ideological Origins of Richard M. Nixon's 'Black Capitalism' Initiative," *Review of Black Political Economy* 29, no. 1 (2001), 53.

83. For a sample, see Ronald W. Bailey, ed., *Black Business Enterprise: Historical and Contemporary Perspectives*(New York: Basic Books, 1971).

84. "Debro to Head Oakland's Model Cities Program," *Oakland Post,* April 10, 1969, 1.

85. Joseph Debro, "The Minority Builder."

86. Dean J. Kotlowski, *Nixon's Civil Rights: Politics, Principle, and Policy* (Cambridge, Mass.: Harvard University Press, 2001), 130.

87. Quoted in "80 Turn Out for Black Jobs Rally," *San Francisco Chronicle,* Oct. 14, 1969, 1.

88. Helen Sause to File, "Notes of Meeting on Demolition Stoppage, December 11, 1969," folder 3, box 17, Joseph L. Alioto Papers, San Francisco History Center, San Francisco Public Library, San Francisco, Calif.; Addendum No. 1 to Specifications for Demolition and Site Clearance Contract No. 26 Western Addition Approved Redevelopment Project Area A-2, folder 3, box 17, Joseph Alioto Papers.

89. My interview with Debro.

90. "Hearings before the Subcommittee on Small Business, June 15, 16, and 17, 1970," 127.

91. "Black Contractor Turns off black pickets," *Engineering News-Record,* April 30, 1970.

92. "$1.7 Million Local Nod Given Bakersfield Firm," *Los Angeles Sentinel,* July 16, 1970.

93. Memorandum, Robert Easley to Herbert Hill, November 13, 1969, Papers of the NAACP, Part 29, Series B, Reel 10.

94. "Black Contractors Form National Organization," *Sun-Reporter,* August 2, 1969, 2.

95. Remarks Given by Samuel J. Simmons at the Annual Convention of the NAACP: "Hud's New Directions in Equal Opportunity," Jackson, Miss., July 1, 1969, Papers of the NAACP, Supplement to Part I, 1966–1970, Reel 9.

96. "Black Contractors Form National Organization," *Sun-Reporter,* August 2, 1969; "Nixon's New Plan to End Job Bias," *San Francisco Chronicle,* July 26, 1969.

97. Memorandum, Howard J. Samuels to "All Affected Personnel," October 1968, NAACP Region I Records, Carton 54, folder 4; *Chicago Defender,* weekend ed., February 8, 1969.

98. Quoted in "Minorities Get Short End of It," *Oakland Post,* September 30, 1971, 1.

99. "Blacks Eye Militancy for Building Jobs," *New York Times,* July 10, 1971, 35.

100. "Comments on N.O. Plan Indicate Wide Confusion," *Times-Picayune,* July 25, 1970.

101. "Minority Contractors Hit Pittsburgh Plan," *New Pittsburgh Courier,* December 12, 1970, 2.

102. "Blacks Eye Militancy for Building Jobs," *New York Times,* July 10, 1971, 35.

103. "A Successful Black Contractor's Advice on How to Succeed: Get Big," *ENR,* September 9, 1971, 19.

104. Testimony of Debro, "Hearings before the Subcommittee on Housing," 400–401; testimony of Debro, "Hearings before the Subcommittee on Small Business, June 15, 16, and 17, 1970," 128–29.

105. Birch Bayh to Roy Wilkins, August 4, 1969, Papers of the NAACP, Part 28, Series A, Reel 9.

106. Robert Easley to Herbert Hill, November 13, 1969, Papers of the NAACP, Part 28, Series B, Reel 10.

107. In 1971 Public Law 91-609 created the "Surety Bonding Guarantee Program," in which the SBA guaranteed bonds up to 90% on government projects.

108. Stuart, "Black Contractors Dilemma," 21.

109. Office of the Assistant Secretary for Equal Opportunity, *Registry of Minority Construction Contractors,* Vol. 6 (Washington, D.C.: Department of Housing and Urban Development, 1970).

110. *Black Enterprise,* January 1974, 22.

111. News clipping from the *Oakland Tribune,* c. 1984 (in Joseph Debro's possession).

112. *Chicago Defender,* daily ed., March 21, 1974; Glover, *Minority Enterprise in Construction,* 89.

113. For a top-down treatment of the plan's origins, see Graham, *Civil Rights Era;* Kotlowski, "Richard Nixon." For a bottom-up account, see Sugrue, "Affirmative Action from Below." For works that argue for the plan's success, see Nancy MacLean, *Freedom Is Not Enough: The Opening of the American Workplace* (Cambridge, Mass.: Harvard University Press, 2006); Jill Quadango, *The Color of Welfare: How Racism Undermined the War on Poverty* (New York: Oxford University Press, 1994). For an opposing view, see Yuill, *Richard Nixon.* For a scathing critique of affirmative action, see Eastland, *Ending Affirmative Action.*

4. COMMUNITY CONTROL OF CONSTRUCTION

1. "'Outlaw' Local 124 Sees Win," *Michigan Chronicle,* Dec. 28, 1968; "Detroit Negroes form Building Trade Local," *Daily World,* January 3, 1969. See also, "Calvin Stubbs Speaks," *Voice of Black Labor,* June 1, 1969, 1.

2. "Eulogy of Henry 'Hank' Rogers," folder 1, box 18, Ken Cockrel Papers [hereafter Cockrel Papers], Walter P. Reuther Archives of Labor and Urban Affairs (ALUA), Detroit. The term *black revolutionaries* specifically refers to members of the Detroit cell of the Revolutionary Action Movement and the League of Revolutionary Black Workers. I make the distinction to show clearly that (1) the Detroit Black Power movement included activists with different backgrounds, approaches, and ideologies and (2) these activists often worked together and established an organizing tradition despite these differences.

3. Philip S. Foner, *Organized Labor and the Black Worker, 1619–1981* (New York: International Publishers, 1982), 401.

4. David Lewis-Colman, *Race against Liberalism: Black Workers and the UAW in Detroit* (Urbana: University of Illinois Press, 2008), 99. See also Heather Thompson, *Whose Detroit?: Politics, Labor, Race in an American City* (Ithaca: Cornell University Press, 2002); Muhammad Ahmad, *We Return in the Whirlwind: Black Radical Organizations, 1960–1975* (Chicago: Kerr Publishing, 2007), 237–306; Dan Georgakas and Marvin Surkin, *Detroit: I Do Mind Dying, a Study in Urban Revolution* (Cambridge, Mass.: South End Press, 1999); James Geschwender, *Race, Class, and Worker Insurgency: The League of Revolutionary Black Workers* (Cambridge, UK: Cambridge University Press, 1977); James Geschwender and Judson Jeffries, "The League of Revolutionary Black Workers," in *Black Power in the Belly of the Beast*, ed. Judson Jeffries, 135–62 (Urbana: University of Illinois Press, 2006); Kieran Taylor, "Turn to the Working Class: The New Left, Black Liberation, and the U.S. Labor Movement (1967–1981)," PhD diss., University of North Carolina, Chapel Hill, 2008, 19–58.

5. "DRUM Spokesmen Claim to Lead All Black Labor," *Michigan Chronicle,* January 11, 1969, 1, 4.

6. Rhonda Y. Williams, "Black Women, Urban Politics, and Engendering Black Power," in *The Black Power Movement: Rethinking the Civil Rights-Black Power Era,* ed. Peniel Joseph (New York: Routledge, 2006), 84.

7. For the organizing tradition of Black Power, see Rhonda Y. Williams, *The Politics of Public Housing: Black Women's Struggles against Urban Inequality* (New York: Oxford University Press, 2004); Matthew Countryman, *Up South: Civil Rights and Black Power in Philadelphia* (Philadelphia: University of Pennsylvania Press, 2006); Komozi Woodard, *A Nation within a Nation: Amiri Baraka (LeRoi Jones) and Black Power Politics* (Chapel Hill: University of North Carolina Press, 1999); Thompson, *Whose Detroit?;* Jeanne Theoharis and Komozi Woodard, eds., *Freedom North: Black Freedom Struggles outside the South, 1940–1980* (New York: Palgrave Macmillian, 2003); Jeanne Theoharis and Komozi Woodard, eds., *Groundwork: Local Black Freedom Movements in America* (New York: New York University Press, 2005); Robert Self, *American Babylon: Race and the Struggle for Postwar Oakland* (Princeton: Princeton University Press, 2003); Peniel Joseph, *The Black Power Movement: Rethinking the Civil Rights–Black Power Era* (New York: Routledge, 2007); Peniel Joseph, *Waiting 'Til the Midnight Hour: A Narrative History of Black Power in America* (New York: Henry Holt, 2006); Annelise Orleck, *Storming Caesar's Palace: How Black Mothers Fought Their Own War on Poverty* (Boston: Beacon, 2005); Yohuru Williams, *Black Politics/White Power: Civil Rights, Black Power and the Black Panthers* (St. James, N.Y.: Brandywine Press, 2000).

8. For recent works that discuss the impact of Black Power on labor struggles, see Peter Levy, *The New Left and Labor in the 1960s* (Urbana: University of Illinois Press, 1994); Ruth Needleman, *Black Freedom Fighters in Steel: The Struggle for Democratic Unionism* (Ithaca: Cornell University Press, 2003); William Van Deburg, *New Day in Babylon: The Black Power Movement and American Culture, 1965–1975* (Chicago: University of Chicago Press, 1992).

9. For different interpretations of the legacy and significance of the long civil rights movement that largely ignore or downplay the Black Power movement and its impact on civil rights unionism and the struggle for jobs and freedom during the 1960s and

1970s, see Jacquelyn Dowd Hall, "The Long Civil Rights Movement and the Political Uses of the Past," *Journal of American History* 91, no. 4 (2005): 1233–63; Nancy MacLean, *Freedom Is Not Enough: The Opening of the American Workplace* (Cambridge, Mass.: Harvard University Press, 2006); Timothy Minchin, *The Color of Work: The Struggle for Civil Rights in the Southern Paper Industry, 1945–1980* (Chapel Hill: University of North Carolina Press, 2001); Timothy Minchin, *Hiring the Black Worker: The Racial Integration of the Southern Textile Industry, 1960–1980* (Chapel Hill: University of North Carolina Press, 1999).

10. For the 1967 rebellion, see Sidney Fine, *Violence in the Model City: The Cavanagh Administration, Race Relations, and the Detroit Riot of 1967* (East Lansing: Michigan State University Press, 2007 [1989]), which remains the most exhaustive study of this period of Detroit history. For race relations in Detroit during World War II, see Dominic Capeci, *Race Relations in Wartime Detroit: The Sojourner Truth Housing Controversy of 1942* (Philadelphia: Temple University Press, 1984); Dominic Capeci and Martha Wilkerson, *Layered Violence: The Detroit Rioters of 1943* (Jackson: University of Mississippi Press, 1991); Harvard Sitkoff, "Detroit Race Riot of 1943," *Michigan History* 53 (fall 1969): 183–206; Angela Dillard, *Faith in the City: Preaching Radical Social Change in Detroit* (Ann Arbor: University of Michigan Press, 2007), 148–58. The national reputation of Detroit as the Model City was also due to the role played by Mayor Jerome Cavanagh and Walter Reuther in the development of the federal Demonstration Cities Programs, which provided the template for Model Cities programs. See Bernard Frieden and Marshall Kaplan, *The Politics of Neglect: Urban Aid from Model Cities to Revenue Sharing* (Cambridge, Mass.: MIT Press, 1977), 38.

11. Thomas Sugrue, *The Origins of the Urban Crisis: Race and Inequality in Postwar Detroit* (Princeton: Princeton University Press, 2005), 259; Van Gordon Sauter and Burleigh Hines, *Nightmare in Detroit: A Rebellion and Its Victims* (Chicago: Henry Regnery, 1968); John Hersey, *The Algiers Motel Incident* (Baltimore: Johns Hopkins University Press, 1997).

12. See Thompson, *Whose Detroit?*, quotation on 72.

13. Grace Boggs, *Living for Change: An Autobiography* (Minneapolis: University of Minnesota Press, 1998), 139. For Glanton Dowdell, see folder 9, box 7, New Detroit Committee Papers [hereafter NDC Papers], ALUA; folder 25, box 6, Cockrel Papers; "A Profile of Glanton Dowdell (at Home and Abroad)," *Inner City Voice*, February 1971; "Bro. Glanton Dowdell," *Inner City Voice*, October 1969; my interview with Karl Gregory, October 3, 2006, Southfield, Mich.; my interview with General Baker, August 3, 2006, Highland Park, Mich. For Cleage's interactions with the NDC, see Fine, *Violence in the Model City*, 372–73; Helen Graves, "New Detroit Committee/New Detroit, Inc.: A Case Study of an Urban Coalition, 1967–1972," PhD diss., Wayne State University, 1975, 60–64; Richard Thomas, "The Black Community Building Process in Post-Urban Disorder Detroit, 1967–1997," in *The African American Urban Experience*, ed. Joe W. Trotter, Earl Lewis, and Tera W. Hunter (New York: Palgrave Macmillan, 2004), 217.

14. "Goodman Brothers Sells Apartments for Co-ops, *Michigan Chronicle*, November, 25, 1967; "CCAC to Protest Quast Co-op Plan," *Michigan Chronicle*, November 29, 1967; Stoner to Marks, City of Detroit: Inter-Office Correspondence, November 30,1967, folder 23, box 18, Detroit Commission on Community Relations Papers [hereafter DCCR], ALUA, Detroit.

15. Graves, "New Detroit Committee/New Detroit, Inc.," 64–65; Fine, *Violence in the Model City*, 377.

16. "No Real Split in Black Community," *Michigan Chronicle*, Dec. 30, 1967; Graves, "New Detroit Committee/New Detroit, Inc.," 64–65; Fine, *Violence in the Model City*, 377–79; Leonard Gordon, *A City in Racial Crisis: The Case of Detroit Pre- and Post- the 1967 Riot* (New York: Wm. C. Brown, 1971), 107–10.

17. My Interview with Karl Gregory.

18. Fine, *Violence in the Model City,* 378; Graves, "New Detroit," 72–73; See also "City of Detroit, Inter-Office Correspondence," folder 23, box 18, DCCR Papers; "CCAC to Receive Grant for $85,000 from IFCO," *Michigan Chronicle,* Dec. 23, 1967; "CCAC Receives $85,000," *Michigan Chronicle,* Dec. 30, 1967; my interview with Gregory; Citywide Citizens Action Committee (CCAC), "Report to the Annual Meeting," January 22, 1969, folder 16, box 178, NDC Papers.

19. For the number of urban disorders in spring 1968, see Doug McAdam, *Political Process and the Development of Black Insurgency, 1930–1970* (Chicago: University of Chicago Press, 1982), 182. For the dissolution of the FSD, see "Federation Explains Reason for Dissolution," *Michigan Chronicle,* May 11, 1968; "Militants to Enter New Cycle," *Michigan Chronicle,* April 27, 1968; "Power Struggle among the Black Militants: Cleage's Been Dumped," *Detroit Scope Magazine,* May 11, 1968, 12–14.

20. "Report to the New Detroit Committee," November 16, 1967, folder 7, box, 5, NDC Papers; Redevelopment Subcommittee to Education and Employment Subcommittee, November 21, 1967, folder 7, box, 5, NDC Papers; "A Building Strike Ties Up Michigan," *New York Times,* June 23 1968; Marc Linder, *Wars of Attrition: Vietnam, the Business Roundtable, and the Decline of Construction Unions* (Iowa City: Fanpihua Press, 1999), 28–32.

21. For general information on these early campaigns, see folder 22, box 74, DCCR Papers. For statistical information on blacks in the Detroit building trades during the 1960s, see Michigan Civil Rights Commission, *Employment Distribution Study of the Construction Industry in Michigan* (Detroit: Michigan Civil Rights Commission, 1966), 25

22. Ray Marshall and Vernon Briggs Jr., *The Negro and Apprenticeship* (Baltimore: Johns Hopkins University Press, 1967), 141; interview with Horace Sheffield conducted by Herbert Hill, typed transcript, July 24, 1968, ALUA, 34–36; interview with Buddy Battle conducted by Herbert Hill, typed transcript, n.d., ALUA, 60–67; "Building Trades Opening Doors for Negro Workers," *Detroit Free Press,* Dec. 28 1968.

23. For ONE, see "Report on Meeting at TULC: ONE," July 11, 1963, folder 42, box 21, DCCR Papers; ONE, "Minutes," "Agenda," and "Statement of Purpose," June 19, 1963, folder 43, box 21, DCCR Papers; "Start Push for Equal Job Rights," *Detroit Free Press,* July 11, 1963; Fine, *Violence in the Model City,* 72; Lewis-Coleman, *Race against Liberalism,* 84; Dillard, *Faith in the City,* 257–56. GOAL included Reverend Cleage, the Henry brothers (who later went on to form the Republic of New Africa), and James and Grace Boggs. Students at Wayne State University, several of whom later aligned with the Revolutionary Action Movement and/or DRUM and the LRBW, formed UHURU in 1963.

24. Tom McNamara to W. Willard Wirtz, July 10, 1963, Record Group (RG) 9-001, Apprenticeship Series, AFL-CIO Civil Rights Division Papers, Unprocessed Records at the George Meany Memorial Archives, Silver Spring, Md.; "Racial Bars in Trades Fall Slowly," *Detroit News,* September 22, 1968.

25. "Detroit Unions Act," *New York Times,* August 9, 1963; interview with Battle conducted by Hill; "Apprenticeship Grant Totaling $84,000 Received by TULC," *Michigan Chronicle,* November 30, 1968; "TULC Head Predicts More Skilled Blacks," *Michigan Chronicle,* December 14, 1968; "Racial Bars in Trades Fall Slowly;" interview with Sheffield conducted by Hill.

26. Marshall and Briggs, *The Negro and Apprenticeship,* 139–40; "Construction Jobs Elude Negroes," *Detroit Free Press,* Dec. 26, 1968; Michigan Civil Rights Commission, *Employment Distribution Study,* 25; William Zick, "Equal Employment Opportunity in the Building Trades in Detroit," MA thesis, Wayne State University, 1969, 24. According to Zick, 70 percent of journeymen electrician, plasterers, and sprinkler fitters secured journeymen cards via this informal process, as had 50–69 percent of bricklayers, lathers, tile fitters, plumbers, pipe fitters, and sheet metal workers.

27. "'Outlaw' Local 124 Sees Win" 4; See also "The 20 Years Is Up—Calvin Stubbs Is Back," *Detroit News Sunday Magazine*, January 3, 1971, 9.

28. Accord, Inc., press release, June 11, 1968, folder 8, box 5, NDC Papers; "Accord Formed: Rehabilitation Aim of New Organization," *Michigan Chronicle*, June 15, 1968; "Dr. Gregory: Accord Helpful, 'But No Black Cure-All'" and "ACCORD Another Approach," *Michigan Chronicle*, July 27, 1968; Fine, *Violence in the Model City*, 383; my interviews with Gregory and Baker. In New York, for example, high union wages and corresponding nonunion wage parity caused rents of rehabilitated properties to skyrocket beyond the means of over 50 percent of the black families in the city. Rents would have gone up an extra 12.5 percent if union labor had been used exclusively. See Arnold Schuchter, *White Power, Black Freedom: Planning the Future of Urban America* (Boston: Beacon Press, 1968), 114–15.

29. For the Allied International Workers Union in Indiana, see "Construction Workers Officials," *Chicago Daily Defender*, August 1, 1968; "26 at Hospital in Gary Walk Out in Strike," *Chicago Tribune*, January 3, 1967; "Gary Unions Remain 100 Per Cent White despite U.S. Ruling on Bias," *Chicago Daily Defender*, October 1967.

30. My interviews with Baker and Gregory. For the founding of Local 124, see Herbert Hill, "Black Protest and the Struggle for Union Democracy," *Issues in Urban Society* 1, no. 1 (1969), 23; Ozell Bonds, "The Case for Independent Black Trade Unions," *Ebony* (August 1970), 142–44; "Black Power Struggle Hits Detroit Job," folder 7, box 5, unidentified press clipping, NDC Papers. A conflicting account appears in Foner, *Organized Labor and the Black Worker*, 409. Foner claims that Local 124 formed in 1967. I have found no information that corroborates this claim, including Stubbs's own recollections. The available evidence suggests that Local 124 received National Labor Relations Board (NLRB) recognition in August but had received its charter from the Allied Workers International Union (AWIU) several months prior. See "Construction Workers Officials," *Chicago Daily Defender*, August 1, 1968, 5.

31. Quotations from "20 Years Is Up," 9. See also "Union Rivalry on Project Is Threat to 'Black Local,'" *Detroit News*, November 19, 1968.

32. "Union Rivalry"; Hill, "Black Protest," 23."; "Black Power Struggle Hits Detroit Job"; "Detroit Negroes Form Building Trade Local," *Daily World*, January 1, 1969.

33. Hill, "Black Protest," 23; "Union Rivalry"; "Black Power Struggle"; "Black Union Battles AFL," *Michigan Chronicle*, November 23, 1968; "Inner City Labor Rift Widens," *Detroit Free Press*, December 3, 1968; "'Outlaw' Local 124 Hires during Talks, *Michigan Chronicle*, December 14, 1968; "'Outlaw' Local 124 Sees Win."

34. "20 Years Is Up, 9;" interview with Battle conducted by Hill; "'Outlaw' Local 124 Sees Win, 1, 4"; "DRUM Spokesman Claim," 4.

35. "DRUM Spokesman Claim," 4.

36. My interview with Baker; my interview with Mike Hamlin, October 23, 2007, Detroit, MI; "Profile of Glanton Dowdell." For the ELRUM wildcat strike, see Geschwender, *Class, Race, and Worker Insurgency*, 93–95; Georgakas and Surkin, *Detroit*, 85–106. For a critique of the construction movement as an important but subsidiary part of black liberation struggles in Detroit, see "T.U.L.C.," *Inner City Voice*, July 15, 1970; "AFL Wages War on Blacks," *Sauti*, September 1969, 3.

37. "Black Self-Help Project Snagged on Labor Dispute," *Detroit Free Press*, May 28, 1969, 3A, 4A.

38. "Unionists Picket Renovation Job," *Detroit News*, May 14, 1969; my interview with Gregory; "Black Workers to Fight Racist A.F.L.-C.I.O.," *South End*, May 22, 1969.

39. Theodore Stephens to Jack Wood, June 19, 1969, Building Trades Clippings File, ALUA; "Black Self-Help Project Snagged," 4A; my interview with Baker; "Pickets Delay Low Cost Housing Work," *Detroit News*, May 29, 1969.

40. The foray by Local 124 into independent apprenticeship training in Detroit was not the first. In 1966, the Associated Electricians of Detroit (AED), a black nonunion group of journeymen and contractors formed in 1937, attempted to establish an apprenticeship program "independent of the IBEW and if necessary for BAT." This program was limited to a single trade and was designed to train black apprentices to enter the IBEW. These efforts, however, were blocked when the IBEW would only agree to allow AED apprentices to work with AED contractors, Jim Crow terms that the AED refused; Marshall and Briggs, The *Negro in Apprenticeship*, 145.

41. "First Step in Minority Training," *Voice of Black Labor*, June 1, 1969. Also see Zick, "Equal Employment Opportunity," 22; "Allied Trades Apprenticeship," folder 1, box 18, Cockrel Papers.

42. "Blacks to Stay in Union," *Detroit Free Press*, June 11, 1969.

43. For Accord, see Fine, *Violence in the Model City*, 383; my interview with Gregory. See also "Stanley Winkelman to Mayor Roman Gribbs," February 24, 1971, Building Trades Vertical File, ALUA.

44. "Detroit NAACP Sets Sights on Building Jobs," *Detroit News*, September 22, 1969.

45. "Detroit Negroes Press for Jobs: Solution Sought to Demand for Building Trades Role," *New York Times*, October 26, 1969.

46. "Blacks May 'Halt' Construction," *Detroit Free Press*, October 4, 1969; my interview with Ron Scott, March 16, 2007, Detroit; my interview with Gregory.

47. For the "Black Manifesto," see Georgakas and Surkin, *Detroit*, 78–83; Keith Dye, "The Detroit Beginnings of the Black Manifesto for Reparations Controversy, 1968–1969," PhD diss., University of Toledo, 2007. Hank Rogers of the AHCC had helped organize the Black Economic Development Conference. Initially designed as a means to discuss autonomous noncapitalist development strategies for black communities, Foreman's "Manifesto" and call for reparations dominated the event as well as coverage of it. For the AHCC demands and gambit, see "Blacks May 'Halt' Construction"; "A Proclamation to Owner-Sponsors of Building Projects Utilizing Public Funds," October 6, 1969, folder 11, box 31, William Keast Papers, ALUA; "A Proclamation to the City of Detroit Mayor's Office," October 7, 1969, folder 36, box 195, NDC Papers; "Blacks Demand 50 Percent of Building Jobs in Area," *Detroit Free Press*, October 7, 1969.

48. "Proclamation to the City of Detroit Mayor's Office"; William B. Gould, *Black Workers in White Unions: Job Discrimination in the United States* (Ithaca: Cornell University Press, 1977), 308.

49. "Labor Acts to Avert Trades Showdown," *Detroit News*, October 9, 1969; "Blacks Demand 50 Percent"; "Detroit Negroes Press for Jobs"; George Gullen Jr. to William Keast and Edward Cushman, October 8, 1969, folder 11, box 31, Keast Papers; my interview with Scott; "Job Plan for Blacks Revealed," *Detroit Free Press*, October 15, 1969.

50. Rogers, quoted in "Job Plan for Blacks Revealed." See also "Labor Acts to Avert Trades Showdown," *Detroit News*, October 9, 1969; "Blacks Demand 50 Percent."

51. Quoted in "BCC Formulate Plans for All Black Union," *Pittsburgh Courier*, October 25, 1969, 26. For the summit meeting and its origins, see Alex Poinsett, "Crusade against the Craft Unions," *Ebony* (Dec. 1969): 33–42; "Pittsburgh Blacks Call for a 'Summit' on Building Jobs," *Washington Post*, September 20, 1969; "Negroes Plan Talks on Demand for Jobs," *New York Times*, September 20, 1969. For the proposed expansion of the Philadelphia Plan by the Department of Labor, see "U.S. Will Extend Minority Job Aid," *New York Times*, September 30, 1969.

52. "BCC Formulate Plans," 26; "Crusade against the Craft Unions," 42.

53. Quotations from Poinsett, "Crusade against the Craft Unions," 42.

54. Ibid., 42; "BCC Formulate Plans," 26.

55. "Proclamation to the United States Government Department of Labor," October 6, 1969, folder 36, box 195, NDC Papers.

56. For union attempts to block Stubbs, see Calvin Stubbs to Arthur Fletcher, September 4, 1970; Thomas Murphy to Hugh Murphy, June 1, 1970; and Hugh Murphy to Thomas Murphy, June 17, 1970; all in folder PE-4-2 1970 "Fletcher, Arthur," box 52, RG 174, Records of the Secretary of Labor James Hodgson, 1970–72, Dept. of Labor Papers, National Archives Regional Archives (NARA), Silver Springs, Md. I thank Trevor Griffey for sharing these documents with me. For the role of NDC, see "City of Detroit Model Neighborhood Agency, Project Description"; Gloria Pearson to Larry Doss, June 4, 1971; William Patrick to Calvin Stubbs, November 19, 1971; James Jackson and Calvin Stubbs to William Patrick, Dec. 7, 1970; and Sylvester Angel to Calvin Stubbs, November 30, 1970; all in folder 19, box 36, NDC Papers, ALUA.

57. Gloria Pearson to Larry Doss; William Patrick to Calvin Stubbs, November 19, 1971, folder 19, box 36, NDC Papers, ALUA.

58. Grace Palladino, *Skilled Hands, Strong Spirits: A Century of Building Trades History* (Ithaca: Cornell University Press, 2005), 170.

59. Ed Koch to William Patrick, October 23, 1970, folder 19, box 36, NDC Papers, ALUA. For the summer agreements, see "Building Trades Accord Spares Detroit Strikes," *Detroit News,* May 3, 1970; "Plumbers Reach 3-County Pact, *Detroit News,* July 29, 1970.

60. Ed Koch to William Patrick.

61. Ibid.

62. Ibid.

63. William Gould, "Critique of the Detroit Plan," folder 16, box 78, DCCR Papers; Sheffield quoted in "Detroit Plan to Integrate Trades Sure of Adoption," *Detroit News,* February 26, 1971. See also "MCRC Rejects Bid to Integrate Trades," *Detroit News,* March 23, 1971; "Civil Rights Unite Votes 'No,'" *Detroit News,* March 27, 1971; "Five Black Leaders Stake Reputations on Union Integration Plan," *Detroit Free Press,* March 7, 1971.

64. "Service in Memory of Henry 'Hank Rogers,'" March 6, 1971, folder 1, box 18, Cockrel Papers; "Some Sort of Street Cat," *South End,* March 17, 1971.

65. Federal Bureau of Investigations FOIA Request, Subject: Local 124, FOIPA No. 1059768-00, Washington D.C.; Gould, *Black Workers in White Unions,* 308.

66. "Ex-Union Aides Told to Begin Extortion Sentences," *Detroit Free Press,* June 5, 1973; "Union Chief Charged with Filing False Statements," *Detroit Free Press,* January 18, 1971; "U.S. Indicts Union Boss, Builder," *Detroit Free Press,* April 2, 1971; "Union Leader Indicted on Extortion Charge," *Detroit News,* April 1, 1971; *Liberty State Bank v. Allied Trades Apprenticeship,* Wayne County Circuit Court, Michigan, Civil Action No. 156 239, 1970, transcript in Building Trades Vertical File, ALUA.

67. Gould, *Black Workers in White Unions,* 309.

68. *Next Detroit* is a term recently used by the Kwame Kilpatrick administration. For data regarding racial representation in the Detroit construction workforce when compared to eighteen other metropolitan areas, see Todd Swanstrom, "The Road to Jobs: Patterns of Employment in the Construction Industry in Eighteen Metropolitan Areas," August 30, 2007, available at: http://www.gamaliel.org/TEN/TEN_Road_to_Jobs_study.pdf.

5. "THE STONE WALL BEHIND"

1. See C. T. Vivian, *Black Power and the American Myth* (Philadelphia: Fortress Press, 1970), 5–6, 75, 76, 83, 109, 130.

2. Harold Baron and Bennett Hymer, "The Negro Worker in the Chicago Labor Market: A Case Study of *De Facto* Segregation," in *The Negro and the American Labor Movement,* ed. Julius Jacobson (Garden City, N.Y.: Anchor Books, 1968), 233, 237, 252.

3. See Frank Cassell, "Chicago 1960–1970: One Small Step Forward," *Industrial Relations* 9 (May 1970), 277–78, 282.

4. See James Ralph, *Northern Protest: Martin Luther King, Jr., Chicago, and the Civil Rights Movement* (Cambridge, Mass.: Harvard University Press, 1993); David Garrow, ed., *Chicago 1966: Open Housing Marches, Summit Negotiations, and Operation Breadbasket* (Brooklyn: Carlson, 1989).

5. William J. Wilson, *When Work Disappears: The World of the New Urban Poor* (New York: Knopf, 1996); Nicholas Lemann, *The Promised Land: The Great Black Migration and How It Changed America* (New York: Vintage Books, 1992).

6. The exception is Sudhir Venkatesh, *American Project: The Rise and Fall of a Modern Ghetto* (Cambridge, Mass.: Harvard University Press, 2000).

7. Quoted in Arthur Fletcher, *The Silent Sell-Out: Government Betrayal of Blacks to the Craft Unions* (New York: Third Press, 1974), 69.

8. "Crisis in the Making," *Daily Defender,* September 11, 1969, 21.

9. See interview with Paul King conducted by Dempsey Travis, July 10, 1981, in Dempsey Travis, *An Autobiography of Black Chicago* (Chicago: Urban Research Institute, 1981), 222–27; "Black Coalition Wary of Job Plan Accord," *Chicago Today,* December 3, 1969.

10. See James F. Short Jr., "Youth, Gangs and Society: Micro- and Macrosocial Processes," *Sociological Quarterly* 15 (winter 1974): 3–19; James F. Short Jr. and John Moland Jr., "Politics and Youth Gangs: A Follow-up Study," *Sociological Quarterly* 17 (spring 1976), 176, 162–79. For more recent work that views gangs in a broader context, see Sudhir Venkatesh, "A Note on Social Theory and the American Street Gang," in *Gangs and Society: Alternative Perspectives,* ed. Louis Kontos, David Brotherton, and Luis Barrios, 3–11 (New York: Columbia University Press, 2003); John Hagedorn, *A World of Gangs: Armed Young Men and Gangsta Culture* (Minneapolis: University of Minnesota Press, 2008).

11. See "Gangs in the Post-World War II North American City: A Forum," *Journal of Urban History* 28, no. 5 (2002): 658–63.

12. Interview with Edward Doty conducted by Herbert Hill, November 2, 1967, Walter P. Reuther Archives of Labor and Urban Affairs, Wayne State University, Detroit [hereafter ALUA]; Erik S. Gellman, "'Death Blow to Jim Crow': The National Negro Congress, 1936–1947," PhD diss., Northwestern University, 2006; "Chicago Plumbers Group Sues A.F. of L. Union for $10,000," *Kansas City Call,* March 31, 1940; "Every Third Bricklayer to be a Negro," *Kansas City Call,* April 5, 1940; folder 1192, box 108, folder 1682, box 153, and folder 1678, box 153, all in series III, Chicago Urban League Papers, University of Illinois, Chicago Special Collections [hereafter CUL Papers].

13. Dennis A. Derryck, *The Construction Industry: A Black Perspective* (Washington, D.C.: Joint Center for Political Studies, 1972), 8; Earl McMahon, *The Chicago Building Trades Council Yesterday and Today* (Chicago: Building Trades Council, 1947), 112.

14. Derryck, *Construction Industry,* 8. See also Oscar Brown, "Panel Discussion," *Home Front Unity in Chicago* (Chicago: Mayor's Committee on Race Relations, May–June, 1945), 28, copy at Harold Washington Public Library, Chicago; St. Clair Drake and Horace R. Cayton, *Black Metropolis: A Study of Negro Life in a Northern City* (New York: Harcourt Brace, 1945), 260.

15. "1,000 Labor Leaders Move toward Equality," *Daily Defender,* June 6, 1960, 4, 22; *De Facto Segregation: Hearings Before a Subcommittee of the House Committee on Education and Labor* (Washington, D.C.: U.S. Government Printing Office, 1965), 200–203, 322–25.

16. Catherine Weidner, "Debating the Future of Chicago's Black Youth: Black Professionals, Black Labor and Educational Politics during the Civil Rights Era, 1950–1965," PhD diss., Northwestern University, 1989, 295–367.

17. "Pickets to Hit Bias at $25 Million Skyscraper," and "Trade Union Bias," *Chicago Defender*, national ed., October 7, 1964; "Trade Unions Under Fire by ACT Group," *Chicago Defender*, national ed., October 13, 1964.

18. "Chicago Rights Fight Seen in Sad Shape," *Chicago Defender*, June 6, 1964, 1–2.

19. Bill Berry to CUL Staff, "Direction Action Demonstrations and Political Action," March 15, 1965, folder 1856, box 170, series III, CUL Papers.

20. Hampton McKinney, director, CUL Employment and Guidance Department, "Career Opportunities," column 206, May 9, 1967, folder 1199, box 108, series 3, CUL Papers; Sanford Kanter for the CUL, "Blacks and the Construction Industry: Which Way Now," 1975 report, folder 1689, box 154, series III, CUL Papers.

21. James Bevel and SCLC, "A Proposal by the Southern Christian Leadership Conference for the Development of a Nonviolent Action Movement for the Greater Chicago Area" and "Proposals of the Freedom Movement," July 1966, 2, 9–10, folder 2934, box 278, series III, CUL Papers.

22. Martin Luther King Jr., transcript of address at the Chicago Freedom Festival, The Amphitheatre, Chicago, March 12, 1966, folder 2932, box 6, series III, CUL Papers.

23. Ralph, *Northern Protest*, 70–71, 204; Adam Cohen and Elizabeth Taylor, *American Pharaoh: Mayor Richard J. Daley and His Battle for Chicago and the Nation* (New York: Little, Brown, 2000), 125, 161–62.

24. Federal Ad Hoc Committee on the Building Trades (FAHC), "Factors Precipitating September Compliance Review," 1969, in *U.S. Task Force on Building Trades: Minority Participation in Construction Trades*, Vol. 5, copy filed at Law Library, Northwestern University, Chicago.

25. "Protest Shuts 4 Building Sites; Bias Foe Says Loop Is Next," *Chicago Daily News*, July 28, 1969; "Unions Facing Court Action," *Daily Defender*, July 24, 1969; "Construction Sites Shut," *Daily Defender*, July 29, 1969; "The Black Coalition and the Chicago Construction Industry: Bargaining in the Streets," Northwestern University Graduate School of Management report, 1970, 1–2, copy in box 37, #2, Wharton School Industrial Research Unit Records, 1900–1996, University of Pennsylvania Archives and Records Center, Philadelphia.

26. See Felix Padilla, *Latino Ethnic Consciousness: The Case of Mexican Americans and Puerto Ricans in Chicago* (Notre Dame: Notre Dame University Press, 1985), 110–13.

27. Lydia Walker, *Challenge and Change: The Story of Civil Rights Activist C.T. Vivian* (Alpharetta, Ga.: Dreamkeeper Press, 1993); "Black Curfew Leader a Fighter," *Chicago Today*, December 18, 1969.

28. "One Way," UTC Newsletter, Spring 1968, folder 1731, box 158, series III, CUL Papers; other UTC "alumni" became involved with CUCA, including Willie Barrow, Curtis Burrell, Jesse Jackson, and some Disciples gang members. See my interview with Sally Johnson, Chicago, April 13, 2005. For more on the Urban Training Center, see folder 1731, box 158, series III, CUL Papers; Kay Winterowd, "The Role of Para-Ecclesial Agencies in the Renewal of the Church and Society: An Analytical Student of the Mission Training Programs of Three Models," PhD diss., South Baptist Theological Seminary, Louisville, 1971, 109–23, 172–77.

29. R. Calvin Lockridge, chairman, Black Consortium, to "members," August 7, 1968, Gang Intelligence Unit report [hereafter GIU Report], Blackstone Rangers, folder Vol. 11, box 424, Chicago Red Squad files [hereafter CRS], Chicago History Museum.

30. "Construction Sites Shut," *Daily Defender*, July 29, 1969; Vivian, *Black Power and the American Myth*. CUCA, "It's Our Thang," press release attached to Red Squad surveillance report on CUCA, August 8, 1969, file 1158, f 1, box 238, CRS.

31. CUCA, "It's Our Thang," flyer/press release, n.d. [August 8, 1969], copy in *U.S. Task Force*, Vol. 3; "Pickets Halt New Construction on S. Side," *Daily Defender*,

August 5, 1969; "Negroes Vow to Continue Construction-Job Shutdowns," *Chicago Daily News,* August 6, 1969.

32. My interview with Johnson; Berry quoted by Martin Luther King Jr. transcript of address at the "Chicago Freedom Festival," The Amphitheatre, Chicago, March 12, 1966, folder 2932, box 6, series III, CUL Papers; my interview with Bob Taylor, Chicago, April 14, 2005; Aleta D. Styers, Chicago Chapter NOW, to Thomas Jenkins, Division of Contract Compliance, September 13, 1969, *U.S. Task Force,* Vol. 7; Nancy MacLean, *Freedom Is Not Enough: The Opening of the American Workplace* (Cambridge, Mass.: Harvard Press, 2006), 91–92.

33. See Elliot Leibow, *Tally's Corner: A Study of Negro Streetcorner Men* (Boston: Little Brown, 1967); Wilson, *When Work Disappears,* 123–26.

34. David Dawley, *A Nation of Lords: The Autobiography of the Vice Lords* (Garden City, N.Y.: Anchor Press, 1973), 113. See also "Lawndale Violence Dies Out; 15 Beaten," *Chicago Tribune,* July 15, 1961; "9 Youths Held at Farragut," *Chicago Tribune,* October 22, 1963; "Coroner Jury Asks Trial in Cicero Death," *Chicago Tribune,* June 3, 1966; "School Gangs Fight Cops," *Chicago Tribune,* November 22, 1967.

35. "The Talk of the Town: Notes and Comments," *New Yorker* 42 (July 16, 1966), 25.

36. [First Presbyterian Church], "History of Ranger Activity, Summer, 1966," GIU Report, Blackstone Rangers, folder Vol. 1, box 423, CRS; Special Investigator to Assistant Supervisor in Charge, Enforcement, August 4, 1966, Blackstone Rangers, folder Vol. 2, box 423, CRS; John Fry, "Eyeball to Eyeball with the Rangers," *Arena One* 1, no. 5 (1967), copy in Blackstone Rangers, folder Vol. 3, box 423, CRS; James McPherson, "All Mighty Blackstone: And What Does That Mean? Part I," *Atlantic Monthly* 223, no. 5 (1969), 76; "Organization Man," *Newsweek,* June 5, 1967; John Fry, *Locked-Out Americans: A Memoir* (Evanston, Ill.: Harper and Row, 1973), chap. 6.

37. Frank Donner, *Protectors of Privilege: Red Squads and Police Repression in Urban America* (Berkeley: University of California Press, 1990), 49–52, 90–104, 135.

38. GIU, "Informational Report," Blackstone Rangers, June 21, July 13, July 24 and July 27, 1967, in folder Vol. 4, September 27 and October 23, 1967 in folder Vol. 5, November 2 and December 19, 1967 and January 26, March 20, March 24, March 28, March 29, and April 3, 1968, folder Vol. 6, all in box 424, CRS; John Hall Fish, *Black Power/White Control: The Struggle of the Woodlawn Organization in Chicago* (Princeton: Princeton University Press, 1973), chap. 3.

39. "Negro Gang Leader Tells of Arms Offer," *Chicago Tribune,* March 10, 1969; McPherson, "All Mighty Blackstone"; Fish, *Black Power/White Control;* U.S. Congress, Committee on Government Operations, "Riots, Civil and Criminal Disorders: Hearings Before the Senate Permanent Subcommittee on Investigations," 91st Cong., 1st and 2nd sess., 1967–1968; Fernando Carbajal, "'We Do Not Profess to Being Angels . . .': The T.W.O. Youth Project, the Chicago Red Squad, and the End of the War on Poverty," MA thesis, Northwestern University, 2007, 3.

40. Into the early 1970s, the district attorney pursued 132 indictments against twenty-four gang members, three of whom were eventually found guilty of conspiracy. See Fry, *Locked-Out Americans,* 106–8.

41. "Businessmen Support Gang Efforts to Keep Peace on Southside," *Daily Defender,* April 17, 1968; GIU, "Informational Report," Blackstone Rangers, April 25, 1968, folder Vol. 8, box 424, CRS; "Two Business Leaders Defend Rangers, Deny Shakedowns," *Chicago Tribune,* April 17, 1968; McPherson, "All Mighty Blackstone"; Anthony Gibbs, *Final Report: The Woodlawn Organization Youth Project* (Chicago: Woodlawn Organization, Office of Economic Opportunity, 1968); Fry, *Locked-Out Americans,* 118–19.

42. R. Lincoln Keiser, *Vice Lords: Warriors of the Streets* (New York: Holt, Rinehart, and Winston, 1969), 4–10.

43. My interview with Taylor; interview with Robert Lucas conducted by Dempsey Travis, July 9, 1981, in Travis, *Autobiography of Black Chicago,* 244–55.

44. GIU, "Information Report," Blackstone Rangers, April 2, 1967, Vol. 3, box 423, CRS; my interview with Taylor; Dawley, *Nation of Lords;* "Unions Facing Court Action," *Daily Defender,* July 24, 1969; "Tentative Pact Here in Building Jobs for Blacks," *Chicago Sun-Times,* November 7, 1969.

45. My interview with C. T. Vivian, Atlanta, Ga., May 2, 2005; "Black Curfew Leader a Fighter"; and Walker, *Challenge and Change,* 52.

46. "Time for Action," editorial, *Chicago Tribune,* August 12, 1969; "Jobs for Blacks Demanded" *Chicago Daily News,* August 6, 1969.

47. "Teen Gang Coalition Lending a Big Hand," *Daily Defender,* October 9, 1969; interview with Paul King by Travis.

48. Edwin Berry, "The Building Trades Situation," September 15, 1969, *U.S. Task Force,* Vol. 7, p. 1; "Negroes and the Craft Unions," editorial, *Chicago Tribune,* August 1, 1969, p. 12; "Building Trades Unit Answers Protesters," *Chicago Tribune,* July 28, 1969, 12.

49. "Black Demonstrators Halt 3 S. Side Building Projects," *Chicago Sun-Times,* August 8, 1969, clipping in CUCA file, folder 1158-A, box 238, CRS.

50. My interview with Taylor.

51. "Blacks Carrying Clubs March on Civic Center," *Chicago Tribune,* August 14, 1969; "7 Protestors Arrested at Building Job," *Chicago Tribune,* August 13, 1969; "Coalition Fights Police Pressure," *Chicago Defender,* August 13, 1969.

52. "C.U.C.A. Chief Uses Reason, Passion," *Chicago Today,* August 14, 1969, 17.

53. "Time for Action," 14.

54. "Trades Ask for Aid in Threat by Negroes," *Chicago Tribune,* August 8, 1969; "Black Demonstrators Halt."

55. "Guard Building Jobs, Sheriff Urged," *Chicago Tribune,* August 1, 1969, 14; "Youths Shut Down 2 More Projects," *Chicago Daily News,* August 4, 1969; "City Building Unit, Blacks Set Meeting: Gang Halts Work at S. Side Site," *Chicago Tribune,* August 5, 1969, 3; "Jobs for Blacks Demanded: Beret-Wearing Youths Stop S. Side Construction Projects," *Chicago Daily News,* August 6, 1969, 6; "Trades Ask for Aid in Threat by Negroes," *Chicago Tribune,* August 8, 1969; "Judge Restrains Job Protests," *Chicago Tribune,* August 15, 1969, 5.

56. Judge Walker Butler, Circuit Court, State of Illinois, County of Cook, "Temporary Injunction Order," August 14, 1969, copy in *U.S. Task Force,* Vol. 8.

57. Quoted in "Tensions Mount over Job Fight," *Chicago Defender,* August 18, 1969, 20.

58. "Blacks vs. Trades: Is a Showdown Due This Week?" *Chicago Sun-Times,* August 17, 1969, p. 8; "Black Coalition Vows to Defy Ban on Building Pickets," *Chicago Daily News,* August 15, 1969, clipping in CUCA file, folder 1158-A, box 238, CRS.

59. Chicago Freedom Movement, Minutes of Meeting, Conrad Hilton, July 28, [1966], copy in folder 1851, box 170, series III, CUL Papers; "Negroes Chant, Pray in Chicago to 'Build,'" *Washington Post,* August 22, 1969; "Protestors Are Halted in Chicago," *Washington Post,* September 9, 1969; "Jail Jackson in Job Clash: Bottles, Stones Hurled at Cops," *Chicago Tribune,* September 9, 1969; my interview with Taylor.

60. "U.S. Aid Called Key to Black Jobs," *Chicago Today,* August 22, 1969, 4; CRS, "Surveillance Report," CUCA, August 21, 1969, folder 1158-A, box 238, CRS.

61. FAHC, U.S. Government Agencies Meeting Minutes, Office of Economic Opportunity, Chicago, August 19, 1969, in *U.S. Task Force,* Vol. 1.

62. FAHC, "Summary: Labor Shortage Minority Representation Report," in *U.S. Task Force,* Vol. 2.

63. FAHC, U.S. Government Agencies Meeting Minutes, Office of Economic Opportunity, Chicago, August 20, 1969, in *U.S. Task Force,* Vol. 1.

64. Berry, "Building Trades Situation."

65. Richard A. Salem, Midwest Regional Director, Department of Justice, to Robert Tucker, Chairman, Ad Hoc Task Force, September 8, 1969, *Task Force on Building Trades,* Vol. 7; Salem to Tucker, September 10, 1969, *Task Force on Building, Trades,* Vol. 12.

66. "Rev. C.T. Vivian Firms Up Stand," *Weekly Defender,* August 23–29, 1969; "Blacks Vow Picketing as Labor Talks Break Up," *Today,* September 8, 1969; interview with Paul King by Travis.

67. "Coalition Fights City Hall," *Daily Defender,* August 7, 1969.

68. Quoted in "Teen Gang Coalition," 16.

69. FAHC, Meeting Minutes of Building Construction Employers Association (BCEA) and CUCA, Sherman House, Chicago, August 21 and September 4, 1969, in *U.S. Task Force,* Vol. 9.

70. "Blacks Vow Picketing as Labor Talks Break Up," *Chicago Today,* September 8, 1969; CRS, "Surveillance Reports," CUCA, September 30 and October 2, 3, 6, 8, 10, 1969, folder 1158-B, box 238, CRS; "Circle Campus Teachers Ask Building Halt," *Daily Defender,* October 9, 1969.

71. Fletcher, *Silent Sell-Out,* 70–73.

72. Ibid.; Alex Poinsett, "Blacks Battle Blatant Racism in High-Paying Building Jobs," *Ebony* 25, no. 2 (1969), 40; "Black Coalition," 27–34.

73. "The Black Coalition," 23, 29–34, 54–59; "Unions Facing Court Action," *Daily Defender,* October 4, 1969; Fletcher, *Silent Sell-Out,* 71–73.

74. "Chicago Plan," in "Manual for the Planning and Implementation Minority Employment Programs," Chicago Urban League, 1970, folder 1216, box 110, series III, CUL Papers.

75. FAHC, U.S. Government Agencies Meeting Minutes, Office of Economic Opportunity, Chicago, August 19 and August 20, 1969 and Federal Building, Chicago, September 2 and 22, 1969, *U.S. Task Force,* Vol. 1.

76. "Oscar Brown, Jean Pace to Play 'Soul Impact 1969' for Coalition," *Daily Defender,* December 18, 1969.

77. FAHC, Meeting Minutes of BCEA and CUCA, August 21 and September 4, 1969; Meeting Minutes of Unions-Contractors-Builders and CUCA, Mayor's Office, City Hall, Chicago, October 2 and October 15, 1969, *U.S. Task Force,* Vol. 9–11; "More Work and Training for Blacks," *Chicago Tribune,* November 7, 1969; "Tell Details of Chicago Plan," *Daily Defender,* November 10, 1969; "Building Jobs Plan Won't Be Stopped," *Today,* November 12, 1969.

78. "Tentative Pact Here," *Chicago Sun-Times,* November 7, 1969; and "Chicago Plan Gains Washington Favor," *Chicago Sun-Times,* January 20, 1970, clippings found in CUCA file, folder 1158-A, box 238, CRS.

79. "Police Strive to Halt Teen Gang Violence," *Chicago Tribune,* May 9, 1969, B25; "Nab Six in Gang Murders: Form a New Court to Try Terrorists," *Chicago Tribune,* May 30, 1969, 1; "Gang Leader Charged with S. Side Killing," *Chicago Tribune,* December 5, 1969.

80. "Ranger Too Slippery for Big Police Net," *Chicago American,* December 19, 1968.

81. Dawley, *Nation of Lords,* 160–69; "Blacks OK 9-Point Plan," *Chicago Daily News,* December 17, 1969; my interview with Taylor; my interview with Johnson; United Front of Black Community Organizations, press release, December 15, 1969, and Pick Congress Hotel, Washington Room, Chicago and Rose Committee for Bobby Gore, press release, May 29, 1970, CUCA, folder 1158-B and 1158-C, box 239, CRS.

82. My interview with Taylor.

83. Fletcher, *Silent Sell-Out,* 73.

84. FAHC, meeting minutes of BCEA and CUCA, August 21, 1969, 93, 129; Meeting Minutes of Unions-Contractors-Builders and CUCA, Mayor's Office, City Hall, Chicago,

October 2, 1969, 10, 17–19, and October 15, 1969, 96–97. For an estimate of the number of sustained jobs created, see "'Chicago Plan' Probe Asks Fund Holdup," *Chicago Tribune,* July 29, 1970; "New Chicago Plan Goal Is 10,000 Building Jobs," *Chicago Daily News,* October 17, 1972.

85. My interview with Taylor.

86. Ibid.; my interview with Johnson.

87. "Time Running Out for Chicago Plan," *Chicago Today,* September 8, 1970; "'Chicago Plan' Critics Assailed," *Chicago Today,* August 7, 1970; "'Chicago Plan' Probe Asks Fund Holdup"; "Fletcher Hails Nixon Construction Statement," press release, week of March 30, 1970, copy in folder 1217, box 110, CUL Papers; "Negro Drive for Jobs Is Gathering Momentum," press clipping, n.d., *U.S. Task Force,* Vol. 4.

88. "Chicago Plan Revival Talk Stirs Row," *Chicago News,* October 29, 1971; "Chicago Aide Indicted as Embezzler," *Washington Post,* August 12, 1971; "Ex-Alderman from Chicago Caught in L.A.," *Washington Post,* August 23, 1972.

89. Peter Stahl, Department of Justice, to Clark G. Roberts, February 19, 1970, *U.S. Task Force,* Vol. 12.

90. "Ald. Hubbard Heads Job Equality Plan," *Daily Defender,* April 18–19, 1970; "Time Running Out on Chicago Plan"; "New Chicago Plan Goal."

91. "New Chicago Plan Goal is 10,000 Building Jobs," *Daily News,* October 18, 1972, clipping found in CUCA file, folder 1158-B, box 238, CRS; "CUCA Backed in Chicago Plan Deal," *Daily Defender,* August 4, 1972; "Hit Building Row," *Daily Defender,* August 7, 1973.

92. "U.S., CUCA Officials Meet on Work Halt," *Daily Defender,* September 21, 1973; "Coalition's Top Leaders Face Ouster," *Chicago Daily News,* September 21, 1973; "Hit Building Row," *Daily Defender,* August 7, 1973; "Feds to Aid Push for Minority Jobs," *Daily Defender,* October 1, 1973; Bernard DeLury, Assistant Secretary of Labor, press statement, October 18, 1973, folder 1686, box 153, series III, CUL Papers.

93. "Feds to Aid Push for Minority Jobs," *Daily Defender,* October 1, 1973; "League Quits Chi Plan," *Daily Defender,* June 27, 1973; Chicago Urban League, "Statement of the New Chicago Plan," n.d. [1973], folder 1686, box 153, series III, CUL Papers; James Compton, Executive Director of Chicago Urban League, press conference statement, August 15, 1974, folder 1692, box 154, series III, CUL Papers.

94. For more information about the internal CUCA split in 1973, see folder 1226, box 111, and folder 1690, box 154, series III, CUL Papers; Noah Robinson, "A Review of the New Chicago Plan—One Year Later," May 1973, folder 1686, box 153, series III, CUL Papers; Hector Franco, Noah Robinson, and Chester Robinson, "Proposal and Position Paper to the U.S. Department of Labor," May 1973, folder 1237, box 112, series III, CUL Papers.

95. CUCA granted a request for a nonvoting observer from the Latino community to attend negotiations for the first Chicago Plan. See Meeting Minutes of Unions-Contractors-Builders and CUCA, October 2, 1969, *U.S. Task Force,* Vol. 10. Hector Franco, backed by the resources of the Black Strategy Center, made the Spanish Coalition for Jobs into a network that combined the forces of previously separate Latin American groups that had waged successful campaigns against Jewel Tea and the Illinois Bell Telephone Company. See Padilla, *Latino Ethnic Consciousness,* 110–14. For the LATF and its leader, Jose Ovalle, participation in the New Chicago Plan ended in a bitter withdrawal from an alliance with Urban League. See Jose Ovalle, correspondence, in folder 1226, box 111, series III, CUL Papers; Jose Ovalle to Mrs. Carey Preston, Chicago Urban League, December 25, 1973, folder 1681, box 154, series III, CUL Papers.

96. Paul King, *Reflections on Affirmative Action Construction* (Bloomington, Indiana: Authorhouse, 2009); and Stephen Dunphy, "Minority-Hiring Drive Gets Help from Chicago," *Seattle Times,* September 13, 1970, H4.

97. "Negroes Pack Civic Center Plaza in Protest of Job Discrimination," *Chicago Tribune,* September 23, 1969; Attendance Lists, Minority Construction Committee, n.d. [1970s], folder 1687, box 153, series III, CUL Papers.

98. "Ruling Offers Welcome Chance to Revisit Set-Aside Contracts," *Chicago Sun-Times,* December 31, 2003; "City Told to Change Law on Set-Asides for Minorities, Women," *Chicago Sun-Times,* December 30, 2003.

99. My interview with Taylor.

100. Vivian, *Black Power and the American Myth,* 75.

101. Richard Nixon, White House telephone conversation with Tricia Nixon Cox, April 18, 1972, no. 23–21, available at: http://nixontapes.org.

6. "THE BLACKS SHOULD NOT BE ADMINISTERING THE PHILADELPHIA PLAN"

1. For an example of this conventional narrative, see Terry H. Anderson, *The Pursuit of Fairness: A History of Affirmative Action* (New York: Oxford, 2004).

2. Thomas J. Sugrue, "Affirmative Action from Below: Civil Rights, the Building Trades, and the Politics of Racial Equality in the Urban North, 1945–1969," *Journal of American History* 91 (June 2004): 145–73.

3. Chris Bonastia, *Knocking on the Door: The Federal Government's Attempt to Desegregate the Suburbs* (Princeton: Princeton University Press, 2006); Gareth Davies, "Richard Nixon and the Desegregation of Southern Schools," *Journal of Policy History* 19, no. 4 (2007): 367–94.

4. Nixon White House Tapes (NWHT) 6-93, July 2, 1971, Nixon Library, National Archives and Records Administration, College Park, Md. [hereafter NL]. (All transcriptions are my own.)

5. Kevin Yuill, *Richard Nixon and the Rise of Affirmative Action: The Pursuit of Racial Equality in an Era of Limits* (Lanham, Md.: Rowman & Littlefield, 2006), 5.

6. Thomas Sugrue and John Skrentny, "The White Ethnic Strategy," in *Rightward Bound: Making America Conservative in the 1970s,* ed. Bruce Schulman and Julian Zelizer, 171–92 (Cambridge, Mass.: Harvard University Press, 2008); Paul Frymer and John Skrentny, "Coalition-Building and the Politics of Electoral Capture during the Nixon Administration: African Americans, Labor, Latinos," *Studies in American Political Development* 12 (spring 1998): 131–61; Joe Merton, "The Politics of Symbolism: Richard Nixon's Appeal to White Ethnics and the Frustration of Realignment, 1969–72," *European Journal of American Culture* 26, no. 3 (2007): 181–98; Edmund Wehrle, "'Partisan for the Hard Hats': Charles Colson, George Meany, and the Failed Blue-Collar Strategy," *Labor: Studies in Working-Class History of the Americas* 5, no. 3 (2008): 45–66; Jefferson Cowie, "Nixon's Class Struggle: Romancing the New Right Worker, 1969–1973," *Labor History* 43, no. 3 (2002): 257–83.

7. Jefferson Cowie, "'Vigorously Left, Right, and Center': The Crosscurrents of Working-Class America in the 1970s," in *America in the Seventies,* ed. Beth Bailey and David Farber (Lawrence: Kansas University Press, 2004), 87; Nancy Banks, "'The Last Bastion of Discrimination': The New York City Building Trades and the Struggle over Affirmative Action," PhD diss., Columbia University, 2006; Joshua Freeman, "Hardhats: Construction Workers, Manliness, and the 1970 Pro-War Demonstrations," *Journal of Social History* 26 (summer 1993): 725–44.

8. Hugh Davis Graham, *The Civil Rights Era: Origins and Development of National Policy, 1960–1972* (New York: Oxford University Press, 1990), 278–300, 322–45; Dean J. Kotlowski, *Nixon's Civil Rights: Politics, Principle and Policy* (Cambridge, Mass.: Harvard University Press, 2002), 97–124; John Skrentny, *The Ironies of Affirmative Action: Politics, Culture, and Justice in America* (Chicago: University of Chicago Press, 1996), 193–221; Yuill, *Richard Nixon,* 135–58; Judith Stein, "Affirmative Action and the Conservative

Agenda: President Richard M. Nixon's Philadelphia Plan of 1969," in *Labor in the Modern South,* ed. Glenn Eskew, 182–206 (Athens: University of Georgia Press, 2001).

9. Stein, "Affirmative Action and the Conservative Agenda," 186–90.

10. Kotlowski, *Nixon's Civil Rights,* 106–9.

11. Hugh Davis Graham, "The Incoherence of the Civil Rights Policy in the Nixon Administration," in *Richard M. Nixon: Politician, President, Administrator,* ed. Leon Friedman and William Levantrosser, 159–72 (Westport, Conn.: Greenwood Press, 1991).

12. Robert Smith and Ronald Walters, *We Have No Leaders: African Americans in the Post-Civil Rights Era* (Albany: SUNY Press, 1996), 145. Fletcher ended up appointing John Wilks, a black Republican from San Francisco whom Fletcher knew from his days in the San Francisco Bay Area.

13. Graham, *Civil Rights Era,* 297; "Wirtz Says No to Race Quotas," *Washington Post,* June 27, 1968; Arthur Fletcher, *The Silent Sell-Out: Government Betrayal of Blacks to the Craft Unions* (New York: Third Press, 1974), 64.

14. "Potomac Profile: Arthur A. Fletcher, Who Has a Degree from Malcolm X College, Is a Rare Bureaucrat," *Washington Post, Potomac Magazine,* February 7, 1971, 250; Graham, *Civil Rights Era,* 326.

15. William Gould, *Black Workers in White Unions: Job Discrimination in the United States* (Ithaca: Cornell University Press, 1977), 339–40; Skrentny, *Ironies of Affirmative Action,* 67–110.

16. "Idled Workers Protest Shutdown in Pittsburgh," *Washington Post,* August 30, 1969; "Labor's Double Standard Accented by Pittsburgh Protest over Bias," *Washington Post,* September 2, 1969; "Thousands of White Workers Boo and Jeer Evans in Olympia," *Seattle Times,* October 16, 1969.

17. Fletcher, *Silent Sell-Out,* 70–72; NBC News, September 25, 1969, available at: Vanderbilt University TV News Archive, http://tvnews.vanderbilt.edu/.

18. Fletcher, *Silent Sell-Out,* 71.

19. For example, Judith Stein mischaracterizes Fletcher's politics as "gleeful anti-unionism." Stein, "Affirmative Action and the Conservative Agenda," 199.

20. Charles Colson, "The Silent Majority: Support for the President," in *Richard M. Nixon: Politician, President, Administrator,* ed. Leon Friedman and William Levantrosser (Westport, Conn.: Greenwood Press, 1991), 275.

21. Kevin Phillips, *The Emerging Republican Majority* (New Rochelle: Arlington House, 1969); quoted in Dan Carter, *The Politics of Rage: George Wallace, The Origins of the New Conservatism, and the Transformation of American Politics* (New York: Simon and Schuster, 1995), 380.

22. "Nixon Minority-Hiring Plan Divides Liberal Democrats," *Washington Post,* January 5, 1970, 19; "Meany Hits Hiring Plan, as Politics," *Washington Post,* January 13, 1970, A-1; John Brown to Ehrlichman and Garment, January 14, 1970, folder "Philadelphia Plan [1 of 2]," box 142, White House Special Files [hereafter WHSF], Len Garment Papers [hereafter LG], NL; Wehrle, "'Partisan for the Hard Hats,'" 47; Kevin Phillips, "Post-Southern Strategy," *Washington Post,* September 25, 1970, A-25; "Nixon, Intellectuals Far Apart on Race," *Washington Post,* March 15, 1970, 39; Harry R. Haldeman, *The Haldeman Diaries: Inside the Nixon White House* (New York: Putnam, 1994), 145.

23. "9 Big Cities Seeking U.S. Job-Quota Plan," *Washington Post,* October 1, 1969.

24. "Address by Assistant Secretary of Labor Arthur A. Fletcher before the Pennsylvania League of Cities, Philadelphia, PA, August 11, 1969," folder "Fletcher, Arthur," box 88, WHSF, LG, NL; Wehrle, "'Partisan for the Hard Hats,'" 50.

25. "U.S. Willing to Ease Minority Job Plan," *Washington Post,* January 27, 1970.

26. "U.S. Softens Ruling on Hiring Minorities in Nonbuilding Jobs," *New York Times,* February 4, 1970, 26.

27. "Shultz Picks 19 Cities for Job-Equality Push in Construction Work," *Wall Street Journal,* February 10, 1970.

28. The Third District U.S. Court of Appeals ruled the Philadelphia Plan constitutional in *Contractors Association of Eastern Pennsylvania v. Secretary of Labor* on April 22, 1971. The Supreme Court denied certiorari on October 12, 1971.

29. Fletcher, *Silent Sell-Out,* 73; Yuill, *Richard Nixon,* 148–52.

30. Yuill, *Richard Nixon,* 100.

31. John Ehrlichman, *Witness to Power: The Nixon Years* (New York: Simon and Schuster, 1982), 228–29.

32. Charles Colson to Jim Keogh, Mach. 23, 1970, folder "AFL/CIO Building Trades Council," box 28, WHSF, Charles W. Colson Papers [hereafter Colson Papers], NL.

33. "Hard Hats: The Rampaging Patriots," *Nation,* June 15, 1970, 715; "War Foes Here Attacked by Construction Workers," *New York Times,* March 9, 1970, 1.

34. Marc Linder, *Wars of Attrition: Vietnam, the Business Roundtable, and the Decline of Construction Unions* (Iowa City: Fanpihua Press, 1999), 278, 284; "Hard Hats"; "After 'Bloody Friday', New York Wonders If Wall Street Is Becoming a Battleground," *Wall Street Journal,* May 11, 1970, 10.

35. Wehrle, "'Partisan for the Hard Hats,'" 45, 55; Colson to Haldeman, May 28, 1971, folder 4, box 3, Contested Materials [hereafter CM], WHSF, NL-Yorba Linda [hereafter YL]; Anthony Summers, *The Arrogance of Power: The Secret World of Richard Nixon* (New York: Viking, 2000), 361–73.

36. Philip Foner, *U.S. Labor and the Vietnam War* (New York: International Publishers, 1989), 99; Edmund Wehrle, *Between a River and a Mountain: The AFL-CIO and the Vietnam War* (Ann Arbor: University of Michigan Press, 2005), 157–60; "Workers against the War," *Ramparts* 9 (1970), 31.

37. Tom Huston to Ehrlichman, Haldeman, Dent, and Colson, May 12, 1970, folder "New York Construction Workers," box 95, WHSF, Colson Papers, NL; Banks, "'Last Bastion of Discrimination,'" 312–13.

38. Linder, *Wars of Attrition,* 279–81; "Hard Hats on the March—Fists Swinging," *New York Times,* May 17, 1970, 164.

39. Thomas Nolan (Bus. Manager, Operating Engineers Local 14), letter to members, May 18, 1970, folder "Hard Hats—Building and Construction Trades," box 69, WHSF, Colson Papers, NL; Haldeman, *Haldeman Diaries,* 165; Wehrle, "'Partisan for the Hard Hats,'" 55; Colson to President, May 26, 1970, folder "Building and Construction Trades Council Mtg. with President, 5/26/70," box 20, WHSF, Colson Papers, NL.

40. Freeman, "Hardhats"; Colson to President, May 26, 1970; "Buffalo Workers Protest," *New York Times,* May 21, 1970.

41. Colson, "Silent Majority," 276; Bull to Colson, May 22, 1970, folder "Hard Hats—Building and Construction Trades," box 69, WHSF, Colson Papers, NL.

42. Colson to Haldeman, July 2, 1970, folder "Mt. With President, Sec. Volpe, Flanigan, Dick Moore, 7/13/70," box 21, WHSF, Colson Papers, NL; Colson to Bell, folder "New York Construction Workers Building & Con. Trades Coun.," box 95, WHSF, Colson Papers, NL; Colson, "Silent Majority," 276; Colson, "Memorandum for President's File: Building & Construction Trades Meeting with President, May 26, 1970," September 12, 1970, box 20, WHSF, Colson Papers, NL.

43. Colson to President, July 7, 1970, folder "Hard Hats—Building and Construction Trades," box 69, WHSF, Colson Papers, NL; "Fights at Arizona Peace Rally," *New York Times,* June 1, 1970; "Antiwar Youth Seriously Hurt by Hard Hat Demonstrators," *Washington Post,* June 8, 1970; "Protest!" *Washington Post,* June 8, 1970; "Building Workers to Protest 'Law Breakdown' at Meeting," *Seattle Times,* June 4, 1970; "Hard-Hat Workers Stage Flag March," *Washington Post,* June 16, 1970; "Nixon, Cheered in St. Louis, Hails 'What's Right' with U.S.: Thousands Cheer Nixon in St. Louis," *Washington Post,* June 26,

1970; Colson to President, July 7, 1970, folder "Hard Hats—Building and Construction Trades," box 69, WHSF, Colson Papers, NL.

44. "A Hickel Request," *Washington Post,* May 28, 1970, G-1; Cowie, "Nixon's Class Struggle," 263; James Gregory, *American Exodus: The Dust Bowl Migration and Okie Culture in California* (New York: Oxford University Press, 1989), 239; "Avoiding 'Hard-Hat' Haircuts," *Washington Post,* October 18, 1970, 97; Derek Nystrom, "Hard Hats and Movie Brats: Auteurism and the Class Politics of the New Hollywood," *Cinema Journal* 43, no. 3 (2004): 18–41; "Archie Bunker Has Two Kinds of Viewers," *Washington Post,* December 19, 1971, 193.

45. Colson to Nixon, folder 36, box 3, CM, WHSF, NL-YL.

46. Haldeman to Buchanan, June 29, 1970, folder 43, box 6, CM, WHSF, NL-YL; Colson to Haldeman, and Colson to William J. O'Hara, September 21, 1970, folder "Labor Campaign [2 of 2]," box 77, WHSF, Colson Papers, NL.

47. Wehrle, *Between a River and a Mountain,* 161; Colson to Haldeman, February 10, 1971, folder 5, box 3, CM, WHSF, NL-YL.

48. Banks, "'Last Bastion of Discrimination,'" 326–28; Cowie, "Nixon's Class Struggle," 271–73.

49. Linder, *Wars of Attrition,* 305–27.

50. "President, Visiting Iowa, Gets Cool Reception," *Washington Post,* March 2, 1971, A-3; "Wage-Price Curbs for Building Industry Are Nixon Victory, but Impact Is Unclear," *Wall Street Journal,* March 30, 1971, 3.

51. "Wage-Price Curbs for Building Industry," 3.

52. Chapin to Haldeman, March 2, 1971, folder "New York Construction Workers Building & Con. Trades Coun.," box 95, WHSF, Colson Papers, NL.

53. Hodgson to Colson, March 1, 1971, folder "Hard Hats—Building and Construction Trades," box 69, WHSF, Colson Papers, NL.

54. Colson to President, folder "Mtg Peter Brennan/ w President, 7/2/71," box 23, WHSF, Colson Papers, NL.

55. Banks, "'Last Bastion of Discrimination,'" 329–41; misc. docs. in folder "NY Plan," box 20, Undersecretary Laurence Silberman Papers, RG 174, National Archives and Records Administration (NARA).

56. "Address by Assistant Secretary of Labor Arthur A. Fletcher before the Annual Meeting and Legislative Conference of the Associated Builders and Contractors, Inc.," March 12, 1971, folder "Fletcher, Arthur," box 147, Secretary Hodgson Papers [hereafter Hodgson Papers], RG 174, NARA; Jill Quadagno, *The Color of Welfare: How Racism Undermined the War on Poverty* (New York: Oxford University Press, 1994), 81; Fletcher, *Silent Sell-Out,* 78.

57. "U.S. Agencies Cited in Failure to Enforce Minority Jobs Plan," *Washington Post,* March 18, 1971; Fletcher, *Silent Sell-Out,* 78.

58. Fletcher to Hodgson and Silberman, February 26, 1971, folder "PE-4–2 1971: Fletcher, Arthur A," box 147, Hodgson Papers, RG 174, NARA.

59. "Address by Assistant Secretary of Labor," March 12, 1971, 1–2, 9–10.

60. "Unions Seen Ending Bias in Building," *Washington Post,* March 13, 1971.

61. "Union Asks Firing of U.S. Aide," *Washington Post,* April 5, 1971.

62. Rodgers to Cashen, April 5, 1971, and Cashen to Colson, April 28, 1971, folder "Hard Hats—Building and Construction Trades," box 69, WHSF, Colson Papers, NL.

63. Colson to Haldeman, May 6, 1971, folder "Arthur Fletcher," box 65, WHSF, Colson Papers, NL.

64. NWHT 2-121, May 7, 1971, NL; NWHT 495-21, May 7, 1971, NL.

65. Fletcher, *Silent Sell-Out,* 79–80.

66. Colson to Ehrlichman, May 5, 1971, folder "Hard Hats—Building and Construction Trades," box 69, WHSF, Colson Papers, NL; Colson to Ehrlichman, May 14, 1971,

folder "Building and Construction Trades," box 40, WHSF, Colson Papers, NL; Colson to Haldeman, May 21, 1971, folder 22, box 55, CM, WHSF, NL-YL; Colson to Ehrlichman, June 7, 1971, folder "Arthur Fletcher," box 65, WHSF, Colson Papers, NL.

67. NWHT 2-121, May 7, 1971, NL; NWHT 6-93, July 2, 1971, NL.

68. Colson to Nixon, July 2, 1971, available at: http://www.nixonlibrary.gov/virtual-library/documents/jun09/070271_Colson_President.pdf.

69. Untitled document, folder "Brennan, Peter," box 6, White House Central Files [hereafter WHCF]: President's Personal File, NL.

70. NWHT 535-5, July 2, 1971, NL.

71. "Memo for President's File," July 26, 1971, folder "Nixon and Labor/ Political," box 96, WHSF, Colson Papers, NL.

72. Banks, "'Last Bastion of Discrimination,'" 347; "Blacks Dismayed by Resignations," *New York Times,* May 5, 1971; NWHT 590-3, October 13, 1971, NL.

73. Bull to Colson, September 20, 1971, folder 32, box 3, CM, WHSF, NL-YL; Colson to Haldeman, July 23, 1971, folder 28, box 4, and Colson to Haldeman, August 11, 1971, folder 12, box 3, CM, WHSF, NL-YL.

74. Rodgers to Colson, October 12, 1972, folder "Nixon and Labor/Political," box 96, WHSF, Colson Papers, NL; Colson to Haldeman, May 2, 1972, folder 12, box 3, CM, WHSF, NL-YL; misc. memos in folder "Don Rodgers," box 11, WHSF, Colson Papers, NL; John Dean, *Blind Ambition: The White House Years* (New York: Simon and Schuster, 1976), 111.

75. "Nixon and the Bums: An Editorial," *Scanlan's Monthly,* September 1970; Colson to Brennan, April 17, 1971, folder "Hard Hats—Building and Construction Trades," box 69, WHSF, Colson Papers, NL; James Jacobs, *Gotham Unbound: How New York City Was Liberated from the Grip of Organized Crime* (New York: New York University Press, 1999), chap. 7; Ronald Goldstock, *Corruption and Racketeering in the New York City Construction Industry: Final Report to Governor Mario M. Cuomo from the New York State Organized Crime Task Force* (New York: New York University Press, 1990), 79–82; James Jacobs, *Mobsters, Unions, and Feds: The Mafia and the American Labor Movement* (New York: New York University Press, 2006), 183–84; Summers, *Arrogance of Power,* 358.

76. Colson to Rodgers, June 15, 1972, folder "Don Rodgers," box 11, WHSF, Colson Papers, NL.

77. Misc. memos in folder "Don Rodgers," box 11, and folder "Nixon and Labor/ Political," box 96 in WHSF, Colson Papers, NL; Wehrle, "'Partisan for the Hard Hats,'" 62–66; Colson to Haldeman, May 2, 1972, folder 12, box 3, CM, WHSF, NL-YL.

78. Lovestone told Colson in 1971 that "unless [Henry] Jackson is nominated, the labor machinery will be relatively inactive." Colson to Haldeman, May 28, 1971, folder 4, box 3, CM, WHSF, NL-YL; Colson to Nixon, May 19, 1972, folder 1, box 3, CM, WHSF, NL-YL; Charles Colson, *Born Again* (Old Tappan, N.J.: Chosen Books, 1976), 15.

79. Colson to Haldeman, November 10, 1972, available at: http://www.nixonlibrary.gov/virtuallibrary/documents/jun09/111072_Colson.pdf.

80. Ibid.

81. Ibid.

82. This conclusion cuts against Nixon revisionists, such as Dean Kotlowski, who downplay the effect of Nixon's choice to defer civil rights law enforcement to the courts on most issues, and against labor historians, such as Edmund Wehrle, who downplay the role that conservative unions had in shaping Nixon's campaign strategies.

83. Political scientists, by ignoring Fletcher's unsuccessful attempts to restructure the OFCC, have provided overdetermined explanations for why the courts became the lead enforcement agency for equal employment law. See, for example, Anthony Chen, *The Fifth Freedom: Jobs, Politics, and Civil Rights in the United States, 1941–72* (Princeton: Princeton University Press, 2009).

84. Michael P. Balzano, "The Silent versus the New Majority," in *Richard M. Nixon: Politician, President, Administrator*, ed. Leon Friedman and William Levantrosser, 159–72 (Westport, Conn.: Greenwood Press, 1991), 271–72.

85. David Roediger, *The Wages of Whiteness: Race and the Making of the American Working Class* (New York: Verso, 1991); Linder, *Wars of Attrition;* Herbert Northrup, *Doublebreasted Operations and Pre-Hire Agreements in Construction: The Facts and the Law* (Philadelphia: University of Pennsylvania, 1987); Kris Paap, *Working Construction: Why White Working Class Men Put Themselves—and the Labor Movement—In Harm's Way* (Ithaca: Cornell University Press, 2006).

7. FROM JOBS TO POWER

1. "Pressure On for Minority Trainee Jobs by Monday," *Seattle Post-Intelligencer*, June 10, 1972, A-1.

2. *United States v. Ironworkers, Local 86*, Civil Case 8618, June 5, 1970.

3. "UCWA Struggle: Understanding How to Win," *Seattle Flag*, July 5, 1972, 32.

4. Minutes of the Court Order Advisory Committee [hereafter COAC Minutes], June 7, 1972, folder "1972 Minutes," box 12, Tyree Scott Papers [hereafter TS], University of Washington Libraries Special Collections [hereafter UWSC].

5. "Scott Pledges a New Site Closure," *Seattle Post-Intelligencer*, June 21, 1972, A-3.

6. Herbert Hill, "Labor Union Control of Job Training: A Critical Analysis of Apprenticeship Outreach Programs and the Hometown Plans," Institute for Urban Affairs and Research, Howard University, 1974.

7. On Harlem Fight Back, see Gregory Butler, *Disunited Brotherhoods: Race, Racketeering and the Fall of the New York Construction Unions* (Lincoln: iUniverse, 2006). On the UCCW, see Mel King, *Chain of Change: Struggles for Black Community Development* (Boston: South End Press, 1981), 95–100, 169–94. On the UCWA, see William Little, "Community Organization and Leadership: A Case Study of Minority Workers in Seattle," PhD diss., University of Washington, 1976); William Gould, *Black Workers in White Unions: Job Discrimination in the United States* (Ithaca: Cornell University Press, 1977), 338–62; Vanessa Tait, *Poor Workers' Unions: Rebuilding Labor from Below* (Cambridge, Mass.: South End Press, 2005).

8. Interview with Michael Fox conducted by William Little, 1975, box 1, William A. Little Papers, Acc. 2610-3 [hereafter WL], UWSC.

9. Nancy MacLean, *Freedom Is Not Enough: The Opening of the American Workplace* (Cambridge, Mass.: Harvard University Press, 2006), 76; Hanes Walton, *When the Marching Stopped: The Politics of Civil Rights Regulatory Agencies* (Albany: SUNY Press, 1988); Bayard Rustin, "From Protest to Politics: The Future of the Civil Rights Movement," in *To Redeem A Nation: A History and Anthology of the Civil Rights Movement, ed.* Thomas West (New York: Brandywine Press, 1993), 232–35; Paul Moreno, *From Direct Action to Affirmative Action: Fair Employment Law and Policy in America, 1933–1972* (Baton Rouge: Louisiana State University Press, 1997). MacLean misleadingly refers to all Title VII organizing as "movements for inclusion," thereby overlooking the role of the left in organizing campaigns to enforce Title VII law; *Freedom Is Not Enough*, 332.

10. "4/6/49 Building Trades Council," folder 21, box 34, Seattle Urban League Papers [hereafter SULP], UWSC.

11. Little, "Community Organization and Leadership," 75; *Howard Lewis and Jettie J. Murray v. Ironworkers Local No. 86*, Washington State Board Against Discrimination Tribunal, March 12, 1969, 32, RG AR74-1-1, Washington State Archives, Olympia [hereafter WSA].

12. Deposition of Donald Kelly, box 102, Record Group (RG) 403, National Archives and Records Administration (NARA), Seattle.

13. Deposition of Junior Lee, box 102, RG 403, NARA, Seattle.

14. Deposition summary of Robert E Lucas, box 101, RG 403, NARA, Seattle.

15. *Howard Lewis and Jettie J. Murray v. Ironworkers Local No. 86;* letter to Donald Slaiman, March 20, 1969, Apprenticeship Series, RG 009-2, AFL-CIO Civil Rights Department Papers, unprocessed records at the George Meany Memorial Archives, Silver Spring, Md.; "Construction Men Plan March on Olympia," *Seattle Post-Intelligencer,* October 14, 1969, 1.

16. Gould, *Black Workers in White Unions,* 338–40.

17. "2,000 White Workers March in Mass Protest," *Seattle Times,* October 8, 1969, A-1.

18. "Options Paper: Seattle Project," February 1, 1971, folder "Seattle Plan," box 21, Records of Undersecretary Laurence Silberman, RG 174, NARA, College Park, Md.; "U.S. Files Suit against 5 Unions Here," *Seattle Times,* October 31, 1969, 1.

19. Shultz to Evans, May 5, 1970, folder "WF-2 Inquiries & Information (May)," box 213, Records of Secretary George Shultz, RG 174, NARA, College Park, Md. Governor Evans's staff wrote at the time, "Either by court action or through policies adopted by public agencies, or a combination, the unions are going to be forced to agree to more effective forms of affirmative action." Glen Paschall to Jim Dolliver, September 25, 1969, folder, "Black Contractors Dispute 1969 Sept-Dec," box 2S-2–600, Governor Dan Evans Papers [hereafter DEP], WSA.

20. "Judge William Lindberg Dies at 76 of Heart Attack," *Seattle Post-Intelligencer,* December 16, 1981; Gould, *Black Workers in White Unions,* 340.

21. See, for instance, the diverse works of Arthur Blumrosen, F. Ray Marshall, Herbert Northrup, and Richard Rowan on apprenticeship and job training during the 1960s.

22. Jeffrey Riemer, *Hard Hats: The Work World of Construction Workers* (Beverly Hills: Sage, 1979), 86; Herbert Applebaum, *Royal Blue: The Culture of Construction Workers* (Orlando: Holt, Tinehart, and Winston, 1981), 33. (Some of Applebaum's work clearly plagiarizes Riemer's.)

23. Riemer, *Hard Hats,* 71, 32–33.

24. NBC Evening News, October 16, 1969, available at: Vanderbilt TV News Archive, http://tvnews.vanderbilt.edu/.

25. "An Idea Whose Time Has Come," unpublished document, 6–7 (in author's possession).

26. Ibid.

27. Ibid.

28. Arnold Weber to John Ehrlichman, undated, folder Seattle, box 34 of Numerical Subject File, White House Special Files: John D. Ehrlichman Papers, Richard Nixon Memorial Archives, NARA, College Park, Md.; "News Release: Evans Plans No New Taxes for 1973-75 Biennium", October 2, 1972, folder "income tax issues," box 2S-01-039, DEP, WSA.

29. Interview with Michael Fox by William Little, 1975, Seattle, Wash., box 1, WL, UWSC, 8; my interview with Henry Andes, December 10, 2003, Mountlake Terrace, Wash.

30. Interview with Todd Hawkins by William Little, 1975, Seattle, Wash., box 1, WL, UWSC, 1.

31. My interview with Todd Hawkins, August 21, 2006, Seattle, Wash.

32. Ibid.

33. Arthur Dye to AFSC Executive Committee, July 21, 1972, Unprocessed Pacific Northwest Region Papers [hereafter PNW], American Friends Service Committee Archives, Philadelphia [hereafter AFSCA].

34. "An Idea Whose Time Has Come."

35. Interview with Luvern Rieke by William Little, 1975, Seattle, Wash., box 1, WL, UWSC.

36. "Court Ordered Advisory Committee," August 15, 1972, folder 16, box 68, SULP, UWSC.

37. COAC Minutes, December 7, 1971, folder "1970–71: Minutes," and COAC Minutes, January 7, 1972, folder "1972 Minutes," box 12, TS, UWSC.

38. Interview with Tyree Scott by William Little, 1975, Seattle, Wash., interview #7, box 1, WL, UWSC.

39. "An Issue Whose Time Has Come."

40. "A Progress Report: December 9 through January 2," and Alice Paine to the Urban Affairs Subcommittee on Minority Employment in the Construction Industry, January 20, 1970, PNW, AFSCA; interview with Tyree Scott by William Little, 1975, Seattle, Wash., interview #8, WL, UWSC.

41. "United Construction Workers Association, One Year Later," 3, PNW, AFSCA.

42. "Progress Report"; Alice Paine to Urban Affairs Committee, April 24, 1970, and Arthur Dye to Barbara Moffett, September 9, 1970, PNW, AFSCA; "Seattle Employment Program Changes Slogans into Facts," *Quaker Service* (winter 1970), 1, Pacific Northwest AFSC Papers, UWSC.

43. Interview with Tyree Scott by William Little, 1975, Seattle, Wash., interview #6, 9, and interview #2, 4–5, WL, UWSC.

44. Minutes of the Urban Affairs Committee of the Pacific, November 11, 1970, PNW, AFSCA; interview with Tyree Scott by William Little, 1975, Seattle, Wash., interview #1, 9–10, WL, UWSC.

45. Interview with Scott #1, 11.

46. Interview with Michael Woo conducted by author and Nicole Grant, Seattle Civil Rights and Labor History Project, available at: http://depts.washington.edu/civilr/woo.htm.

47. Ibid.

48. Interview with Scott #6, 8.

49. COAC Minutes, December 7, 1971; COAC Minutes, February 17, 1971, folder, "1971 Minutes," box 12, TS, UWSC; "Court Ordered Advisory Committee," August 15, 1972, folder 16, box 68, SULP, UWSC.

50. Interview with Scott #6, 11–12.

51. "UCWA Struggle: Understanding How to Win," 32; interview with Scott #6, 11–12.

52. "Mercer Island Span Locked Open Briefly," *Seattle Times,* June 1, 1972; "Two Projects Shut Down by Minority Workers," *Seattle Times,* June 2, 1972; "Charges Challenged by Highway Director," *Seattle Times,* June 2, 1972.

53. COAC Minutes, June 5, 1972, folder, "1972 Minutes," box 12, TS, UWSC.

54. "Violence Flares in Jobs Dispute," *Seattle Times,* June 6, 1972, A-1; "More Building to Be Halted—Despite Court Order," *Seattle Post-Intelligencer,* June 6, 1972, A-3; my interview with Hawkins.

55. "Violence Flares in Jobs Dispute," *Seattle Times,* June 6, 1972; "UCWA Still Tough: Jobs or Shutdowns," *Seattle Post-Intelligencer,* June 7, 1972.

56. My interview with Andes; "More Shutdowns Threatened after Rampage at SCC," *Seattle Post-Intelligencer,* June 8, 1972; "Crash of Glass—Nervous Sequel to Final Exams at S.C.C.C.," *Seattle Times,* June 8, 1972; "Police and Demonstrators Engaged in Combat," *Seattle Times,* June 8, 1972.

57. "Supplemental Order Relating to the Authority of the Advisory Committee, Dispatch Ratio and Collective Bargaining Agreement Ratio," June 7, 1972, PNW, AFSCA.

58. Interview with Scott #6, 19; "Scott Calls Off Closures, Goes to Jail," *Seattle Times,* June 8, 1972, A-1; "Tyree Scott 'Thrown Out' of County Jail," *Seattle Times,* June 9, 1972, A-1.

59. "Scott Says, 'We'll be Out in the Streets Again,' Unless…" *Seattle Times,* June 12, 1972, A-4.

60. "Minority-Workers Group Clears First Hurdle," *Seattle Times,* June 13, 1972.

61. "Job Vigil Begins at Courthouse: 'Could Have 1000 Demonstrators,'" *Seattle Post-Intelligencer,* June 14, 1972, A-3.

62. Austin St. Laurent to William Lindberg and Luvern Rieke, June 13, 1972, PNW, AFSCA.

63. "As Police Follow, Marchers Close Jobs," *Seattle Post-Intelligencer,* June 17, 1972; "Demonstrators March, Shut Down 6 Job Sites," *Seattle Times,* June 16, 1972.

64. *U.S. v. Ironworkers, Local 86,* Civil Action 8618, July 5, 13, and 17, 1972.

65. Maxine Daley to Laurence Silberman. "Status of Affirmative Action Plans in Seattle," July 25, 1975, folder, "Seattle Plan," box 21, Records of Undersecretary Laurence Silberman, RG 174, NARA, College Park, Md.

66. Terry Anderson, *The Pursuit of Fairness: A History of Affirmative Action* (New York: Oxford University Press, 2004), 125; Irwin Dubinsky, *Reform in Trade Union Discrimination in the Construction Industry: Operation Dig and Its Legacy* (New York: Praeger, 1973), 165; Hill, "Labor Union Control of Job Training," 103; "U.S. Inaction Seen on Minority Jobs: Officials Say Administration Lets Contractors Evade Hiring Requirements," *New York Times,* December 19, 1972, 89.

67. "Blacks and the General Lockout: In Spite of the Various Plans Put Forward in the Trades, Minorities Are Still Blocked," *New York Times,* July 17, 1971; William Gould, "The Seattle Building Trades Order: The First Comprehensive Relief against Employment Discrimination in the Construction Industry," *Stanford Law Review* 26, no. 4 (1974): 773–813; Hill, "Labor Union Control of Job Training," 108–9; Ray Marshall, Charles Knapp, Malcolm Liggett, and Robert Glover, *Employment Discrimination: The Impact of Legal and Administrative Remedies* (New York: Praeger, 1978), 144–46.

68. "U.S. Asks Changes in Court Order on Building-Trade Jobs for Blacks," *Seattle Times,* December 21, 1972.

69. UCWA History Project interviews, December 2002 (in author's possession).

70. My interview with Michael Simmons, September 25, 2007, Philadelphia, Penn.; Tyree Scott to Frank Quinn, January 31, 1974, folder "Committees and Organizations— Southwest Workers Federation," box "CRD—Housing and Employment, 1974," AFSCA; SWF newsletters (in author's possession), 1973–78; My interviews with James Pannell in Shreveport, La. and Michael Conley in Tulsa, Okla., August 2009.

71. On the U.S. Third World Left as a distinct social formation, see Cynthia Young, *Soul Power: Culture, Radicalism, and the Making of a U.S. Third World Left* (Durham: Duke University Press, 2006). On the U.S. Third World Left in Seattle, see Bob Santos, *Humbows, Not Hot Dogs!: Memoirs of a Savvy Asian American Activist* (Seattle: International Examiner Press, 2002), 46–73.

72. Kieran Taylor, "Turn to the Working Class: The New Left, Black Liberation, and the U.S. Labor Movement (1967–1981)," PhD diss., University of North Carolina, Chapel Hill, 2007, 198–245; Helen Zia, *Asian American Dreams: The Emergence of an American People* (New York: Farrar, Straus, and Giroux, 2000), 139–65.

73. Misc. LELO papers, TS, UWSC.

74. Misc. AFSC Third World Coalition papers (in author's possession).

75. My interview with Simmons; David Hostetter, "Movement Matters: American Antiapartheid Activism and the Rise of Multicultural Politics," PhD diss., University of Maryland, 2004, 77–116.

76. *No Separate Peace,* available at: Seattle Civil Rights and Labor History Project, http://depts.washington.edu/civilr/NSP.htm.

77. My interview with Walter Block, August 21, 2009, Tulsa, Okla.

78. COAC minutes, May 18, 1978, folder "1976–79 Minutes," box 12, TS, UWSC.

79. My interview with William B. Gould, March 2005, Palo Alto, Calif.

80. "Out Cold: Privatization Puts Freeze on Workers," *Real Change*, January 10, 2002.

CONCLUSION

1. "Conservative Media Figures Falsely Suggest That Reich Proposed Excluding White Males from Stimulus Package," Media Matters for America, available at: http://mediamatters.org/research/200901230015?f=h_latest.

2. Ibid.

3. Ibid.

4. Kenneth O'Reilly, *Nixon's Piano: Presidents and Racial Politics from Washington to Clinton* (New York: Free Press, 1995), 315.

5. Quoted in "Dr. Cornel West Pushes for Obama, 'New World Order,'" *Chicago Defender*, February 6, 2008.

6. Robert Weems and Lewis Randolph, "The Ideological Origins of Richard Nixon's 'Black Capitalism' Initiative," *Review of Black Political Economy* 29, no. 1 (June 2001): 49–61; Dean Kotlowski, "Black Power—Nixon Style: The Nixon Administration and Minority Business Enterprise," *Business History Review* 72 (autumn 1998): 409–45; Philip Rubio, *A History of Affirmative Action, 1619–2000* (Jackson: University of Mississippi Press, 2001), 154; O'Reilly, *Nixon's Piano*, 315.

7. Gregory Butler, *Disunited Brotherhoods: Race, Racketeering and the Fall of the New York Construction Unions* (New York: iUniverse, 2006), 55–57.

8. Herbert Northrup, *Open Shop Construction Revisited* (Philadelphia: University of Pennsylvania, 1984), 530–32. Northrup shows some change in the overall industry, but not much, whereas the data on union desegregation is even worse (555–58).

9. Melvin Oliver and Thomas Shapiro, *Black Wealth/White Wealth: A New Perspective on Racial Equality* (New York: Routledge, 1995); Douglas Massey and Nancy Denton, *American Apartheid: Segregation and the Making of the Underclass* (Cambridge, Mass.: Harvard University Press, 1993); William J. Wilson, *When Work Disappears: The New World of the Urban Poor* (New York: Knopf, 1996).

10. Roger Waldinger and Thomas Bailey, "The Continuing Significance of Race: Racial Conflict and Racial Discrimination in Construction," *Politics and Society* 19, no. 3 (1991): 292.

11. Herbert Hill, "Affirmative Action and the Quest for Job Equality," *Review of Black Political Economy* 6, no. 3 (1976): 263–78.

12. Michael Kazin, *Barons of Labor: The San Francisco Building Trades and Union Power in the Progressive Era* (Urbana: University of Illinois Press, 1987).

13. Northrup, *Open Shop Construction Revisited*, 575.

14. Herbert Northrup, *Doublebreasted Operations and Pre-Hire Agreements in Construction: The Facts and the Law* (Philadelphia: University of Pennsylvania, 1987), 2–3.

15. Northrup, *Open Shop Construction Revisited*, 533.

16. Ibid., 539.

17. Ibid., 535.

18. Ibid., 537.

19. "Construction," in "Career Guide to Industries," Bureau of Labor Statistics, 2006, available at: http://www.bls.gov/oco/cg/cgs003.htm.

20. Deirdre A. Royster, *Race and the Invisible Hand: How White Networks Exclude Black Men from Blue-Collar Jobs* (Berkeley: University of California Press, 2003), 12, 15, 178.

21. Kris Paap, *Working Construction: Why White Working-Class Men Put Themselves—and the Labor Movement—in Harm's Way* (Ithaca: Cornell University Press, 2006), 5.

22. Ibid., 180.

23. Ibid., 9.

24. Dennis Deslippe, "Organized Labor, National Politics, and Second-Wave Feminism in the United States, 1965–1975," *International Labor and Working-Class History* 49 (1996): 143–65.

25. Kathleen Laughlin, *Women's Work and Public Policy: A History of the Women's Bureau* (Boston: Northeastern University Press, 2000), 9.

26. One exception, although it overstates the inclusion of women in the Department of Labor guidelines, is John Skrentny, *The Minority Rights Revolution* (Cambridge, Mass.: Harvard University Press, 2002), 138–42, 400.

27. Hugh Davis Graham, *The Civil Rights Era: The Origins and Development of National Policy, 1960–1972* (New York: Oxford University Press, 1990), 410.

28. Dean J. Kotlowski, *Nixon's Civil Rights: Politics, Principle, and Policy* (Cambridge, Mass.: Harvard University Press, 2002), 241–42.

29. Misc. docs, folder "WF-1 Summary Plans and Reports," box 60, Hodgson, Department of Labor Papers, Record Group (RG) 174, National Archives Regional Archives (NARA).

30. Graham, *Civil Rights Era,* 412.

31. Kotlowski, *Nixon's Civil Rights,* 243; Kotlowski is borrowing from ibid., 410.

32. Graham, *Civil Rights Era,* 413.

33. Nancy MacLean, *Freedom Is Not Enough: The Opening of the American Workplace* (Cambridge, Mass.: Harvard University Press, 2006), 270.

34. Susan Eisenberg, *We'll Call You If We Need You: Experiences of Women Working in Construction* (Ithaca: ILR Press, 1998); MacLean, *Freedom Is Not Enough,* 269–70.

35. See Paap, *Working Construction;* Trudi Ferguson and Madeline Sharples, *Blue Collar Women: Trailblazing Women Take on Men-Only Jobs* (Liberty Corner, N.J.: New Horizon, 1994); Molly Martin, ed., *Hard Hatted Women: Stories of Struggle and Success in the Trades* (Seattle: Seal Press, 1988); Jean Reith Schroedel, *Alone in a Crowd: Women in the Trades Tell Their Stories* (Philadelphia: Temple University Press, 1985); Susan Eisenberg, "Still Waiting after All These Years: Women in the US Construction Industry," in *Women in Construction* (Construction Labour Research Studies 2), ed. Linda Clarke, Elsebet Pedersen, Elisabeth Michielsens, Barbara Susman, and Christine Wall, 188–201 (Brussels: CLR and Reed International, 2004); Susan Eisenberg, "Tradeswomen: An Endangered Species?" in *Frontline Feminism, 1975–1995: Essays from Sojourner's First Twenty Years,* ed. Karen Hahn, 94–96 (San Francisco: Aunt Lute Books, 1995). For a notable exception, see Maclean, *Freedom Is Not Enough,* 117–54, 265–300.

36. "Construction Industry Plays Important Role in Building Economy," *St. Louis Daily Record and St. Louis Countian,* December 12, 2003.

37. Todd Swanstrom, "The Road to Jobs: Patterns of Employment in the Construction Industry in Eighteen Metropolitan Areas," Transportation Equity Network, 2007, Saint Louis.

38. "Construction"; "Fitch Confirms Negative Outlook for City of Detroit," *Crain's Detroit Business,* July 30, 2009; "Michigan Tax Revenues Fall $50M in July," *Detroit News,* August 11, 2009; "Nearly Half of Detroit's Workers are Unemployed," *Detroit News,* December 16, 2009.

39. "$146 Million Film, TV Production Studio Factory Chooses Allen Park and Michigan," Reuters, April 14, 2009; Michigan Economic Development Corporation, "Granholm: Unity Studio Launching New Film, Television and Media Production Studio in Allen Park," press release, available at: http://www.themedc.org/News-Media/Press-Releases/Detail.aspx?ContentId=049eae89–917c-4299–9d63-ed1e78a62020; "Allen Park: City Unveils Plans for $146M Film Production Studio, *News-Herald,* April 14, 2009; "Film Industry," City of Allen Park, Michigan, available at: http://www.cityofallenpark.org/news-film-industry.php.

40. "Judge Blocks Regional Authority Plan for Detroit's Cobo Center; Cockrel Says Appeal Is Planned," *Crain's Detroit Business*, April 9, 2009; "Patterson: What Oakland County Needs to Support Cobo Plan," *Crain's Business Detroit*, October 27, 2003; "Cobo Center Expansion Set to Move Forward as Detroit City Council Refuses to Vote against Plan," *MLive*, July 28, 2009.

41. "Krugman: U.S. Headed for 'Jobless' Recovery," July 1, 2009, ABC News, available at: http://abcnews.go.com/ThisWeek/Politics/story?id=7966402&page=1.

42. "The Economic Fallout Has Decimated the Black Middle Class," AlterNet, August 10, 2009, available at: http://www.alternet.org/workplace/141825.

43. Trevor Griffey, "New Economy, New Rules to Work By," interview with Van Jones, *Real Change*, November 5, 2008, available at: http://www.realchangenews.org/index.php/site/archives/1826/.

44. Van Jones, *The Green Collar Economy: How One Solution Can Fix Our Two Biggest Problems* (New York: Harper Collins, 2008).

45. Green for All, "Recommendations for Senate Climate and Energy Legislation," available at: http://www.greenforall.org/what-we-do/working-with-washington/ameri can-clean-energy-and-security-act/recommendations-for-senate-climate-and-energy-legislation/.

46. Griffey, "New Economy."

47. For example, the June 21, 2008, conference on Good, Green Jobs at the University of Washington brought together the governor of Washington, the executive of King County, a member of the U.S. House of Representatives, and prominent labor and environmental leaders. But prominent community organizations representing people of color were not included in the conference planning.

48. "Author-Activist Tapped as White House 'Green' Jobs Advisor," *New York Times*, March 10, 2009. See also Jones, *Green Collar Economy*. For Green for All, see its website, available at: http://www.greenforall.org/. For Jones's sacking and conservative opposition to his appointment, see "White House Official Resigns after G.O.P. Criticism," *New York Times*, September 6, 2009.

49. Reich's transcribed testimony appeared in "Conservative Media." See also Robert Reich, "The Stimulus: How to Create Jobs without Them All Going to Skilled Professionals and White Male Construction Workers," available at: http://robertreich.blogspot.com/2009/01/stimulus-how-to-create-jobs-without.html.

50. Swanstrom, "The Road to Jobs."

51. Ibid.

52. "Jobs Now Campaign," Gamaliel Foundation, available at: http://www.gamaliel.org/Issues/IssueWork/JobsNow.htm.

53. Ibid.; "Alameda Corridor Jobs Coalition—Los Angeles," Working for America AFL-CIO Institute, available at: http://www.workingforamerica.org/documents/journal2/alameda.htm.

54. "Alameda Corridor Jobs Coalition."

55. "Time to Break Cycle of No Skills, No Jobs," *Detroit Free Press*, July 31, 2009, available at: http://www.freep.com/article/20090731/COL10/907310368/Time-to-break-cycle-of-no-skills--no-jobs.

56. Stephen Pitts, "Organize…to Improve the Quality of Jobs in the Black Community: A Report on Jobs and Activism in the African American Community," University of California Berkeley Center for Labor Research and Education, Berkeley, May 2004.

57. Bill Fletcher Jr. and Fernando Gapasin, *Solidarity Divided: the Crisis in Organized Labor and a New Path Forward* (Berkeley: University of California Press, 2008), 10–11.

About the Contributors

Erik S. Gellman is an assistant professor of history at Roosevelt University. He is the author of recent articles in the *Journal of Southern History* and *Labor* and of two forthcoming books that examine the convergence civil rights and labor movements during the New Deal era, *Labor's New Deal Prophets* (with Jarod Roll) and *Death Blow, Jim Crow!*

David Goldberg is an assistant professor of Africana studies at Wayne State University and the director of Beyond the Urban Crisis: The Detroit Civil Rights, Community Activism, and Labor History Project.

Trevor Griffey is a PhD candidate in U.S. history at the University of Washington and the cofounder of the Seattle Civil Rights and Labor History Project (http://www.civilrights. washington.edu). His dissertation, "No Separate Peace: The United Construction Workers Association and the U.S. Third World Left," describes the radicalizing effect that struggles to desegregate the building trades in Seattle had on the left in the 1970s.

Brian Purnell is an assistant professor of African and African American studies at Fordham University and research director of the Bronx African-American History Project. His articles and essays have appeared in *Afro-Americans in New York Life and History, Souls: The Journal of African American History,* and *Groundwork: Local Black Freedom Movements in America.* His forthcoming book is *A Movement Grows in Brooklyn: Civil Rights and Black Power in Brooklyn, New York* (University Press of Kentucky).

Julia Rabig received her PhD in history from the University of Pennsylvania in 2007 and is a visiting lecturer at Boston University. Her dissertation, "The Fixers: Devolution, Development, and Civil Society in Newark, New Jersey, 1960–1990," is currently under review for publication. She is also co-editor of a forthcoming a collection of essays entitled *The Business of Black Power: Corporations, Public Policy, and Community Development.*

John J. Rosen is a PhD candidate in history at the University of Illinois at Chicago. His research interests include U.S. political, labor, and race and ethnic history. He has published book reviews in *Historical Methods* and the *North Carolina Historical Review.* His dissertation examines African American trade unionists' social and political activism in postwar San Francisco.

Index